# LIBRARY OF HEBREW BIBLE/ OLD TESTAMENT STUDIES

## 568

*Formerly Journal for the Study of the Old Testament Supplement Series*

### Editors
Claudia V. Camp, Texas Christian University
Andrew Mein, Westcott House, Cambridge

### Founding Editors
David J. A. Clines, Philip R. Davies and David M. Gunn

# WEIGHING HEARTS

## Character, Judgment, and the Ethics of Reading the Bible

Stuart Lasine

t &t clark

Published by T & T Clark International
*A Continuum imprint*
80 Maiden Lane, New York, NY 10038
The Tower Building, 11 York Road, London SE1 7NX

www.continuumbooks.com

Visit the T & T Clark blog at www.tandtclarkblog.com

**Library of Congress Cataloging-in-Publication Data**
A catalog record for this book is available from the Library of Congress.

ISBN: HB: 978-0-567-43081-6


Typeset by Forthcoming Publications Ltd (www.forthpub.com)
Printed and bound in the United States of America

*To my wife, Rannfrid Thelle*

# CONTENTS

Part II
PROPHETS AND PERSONALITY

Part III
CHARACTERIZING KINGS

# Part IV
## CHARACTER AND THE ETHICS OF READING THE BIBLE

# PREFACE

Every way of a man is right in his own eyes, but Yahweh weighs the hearts. (Prov 21:2)

O you who weighs (*ḫȝi*) everything
who counts…their characters,
who knows what is in hearts…
Thoth…upon the balance
Will count each man for his deeds on earth.
       (Egyptian Coffin Texts Spell 768; De Buck 1935, VI 399u-400c;
          Tomb of Petosiris, inscription 81; Lichtheim 1992, 96-97)

In [earlier times] there were…living men to judge the living, on the day when each was to die…Zeus said: "the cases are now judged badly, because those on trial have their clothes on, for they are judged alive. Now many who have evil souls are dressed in beautiful bodies, and ancestry and wealth, and at the judgment many witnesses…testify that they have lived justly. The judges are dazzled by this, and by being clothed themselves when judging, [with] their eyes and ears and whole body…[being] a veil before their own souls… [Those judged] must be stripped naked of all these things, for they must be tried when dead. The judge also must be naked, dead…in order that the judgment be just."
(Plato, *Gorg.* 523b-e)

Let me remind you of the old legal maxim: for a suspect, motion is better than rest, for he who is at rest can always be on a scale pan without knowing it, being weighed with his sins.
       —Block, in Kafka's *Der Proceß* (1994, 202–3)

In Egyptian mortuary literature, one or more deities weigh the deceased in the balance, counting their deeds and reckoning their character. When we mortals evaluate the people with whom we interact in our quotidian world—*and* the characters we encounter in ancient and modern narratives—it is we who are the judges, but without the divine knowledge of the "secrets of the heart" (Ps 44:22). To make matters worse, those whom we judge are alive, and may attempt to evade judgment by refusing to stand still in the pans of the scale. "Life" in this sense is also granted to literary characters whose elusiveness and unfathomability are enhanced by a variety of rhetorical devices. Moreover, when we judge "clothed" individuals we can be misled by their physical appearance, wealth, connections, and others' assessments of their character, as well as by their own confident assumption that all their actions are right. Thus, while the departed in the Egyptian *Book of the Dead* fear that their heart may reveal their guilty secrets, the hearts of those whom we evaluate—both in our life-world and the fictional worlds we choose to inhabit—tend to resist any compulsion to confess, making our job as judges more difficult to perform.

In the epigraph from Plato's *Gorgias*, Socrates points out yet another complication: like the judges of Kronos's time, we ourselves are also clothed, that is, alive, when we evaluate the character of others. Zeus believes that judges as well as those judged must be naked and dead, in order for a just judgment to be possible. However, few of us wait until we're dead to judge those around us or the characters in the books we read. As I will discuss in Chapter 1, empirical evidence suggests that we attribute character traits to others at the first opportunity upon meeting them (if not *before* a real opportunity arises). This is not the only facet of human perception and social life which "veils" us from assessing others accurately, however we may be clothed. Many others will be discussed in the following pages. In the end, if we are to weigh biblical characters "in scales of righteousness," as Job asks of God (Job 31:6), we will need to thoroughly investigate how people go about judging one another in daily life and how we construe the character of personages in narrative. This will allow us to consider how we might go about correcting for any patterns of distortion we impose on our assessments of others in normal practice, and, hopefully, allow us to disrobe them with our naked eyes.

The first chapters of this book are devoted to this investigation. What we learn there about character and judgment will inform the specific studies of biblical character evaluation that follow. Along the way we will encounter again the texts with which this preface is headed. I will also be adding other theoretical perspectives, as well as texts from other times and cultures, into the analyses when appropriate and helpful. One last, rather disquieting fact: because we tend to expose our own character in how we judge others, our evaluations of biblical characters may end up revealing our own "nakedness," allowing us to weigh *ourselves* in the balance while still alive.

I would like to thank LHBOTS editor Claudia Camp for her consistent support for this project since I first mentioned the idea to her at the 2003 International SBL meeting in Cambridge. More recently, she and her co-editor Andrew Mein have gone out of their way to ensure that my longish volume could appear in their series. David Gunn and Stephen Moore offered moral support for the project, stressing the need for a fresh approach to the knotty problems involving character and characterization in literary and biblical studies. Most of the material which is now in the book was field-tested at various meetings of the SBL and the Southwest Commission on Religious Studies; I am grateful for the valuable feedback I received from the audiences at those sessions. My thanks also to Terje Stordalen, for inviting me to give a lecture on the themes of this study at the 2008 meeting of OTSEM (the Nordic-German network for Old Testament studies) in Granavolden, Norway. Closer to home, I want to thank my former Wichita State student and research assistant Alisa Hardy for ensuring that I received the books, articles and other research materials I needed for this project.

Most of all I want to thank Rannfrid Thelle, my wife, colleague and muse, for all the help she has so generously offered me as I labored on this manuscript. Her insightful comments on drafts of the various chapters have proven invaluable to me, and our daily conversations on the Bible and the vagaries of human behavior are a constant source of inspiration. It is to Rannfrid that this book, and my life, are dedicated.

# ABBREVIATIONS

| | |
|---|---|
| AB | Anchor Bible |
| *ABD* | *Anchor Bible Dictionary*. Edited by D. N. Freedman. 6 vols. New York, 1992 |
| *AEL* | *Ancient Egyptian Literature* M. Lichtheim. 3 vols. Berkeley, 1971–80 |
| *AHR* | *American Historical Review* |
| *AJP* | *American Journal of Philology* |
| *ANET* | *Ancient Near Eastern Texts Relating to the Old Testament*. Edited by J. B. Pritchard. 3rd edn. Princeton, 1969 |
| *Ant.* | Josephus, *Jewish Antiquities* |
| AOE | Actor-Observer Effect |
| ATANT | Abhandlungen zur Theologie des Alten und Neuen Testaments |
| ATD | Das Alte Testament Deutsch |
| *b.* | Babylonian Talmud |
| *BAR* | *Biblical Archaeology Review* |
| *BASOR* | *Bulletin of the American Schools of Oriental Research* |
| *BD* | The Egyptian *Book of the Dead* (*Book of Going Forth by Day*) |
| BDB | Brown, F., S. R. Driver, and C. A. Briggs. *A Hebrew and English Lexicon of the Old Testament*. Oxford, 1907 |
| *Bib* | *Biblica* |
| BJS | Brown Judaic Studies |
| BKAT | Biblischer Kommentar, Altes Testament. Edited by M. Noth and H. W. Wolff |
| *BN* | *Biblische Notizen* |
| *BRCW* | *Bryn Mawr Classical Review* |
| *BRev* | *Bible Review* |
| *BZ* | *Biblische Zeitschrift* |
| BZAW | Beihefte zur Zeitschrift für die alttestamentliche Wissenschaft |
| CBC | Cambridge Bible Commentary |
| *CBQ* | *Catholic Biblical Quarterly* |
| CBQMS | Catholic Biblical Quarterly Monograph Series |
| *CDMEA* | *Concise Dictionary of Middle Egyptian*. Edited by R. O. Faulkner. Oxford, 1962 |
| *CJ* | *Classical Journal* |
| CTHPT | Cambridge Texts in the History of Political Thought |
| *CW* | *Classical World* |

| | |
|---|---|
| CWS | Classics of Western Spirituality |
| *DCH* | *Dictionary of Classical Hebrew.* Edited by D. J. A. Clines. Sheffield, 1993– |
| DSB | Daily Study Bible |
| *DSM* | *Diagnostic and Statistical Manual of Mental Disorders* |
| *ECT* | *Egyptian Coffin Texts.* Edited by A. de Buck and A. H. Gardiner. Chicago, 1935–47 |
| *EDB* | *Eerdmans Dictionary of the Bible.* Edited by D. N. Freedman, A. C. Myers and A. B. Beck. Grand Rapids, Mich., 2000 |
| EHAT | Exegetisches Handbuch zum Alten Testament |
| *EJSP* | *European Journal of Social Psychology* |
| *ELH* | *ELH: English Literary History* |
| ESV | English Standard Version |
| *Eth. nic.* | Aristotle, *Nichomachean Ethics* |
| FAT | Forschungen zum Alten Testament |
| FOTL | Forms of the Old Testament Literature |
| *Gen. Rab.* | *Genesis Rabbah* |
| *Gorg.* | Plato, *Gorgias* |
| Gr. | Greek |
| *GW* | Sigmund Freud, *Gesammelte Werke.* Edited by Anna Freud. London, 1940– |
| *HAR* | *Hebrew Annual Review* |
| HCOT | Historical Commentary on the Old Testament |
| Heb. | Hebrew |
| *Hipp. min.* | Plato, *Lesser Hippias* |
| *Hist.* | Herodotus, *Histories* |
| *HS* | *Hebrew Studies* |
| HSM | Harvard Semitic Monographs |
| *HTR* | *Harvard Theological Review* |
| *HUCA* | *Hebrew Union College Annual* |
| IBC | Interpretation: A Bible Commentary for Teaching and Preaching |
| ICC | International Critical Commentary |
| *IDB* | *The Interpreter's Dictionary of the Bible.* Edited by G. A. Buttrick. 4 vols. Nashville, 1962 |
| *Il.* | Homer, *Iliad* |
| *Int* | *Interpretation* |
| *JAOS* | *Journal of the American Oriental Society* |
| *JAP* | *Journal of Abnormal Psychology* |
| *JBL* | *Journal of Biblical Literature* |
| *JBQ* | *Jewish Bible Quarterly* |
| *JHI* | *Journal of the History of Ideas* |
| *JNES* | *Journal of Near Eastern Studies* |
| JPS | Jewish Publication Society of America Version |
| *JQR* | *Jewish Quarterly Review* |

| | |
|---|---|
| *JRE* | *Journal of Religious Ethics* |
| *JSOT* | *Journal for the Study of the Old Testament* |
| JSOTSup | Journal for the Study of the Old Testament: Supplement Series |
| KBL | Koehler, L., and W. Baumgartner, *Lexicon in Veteris Testamenti libros*. 2d ed. Leiden, 1958 |
| KJV | King James Version |
| LCL | Loeb Classical Library |
| *LD* | *Lectura Dantis* |
| *Leg.* | Plato, *Laws* |
| LHBOTS | Library of Hebrew Bible/Old Testament Studies |
| LXX | Septuagint (the Greek Old Testament) |
| *Mek.* | *Mekilta* |
| *MLR* | *Modern Language Review* |
| MT | Masoretic Text (of the Hebrew Bible) |
| NAB | New American Bible |
| NASB | New American Standard Bible |
| NCBC | New Century Bible Commentary |
| n.d. | no date |
| *NEAEHL* | *The New Encyclopedia of Archaeological Excavations in the Holy Land*. Edited by E. Stern. 4 vols. Jerusalem, 1993 |
| *NIB* | *The New Interpreter's Bible*. Nashville: Abingdon, 1994– |
| NIBCOT | New International Biblical Commentary on the Old Testament |
| NIV | New International Version |
| NJPS | *Tanakh: The Holy Scriptures: The New JPS Translation According to the Traditional Hebrew Text* |
| NKJV | New King James Version |
| n.p. | no page |
| NRSV | New Revised Standard Version |
| *Numen* | *Numen: International Review for the History of Religions* |
| *OBO* | *Orbisbiblicus et orientalis* |
| *Od.* | Homer, *Odyssey* |
| OTL | Old Testament Library |
| *OtSt* | *OudtestamentischeStudiën* |
| *PB* | *Psychological Bulletin* |
| *Phaed.* | Plato, *Phaedo* |
| *Pirqe R. El.* | *Pirqe Rabbi Eliezer* |
| *Pol.* | Aristotle, *Politics* |
| *PR* | *Psychological Review* |
| *Proof* | *Prooftexts: A Journal of Jewish Literary History* |
| *PT* | *Poetics Today* |
| QD | Quaestiones disputatae |
| *RB* | *Revue biblique* |
| *Resp.* | Plato, *Republic* |
| *Šabb.* | *Shabbat* |

| | |
|---|---|
| *Sanh.* | *Sanhedrin* |
| SANT | Studien zum Alten und Neuen Testaments |
| SBL | Society of Biblical Literature |
| SBLMS | Society of Biblical Literature Monograph Series |
| *SE* | *The Standard Edition of the Complete Psychological Works of Sigmund Freud.* Edited and translated by J. Strachey. London, 1953– |
| SemeiaSt | Semeia Studies |
| *SJOT* | *Scandinavian Journal of the Old Testament* |
| SOTSMS | Society for Old Testament Studies Monograph Series |
| SSN | Studia semitica neerlandica |
| *ST* | *Studiatheologica* |
| SubBi | Subsidia biblica |
| Syr. | Syriac |
| SWZBF | Nietzsche, F. W. *Sämtliche Werke in zwölf Bänden.* Stuttgart, 1964– |
| *Ta'an.* | *Ta'anit* |
| *TBT* | *The Bible Today* |
| *TDOT* | *Theological Dictionary of the Old Testament.* Edited by G. J. Botterweck and H. Ringgren. Translated by J. T. Willis, G. W. Bromiley, and D. E. Green. 8 vols. Grand Rapids, 1974– |
| *Tg. J.* | *Targum Jonathan* |
| *Urk.* | *Urkunden der 18. Dynastie: Historisch-Biographische Urkunden.* Edited by Kurt Sethe. Vol. 4 of *Urkunden des ägyptischen Altertums.* Leipzig, 1905 |
| Vg | Vulgate |
| *VT* | *Vetus Testamentum* |
| VTSup | Supplements to Vetus Testamentum |
| WBC | Word Biblical Commentary |
| WBCom | Westminster Bible Companion |
| *WHJP* | *World History of the Jewish People* |
| WMANT | Wissenschaftliche Monographien zum Alten und Neuen Testament |
| *ZÄS* | *Zeitschrift für ägyptische Sprache und Altertumskunde* |
| *ZAW* | *Zeitschrift für die alttestamentliche Wissenschaft* |

Part I

## METHODS, THEORIES, AND TEXTS

Chapter 1

# INTRODUCTION:
## SEEING WITH THE EYES OF EVALUATION

1. *Judging Character: Methodology at the Intersection of Psychology,
Literary Theory, and Moral Philosophy*

We see people with the eyes of evaluation.

—Palmer (1992, 81)

From the moment I grasped that there was in me something to judge, I
understood,…that there was in [my fellows] an irresistible vocation for
judgment.

—Camus, *La Chute* (1956, 92)

"My dear Strong," said Mr. Wickfield in a tremulous voice, "my good
friend, I needn't tell you that it has been my vice to look for some one
master motive in everybody, and to try all actions by one narrow test."

—Dickens, *David Copperfield* (2004, 622)

In Dickens's *David Copperfield*, the lawyer Mr. Wickfield realizes that
he has seriously misconstrued the situation of his friend Dr. Strong and
the character of Strong's young wife. He blames these errors on his habit
of looking for "some one master motive in everybody," a "narrow test"
which another character later calls "his one poor little inch-rule" (Dickens
2004, 842).[1] The process by which people (and literary characters like
Mr. Wickfield) attribute traits to others—often by using our own "inch-
rules"—also has profound implications for the interpretation of biblical
narrative. Just as a person's character can only be judged in relation to

---

1.   This character is David's aunt. She informs her nephew that Mr. Wickfield is a
"reclaimed man," whom David will no longer find "measuring all human interests,
and joys, and sorrows, with his one poor little inch-rule" (Dickens 2004, 842; cf.
229–31, 233, 236–37, 583). Not all Dickens scholars agree that Wickfield *has*
misread the character of Dr. Strong's wife; see, e.g., Joseph 2000, 688–91. On the
"David and Uriah theme" in *David Copperfield*, see Chapter 9, §7, below.

the situations in which they act, the same is true when we evaluate literary characters in terms of plot. Analyzing character from this perspective means more than charting the rhetorical strategies employed by the biblical authors to construct their characters. Many of these strategies have already been extensively studied by biblical narratologists.[2] To investigate character in the sense of this study means that one must also deal with the intricacies of human perception and social interaction, the dynamics of the reading process, and what has come to be called "character ethics"[3] and the ethics of reading.

Not surprisingly, the distinction between "character" and "personality"[4] is understood differently by different writers in these fields. In general, when one speaks of "character" one has in mind matters involving the ethics, principles, integrity, or code of conduct of a person or literary character. When one speaks of "personality," one is usually referring to

2. A number of important studies in English have appeared since the 1980s. For a detailed bibliography of such works, see Gunn and Fewell 1993, 206–52. For more recent studies by biblicists, see below. On the growing interest in "post-classical narratology" among literary scholars, see Herman, who describes this project as "inherently interdisciplinary" (1999, 20; cf. 14). For a critique of this "contextualist turn in narratology," see Kindt and Müller (2003, 415).

3. This includes what has come to be called character ethics, character psychology, and virtue ethics. According to Schneewind, "a virtue-centered view sees character at the core of morality… the primary or central moral judgments are judgments about the character of agents" (1997, 179; cf. Fleming 2006, 25). Hursthouse (1997, 219) contends that in a "skeletal" virtue theory "an action is right iff it is what a virtuous agent would do in the circumstances." On "character ethics," see, e.g., W. Brown 2002, xi–xiii and Chapters 2 and 9, below.

4. Influential psychologist Gordon Allport defines personality as the dynamic organization within the individual of those psychophysical systems that determine individuals' unique adjustments to their environments. In contrast, character is an ethical concept, which is unnecessary for psychology; character is "personality evaluated, and personality is character devaluated" (Allport 1937, 48, 51–53). Similarly, philosopher John Doris (2002, 19) observes that "character traits appear to have an evaluative dimension that personality traits need not." Aristotle (*Eth. nic.* 1450b) famously asserts that character is what makes the choice evident; that is, what sort of action is chosen or avoided in cases not evident in themselves (see, e.g., Telford 1961, 14). A person must be shown in the exercise of his or her will, placed in circumstances in which the choice is not obvious, i.e., circumstances in which everybody's choice would not be the same. As Halliwell points out (1990, 151; cf. 154, 156), in Aristotle "*ethos/ethe* is a specific moral factor in relation to action, *not* a vague or pervasive notion equivalent to modern ideas of personality or individuality—least of all to individuality, since *ethos* is a matter of generic qualities (virtues and vices)." For more definitions of personality, see, e.g., Costa and McCrae 1994, 22–25.

an individual's particular way of presenting him- or herself to others, one's particular way of thinking and speaking, one's emotions, one's "lively personal identity," or one's particular coping style; in short, one's uniqueness (see R. Williams 1983, 233).

As Worman has demonstrated, in the ancient Greek context the term *charaktêr* involves "whatever can be witnessed by an onlooker," just as its original meaning of stamp on a genuine coin concerns "surface effects and authenticity." In contrast, *êthos* "is more ambiguous between internal disposition and external characteristics" (2003, 17, 29; cf. 32).[5] According to Raymond Williams, a personality or a character, once an outward sign, "has been decisively internalized, yet internalized as a possession, and therefore as something which can be either displayed or interpreted" (1983, 235). Literary critic Deidre Lynch also traces historical changes in the two concepts. Novels of the eighteenth century have "unsuspected complexities and depths in the impersonality that we tend to explain away," while in nineteenth-century novels "the truths of character" become "redefined as matters of inner meaning; character has become personality" (1998, 13).

Character and character evaluation are of increasing interest to scholars in various branches of psychology,[6] literary studies and moral philosophy. Within literary studies, characterization has long been considered "the *bête noire* of narratology" (Woloch 2003, 14). For many years, a good number of influential literary theorists have argued that the concept of a coherent character or self is obsolescent, illusory, or a pernicious tool of ideology, whether we are speaking about "characters" in fiction or the character of "real people."[7] Woloch notes that the tendency

5.  Worman cites Gill's view that in the classical period the term arose "from traditional notions of types of people, denoting 'character-markers' such as a person's speeches that indicate moral stances, significant actions, and type-revealing statements made by others" (Worman 2003, 32; cf. Gill, 1990, 6–7).

6.  This includes moral psychology. According to Doris (2002, 3), "moral psychology is the study of motivational, affective, and cognitive capacities manifested in moral contexts;…[it] investigates the psychological properties of moral agents." Doris's attempt to incorporate the findings of empirical psychologists in his discussions of virtue ethics has raised the ire of some academic philosophers; see n. 15 below.

7.  Many kinds of critics have joined in what Hochman (1985, 14) calls this "ritual of cannibalization." In the 1970s, Barthes (1974, 95) proclaimed that "what is obsolescent in today's novel is…the character," and Cixous (1974, 385) argued that "the ideology underlying this fetishization of 'character' is that of 'I' who is a *whole* subject." More recently, Belsey called "classic realism" the "accomplice of ideology," in part because "it tends to offer…the assumption that character, unified and coherent, is the source of action" (2002, 67; cf. 44–48).

to reduce characters to functions has a long history: "Beginning with Russian formalism, literary characters are decoupled from their implied humanness as the price of entry into a theoretical perspective on characterization" (2003, 15). However, in the "post-theory" world we are now said to inhabit,[8] literary analyses of character have again begun to appear. A number of scholars have pointed out problems with these attempts to make character "dissolve or disappear" (Lynch 1998, 15), and insisted that "human action is intelligible only if motivation is taken into account" (Breden 1982, 296–97).[9] Even those who oppose traditional views of character must concede that much "realistic" narrative art over the centuries invites readers to reconstruct characters as coherent "readable" personalities (Bersani 1976, 69), although they and other scholars differ on how interaction between textual cues[10] and reader imagination[11] produces this effect.

Among psychologists, Lupfer and his colleagues have recently called for a restoration of character as a social psychological construct, because it is "the basis for a distinctive and important form of social judgment."[12]

8.   See, e.g., Davis 2004, 164–68, Eagleton 2003, the essays in Payne and Schad 2003, and, in relation to biblical studies, Moore and Sherwood 2011, 2–31. Writing in 2007, Weitzman predicts an uncertain future for literary study of the Bible, noting that it is unclear whether "living in a 'post-theory' age…means that theory has prevailed…or…failed" (193–94, 201–2).

9.   Breden is replying to theorists like Propp, Bremond, and Barthes, who "unite in displacing character from story." Lynch observes that in their tendency to "glamorise the unconventional," the arguments against realism often "rehabilitated the very individualism that they sought to contest." In the end, "the merely demystificatory critique of the psychologized character dismisses the plentitude it should explain" (1998, 15–16).

10.   Textual cues include direct descriptions by the narrator as well as the narrator granting readers direct access to the thoughts and perceptions of a character. Other cues include quoted speech, gestures, actions, the judgments a character makes about other characters, and what the other characters say about a given personage. In Chatman's influential formulation, by means of such textual indicators readers construct a "paradigm of traits" for round characters, "through highly coded psychological information that we have picked up in ordinary living, including our experiences of art" (1978, 126). When textual cues allow readers to form an impression of a character's personality, the terms in which that personality is described will tend to imply a positive or negative judgment on the character. Authors can attempt to shape reader judgment by encouraging or blocking identification and sympathy for the character.

11.   On the role of imagination in this process, see Cohan 1990, 115–31.

12.   Lupfer and Gingrich 1999, 166; cf. Lupfer et al. 2000, 1355. Lupfer and Gingrich argue that "appraisal of others' character influences judgments about their 'deservingness'" (1999, 178; cf. 166). That is, those whose character is judged as

Social psychologists focus on the fact that "character, motive, belief, desire, and intention play leading roles in people's construal of others" (Gilbert and Malone 1995, 21). Because none of these constructs can actually be observed, people must infer them from words and deeds. When adults in modern Western cultures are "forced into inferring... intangibles," they often commit the "fundamental attribution error," that is, they explain behavior in terms of a person's disposition and personality traits, even when evidence points to the situation being the cause.[13] Research increasingly indicates that this "bias" is much less prevalent in Eastern cultures. According to Choi et al. (1999, 60; cf. 57), in the West inconsistency in behavior is taken as evidence of a person's dishonesty or inauthenticity, while in the East people are far more willing to attribute variability to situational constraints.[14]

Among moral philosophers there is deep disagreement about the relevance of psychology to their study of character. Some dismiss social psychological insights as misguided and/or irrelevant to virtue ethics,[15]

possessing "good" traits (according to the "assessors'" moral standards) deserve a positive outcome for their behavior. When people are perceived as having little control over their actions, interpretation of the outcome may depend upon the valences attached to their personal traits (1999, 185). These findings are the result of having subjects respond to invented "vignettes" which illustrate good and bad behaviors and trait attributions made by other characters. Unfortunately, these vignettes tend to make the characters' traits unmistakably univocal and readable, so that the subjects had no choice but to make black and white attributions about them. In order to gauge how people *really* attempt to flatten and make economical judgments about the behavior of real people or complex literary characters, the investigators would have had to expose their subjects to much more sophisticated narratives.

13.   Gilbert and Malone 1995, 21; Ross, 1977, 184–85. Bierbrauer notes that even when the "situational awareness" of subjects was increased, it did not decrease their tendency to make dispositional judgments about participants in the Milgram experiments (1979, 76, 81–82). Many psychologists would say that both the Milgram experiments and real-world catastrophes like the Holocaust refute the view that "monstrous deeds presuppose a monstrous character" (Roger Brown, quoted in A. G. Miller, 1986, 184). For a critique of the character–situation dichotomy and causal attribution model, see Malle 2004, 91.

14.   Cf. Markus and Kitayama 1991, 231–35. As J. Miller puts it, "in non-Western cultures, emphasizing the situational variability of behavior and treating the social role rather than the individual as the primary normative unit, make their attributors more sensitive to the contextual determinants of actions" (1984, 963–64; cf. 972). It should be noted that these studies are looking for typical patterns, not different individual patterns of attribution within a specific group. This tends to overlook individuals whose style of attribution is atypical for a group.

15.   Julia Annas's critique of psychological approaches to virtue ethics is directed not only at psychologists like Ross and Nisbett (1991), but also at philosophers such

while others are beginning to take note of psychological studies, although very few have heeded Anscombe's 1958 call to cease doing moral philosophy "until we have an adequate [and sound] philosophy of psychology...in which we are conspicuously lacking" (Anscombe 1997, 26, 29–30).[16] Not surprisingly, moral psychologists also recommend that we *"psychologize* morality" (Lapsley and Narvaez 2005, 21).

Whomever we might favor in the turf wars among psychologists, literary critics and philosophers, the problem of literary characterization remains an *ethical* one. As Ricoeur puts it, "there is no ethically neutral narrative" (1990, 139; cf. 1983, 94). Iris Murdoch (1999, 257) notes that works of fiction are "concerned with judgements which we make in ordinary life [as well as] judgements which we make upon people in literature."[17] And any attribution errors we might make about others in

as Harman (2000) and Doris (2002), who take note of attribution theory and other insights from social psychology (Annas 2003, n. p.). According to Annas, there are three attacks on virtue ethics: that it falsely assumes we have character traits, that it is egoistic, and that it is conservative. She says all these attacks are based on a misunderstanding of what virtue ethics is. Unfortunately, Annas's counter-attack is based on a reductive and uninformed notion of social psychological research. This includes her criticism of what she calls Milgram's "infamous" obedience experiments (Milgram 1974; 1977; see Chapter 4, below). Fleming also questions much of the empirical evidence against robust traits, adding that whatever evidence *does* exist "can easily be accommodated by virtue ethics," which is "grounded in the notion of character-traits." However, Fleming's definition of "character-trait" is unusually broad and weak: "a structure of some kind that is internal and/or peculiar to an individual agent, and which may be used to account for much of that agent's characteristic behavior, information processing, and subjective experience and so forth" (2006, 30–31, 38). Most recently, philosopher Gregory Currie's essay on narrative and the psychology of character relies almost entirely on a few of the psychological studies cited in Doris's book (Currie, 2009, 61–67, 71 nn. 1, 23, 25, 27 and 31).

16.  According to Crisp and Slote (1997, 2), Anscombe's article had a huge effect, although on the whole it did not turn philosophers in the direction of doing psychology. As recently as 2010, Briggs's attempt to build up a "character portrait" of the Old Testament's implied "virtuous reader" using virtue ethics makes no mention of the important empirical studies of ethical reading conducted by psychologists. Nor does it acknowledge the recent critiques of virtue ethics by moral psychologists. See further in Lasine 2011a.

17.  Murdoch believes that "in a novel the reader rightly expects some indication of how to read the relation, or apparent lack of relation, to the ordinary world" (1999, 257). As I will discuss in Chapter 9, readers' own values "surface" when they judge characters, and when they defend their readings to others who disagree about the character. In a way, reading character in books becomes a way of reading our own character, if we listen to ourselves (or if others *force* us to listen, as the prophet Nathan does with King David).

"real life" can also be made about characters in narrative, if we don't attend to the situational constraints in which characters are placed by authors.

Philosophers like Nussbaum believe that "literary theory needs ethical theory," if we are to answer the age-old ethical question, "How should one live?" (1992, 15–29, 36, 168, 191). While Nussbaum is primarily interested in "the moral vision" of the novelist (e.g. 1992, 142, 189),[18] Cora Diamond points out that most moral philosophers focus on "the characters—their dilemmas, their deliberation, their choices, their judgments, their conception of their situation." This will also be my primary focus in this book.[19]

At the same time, the ethical question "How should one live?" is certainly generated by biblical narrative. One's life may depend upon *how* one interprets these narratives. As Moses reminds his listeners, "it is no vain thing for you (מכם), for it is your life" (Deut 32:47).[20] Many

18. Many literary scholars and moral philosophers believe that the focus of ethical criticism should be on the ways in which literature makes readers "better" people, if not assigning value to works of literature. C. Diamond argues that Nussbaum's primary interest is not in the moral relevance of what characters do in literature, but in the novelist's "moral vision, his moral achievement" (1998, 42). It has been argued that the discipline of "English," with its focus on literary criticism, has been based on a desire to inculcate specific ethical and moral views in the readers of literature from its inception (see Eaglestone 1997, 11–19).

19. Nussbaum (1992, 48) cites Trilling's view that the enterprise of reading brings readers together "in a particular way that is constitutive of a particular sort of community, in which each person's views are respected as morally valuable." Cf. Booth's notion of "coduction" (what we do when we compare our experience of works with other more or less qualified observers, saying whether a given work seems to the individual better or worse than other works of the same general kind, and why; 1988, 72–73). In contrast to Booth and Nussbaum, my emphasis will be on the ways in which conversing about a work with others leads us to re-view the characters and events in response to how our conversation partners have construed them, and to give an account of why we favor our own view. This setting opens one up to be challenged in a way one could not do for oneself. For a collection of texts like the Bible, which over the centuries has been fundamental to the identity of various communities, discussing and debating the actions of characters can be a way of defining and placing oneself within that special interpretive community, including one's moral position within the group. Interpreting characters in shared stories can aid the formation of a group identity by creating shared ways of viewing traditional characters and by debating divergent reactions to the same characters.

20. And the rabbis add, "if it is vain, it is from you" (מכם; *y. Pe'ah* 1:1; cf. *Genesis Rabbah* on Gen 4:1). Compare Plato, *Resp.* 344d; 352d: "[this is] no small…ordinary matter, but how one should live." On these issues, see Lasine 1989b and Chapter 9, below.

voices within the Hebrew Bible *tell* readers how they should live—*or else*! What the texts themselves *show* is another matter. Biblical narratives are not *romans à these*, and their ethical implications remain open to debate. As I will discuss in later chapters, this openness, can—but does not always—keep readers honest, by continually calling their attention to the problematic nature of the reported events, the judgments pronounced by seemingly reliable characters, and their own tendency to seek premature closure.

Ethical criticism of narrative has gone out of fashion and come back in again. In 1988, Booth (25) lamented the fact that ethical criticism had suffered "theoretical ostracism." More recently, Nussbaum (1992, 29 n. 52) noted a "marked turn toward the ethical" within literary studies, and David Parker (1994, 33) pointed out that this development "is closely connected to a turn to the literary within ethics."[21] And just as opinions differ about the future of literary study "after theory," scholars envision different futures for so-called "post-theoretical, ethical criticism" (Gibson 1999, 12). For their part, psychologists have begun conducting empirical studies of how narratives affect the moral stance of readers, often by focusing on the highly debated processes of reader identification and empathy.[22] In fact, psychologist Frank Hakemulder, philosopher Paul Ricoeur, and novelist and critic Robert Musil have all called the reading of narrative a "moral laboratory."[23]

Moral philosopher Frank Palmer (1992, 81, 99) notes that "we see people with the eyes of evaluation"; in fact, "our moral expectations are built into our very conception of what they are doing." Similarly, studies by psychologist Lupfer and his team (2000, 1363) demonstrate that when people are first exposed to others they "promptly appraise their character if provided even a modicum of morally relevant information about them." As Fritz Heider observes, even people's successes and failure are

21.   In 2004 Martin Eskin commented that a strong interest in the question of "ethics and literature" had recently "celebrated its twentieth birthday," after having "gone public" in "*New Literary History*'s pioneering special issue 'Literature and/as Moral Philosophy'" in 1983. Eskin notes the repeated use of the metaphor of a double "turn" to describe this "burgeoning subdiscipline," but finds it to be inappropriate, since this movement does not really represent "a (radical) veering off from hitherto accepted intellectual practices" (2004, 557–58).

22.   Most recently (2007) Keen has studied the role of empathy in novel-reading, in part by appealing to developmental and social psychology, as well as neuroscience. She also gathers anecdotal evidence from other readers, which she compares to existing empirical studies of reading. For other empirical studies, see Hakemulder 2000; Polichak and Gerrig 2002; Batson et al. 2004; and Kuiken et al. 2004.

23.   Hakemulder 2000, 11; Ricoeur 1990, 139; cf. 188, 194; 1983, 94; Musil 1978a, 1351. Also see Collins and Zbikowski 2005, 845, 849.

"morally relevant" in this sense: "there probably exists a tendency to be "intropunitive" in regard to other persons, that is, to see the cause of their successes and failures in their personal characteristics and not in other conditions" (1944, 361). Literary scholars like Patricia Spacks believe that the same is true when we read about characters in narrative; that is, we "inevitably construct judgments" about the characters, employing the same "ethical categories" as when we "function as moral agents in the world" (1990, 202). Finally, Iris Murdoch (1993, 315) points out that even how we see *our own* situation "is itself, already, a moral activity."[24] This "we" includes not only ourselves in our everyday lives, but we as evaluators of characters in narrative, including biblical narrative.

In other words, "psychologizing" is a fact of life. It is also a fact of reading, even though the word is used pejoratively by some biblicists, as though we could (and should) entirely abstain from attempting to understand why characters (and real people) behave as they do.[25] Gunn

24. In fact, "perception itself is a mode of evaluation" (Murdoch, 1993, 315). Murdoch (1999, 91) observes that "although…the information which we have about [fictitious characters] is limited, this may be so also in the case of real people, and anyway the information is endlessly open to interpretation." Similarly, Rashkow notes that with biblical characters, "as with real people, we can't always 'know' why people act the way they do" (1993, 106). Cognitive psychologist Jerome Bruner (1986, 37) notes a different sort of similarity between life and narrative art: "character is an extraordinarily elusive literary idea…even in 'real life' it's always a moot question whether the actions of persons should be attributed to circumstances or to their 'enduring dispositions.'" Currie (2009, 63–64) believes that the similarity is not so great: "in real life and real time, we may count ourselves as doing well if we gain (we think) some vague, working understanding of a person's Character. Within a narrative, we may expect to do much better: getting ourselves, within a space of hours, into the position of making confident evaluative judgments about a person's deepest motives." One obvious difference between life and narrative is that "real life" isn't narrated, while narrators in literary works often make direct dispositional attributions about characters, just as various characters within the textual world make attributions about one another. These factors, together with the narrator's manipulation of situations she describes and the actions she chooses to report, create a reduced world whose inhabitants readers must evaluate. This might seem like a stacked deck, but we must also ask whether our perceptual world in "real life" is not itself already a stacked deck, in terms of our limited perspective, our expectations determining what we see, our ways of masking and "reducing" ourselves before others, and the reductive and typifying judgments others make about us. In the end, one must ask whether all our experience is mediated, constructed and reductive, both in quotidian life and in our experience of imaginary worlds in narrative.
25. In the history of literary criticism, L. C. Knights's influential 1933 work, *How Many Children Had Lady Macbeth?*, is perhaps the best-known attack on psychologizing literary characters and treating them as "friends for life" or "deceased acquaintances" (1933, 23, 27; cf. Woloch 2003, 16–17).

and Fewell (1993, 51) contend that biblical characters are constructed in a way which "compels" readers to psychologize about what "makes them tick" as "people." Speaking of Bathsheba, Walsh (1996, xxi) argues that even the narrator's silence about a character's motivation can make us "feel compelled to conjecture character traits to explain her actions."[26] I would suggest that it is not necessary to compel people to do what they ordinarily do. The question is which "inch-rules"[27] they will apply, and which traits this will lead them to attribute to a specific character.

It has become a commonplace of biblical literary studies that "round characters, like the real people in our lives, are elusive" and "slippery," if not "an abiding mystery."[28] However, this perspective overlooks the fact that "real people" also type one another all the time. As Hochman (1985, 46) puts it, our perception of people is typological in life as well as in literature, even with characters who are presented as radically individual. Studies of person perception have repeatedly shown that people tend to

---

26.   On the other hand, we need to leave open the possibility that silence may just be silence, just as "sometimes a cigar is just a cigar," according to the oft-quoted but apocryphal statement by Freud (see Elms 2001, 96–97). Not every action taken by a person shows that person's character. Walsh is certainly correct to point out that "although it is sometimes difficult for a modern reader to draw the line between appreciating the narrator's subtleties of characterization and over-psychologizing the characters, Hebrew narrative is clearly capable of deep psychological insight" (1996, 321). The question is where to draw the line between appropriate psychological analysis of character and "over-psychologizing," in a given case. We will find cause to draw that line in very different places when discussing different types of biblical characters.

27.   Dickens's Wickfield is not the only nineteenth-century literary character who illustrates observational and moral myopia through his total reliance on "inch-rules." Another is Hugo's Inspector Javert in *Les Misérables*. When Javert is forced to recognize that his "lifelong principles" of authority and duty are inadequate to the task of assessing the character of others (specifically Jean Valjean), "his blinkered, one-track mind" becomes so disturbed that the cognitive dissonance drives him to suicide (Hugo 1982, 1104–7). A similar form of potentially destructive single-mindedness which is illustrated in both *David Copperfield* and *Les Misérables* is the obsessive devotion of the father-figures Valjean and Wickfield for their daughters Cosette and Agnes. On Agnes, see Chapter 9, §7, below.

28.   Gunn and Fewell (1993, 75) contend that these elusive round characters are "always evading complete definition or explanation." Alter describes the "abiding mystery" of human character in the Bible as an imitation of the "abiding perplexities [of] man's [*sic*] creaturely condition" in history (1981, 126, 154, 176; for a critique, see Lasine 1986, 49). Responding to five papers included in the 1993 *Semeia* volume devoted to characterization, Robert Fowler (100) observed that all have "the slipperiness of biblical characters" as their theme.

"type" others, or classify them according to salient, concrete features such as gender, ethnicity, religion, and occupation (Hoffner and Cantor 1991, 77). That is, our perception of *other* people tends to be typological. As literary critic John Bayley puts it, "'character'...is what other people have, 'consciousness' is ourselves" (1960, 45).[29] Social psychologists call this "the actor-observer effect."[30] Literary scholar Hochman warns that "we are mistaken if we think that we are 'round'—that is, rich, inward, ambiguous and developing—whereas others, in their mechanical, attenuated, compulsive limitedness, are 'flat.'"[31]

In daily life, we *need* to categorize others by disposition in order to navigate our way through potential dangers efficiently. Making dispositional inferences and viewing "persons" as "absolute causal origins" is both economical and comforting, because it affords the perceiver a sense of control over reality (Heider 1944, 361).[32] As McAdams puts it,

29. Ricks (1988, 88) points to a similar bias among members of opposing academic groups: "You are a prejudiced clique, we are an interpretive community."

30. The actor–observer effect (AOE) refers to the fact that actors are less likely than were their observers to attribute their own behavior to dispositional causes (see, e.g., Gilbert and Malone 1995, 32; Försterling 2001, 94–96). In terms of the ethics of reading, we need to correct for the AOE when we judge characters by opposing their behavior to what we imagine we might have done in similar situations. Several recent studies have concluded that the AOE holds in some, but not all, circumstances; see Robins et al. 1996; D. Watson 1982; and Malle 2004, 188. Robins et al. (1996, 385) found that personality differences among attributors influenced the degree to which they displayed the AOE.

31. Hochman 1985, 44. Hochman believes that "any adequate view of character in life must allow that we tend to see ourselves as unique and with intrinsic knowledge." Cf. Bayley (1960, 34): "We really do not think of ourselves as fat, kind, irritable etc.—these are the qualities by which we are known to other people and which we may play upon and cultivate as a conscious *persona*." Bayley believes that "the great author can make us see his characters both as we see ourselves *and* as we see other people" (emphasis added). We will consider the effects of reading the Bible on self-perception in Chapter 9, §§7–9, below.

32. It is comforting because it allows "simplicity of organization," which enables us "to reinstate an equilibrium even when otherwise irreversible changes have disturbed it" (Heider 1944, 361). Heider contends that humans grasp, predict, and control reality "by referring transient and variable behavior and events to relatively unchanging underlying conditions, the...dispositional properties of his world" (1958, 79). Gilbert and Malone (1995, 35; cf. 32, 34) point out that while "drawing dispositional inferences may be the only one way of satisfying the need for control,...it seems to be the one way prescribed by Western culture." However illusory dispositional inferences may be, they "afford the observer a culturally acceptable way of gaining a sense of control over her or his environment," yielding "greater

attributing traits to people "essentially provides a psychology of the stranger, nothing more, nothing less" (1994, 303).[33] That the inability to detect the true character of strangers is also a danger for biblical characters is made unmistakably clear by the story of the man of God from Judah in 1 Kgs 13 (see Chapter 4, below).

E. M. Forster defines "round" characters as being "capable of surprising in a convincing way" (1927, 118). In contrast, "flattening" people and characters makes life easier by cutting down on the number of surprises we might encounter. As for literary art surprising us, Tristan Bernard astutely notes that "in the theatre people doubtless want to be surprised, but often by what they expect" (1909, 127). According to psychologist Wulf-Uwe Meyer (1988, 143, 136), surprise is elicited by unexpected events which are "discrepant with" or "contrary to" the schemata by means of which we make sense of our everyday surroundings. This prompts us to focus our attention on the schema-discrepant event, and, if necessary, to revise the relevant schemata in order to increase the effectiveness of our actions and attributions.[34]

psychological benefits than would logically impeccable inferences." In addition, dispositional inferences are "easy to make," and even when they are logically incorrect, "they may have few unfavorable and many favorable consequences." Försterling points out that tracing back an event to the motives or the intention of a person allows one to structure a multitude of stimuli in a simple, parsimonious, and unifying manner; attributions to the person follow the *Gestalt* principle of *Prägnanz* (2001, 28; cf. Bruner 1986, 38; M. Ash 1995, 184–85, 224). R. L. Gregory calls attention to an uncomfortable aspect of perceptual economy: "human prejudice is useful in saving thinking time: clearly it would be intolerable to have to consider all relevant possibilities" (1974, 639; cf. 533). To the data assembled by these psychologists we can add the specific type of moral attribution exhibited by gossip. Gossipers type and judge the subjects of the gossip, generalizing a defining personality trait from a single negative action (see Bergmann 1993, 121, 127; cf. 36; Lasine 2001, 101–5, 118–21).

33.  Cf. Gilbert and Malone 1995, 29; Bruner 1986, 39. McAdams adds that trait psychology is a legitimate paradigm for observing strangers because the "Big Five model of personality traits…encapsules [the] most general and encompassing attributions…that one might wish to make when one knows virtually nothing else about a person." The "Big Five" traits are neuroticism, extraversion, openness, agreeableness, and conscientiousness; see Matthews et al. 2003, 23–38. We might ask whether literary characters are "strangers" in McAdams's sense when readers encounter them. If so, in some cases they are only strangers in the sense that narrators prepare us for meeting them like friends who are fixing us up with a "blind date."

34.  Meyer 1988, 136, 144–46. Meyer describes this process as having several stages. The first involves the interruption of normal processing of schemata in order to focus on the discrepant event. The second is examining and evaluating the event's cause. Finally, when necessary, it leads to the updating or revision of the relevant

Nietzsche, the self-proclaimed psychologist "without equal" (1964a, 343), is not so optimistic about the likelihood of surprising events making our explanatory schemata more realistic and adaptive. He contends that new, foreign, unmotivated and unexplained feelings and events oppress and worry us, making us fearful and uneasy. They therefore "excite our causal instinct"—but not to initiate a search for truth. Rather, the first principle of such investigations is that "any explanation is better than none." We seek only a certain kind of explanation, the kind which is most familiar to us and which can most quickly rid us of the feeling of the strange and unexperienced. To explain the unknown in terms of the known is comforting and liberating—and it also inhibits and excludes the possibility of investigating the actual cause of surprising and unexpected phenomena (1964b, 111–13).

When, as biblical interpreters, we evaluate (and thereby achieve closure on) a biblical character, we must ask ourselves whether we have chosen to explain their behavior in the way that is most comforting and familiar (including methodologically familiar[35]) to *us*, as opposed to the most accurate way of understanding the role of disposition and situational constraints in the character's reported behavior. We must also ask whether the narrative in question has been rhetorically designed to prompt us to "naturalize"[36] the text in this way, or to prevent easy closure

---

schemata in order to more effectively direct one's actions, and, in some cases, the manner in which one makes attributions. Meyer et al. (1997, 253) add that the first two steps of this process "can be identified with the workings of the surprise mechanism proper, which we take to be an evolutionary old mechanism." Lewis (2000, 277) notes that surprise appears in the first six months of life. Children show surprise "when there is…either a violation or a confirmation of expectancy."

35.  Throughout this book I will have occasion to examine the wide variety of contradictory responses which commentators have made to the same biblical characters. How should one decide which response to affirm, if any? Should we privilege the interpretations of scholars whose methodological assumptions we share, or with which we are most familiar? Should we pick the response which seems to us to accord best with the text's narrative rhetoric, or come up with a new judgment which we believe is better supported by textual evidence, or which is more in line with the way we personally interpret people's character in daily life? Should we expose the ideological assumptions behind previous readings and then confess our own, arguing that they are in accord with the ideology projected by the text and its presumed author, or, if not, that we have bracketed them out when making our interpretations? All these strategies have been applied to biblical narratives, as we will see. I will employ many of them myself, knowingly or unknowingly. (I am well aware of my inability to bracket out successfully [or even to acknowledge] all of my ideological biases.)

36.  On "naturalization," see Culler 1975, 137–40.

by increasing our sensitivity to the complexity of interpersonal realities.[37] As noted by Ross and others, even psychologists are capable of
"surprising themselves" when they underestimate the role of situations.[38]
Because "we" humans differ in our tolerance for ambiguity, our preference for consistency, and our ways of reducing cognitive dissonance,
some responses to being surprised by discrepant information may end up
following Einstein's ironic dictum, "if the facts don't fit the theory,
change the facts."[39]

Now, many biblical scholars argue that surprising or seemingly
incoherent[40] character behavior is often *not* the result of a realistically
complex characterization, but the result of redactional layers, each of
which may project a different image of the character's personality. This
possibility must be considered in any discussion of biblical narrative, as
will become clear when we analyze the biblical depiction of kings like
David, Jeroboam and Ahab, prophets like Moses, Elijah and the man of
God from Judah, and the non-biblical figures Agamemnon and Periander.
Some go further, using perceived inconsistencies in characterization as
evidence on which to base a claim that different redactional layers exist
in the first place. For these scholars, "psychologizing" is an anachronistic
and pointless exercise.

Of course, much depends upon one's understanding of "coherence,"
and whether one assumes that the ancients' conceptions of coherence
were identical to those prevalent now.[41] I have already noted researchers

---

37. Sandbank contends that Kafka uses "surprise techniques" to startle his
readers by setting up "certain expectations and cancel[ing] them at once, with the
aim of attaining to the truth by exposing the deception of…conventional thinking"
(1970, 262–63). For a comparison between Kafka's narrative techniques and those
employed by the biblical authors, see Chapter 9, §8, below.

38. As, for example, when making predictions concerning the outcome of the
Milgram obedience experiments; see Ross 1977, 212–13, cf. 186–87; Gilbert and
Malone 1995, 24; Milgram 1977, 118–19; A. G. Miller 1986, 20–36.

39. These processes, and the ways in which readers reduce dissonance involving
the behavior of Yahweh and King David in 2 Sam 24, will be discussed in Chapter
9, §3, below.

40. What constitutes coherent or incoherent behavior in a literary character will
of course depend upon the interpreter's assumptions about the causes of human
behavior in "real life."

41. For example, while Fowler concedes that modern readers perhaps seek
consistency and coherence in reading, readers adopting "a post-modern mode" of
reading do not. He also "doubts that ancient readers did either," adding that if they
did, "those qualities were at least understood far differently than they are today"
(1993, 99). The degree of difference between ancient and modern representations of
mental life is discussed in detail in Chapter 2, below.

who study the need for humans to perceive others as possessing coherent and predictable character traits in order to negotiate their social world with economy and safety. As noted by Furnham (1995, 402), "intolerance of ambiguity…serves a coping function." On the level of object perception, there is ample evidence that we seek coherence and simplicity, in other words, as "good" a *Gestalt* as possible.[42] For social-cognitive psychologists like Cervone and Shoda, personality coherence requires that personality variables function as coherent, integrated systems. An individual's "unique characteristic organization of cognitions and affects… fosters stable patterns of behavior variation and consistency across situations" (1999, 17, 21).[43] This view also posits that people generally achieve a coherent sense of self and develop and update a coherent life story that reflects both their past experience and current aspirations (1999, 17–18).[44]

In terms of our expectations of coherence as readers, I have already mentioned literary theorists who deny that there is such a thing as a stable, coherent self. Cohan argues that "the conventional assumption that character is readable only when grounded in the specific ideology of psychological coherence….obscures the imaginative function of character" (1990, 115). While seemingly incoherent characters might still be "readable," many empirical studies indicate that readers do "attempt to maintain coherence at both a local and a global level" and experience difficulty when they read information which is inconsistent with a protagonist's already established characteristics (Albrecht and O'Brien 1993, 1066).

On the level of the work as a whole, Wayne Booth claims that "we all admire…works that acknowledge their own inconsistencies and thus reflect a genuine encounter with recalcitrant materials" (1988, 193–94). Susan Suleiman's study of ideological literature supports Booth's point: "to the extent that contradictions introduce disruptive elements…they allow the system to test and possibly to reinforce its own coherence. A crisis overcome (or 'weathered')…is also a sign of the system's

---

42. In Gestalt psychology this is referred to as the principle of *Prägnanz*; see n. 32 above.

43. In Chapter 3 I will discuss this notion of "cross-situational coherence" (Cervone 1999, 303–41) in relation to specific biblical characters. Doris (2002, 85) argues that in terms of "familiar understandings of ethical character," the social cognitive conception of personality overemphasizes coherence, and downplays the fragmentation and disorder of human behavior.

44. This last factor recalls Sartre's distinction between facticity and transcendence, which is discussed in Chapter 9, §1, below.

flexibility or 'openness.'" In contrast, genres of literature like the *roman
à these*, which are excessively coherent or "redundant," are "so predictable that it no longer offers the encoded reader any area of uncertainly on
which to exercise his [*sic*] imaginative or guess-making capacities." The
"perfectly readable" characters in such works are caught in "a network
of…redundancy that allows for…no surprises."[45]

While some biblicists take seemingly incoherent characters as an
indication of redaction, others contend that psychological verisimilitude
and logic are sometimes sacrificed by the biblical editors in the service
of an ideological point. Some scholars who choose this strategy assert
that the "iron necessity" of mythical plots causes the subordination of
character, so that figures like Samuel, Jonathan, or Elijah are "rendered
incredible" (Jobling 1998, 6–7)[46] or incoherent (White 1997, 4, 7).[47] In
what follows, I will recommend that we make a careful and sustained
attempt to analyze surprising character behavior in psychological terms
*before* deciding that the portrayal is psychologically or narratively
incoherent due to redaction or other factors.

Before we can inquire about the relationship between literary characters and real people, we have to admit that there is no agreement about
what it means to be a "person." As one classical scholar points out,
"critics usually start from the premise that we know what 'people' are."
And, "in daily life we have to behave and speak…as if everyone knew

---

45.   Suleiman 1983, 172, 194, 180. For more on Booth's point, see Chapter 3,
below. Suleiman (1983, 180–81) contends that readers "rebel" against excessive
coherence. As I have discussed elsewhere (Lasine 1986; 1989a), in certain conditions people are fascinated by the apparent inconsistencies, incoherencies, and
contradictions which challenge our habitual tendencies. Literary forms such as the
folk riddle function to keep societal thinking flexible and adaptable by challenging
categories in this way. Seeming incoherent or inconsistent literary texts can serve the
same function, as can Hebrew scripture.

46.   Referring to Jobling's earlier discussion of Saul and Jonathan, Robert
Gordon argues that Jobling is "looking for a narrative coherence which makes no
concessions to historical reality"; as a result, "Jobling has imposed his own stereotype on the narrative and castigated it for vacuity" (Gordon 2000, 335; cf. Jobling
1986, 29–30). In other words, Gordon believes that Jobling viewed the characters'
behavior using the wrong "inch-rules."

47.   Rashkow (1993, 107) leaves room for both types of explanation: "contradictory behavior in a biblical character may result from psychic complexity, but may…
be more a function of the requirements of the story-line than personality." The
difficult part is to decide which kind of explanation is appropriate for a specific
instance of "contradictory behavior," assuming we can agree that the behavior is
"contradictory" in the first place.

what constitutes a person in the real world" (Easterling 1990, 84).[48]
Literary critic Bayley believes that "the critic's distrust of judging in
terms of 'character' to-day arises from the total absence of agreement
about what people are really like and how they can be portrayed" (1960,
281). Philosopher Murdoch (1999, 255) is more blunt: "people in real
life are very, very odd as soon as one gets to know them at all well."
Once again, it is clear that a rigorous discussion of characterization
requires us to wrestle with psychological and philosophical questions as
well as literary issues.

There is also a fundamental historical question to be addressed in this
connection: How different are "people" now from the "people" represented in ancient Near Eastern narratives like those of the Hebrew Bible?
While it may be inevitable for modern Western readers to view characters in ancient Near Eastern narrative in terms of modern notions of
personality traits and modern styles of attribution, is it *appropriate* to do
so? One might argue that ancient Near Eastern conceptions of the self
differ from the various ones displayed in modern cultures, and even
from, say, ancient Greek, conceptions. Some theorists believe that conceptions of the self are even more fickle than that; one notes that what
strikes readers as real and sincere in literary characters changes like
fashion as the social reality changes (Lynch 1998, 27, 255, 257). How,
then, *should* we answer the question, "How different are they?" Chapter
2 of this study is devoted to answering this question. For now, suffice it
to say that a number of classicists and literary scholars believe that some
"fundamental factors in human experience" (Halliwell 1990, 34–35) are
universal, allowing characters in ancient texts to seem familiar to us.

## 2. *Preview of Chapters 2–9*

In the chapters which follow, I will discuss the remaining methodological and theoretical issues which are raised by my enterprise and then turn
to the analysis of various biblical texts using the interdisciplinary
approach I outlined above. Chapter 2 addresses the difficult core issue I
just noted: How different were the ancients (and the literary characters
they created) from the various types of people who now read the Bible?
What methodological problems must be considered in order to answer
this question? These issues are addressed by making use of insights from
a variety of theorists in different fields, all of whom concern themselves

---

48. According to Easterling, the underlying assumption of these critics is that
"real people" are "relatively stable and definable" in comparison to fictional
personages (1990, 84).

with ancient and modern concepts of selfhood, consciousness and mental space. After surveying previous work on these issues by biblical scholars, I then examine several biblical texts (including Gen 4, Ps 55, and Job's speeches) in order to determine how they represent selfhood, mental space, and consciousness, including phenomena such as inner conflict and deliberation. In this connection I also consider the consequences of biblical characters not being able to imitate Yahweh's ability to penetrate the "secrets of the heart" (Ps 44:22). Chapter 3 then examines another group of biblical narratives in order to illustrate the ways in which readers seek psychological and narrative coherence even when dealing with heavily redacted biblical texts. In effect, this means that even redaction critics need to have a precise understanding of how they and everyone else normally attribute traits to characters, and how they can avoid the pitfalls inherent in our habitual ways of judging character. To illustrate the importance of such precision, I begin by analyzing the interplay between character and situation in the prologue to the book of Job. I then examine in detail narratives involving two prophets (Moses and Elijah) and two kings (David and Zedekiah).

Having forged the theoretical and methodological foundation for what is to follow, Parts II and III of *Weighing Hearts* present detailed studies of specific biblical personages, charting the interplay between character and situation in their presentation, first in texts which focus on prophets and then in texts which report the actions of kings. Different stories call for different approaches to the problem of character. In some cases, an appropriate psychological approach requires insights from attribution theory; in others, the material invites a psychoanalytic approach to personality types.

Chapter 4 deals with characterization and the ethics of obedience in the story of the man of God from Judah in 1 Kgs 13, a narrative which features characters who have been said to be devoid of personality. Many commentators have made strong ethical judgments about these characterless characters, and attributed a number of dispositional traits and intentions to them. In addition, readers have long puzzled over the unhappy fate of the obedient man of God, who is killed by a lion because he believed the lie told by the Bethel prophet. I will focus on the interplay between character (or lack of character) and situation in the story, by analyzing the events in light of the continuing debate over Stanley Milgram's famous obedience experiments and by comparing the man of God with Dante's gullible prophet Virgil, who is the victim of similar deceit. I also examine the equally disconcerting report in 1 Kgs 20 about the prophet who asks his colleague to strike him—without giving any explanation—and then tells the colleague that he will be killed by a lion because he refused to comply. After discussing the so-called folktale elements in 1 Kgs 13, the chapter concludes by revisiting the issues of character, situation, obedience, and divine justice with the help of an actual folk story, the fable of the scorpion and the frog.

Having discussed a prophet who is devoid of personality, I next turn to a series of narratives which feature a character who is typically taken to possess a strong and unique personality: the prophet Elijah. Chapter 5 considers the evidence favoring the many divergent assessments which readers have made concerning Elijah's personality as it is displayed in 1 Kgs 19. Many readers find the prophet's behavior here to be quite puzzling. Although he has just enjoyed a complete victory over the prophets of Baal and escaped Jezebel's attempt to kill him, he begs Yahweh to kill him, saying that he is no better than his fathers. As he construes his situation, he is the only prophet left, a man who is extremely jealous for Yahweh, and a man whose own people want to kill him. Some commentators attempt to explain Elijah's surprising behavior by diagnosing him as suffering from some sort of mental disorder. After showing that such judgments typically lack theoretical rigor in psychological terms, I make an extended analysis of Elijah's wish to die, his reading of his situation vis-à-vis his people, and his ultimate ascension, using psychological studies of the attitudes toward death and jealousy exhibited by people with narcissistic personalities. The final section of the chapter analyzes the relationship between personality, narcissism, and death, taking my lead from the poet Wordsworth's childhood desire to escape death by translation in the manner of Enoch and Elijah, "whatever might become of others."

Part III opens with a fresh analysis of two rulers of the Northern Kingdom about whom I have written in the past. Chapter 6 traces the interplay between character and situation in the Jeroboam and Jehoram narratives in order to understand why readers have reacted so negatively to their reported behavior. Many commentators have explained the Jeroboam's intentions and behavior in terms of negative character traits such as selfishness, cowardice, obduracy, and inability to trust, without considering that Jeroboam's actions in 1 Kgs 12 have more to do with the realities of his political situation than they do with his personal disposition. In other words, they have engaged in over-attribution. While some social psychologists believe that situations are largely of one's own making, 1 Kgs 11–14 raises the question whether Yahweh put Jeroboam into a no-win situation of *Yahweh's* own making. King Jehoram of Israel is also confronted with a uniquely constraining situation when he encounters a cannibal mother in his besieged capital. While most scholars are quite severe in their assessments of Jehoram's character, both here and elsewhere in 2 Kgs 3–9, I will argue that Jehoram is presented sympathetically, in spite of his desire to kill the prophet Elisha. Readers of 2 Kgs 6 who identify with the desperate king and share his perspective will be led to question a divine justice which is devoid of maternal compassion and punishes the guilty by inverting human nature itself.

Chapter 7 examines the characterization of Ahab, a king who is usually judged to be more wicked than Jeroboam and as weak as Zedekiah. Here I use a comparative approach to gain insight into the portrayal of Ahab as type and individual. In both the biblical portrait of Ahab and Herodotus's depiction of the tyrant Periander, what counts as typical for a wicked king is outlined in speeches made by other characters in the same work. Both Ahab and Periander display behavior which is not in conformity with the expectations set up by their presumed type. And in both cases historical and archaeological information about the king suggests a much different picture of the king's career and character from that which readers usually take away from the texts themselves. I then compare the portrayal of Ahab as a supposedly weak king with Homer's depiction of Agamemnon in *The Iliad*. Both kings complain about a prophet who never tells him anything but evil, and both act as foils for other characters who display strong, if not narcissistic, personalities (Elijah and Achilles). The results of these comparisons will allow me to draw some broader conclusions concerning the depiction of royal character in biblical narrative.

The concluding chapters of the book take Egyptian accounts of postmortem judgment as their starting point. In Chapter 8, Egyptian texts describing the "weighing of the heart" of the deceased are compared with the motif of weighing of the heart in the book of Job. Here the emphasis is on the unusual accuracy of Job's self-evaluation as blameless and righteous, in contrast to the fear of self-betrayal expressed in the *Book of the Dead*. I then focus on other biblical characters who insist that they are righteous or possess laudable character traits, including those who are put into situations in which they are forced to explain and justify themselves. After examining cases which illustrate the various ways in which biblical speakers profess self-knowledge, I turn to an extended discussion of King David's self-presentation as soft or weak in 2 Sam 3.

The final chapter begins by considering another Egyptian text which claims that individuals' deeds are placed beside them in "heaps" when they are judged by a god after death. For the Egyptians, afterlife judgment involves "counting" a person's character and heart. This notion is then compared to Job's recognition that God is "counting his steps" and to the oath of clearance he proceeds to take in ch. 31. Should we "living judges" count and weigh the heaps of information we receive about other people and characters in narrative such as King David, knowing that our judgments will also expose our own moral posture? Because this is a complex and difficult task, I approach it from several angles. First I ask whether it is just to condemn a person as a whole and forever because of one or more wicked act(s) he or she has committed, taking into account the views of both moral philosophers and the social psychologists who study the "negativity bias" we display when judging others. I then examine the role played by cognitive dissonance in determining readers' judgments concerning the behavior of both David and his God Yahweh, using the story of the plague in 2 Sam 24 as my example.

In the remaining sections of the chapter I consider the advice given by Diderot, and much more strongly by Kierkegaard, that we read "sacred texts" personally, through identifying sympathetically with characters in scriptural narrative. After discussing theories about the process of identi-fication and empathy with literary characters, I ask whether it is justifi-able to withhold empathy and condemn King David as a person for his actions against Bathsheba and Uriah, instead of showing understanding for the king as a "fully human" being like ourselves. Is showing mercy toward David actually an evasion of responsibility on our part, and a way to avoid being judged by the text in the way that Nathan's parable judges David? Before making my Osirian decision concerning David's afterlife, I compare the presentation of the biblical David with two characters in modern Western literature. The first is another David who must deal with a Uriah, in Dickens's *David Copperfield*. The second is a character who, like King David, is confronted with a parable which carries life and death implications for him as an individual. This is Josef K. in Kafka's novel *The Trial*. I will argue that both of these modern works resemble the Court History in challenging readers to "break the spell of identification" with a morally suspect protagonist. I then conclude by deciding David's fate (and thereby fixing my own character) on the basis of what we have learned about the implications of judging others in this study as a whole.

Chapter 2

SEARCHING THE INNERMOST PARTS:
CONSCIOUSNESS, SELF, AND MENTAL SPACE
IN ANCIENT LITERATURE

According to Stephen Geller, the revolutionary "invention" of the "indivisible, united self" happened in Israel (2000, 298; cf. 337).[1] Geller believes that this was the achievement of deuteronomic covenant religion and its prophetic sponsors. Other biblical scholars share this opinion, although classicists like Bruno Snell contend that the revolution happened in Greece, where the human *Geist*[2] was "invented" on the basis of a new self-conception. Both Geller and Snell also describe this innovation as a "discovery."[3] Not to be outdone, some Egyptologists claim that "man...discovered himself" in Egypt,[4] a process which involved both the

---

1. On Geller's view, see further in §4b below. Cf. Assmann (1993b, 154), who asserts that Israel's walking in scripture and "living by citation" is tantamount to a revolution in human history. "Living by citation" (*das zitathafte Leben*) is Thomas Mann's expression; see Mann 1972, 146–47.

2. This term is always difficult to translate into English. Snell at times uses the word in the sense of "spirit," "mind," or "intellect."

3. As Snell (1975, 7) puts it, the *Geist* and new self-conception were not only "invented" (*erfunden*) but truly "discovered" (*entdeckt*). My translations are based on the 4th German edition (the English version is based on the 2d German edition). The term "revolution" is used in the English version (1960, vii), but not in the 4th German edition.

4. Lichtheim, 1988, 142. Lichtheim (1992, 23) contends that the Egyptians "discovered the sources of their selfhood" and their "inner-directedness" with the rise of the 11th dynasty, manifested by the focus on the heart (*ib*) and the character (*qd*). She believes that after the Old Kingdom, the brief kingless period liberated the individual. Everybody had tombs and memorial stones with self-presentations. When vigorous kingship returned in the 11th Dynasty, the gain in self-awareness had been so large that there was a "pride of self" expressing itself in new way. As evidence she points to the growing vocabulary related to the self and autobiographies of the period (1988, 142–43). Elsewhere Lichtheim observes that "what comes to fruition in the New Kingdom is "conscious...evolved individualism" (1976, 104).

discovery of the "inner self" or "inner man,"[5] and the "discovery" of character and the "dawn of conscience."[6]

While such claims are dramatic and stimulating, the prosaic truth is that fundamental methodological difficulties have to be confronted and overcome before one could even *begin* to debate whether the invention of the "self" happened in Israel, Greece, or Egypt—or some other place much farther from the Mediterranean. Among them is the question whether modern assumptions about mental space skew our understanding of the way ancient texts portray individuals and their consciousness, particularly when it comes to topological factors such as the relations between inside and outside, separation, enclosure, and connectivity (see Lasine 1977, 81–85). After discussing this issue, and several other basic methodological problems in general terms, I will focus on representations of mental space and selfhood in the Hebrew Bible.

## 1. *"How different were the ancients?"*

Classicist Michael Halleran (1992) voices a question many scholars have asked themselves about the ancient world as a whole: "while it is unquestionably true that our categories are not the same as the Greeks', just how different are they?"[7] This question has been asked in various ways by classicists, historians, philosophers, historical sociologists, psychologists, and even literary artists. Classicists basically fall into two groups, one arguing that differences exist but are smaller than is usually assumed, and the other insisting on the "chasm" or "axial break-throughs"

5.  Assmann 1993a, 96. For Assmann, this includes the attendant "invention" of the "guiding, hearing, heart weighed-in-the-balance" (*das leitende, hörende, auf der Waage gewogene Herz*). He, like Lichtheim, traces "the discovery (*Entdeckung*) of the inside" to the 11th Dynasty, although the "invention" (*Erfindung*) of the heart as a symbol for internal guidance and moral accountability is the result of a long process which began at the end of the Old Kingdom (1993a, 96–97). Elsewhere, Assmann asserts that the discovery and development of the idea of "the inner man" constituted an "axial break-through" (2005b, 135). Similarly, the idea of the judgment of the dead by a divine court constituted a "break-through" which signaled an "important shift in history of the heart" (2005b, 139).

6.  Breasted proclaims that "two thousand years before the theologians' age of revelation began,…the dawn of the age of conscience and character broke upon the world… [T]he discovery of character [is] the greatest discovery…of the evolutionary process" (1968, xv–xvi; cf. 139–40).

7.  Cf. Izre'el (2001, 135), who asks "are we indeed so different from these allegedly remote cultures [of ancient Mesopotamia]?" Izre'el's answer is that we are not at all remote from the ancients in most ways, including "in our understanding of human nature."

separating moderns from the ancients.[8] Bernard Williams concludes that "in important ways, we are, in our ethical situation, more like human beings in antiquity than any Western people have been in the meantime" (1993, 166).[9] James Redfield (1975, 20–22) focuses on "Homeric social psychology" and suggests that we may be "more like Homer's Achilles than we like to think."[10] Momigliano (1985, 89) contends that "Greek and Roman historians talked about individuals in a manner which is not distant from our own." And while Pelling (1990, 249) concedes that the Greeks may not have felt their emotions quite as we do, he adds that "such imaginative cultural leaps may not be different in type from those we make every day in seeking to engage sympathetically with people of different ages, cultures, and moral or religious values."

Among the scholars who emphasize difference, Ruth Padel advises that it is difficult but rewarding to think of the ancient Greeks as "astoundingly alien from ourselves"; it is we, not they, who are "the cultural oddity" (1992, 10, 35).[11] Among classicists of earlier generations, Fränkel (1951, 108) asserts that "the homeric person actually had a different structure from that with which we are acquainted today. People are by no means always the same in all periods and all regions." Snell (1975, 7) warns that because Homer's works speak to us and strongly move us, we can easily overlook how fundamentally different everything is from what we are accustomed to experience. Snell argues that in the early period consciousness of the "character" of an individual person is lacking, as is self-awareness in general. People in Homer do not yet have a *Geist* or soul, or even a body in the precise sense of the word. Inner dialogue, genuine reflection, and genuine personal decisions are also lacking (1975, 10, 18, 27–28).

8.   Padel (1992, 34) suggests that there is likely a "profound chasm" between "our" approach to metaphor and that of pre-Aristotelian Greeks. Wheeler Robinson's discussion of metaphor in the Bible (1911, 21–22) is quite similar to Padel's view of the early Greek attitude toward metaphor. On axial break-throughs, see n. 5 above and n. 13 below.

9.   B. Williams assures his readers that he does not "want to deny the otherness of the Greek world" (1993, 2; cf. 4); however, he admits that his stress will be on "some unacknowledged similarities" between Greek conceptions of responsible action, justice, and intention and modern Western ideas.

10.   Redfield means this in the sense that "our lives could also be described as consisting of transparently socially conditioned speech and action" (1975, 22).

11.   She adds that another "core difference" between "us" and fifth-century Athenians is our tolerance for "extraordinary dissociations between what we think is inside us and what we imply is inside us when we speak of our feelings" (1992, 35).

Among Egyptologists, Breasted believes that before the Egyptians discovered character and conscience, humans lived in a "characterless universe."[12] Brunner-Traut (1990, 71–79) contends that the Egyptians viewed the person as simply the aggregate of qualities without a center. She accepts Snell's lexical argument that the Greeks lacked the concept of a unified "body" and extends this assumption to the Egyptians, who viewed the body as a "jointed doll" or "mannequin" (1990, 72).[13] And while Assmann takes issue with Brunner-Traut's view,[14] he assumes that neither the early Egyptians nor the Homeric Greeks recognized the distinction between inside and outside (see further below).

Historical sociologists and psychologists are also divided on this issue.[15] However, the majority of influential figures tend to see important differences, resulting from an historical process of social change (or development, progress, or evolution). For example, Norbert Elias (1970, 128) attempts to demonstrate that a split between individual and society was caused by a specific experience of self, one which, since the Renaissance, has become characteristic of wider and wider circles of European society. In antiquity, this mode of self-experience was perhaps, at most, exhibited solely by some intellectual elites. And Freud (1948, 332) is in agreement with both Elias and Fränkel when he asserts that "it

12.  Breasted (1968, xv): "man [*sic*] arose to visions of character. That achievement…was…from a characterless universe,…to a world of inner values transcending matter…for the first time conscious of character and striving to attain it." More recently, Karenga (2004, 372–80) has described the ancient Egyptians' focus on "character" in terms of "virtue ethics"; see below.

13.  Like Snell (1975, 17–18), Brunner-Traut compares ancient depictions of the human body to drawings by children. However, rather than contrasting the depictions of the body by children and by the Greeks, she claims that Egyptian "aspective" art is comparable to children's art in its "additive" method of apprehending the whole of the picture gradually, part by part. She also claims that Egyptian art is comparable to the artwork of modern mentally disturbed individuals, primitives (whom she prefers to call "ethnicities"), "Sunday painters" who are inadequate in drawing, modern expressionist painting, and all ancient art prior to the Greek classical period (1990, 7, 59; cf. 69). Brunner-Traut contends that it was in Greece at the turn of the sixth–fifth centuries B.C.E. that a unified view, which subsumed the elements under an overriding whole, first came about during what Jaspers calls the "axial age" (1990, 59; cf. 4).

14.  Assmann (1993a, 87–88) disagrees with Brunner-Traut's view that the Egyptian person is an additive multeity, but he does believe that this description does fit the Homeric image of humanity.

15.  After discussing a variety of opinions, van Krieken (1998, 125) concludes that "the problem remains of *whether* human psychology today is so different from that of earlier historical periods."

is incorrect that the human mind (*Seele*) has undergone no development since the most ancient times." In the course of human development "external force gradually becomes internalized."

As I discuss below, many philosophers also emphasize change over time. Some rely on the opinions of classicists such as Snell and Adkins. For example, Hall (1996, 243) believes that "the human adventure" has gone "from…disparate and unfocused actions, dispositions, and understandings…to the unity of the individual human being," and back again.[16] The "postmodern" self differs from the "original disparate self" only in the sense that "consciousness of self [is now] a candidate for a variety of distinctive interpretations."[17]

Among literary works, Thomas Mann's *Joseph und seine Brüder* has been said to focus on "a psycho-anthropological theory of the development of human consciousness" (Bishop 1996, 143).[18] In both *Joseph* and his lectures, Mann asserts that "the ancient 'I' and its consciousness of itself were different from ours, less exclusive, with less sharply defined boundaries. It stood, as it were, open to the back [*nach hinten offen*] and absorbed much of what had been, which it repeated in the present, so that it was 'again there' with him" (1972, 146; cf. 1964, 90; 1960, 659). In fact, the historical persons of the ancient world lived their lives in myth, as a consecrated repetition. At times, Mann asserts that the self (and *Geist*) has developed, advanced, and become emancipated (1960, 665–68), while the ancients did not quite know who they were (1964, 94; 1960, 659). On other occasions, however, he claims that the ancients had a deeper and more precise way of knowing who they were than modern individuals do (1960, 659).[19]

16. Hall cites classicist Arthur Adkins to support his assumption that "the semantics of selfhood" begin with Homer. As is typical of such discussions among classicists, ancient Near Eastern evidence goes unmentioned. See below for a similar exclusion of Near Eastern evidence by biblicist Sandmel. On Adkins, see Chapter 4, below.

17. In an early work (1964c, 127–28), Nietzsche saw a greater difference: "In the end, the modern person drags around with him an immense multitude of indigestible stones of knowledge." This exposes "the most characteristic trait (*eigenste Eigenschaft*) of this modern person: the curious opposition of an interior with no corresponding exterior, and an exterior with no corresponding interior, an opposition unknown to ancient peoples."

18. Assmann (1993b, 145) considers Mann's novel to be the most significant contribution to this theme prior to Marcel Mauss; on Mauss, see n. 44 below.

19. In Musil's *Der Mann ohne Eigenschaften* (1978b, 150), the character Ulrich reflects that "in former times one was a person with a better conscience than today." In Ulrich's opinion, those early peoples were more vulnerable to being moved by

Anthropologists and cross-cultural psychologists also vary in their assessment of the degree of difference among cultures. Solomon (1996, 111) claims that "the 'Western' conception of the self has...been misconstrued"; this conception is actually "far more social [and interdependent] as well as socially constituted than we are usually willing to recognize."[20] Among anthropologists, Geertz's characterization of the "peculiar" modern Western conception of the person as a "bounded, unique,... integrated motivational and cognitive universe" has been particularly influential with non-anthropologists.[21] Among cross-cultural psychologists, the East is typically said to have a more holistic conception of the person, and to understand dispositions to be flexible and malleable instead of fixed (Choi et al. 1999, 57–58).[22] The West, on the other hand, is assumed to treat the autonomous individual as inherently asocial if not antisocial, rather than viewing individuals as open and interdependent (J. Miller 1984, 963).

## 2. *Methodological Problems Assessing Ancient Selves from Texts*

Drawing conclusions about ancient selves on the basis of textual remains is fraught with methodological difficulties. One set of problems involves assessing evidence about ancient people on the basis of modern assumptions about what constitutes a "self." To give just one example, Snell (1975, 11) argues that "if things do not appear in Homer which we, with our modern thinking, immediately expect, it is to be presumed that he did not yet have knowledge of them." Besides assuming that ancient texts

external forces like God, pestilence and war. But as a whole, in terms of their city or nation—as well as for whatever personal movement was left to them—this could be answered for and was clearly delineated.

20.   His goal is to "challenge our Western view of the 'Western' view of the self and render our conception of ourselves more 'Chinese'" (1996, 112).

21.   Geertz 1983, 21. Geertz's comment has been quoted and used by cross-cultural and social psychologists, social cognitivists, moral philosophers, moral psychologists, as well as interdisciplinarians working on psychology and the arts, American studies and English.

22.   Some go beyond Geertz, leaving the impression that every modern Westerner has a narcissistic personality. For example, Markus and Kitayama (1991, 246) assert that in the Western "independent construal of the self," the self is assumed to be a complete, whole, autonomous entity without others, "conscious of being in control over the surrounding situation," needing to express their own thoughts and feelings, but "less conscious of the need to receive the thoughts [and] feelings and actions of others."

necessarily offer reliable evidence about the mentality of historical peoples, Snell assumes that their failure to offer evidence of what he considers to be an expectable modern psychological trait means that this trait did not exist in the cultural world in which Homer lived. In addition, Snell assumes that there is only one monolithic modern mentality. Padel (1992, 46) suggests that Snell is projecting modern assumptions onto Homer when he argues that in Homer there is no unified self and that internal dialogue shows internal fragmentation.[23] She views this as an example of how we have projected the multiplicity, split, and disunity in our own self-image and images of consciousness onto others in past cultures.

The literary critic E. D. Hirsch criticizes Snell for having committed what Hirsch calls the historicist fallacies of the "inscrutable past" and the "homogeneous past" (1976, 39–40). In the first case, literary historians infer a past state of mind so different from our own that its texts can be understood only by an initiated few practicing "historical sympathy." The second fallacy is assuming that everyone who lived during a specific historical period shared the same mentality. Similarly, Bendix (1952, 301) warns against "the temptation of attributing to the people of another culture a psychological uniformity which we are unable to discover in our own." Hirsch (1976, 41) also describes a third fallacy, which he dubs "the fallacy of the homogeneous present-day perspective." There is no monolithic totally like-minded "us." However, saying that individuals and cultures are often very different from one another is not to deny that one can understand someone with a perspective (or culture) very different from one's own. In fact, the distance between one historical period and another is very small in comparison to the huge metaphysical gap we must leap to understand the perspective of another person in *any* time or place (1976, 42).

Elias is less confident that a modern *homo clausus* has the ability to understand people from a different culture or time. For people who believe that their own self is "inside," closed off from, and independent of, all other people and things which are "outside," it is difficult to ascribe significance to the facts which indicate that individuals live in

---

23. Even though Snell (and those with similar approaches like Fränkel and Adkins) are now rarely cited by classicists without caveats (see, e.g., Sullivan 1988, 2–10 and the studies she cites on p. 18, n. 46), recent studies by experts in other fields tend to be more uncritically accepting of Snell's conclusions (e.g. Green and Groff 2003, vii–viii, 6; Brunner-Traut [n. 13 above], and C. Taylor 1989, 118). Among Snell's critics, B. Williams (1993, 25) is perhaps most blunt, charging that "Snell has some peculiar formulations which help him not to see where he is going."

interdependence with others from childhood on (1997a, 51). Such people are incapable of understanding how it is possible for there to have been a civilizing process spanning many generations in the course of which the personality structure of the individual person changed, without the nature of people changing (1997a, 67–68).[24]

Other scholars point to different aspects of the same basic problem. B. Williams (1993, 5–6) notes that while we assume that we have an entirely adequate control of concepts such as autonomy, inner responsibility, and "developed moral consciousness," we actually have no clear idea of the substance of these conceptions, and hence no clear idea of what it is the Greeks did not have. As noted in Chapter 1, Easterling and Bayley go further, by asserting that in daily life we merely act as if we knew what constitutes a person, and by noting that there is a total absence of agreement about what people are really like.

Another methodological problem concerns the relationship between social institutions, language, and the psychology of the individual. Bendix (1952, 297) warns that if we take the symbols of a culture as a clue to the characteristic personality types of its participants, we will underestimate the incongruity between prevailing social institutions and cultural forms on the one hand, and the psychological habitus of a people on the other.

Nor can we assume congruity between the lexical characteristics of a culture and individual psychology, as do Snell and others like Pedersen and Boman.[25] Thomas Mann's narrator in *Joseph* assumes that the ancients' way of expressing themselves gives a faithful picture of their insight, pointing to the fact that antiquity "knew only such objective designations as 'religion' and 'confession' for the idea of 'personality' and 'individuality'" (1964, 90).[26] In contrast, Solomon (1996, 114) asserts that

24.  Solomon (1996, 115) cautions that self-conceptions, no matter how false, influence and eventually determine the construction of self. Schacht (1994, 444) notes that if individuals accept the socially induced self-identification that they are unitary agents, although this idea is "fundamentally a fiction," it "has the consequence that we not only apprehend ourselves accordingly, but also to a considerable extent cease to *be* creatures of the moment, and *become* such selves—at least in a functional sense, if not substantially."

25.  On Pedersen, see Barr 1961, 181–85; Polk 1984, 25–26. On Boman, see Barr 1961, 46–79 and Penchansky 1995, 17–31. In contrast to Snell, Sullivan's study of Homer's psychological vocabulary indicates that his characters *do* possess a degree of "innerness" and a sense of integrated selfhood (Sullivan 1988, 4–7).

26.  The basic problem with Mann's perspective on ancient Near Eastern people is not that it is based on the usual dichotomy between closed-off moderns and

how we talk about ourselves is only a partial indication of how we *think* about ourselves and how we actually behave... [I]t's possible for a culture to cultivate a way of talking about themselves and the self that is somewhat at odds with the ways in which they actually conceive of themselves and their relationships to one another.

Halliwell (1990, 37–38) uses the term "lexical bias" to refer to the assumption that individual lexical items and locutions or the lack of them are the most significant facts about the way in which a language shapes the conceptions expressible within it. He believes that this assumption is often hazardous, particularly in the psychological sphere. Cross-cultural psychologists like Church and Lonner agree that "some individual differences may not be encoded in the natural language and the structure of the personality lexicon may not be identical to the structure of personality" (1998, 36).

Egyptologists who grapple with ancient mentality also tend to rely on evidence from a "personality lexicon." Lichtheim uses the "expanding moral vocabulary" of Egyptian autobiographies as evidence for the discovery of the self (1988, 142; cf. Assmann 1993a, 97–98). Assmann notes that the Greek language possesses no equivalent for the Hebrew concept of the heart (*lēb, lēbāb*); consequently the LXX uses a variety of Greek words to represent Hebrew *lēb*. He also points out that Greek has not one, but many words to designate the "inner space" of soul, spirit, consciousness, feeling, affect, and drive. While Assmann concedes that this in no way speaks against the acceptance of an outer–inner distinction as such, it makes clear that the Greeks had no concept beyond the "inner"[27] to designate the middle or "personal center" of humans. The latter is the achievement of Hebraic and Egyptian concepts. In this respect, Israel and Egypt stand in contrast to Greece as "cultures of the heart" (Assmann 1993a, 82).

---

simpler "open" ancients, but that it is colored by his assumptions concerning a mode of life which he believes is prevalent universally. In one lecture, Mann (1972, 144) asserts that "life is actually a mixture of formulaic and individual elements... Much extra-personal, much impersonal identification, much which is conventional-schematic is determinant for the experience of...humans in general." He also draws a problematic parallel between the childhood of the individual and "the childhood of humanity, the primitive and the mythical." Even Assmann, who is so sympathetic to Mann's enterprise, concedes that Mann projected back modern artistic trends onto the ancient world (1993b, 153). For Assmann it is the myth of the "unity of the human spirit" which prevented Mann from catching sight of the spiritual world of Egypt in its foreignness (1993b, 156–58; cf. Mann 1960, 664).

27. This would seem to be inconsistent with Assmann's assignment of the early Greeks to the initial stage of "indifference," in which a distinction between inner and outer is not made; see §3, below.

Both Lichtheim and Assmann not only stress the importance of the heart as symbol in this phase of Egyptian history, but the importance of "character" as well. They point out that the expanding moral vocabulary of Egyptian includes several terms for what we call moral character. Although they do not define the sense in which they understand the term "character," in context it is clear that they have in mind "inner qualities" (Assmann 1993a, 98) which resemble durable dispositional traits.[28] In his recent study of the Egyptian concept of *Maat* and associated moral qualities, Karenga makes this explicit. Following modern Western moral philosophers like MacIntyre and Hauerwas, Karenga defines character as "a relatively stable dispositions [*sic*] toward doing good which enables one to live a moral life and thus flourish as a human being" (2004, 373–74). He then interprets selected textual evidence[29] to show that the Egyptians espoused a form of what is now called virtue ethics.

The fact that we must use literary and other texts as evidence for ancient self-conceptions and psychology is itself a fundamental methodological problem. Ancient literary conventions and reader expectations must be surmised from the texts themselves, insofar as they are knowable. Commenting on Fränkel, Redfield (1975, 22) warns that we should be cautious about moving so quickly from poetry to culture; the people of Homer's day may have had more "innerness" than Homer allows his characters. B. Williams (1993, 47) concedes that drawing boundaries between the stylistic and the psychological can be an exceedingly complex and elusive pursuit, above all because of the silences that are imposed by narrative restraint. Pelling (1990, 249) also admits that

28. For example, Lichtheim: "New attitudes of self-reliance and self-reflection mirrored in growing vocabulary. The word *qd* ('form'), available since the Old Kingdom in meanings of 'character,' 'behavior,' and 'good repute,' becomes prominent and continues in all three senses, until it loses some ground to *biȝt*, which is more specifically 'character'" (1988, 142; cf. 45 and 69).

29. In his preface/foreword to Karenga's book, Assmann diplomatically suggests that it is legitimate for a philosopher like Karenga, who wants to apply his findings to modern practice, to restrict himself to evidence which supports his views, unlike historians, who must take into account all relevant evidence (in Karenga 2004, xxi). I would suggest that it is no more legitimate for a philosopher to overlook counter-evidence than it is for an historian to do so. Sullivan finds evidence for "moral character" being expressed in Homer (e.g. 1988, 95, 115, 181, 189–90). In her view, "*phrenes* [are] a location of a person's inner qualities and a seat of his [*sic*] true character," and Homeric heroes are "strong personalities with distinctive traits" (1988, 58, 5). Like many other scholars who examine ancient texts for evidence of character, Sullivan assumes a notion of character which is identical to that of "naive lay dispositionists" in the West today (on this term, see Chapter 4, §3 below).

Greek dramatic conventions are barriers to understanding differences in degree between ourselves and the ancients.[30]

Finally, we might consider the possibility that modern Westerners understand "difference" differently from the ancients. To put it a bit less paradoxically, the ancients might have been aware of what we call differences, but not believe that they made much of a difference, in terms of their general understanding of how the world works and what constitutes meaningful change. Contemporary Western culture tends to be "exclusivist"; we live in a world of excluded middles, mutual exclusion, and exclusivist religions. This is not to affirm the once-popular notion that the ancients were limited to "mythical thinking" as opposed to the logical thinking of modern Westerners. For example, Cassuto is correct to advise us not to read biblical passages "in the light of concepts that came into existence at a later epoch" (1967, 57). But this does not justify his attempt to dismiss the problem of Yahweh punishing Pharaoh after hardening his heart by pointing out that "Greek logic was…non-existent" when this text was written (1967, 55).[31] Problems of theodicy were taken to be very real—and very urgent—in the ancient Near East long before Aristotle.

### 3. *Mental Space Ancient and Modern*

If people in the West have really become less open, more internally divided and more self-restrained or "disciplined" over time, as many theorists contend, the first question becomes "Why?" Many causes have been suggested. A number of social theorists and psychologists continue to call the "totally internalized individual" (Frankfurt Institute 1972, 48) the product of capitalism, the Protestant ethic, democracy, centralization, and/or legal innovations.[32] The ways in which this process is envisioned differ considerably. Theorists such Nietzsche, Elias, and Foucault all

---

30. Nevertheless, they and other classicists tend to be cautiously optimistic about the possibility of deciphering selves from the corpus of Greek texts, even apart from artifactual and other evidence.

31. Cf. Cassuto 1967, 432 on Exod 33:12–23: "this conversation is not conducted in accord with Greek or modern processes of logical thinking, but follows the pattern of eastern dialogues, which convey the intention of the speakers more by…allusion than through explicit statements."

32. On capitalism and the Protestant ethic, see the influential work by Weber (1934) and further below. Social psychologist Nisbett stresses "the Judeo-Christian insistence on individual moral responsibility" (quoted in Gilbert and Malone 1995, 34–35). On the role of centralization, see Elias 2002, 411–12.

stress, in their own fashion, that it is in modern societies' interest for individuals to be calculable. Nietzsche (1999, 293) asserts that for humans to become responsible they had to be bred to be regular, uniform, and thereby calculable and predictable. This was achieved "with the help of the morality of custom (*Sittlichkeit der Sitte*) and the social straightjacket." Once people found themselves enclosed in the captivating power of society and peace, they were reduced to calculating and cause-and-effect thinking; in other words, they were reduced to their poorest and most erring organ, their "consciousness" (1999, 322).

Elias (1997a, 66) also describes a push toward civilization which requires a stronger, more steady, general, and evenly maintained self-constraint, particularly of the emotions, as the social situation involves increasingly large and more complex networks of interdependency. Individuals are also forced to regulate their behavior in more stable fashion, resulting in it becoming increasingly automatic (1997b, 327–28). Elias sees the royal court playing a key role in this "civilizing process," leading to the development of a "psychological view of humanity" in their social situation. Elementary prerequisites for survival and maintaining one's social position at court included masking and controlling one's emotional impulses and delving deeply into others' personal consciousness and emotional structure in order to determine their hidden motives and calculations. These behaviors became integral characteristics of their personality structure (1997b, 383–86; cf. 1997a, 62).

Nietzsche, Elias and many other theorists use spatial metaphors to describe how ancient and modern selves differ from each other. Almost all of these metaphors involve aspects of topological space. Charles Taylor, for one, believes that all cultures distinguish inside from outside. He also contends that our modern notions of inner and outer are strange and without precedent in other cultures and times (1989, 114). Elsewhere I have argued that human beings in general inhabit projective and topological spaces simultaneously, although their experience of this double spatiality may vary widely in different cultures and eras, and among individuals at any given time.[33] In all cases, we must take account

33. Very briefly, I argue that these spatial dimensions are linked with two fundamentally distinct modes of human experience and knowledge. One is based on the model of the body as a "kinaesthetic amoeba" (see n. 36 below) immersed in an enveloping fluid world in topological space. Topological experience is grounded in the biological processes of metabolic exchange, which govern all traffic between outside and inside. The other mode of experience is based on the model of sight at a distance. Here the world is experienced as before and present to a disembodied ocular knower in projective space. Projective experience tends to defend against,

of ways in which the contact boundary separating inside from outside is experienced—or *not* experienced.[34] That boundary may be perceived as being as hard and impermeable as the hull of a ship[35] or as osmotic and permeable, promoting interchange between inside and outside.[36]

Among the classicists I have mentioned it is Fränkel whose use of spatial terminology is most rich and evocative. He begins with an understanding of "Homeric man" as "*ein Ganzes*." While every single organ can develop an energy of its own, each represents the total person at the same time.[37] Nowhere are boundaries to be found. There is no rift (*Zwiespalt*) between emotion and bodily behavior; all the components of the person work together without conflict or complication. The person (*der Mensch*) always remains himself. He has no hidden depths, no hidden motives, no dark undergrounds and he is incapable of developing. He is not "encapsulated" from the outside. On the contrary, his being "radiates freely out into the world." He is like a "force field, whose lines extend out into space and time without boundary or limit. He is unconditionally wide open to the world." In short, a Homeric individual "does

and deny the fact of, bodily immersion in, and open interchange with, the now-threatening fluid world. See further in Lasine 1977, 1–136. On the primordial nature of topological experience, cf. Hyppolite's notion of the "myth of the formation of outside and inside" (1966, 884) and Merleau-Ponty's account of "primordial space as topological (that is to say, carved out in a total voluminosity which surrounds me, in which I am, which is behind me, as well as in front of me)" (1964, 267).

34.  Cf. Simmel: "only he who stands outside his boundary in some sense, in whatever capacity, knows that he stands within it, actually knows it as a boundary. Kaspar Hauser hadn't known that he was in a prison until he came out into the open and could also see the walls from outside" (1918, 3).

35.  This phenomenon is associated with projective withdrawal from the enveloping fluid world. The reified boundary is viewed as protecting the life of the individual (who is "inside") from the dangers outside. The surrounding world is then experienced as "outside" and present to the self, which views that world from within the confines of the reified boundary. In effect, this stance inverts the meanings of life and death. In the primordial topological model of experience, the contact boundary is permeable and life is made possible through the transmission of nutriment (and information) from outside through the boundary and the expelling of waste from the inside to the outside. Preventing such transmission results in death. Projective detachment can also "theatricalize" the seen world and one's place within it, including one's death. On this point, see Lasine 1977, 95–107.

36.  Cf. Michotte (1963, 204): the body is "a sort of *kinaesthetic* amoeba,…[it] is not limited by a clearly defined surface and there is no 'contour.' The limit of the body is…an imprecise frontier."

37.  While A. R. Johnson also discusses body parts referring to "the individual as a whole" in the Bible, he stresses the poetic aspect of such "synecdoche," describing it as "picturesque" and "graphic" (1964, 50–51).

not stand opposed to an outside with an innerness different from it; on the contrary, the whole carries and penetrates him."[38]

In Fränkel's account, the emphasis is on the inside radiating out. In contrast, Snell (1975, 20) describes mental and spiritual acts in Homer in terms of outside forces invading the inside. Humans are the open target of a great many forces which impinge on them, and penetrate their very core. In this sense, the individual's situation resembles that of Freud's simplified organism, a "little bubble" or "vesicle" (*Bläschen*) of substance enveloped by the surrounding external world, bombarded by stimuli until the surface becomes a "baked-through crust" protecting the substance within (1940a, 25). Freud likens this situation to that of human consciousness, with the baked-through crust being analogous to the "shield against stimuli" (*Reizschutz*) by which we protect ourselves from excessive stimulation from the outside. Snell's depiction of the individual in space could also be likened to what Simmel (1957, 228) calls the *Schutzorgan* of intellect which modern big-city dwellers must develop as protection against the threat of the fluctuating stimuli of their "outer milieu."[39]

Among Egyptologists, Assmann (1993a, 81–82) posits three phases in the development of the inner-outer distinction in ancient Egypt. In the initial phase of "indifference," the distinction between inside and outside is not made. In this stage there is no talk of the heart as the embodiment of the human internal world and no abstract concept of such a world. In the second phase, "differentiation," a boundary is drawn between inside and outside, but only to lay all weight on the correspondence between the two spheres; that which is outside only counts if it is also inside. Everything depends on the heart intending that which the mouth says and the hands do. Assmann dubs the third and final phase "hiatus"; here either the internal *or* external constitutes the true essence of the human being.[40]

Assmann's main focus is on what he calls the "history of the heart" in ancient Egypt, particularly during the Middle Kingdom, when Egypt

---

38. Fränkel 1951, 109, 112–14, 118–20. In the end, Fränkel's composite picture of "Homeric man" is quite idealized, and also reductive, in the sense that all males in Homer are exactly the same in all the essential ways he lists.

39. These metaphors (and all the references below to individuals separated from the world by a "shell," "casing," "capsule," etc.) are indicative of what I have described as a projective retreat from the vulnerabilities of topological experience; see nn. 33 and 35 above. Cf. Assmann's "hiatus" phase of inside-outside relations, discussed below.

40. Assmann's highly reductive schema assigns the ancient Greeks to the first phase of the "development," while the Egyptian experience includes both the first and the second stages.

was in the second stage of "differentiation" between inner and outer. Assmann charts another three-stage development in terms of the "king-directed" to the "heart-directed" person, and ultimately to the person whose heart is "god-directed" (1993a, 90–100). In the last two stages the heart exercises a multitude of functions. It is the "organizing center" of the person which grants coherence to the "constellative compositeness" of the individual. It directs or guides a person. It is the seat of inner quali-ties, virtues, and character. It is concerned with consciousness, identity and responsibility, including the "weighing of the heart" in the judgment of the dead.[41]

In terms of the inside–outside distinction, Assmann describes the heart as the site of utmost exposure in relation to influences from outside and drives from inside (1993a, 87). Like Snell's account of humans subjected to bombardment by outside forces, Assmann's description evokes Freud's topography of the human mind. Freud describes the ego (*das Ich*) not only as a surface entity, but as the projection of a surface; above all, it is a "body-ego" (1940b, 253, 255). Yet Assmann also describes the voice of the heart as a kind of "superego" (*Über-Ich*) in the phase in which the heart is "god-directed" (1993a, 99–100; 2005b, 147). Specifi-cally, it is a social superego which is identified with the divine voice, coming very close to our idea of the conscience. It is the internalized voice of the community and tradition, which suppresses spontaneous feelings and drives (1993a, 99–100; cf. 1999, 238; 2005a, 101).[42] While Assmann's depiction of Egyptian individuals' relations with society owe more to the sociologist David Riesman[43] than they do to Freud, the fact that both Snell and Assmann describe ancient mental space in ways typical of twentieth-century psychoanalytic theory raises the question whether they have succeeded in their attempts to describe a mode of consciousness different from modern Western characterizations of mental dynamics and mental space.

---

41.　Assmann 1993a, 84, 87, 91, 96–100. The third motif of the heart-teaching during the Middle Kingdom involves the leading and listening heart; this is the "weighed heart" or "*Psychostasie*" after the first death (1993a, 100). Cf. Assmann 2005a, 30, 75, 89, 102–4 and further in Chapters 8 and 9, below. According to Assmann (2005a, 103–94), the Egyptians feared dissociation between heart and self and connected such dissociation with loss of self-control and death.

42.　Assmann (1993a, 98) stresses that in its mature form this new teaching of the heart has "*eine ausgeprägt anti-individualistische Tendenz*," emphasizing self-control, obedience, and altruism. He does not consider the possibility that the moral values promulgated in these texts might serve the needs of the ruling elite.

43.　E.g. Assmann, 1993a, 97, 99; 2005b, 140.

When modern historical sociologists and philosophers describe changes in self-experience over time, they also tend to employ spatial metaphors. Max Weber famously described individuals in capitalist societies as being enclosed in a "steel-hard casing" or "shell" (1934, 203). Although Nietzsche speaks of consciousness having "doors" and "windows" when describing the process of forgetfulness (1999, 291–92), it is when he describes the process of "internalization" that he uses spatial imagery most forcefully. When humans formed societies, those societies imposed external restraints on their members, forcing the instincts to turn inward: "The entire inner world, originally thin as if stretched tight and flat between two skins,[44] spread out and swelled, gained depth, breadth, height, to the same extent as people's outward discharge has been inhibited" (1999, 322).

Although Nietzsche and Mann (1964, 90) describe modern Westerners as having a "closed" self, it is Norbert Elias who has gone furthest in describing the spatial aspect of the "closed personality" (1997a, 47; cf. 50, 70). Elias's "*homo clausus*" is a "little world for himself," to whom every other person is likewise a *homo clausus* (1997a, 52; cf. 1970, 128). Here the individual "I" is experienced as being shut off[45] from everything outside like a hidden kernel in a shell, "sealed casing," "armoring," "capsule," or "vessel" experienced as an actually existing "invisible wall."[46] Like Nietzsche, Elias posits transformation of the emotions, as well as the "armor of self-constraints" (2002, 408; cf. 409, 427–28) as the causes of this experience. The civilizing process increases the "horizontal fissure" that goes across the whole person (1997b, 342), and makes the "wall of forgetfulness" separating drives and 'consciousness' harder and more impermeable" (1997b, 541).

Elias concedes that these spatial metaphors, with which people ascribe to themselves an unverifiable spatial position in the interior of a container, must express an extraordinarily strong and recurring feeling among people. While he does not doubt the genuineness of this feeling, he doubts that it corresponds with the "facts" (1970, 128–29). The

---

44. In German, "*dünn wie zwischen zwei Häute eingespannt.*" Clark and Swensen (1998, 147) find this image to be puzzling because the verb has several meanings, none of which clearly fits the context. For the idea that there is only a "very thin layer of individual consciousness" between social and bodily life, see Mauss 1968, 289.

45. Elias usually uses the words "*abgekapselt*" and "*abgeschlossen*" here (1997a, 52, 65).

46. Shell: 1997a, 67–68. Sealed casing: 1997a, 64; cf. 68; 1970, 128. Armoring: 2002, 405, 412, 424, 427–28. Capsule: 1997a, 65–66; 1970: 128. Vessel: 1997a, 66; 1970: 128. Invisible wall: 1997a, 52, 63, 64, 66; 1970, 128; 2002, 424.

expression "the inside of the person" is a convenient metaphor, but it can lead one astray. Elias notes that while there is good reason to say that the brain is located in the skull and the heart in the interior of the chest cavity, these figures of speech are inappropriate when referring to personality structures, because the relationship between drive-controls and drive-impulses is not a spatial relationship (1997a, 66). In a sense, Elias's view is ironic, because the ancients did express those relationships in spatial terms using bodily organs, and they were presumably *not* experiencing themselves as closed personalities.[47]

As I noted earlier, Thomas Mann does ascribe a kind of openness to the ancients. In *Joseph und seine Brüder*, characters like Eliezer and Isaac have an "I" which is "not quite firmly circumscribed, and is "open to the back." They have an "open identity." They distinguish less sharply between "I" and "not-I" than we are accustomed to do (Mann 1964, 90, 94). In contrast to Elias, Mann is not talking about an ego which is open in the sense of recognizing its interdependence with others in their shared social figuration. Nor is he using "openness" in the sense of Fränkel, Snell, or Freud, for whom openness brings vulnerability to a potentially dangerous and invasive outside world or bombarding external stimuli. Rather, he is talking about being open to identify with, and incorporate, the identity and the life-story of one's forbears.[48] Mann's narrator asks whether the "I" of a person is *ever* a thing which is solidly closed in itself and strictly sealed up within its temporal-bodily boundaries (1964, 90). Elias would agree that people have never entirely been the closed-up and walled-in autonomous individuals they have thought themselves to be at various points in history and culture.

## 4. *Biblical Selves and Inner Space*

a. *How Different Were They?*

What, then, does the Hebrew Bible—and biblical scholarship—have to say about the difference between ancient Israelites and ourselves? Samuel Sandmel believes that people have been "basically the same…at

47. Elias does envision the possibility of replacing the image of *homo clausus* with an image of "open people" or "*homines aperti*" who have an "open personality" (1970, 147, 135; 1997a, 70), but with whom the disunity of the traditional image has disappeared. Elias does not explicitly ascribe such openness to the ancients.

48. The narrator in *Joseph* (1964, 90) says that the "I" of one character (Eliezer) overflowed outside his own individuality to incorporate experiences which we would take as having been lived by those with whom he is identifying in the past and in myth.

least for the past four thousand years" (1972, 30). Sandmel is referring
to basic human emotions. He *does* concede that some "habits of mind"
differ among peoples. Thus, "the Hebrew mind" has a "bent for the
concrete," has humor as one of its "facets," does not distinguish between
history and non-history, and has an "elasticity" which "we" moderns lack
(1972, 31, 33, 38, 42).

Most biblicists do not acknowledge even this degree of basic "same-
ness" between the ancient Israelites and people today. Among scholars of
previous generations, Gunkel asserts that in ancient Israel personality—
even in the case of an author—was far less developed and the power of
custom was far greater than it is in the modern world (1928, 58–59).
Koch agrees that the inclinations of the individual were much more controlled and strictly regulated by custom and practice (1969, 11). And
Mowinckel believes that "the concept…of a life borne by a unitary
character was altogether lacking in the entire ancient Orient" (1914, 25).

More recently, Di Vito has argued that the "notion of 'self' reflected in
biblical literature presents a striking contrast to modernity" in several
respects.[49] These include the lack of "a true center for the person" and the
absence of "hidden depths."[50] In addition, "the boundaries that mark
personal identity [are] extremely permeable" (1997, 59–61, 66). Other
recent scholarship concludes that the Bible presents a radically new
concept of self. For Alter, the Hebrew Bible illustrates a "monotheistic
revolution in consciousness" (1981, 115; 1983, 114). For Geller (1996,
179), "what biblical religion really represented was a change in human
consciousness." This consciousness and "zeal for self" was "born from
the spirit of prophecy" (1996, 179), although other factors were also
involved.[51] Halpern links Deuteronomic religion with "the social creation
of the individual in Israel," and of the self-consciousness, alienation, and
loneliness that necessarily accompanied it (1991, 76; cf. 84). It began
with the "elite" and political "sophisticates," and then trickled down to
the citizenry in general (1991, 76–79). Others, like Kawashima (2004,
111–14), focus on biblical style and conclude that the writers came up
with new techniques in representing consciousness and "subjective
interiority."

49. Di Vito's model of the modern self is derived from Charles Taylor (Di Vito
1997, 51–52, 59, 71). On Taylor, see above.

50. By "hidden depths" Di Vito is referring to depths which are "hidden from
one's self" (1997, 66).

51. These include the "demotion of seeing in favor of hearing," a new concept of
absolute faith, a turning to text, and the biblical "dynamic of sexuality" (1996, 178,
154).

b. *Methodological Problems*

These studies display the same range of methodological problems I described earlier. Several use literary texts as clues to the psychology of historical persons. Sandmel draws inferences about mentality from repetitions and contradictions in scripture, concluding that Israelites were not bothered by inconsistencies or contradictions. In addition, he speaks in general of the "ancient mind" and the "Hebrew mind" without distinguishing between the two or entertaining the possibility of variations within each group, and assumes a monolithic "Western mind" (1972, 32; cf. Di Vito 1997, 51, 80). Once again, relevant Greek and ancient Near Eastern textual evidence is left unmentioned. Gunkel (1928, 59) points to repeated phrases and metaphors in the psalms to support his contention that personality was far less developed in ancient Israel. Mann uses this strategy as well.[52] Mowinckel's assertion that the concept of a unified character was totally lacking throughout the ancient Near East is grounded on a different problematic assumption. He assumes that the ancients were at a stage of spiritual development (*Geistesstufe*)[53] where this concept could not come into existence, namely, the stage of purely mythical thought (1914, 25).

Methodological problems are also evident in the more recent work of Geller and Halpern. In one essay, Geller states that his aim is "strictly historical," although he later concedes that "the issue is theological" and must be discussed using "literary" strategies (2000, 274, 287). His claim is that biblical religion "demands" that "one achieve unity of the self, both of one's mind (*lēb*) and appetites/emotions/life (*nepeš*), through singular attachment to God." Yet he goes on to caution that he is *not* claiming that *lēb* and *nepeš* were viewed as totally distinct by Israelites before the deuteronomic movement and admits that "we can never know." He also admits that numerical unity of the self is "elusive to find" in the text, adding that the issue is "actually unimportant…and makes no practical difference." Nevertheless, he continues to assert that "psychic unity" was the revolutionary "result of a complete reorganization of the…psychic universe"—in spite of his admission that we don't know whether such a reorganization occurred, *and* that if it did, it is unimportant

52. Hamburger (1965, 69–88) notes that Mann, who was influenced by biblicists of the pan-Babylonian school, believes that certain contradictions and striking repetitions in Genesis allow a particular structure of consciousness to become visible, from which one can draw conclusions about the specific spiritual structure of the ancient Israelite world and its people.

53. This assumption is also made by R. Otto (2004) in his immensely influential analysis of holiness in the Old Testament. For a critique of Otto's approach, see Lasine 2010, 34 n. 9, 47, 51 n. 59.

(2000, 295–96). Finally, he does not explicitly tackle the problem of whether the ideal situation projected by Deuteronomy is evidence for the lived experience of historical individuals in ancient Israel.[54]

Unlike Geller, Halpern (1991, 59–91) focuses on both biblical evidence and Israelite society in the eighth and seventh centuries, as he reconstructs it. His main thesis is that the policies of Hezekiah, Manasseh, and Josiah were designed to marginalize the clan sector, tribal institutions, and rural landowners. In addition to the DtrH and the prophets, Halpern points to "material-cultural indicators" such as the smaller size of ovens, cooking pots, and tombs in the seventh century (1991, 71–72). His use of Deuteronomy is open to the same objections as Geller's, and his reconstruction of Israelite social history leans heavily on models derived from interpretations of modern European history (including the growth of Protestantism, capitalism, and national centralization). Finally, the idea that "moral and legal individuation" (1991, 91) in Israel *necessarily* resulted in individuals who experienced themselves as lonely and alienated is incapable of proof.[55]

In his study of the language of the self in Jeremiah, Timothy Polk notes the danger that "arises when the insight into the historically and culturally conditioned character of human thought is raised to the level of natural law and metaphysical principle... Then the various, oft-cited distinctions between ancient and modern people are transformed into a monolithic singular" (1984, 23). Like some of the classicists mentioned earlier, Polk concedes that "there are many, but *specific*, modes of thought with which certain of the ancients were at home but which are alien to us." But he wisely adds that we should not imagine "the cleft between old and new to be everywhere the same in depth and width, everywhere a virtual chasm, or by ignoring that there are places where... the cleft disappears because the structure of certain features of existence then and now is the same" (1984, 23).

---

54. He focuses more on "biblical religion" than on "Israelite religion." Geller (1996, 180) does warn that the isolation of the believing, aware self should not be thought of in terms of any modern conceit, such as that of an autonomous individual. Instead, the new self immediately became integrated into a society again, but a society of a new type, a group in which each adult is individually and totally committed, and in which each immature member is being trained to undertake that commitment.

55. Contrast the wealth and variety of evidence available to the historians and sociologists who have described such phenomena in modern Western urbanized societies. Halpern would also do well to heed Bendix's warning not to underestimate the possible incongruity between prevailing social institutions and the psychological habitus of a people.

c. *Mental Space in the Hebrew Bible*
(1) *Inner Conflict and Deliberating Decisions.* Narratological studies
of the Bible routinely allude to mental space when characterization is
discussed. Reference is made to "internal" or "inner" motives, "inner
personality," and "inner life" in general.[56] Others stress the limitations
of our access to the characters' "inner selves," which are usually left
"opaque" (Sternberg 1985, 190; Kawashima 2004, 107).

Bar-Efrat (1989, 63) points out that while characters' "considerations
and motivations are given at considerable length," the presentation of
their thoughts "does not reach the dimensions of interior monologue…
no internal argument or discussion is given."[57] If this is correct, it contrasts strongly with the way Homer presents his characters. The Homeric
epics contain a large number of what classicists call "inner dialogues" or
"deliberative monologues." Certainly biblical characters are shown in
situations which seem to call for internal deliberation, even if one
excludes the situation of judges. Typically, they simply announce their
decisions to others or perform actions which would naturally seem to
follow deliberation, without readers having been given any account of
the process of decision-making. To give just one of many possible
examples, after God fails to regard Cain's offering with favor, he gives
Cain some advice to consider (Gen 4:4–7). In the following verses, we
are not shown Cain deliberating over whether he should do well or
attempt to master sin. On the contrary, his actions imply that he has
ignored God's advice altogether.

The Hebrew Bible does include cases in which characters "say things
in their heart" (e.g. Gen 8:21; 17:17; 1 Sam 27:1), but they do not say
things *to* their own heart, and their heart does not say things to them.

---

56.  E.g. Bar-Efrat 1989, 53, 77; Berlin 1983, 37–38; Polzin 1993, 36.

57.  Bar-Efrat does add that on occasion one gains the impression that characters
wish to convince themselves that the action they are taking is the right one, rather
than an alternative course. Kawashima (2004, 105–106) argues that Homer's use of
interior monologue is markedly different from the Bible's. He cites *Od.* 11, stressing its stereotypical nature by using the concept of "type scene," a strategy familiar
from some classicists' analyses of Homer. In contrast, Kawashima accepts Erich
Auerbach's characterization of biblical background style, and goes on to assert that
the biblical writers "break much ground" in the representation of subjective interiority and consciousness by hinting at unexpressed thoughts and psychological depths
(2004, 112–14). For example, he believes that Noah undergoes an "underlying
psychological tempest" when he sees the dove's "leafy symbol of hope" (2004, 113),
even though the biblical narrator gives readers no clue about what Noah might have
said, thought, or felt at this juncture. In fact, Noah is entirely silent in Genesis until
he curses his grandson Canaan after the Flood.

Although there are a few possible exceptions,[58] they are not really parallel to the formulae found in so many Homeric deliberative monologues, namely, "he spoke to his great-hearted spirit" (e.g. *Il.* 11.403) followed by "why does my spirit debate these things with me?" (e.g. *Il.*11.407: ἀλλὰ τί ἤ μοι ταῦτα φίλος διελέξατο θυμός;).[59] The word I translated "spirit" is *thumos*, which is often rendered as "heart" in such passages. Just as *thumos*, *phrēn*, *kēr*, and other Greek terms are often used interchangeably in early Greek poetry,[60] so are Hebrew *lēb/lēbab*, *kᵉlāyōt*, *mē'im*, *qereb*, and *beṭen* at times used synonymously to indicate the deepest inner recesses of a human person (see, e.g., Wolff 1981, 7, 43, 63–66). And if, as most classicists now agree, the Greek terms "belong to a vocabulary in which the person himself plays an essential and irreplaceable role" (B. Williams 1993, 26), the same may be true of the Hebrew terms.

I would therefore disagree with Fox (1989, 240, 88 and 88 n. 15), who believes that Qoheleth "thinks of his heart as an entity distinct from his ego, the 'I,'" thereby "distinguishing the heart from the person," even

58. For example, Ps 27:8, although the text is difficult. Dahood (1966, 168) emends MT לְךָ ("to you") to לְךָ ("Come!"), changes the plural imperative "seek" to a singular, and understands the pronominal suffix before "face" as third-person, so that the line becomes "Come, said my heart, 'Seek his face'" (cf. NRSV). For this verse to be a true exception, the heart would have to be addressing the speaker, quoting to himself what God had said. Cohen (1945, 79) takes it in this sense and paraphrases, "in my peril I hear the promptings of my innermost self." Another possible exception is also a difficult verse. In Neh 5:7, Nehemiah seems to be claiming that he deliberated with himself: "my heart took counsel upon me" (v. 7), often rendered "I consulted with myself" (KJV, NASB, JPS; cf. Luther, NRSV, NKJV). Blenkinsopp (1988, 255) concludes that translators must choose between forms of מלך which are unattested in Biblical Hebrew: מלך meaning "to take counsel with oneself," as in Aramaic, or a Niphal of מלך meaning to "exercise control."

59. Hainsworth (1993, 270) notes that "he spoke then to his great-hearted spirit" (*Il.* 11.403) is the "standard formula that introduces monologues," occurring seven times in the *Iliad* and four in the *Odyssey*. Murray and Wyatt (1999, 523) render *Il.* 11.407 with "why does my spirit debate this with me?" Gill (1996, 15) also refers to "inner dialogues" in Greek literature and philosophy.

60. B. Williams (1993, 26–27, 177 n. 17) notes that people "standardly reflect or deliberate with or in (*kata*) their *phren* and *thumos*." He concludes that "the search for consistent and illuminating distinctions between these terms has not been very successful," pointing to Jahn's 1987 study, which argues that *thumos* and six other terms are semantically interchangeable and exploited according to their metrical possibilities. Padel (1992, 12–48) deals with various Greek terms for "innards" in a manner similar to Wolff's description of Hebrew terms for the inner parts of the body. Padel (1992, 13) notes that Greek *splanchnon* ("innards") can read like "character."

though Qoheleth admittedly "sets" his heart to do things and once "turns together" with it (7:25). These passages do not imply that one psychological function of a person is external to the person as a whole. Not even Leontius in Plato's *Republic* indicates this. Leontius is simultaneously repelled and fascinated when he sees the corpses of executed criminals. For a while he resists looking and then, overpowered by his desire, with his eyes open wide and staring he rushes up to corpses and cries "There you wretches, take your fill of the fine spectacle!" Socrates then states the point of his anecdote: "anger sometimes fights against desires as an alien thing against an alien" (ὡς ἄλλο ὂν ἄλλῳ; *Resp.* 440a; Shorey 1969, 401). Leontius is talking to his eyes, but his eyes—the means by which his desire could be fulfilled—are not external to Leontius's self. The experience is of something *internally* alien; the conflicting forces are all "within him" (*Resp.* 440a–b).

Most classicists now concede that Homer's characters also display internal conflict, both psychological and "psycho-ethical" (Gill 1996, 196). Pointing to the "conflict of impulses" in Homer's Odysseus, Halliwell argues that "far from being an impediment to a coherent conception of the person, it would be unintelligible,…without one" (1990, 39; cf. Padel 1992, 47). Although the Hebrew Bible does not include inner dialogue, conflict—and the experience of an internal alien force—are indicated in other ways.[61] One example is a notoriously difficult verse, Gen 4:7, which I mentioned briefly earlier. Yahweh tells Cain that sin is crouching at the doorway (לפתח חטאת רבץ), that its desire is toward him, but he can rule over it (תמשל־בו); cf. Gen 3:16). As von Rad points out (1972, 105), the statement "does not actually speak of an inner emotion"; rather, sin is described "as an objective power which, as it were, is outside the man."[62] More importantly, the *desire* is attributed to sin, which is "outside the man."

The question is whether sin and its desire stand for an aspect of the person himself, in this case, Cain. Commentators traditionally balk at such an idea. Westermann finds it hard to imagine such personification of sin "in so early a text," especially because "there is nothing like it anywhere in the Old Testament" (1994, 300; cf. 298).[63] Von Rad (1972, 105)

---

61. Saul has to be the best example of an "internal alien" dynamic in the Hebrew Bible, but nothing is said about Saul undergoing a process of conscious, volitional, internal wrestling. Nor does Saul use any alien influence as an excuse when apologizing to David in 1 Sam 24:16–21.

62. Von Rad adds "and over him," but it is difficult to see how this addition can be justified by the Hebrew.

63. Westermann (1994, 299) notes that the phrase "one crouching at the door" is very striking. It is completely outside the admonitory or warning style of the two

also finds this, and the "purely figurative use of 'door,'" to be "strange in such an ancient narrative."[64] Interpretations of this mysterious "doorway" or "entrance" (פתח) are many and varied: "door (or portals) of the heart," "doors of the soul" (i.e. the "countenance"), "door of the house," "door of the sanctuary," "entrance of the grave," and "the door of Paradise."[65] Cassuto (1978, 211) finds all this interpretive effort to be wasted: "The verse simply says 'door' (entrance), and the commentator isn't called upon to determine what Scripture leaves undetermined."[66]

In terms of topological space, a doorway is a boundary phenomenon which allows (or disallows) intercourse between outside and inside. Is God inviting Cain to view his desires as though they were an external danger against which he needs to be vigilant? If so, the advice would anticipate Freud's explanation of the origin of projection: since there can be no shield against stimuli towards the *inside*, we tend to treat internal excitations as though they were acting from the outside, in order to use the *Reizschutz* to protect against them (1940a, 25–27). If Yahweh is implying that the doorway is the boundary between Cain's self and the external world, this is the first biblical occurrence of a person's self being an enclosed space which has an opening to a dangerous outside.[67] Of

---

verses. It has "the effect of a foreign body too inasmuch as there is no similar expression anywhere in the Old Testament."

64. BDB (836) cites two figurative uses in addition to Gen 4:7: Mic 7:5 (guard the doorways of your mouth) and Hos 2:17 (for a doorway of hope).

65. The "door of Paradise" is Azevedo's suggestion (1999, 49, 54–55); the others are all cited by von Rad (1972, 105), Westermann (1994, 301), or Cassuto (1978, 211). Azevedo refers repeatedly to the gate of Paradise or the Garden in 4:7, but a פתח is not even mentioned in Gen 3:24, where one might most expect it. The cherub is guarding the "path" or "way" (דרך) to the tree of life. Other interpretations of פתח in 4:7 which are listed by Westermann include "close at hand," "at the parting of the ways," "out!," "opportunity," an adverbial construction ("clearly perceptible") or, following LXX, an emendation to לנתח. The Piel verb נתח, to "cut up" or "divide," is reflected in the LXX use of διαιρέω ("if you offer rightly but do not divide [διέλῃς] rightly, have you not sinned?").

66. Nevertheless, Cassuto (1978, 211) goes on to offer an interpretation of his own: "It means, apparently, 'your door' in a general sense, that is, the place through which you are wont to go in and out constantly; in other words, it will always be found in your path." He does not attempt to clarify what he means by "the place."

67. In terms of what I call projective and topological experience (see nn. 33, 35, 39 above), it is in projective space that death for the inside results from allowing something from the outside through a boundary opening. Conversely, situations in which allowing something through the boundary is essential for the life of the inside are indicative of topological experience. At times the same boundary can function in both ways. For Yahweh in Gen 3, Adam incorporating the fruit of knowledge into his body in spite of the divine prohibition means death, while according to Prov 3:18

course, the vagueness of Gen 4:7 precludes any definitive explanation of the metaphors. However, Lohfink's contention that Cain is told to protect himself from sin by means of "inner self-mastery" (1989, 196) would be difficult to refute.

Internal conflict and self-mastery are also the focus of another piece of biblical advice: "he who rules over his spirit is better than he who captures a city" (טוב...ומשל ברוחו מלכד עיר; Prov 16:32b).[68] Just as Cain was advised to "rule over" sin, we are advised to rule over our רוח. Interestingly, various rabbinic sources have equated both "sin" in Gen 4:7 and "spirit" in Prov 16:32 with the *yetzer ha-ra'*, the "evil inclination."[69] The thought recalls Plato's references to the "civil war of the soul," in which the "victory over self is of all victories the first and best" (*Resp.* 440e; cf. 444b; *Leg.* 626e).[70] The fact that in Proverbs rule over part of the self is compared to an outside force's victory over a city echoes Job's account of God's army invading and flattening the city of his self, which I will discuss shortly.

(2) *Epistemological inadequacy and the hiddenness of inner space.* The fact that internal deliberation is generally lacking in biblical narrative does not imply that biblical characters make decisions precipitously or unthinkingly. By omitting the process of deliberation, the narrators

wisdom is a tree of life for those who grasp it. Boundary violations bringing death occur in various contexts in the Hebrew Bible, including encroachment on the holy. On Eve's unique "openness," including her nakedness, vulnerability and our access to her motivations in Gen 3, see Lasine 2001, 174–75.

68.   The first part of 16:32 says that a "long-to-anger" man is better than a mighty warrior. This means that both parts of the verse compare a way of *being* to *doing*, and say that it is better to *be* of a self-controlling disposition than to *do* mighty things.

69.   The term is also rendered "evil imagination" or "impulse." With Prov 16:32 compare *Pirqe Avoth* 4.1, which cites this verse and adds that the answer to "who is mighty?" is "he who subdues his *yetzer.*" In reference to Gen 4:7, *Gen. Rab.* 22.6 cites R. Isaac's comment that at the beginning sin is like a visitor who drops in, then it becomes like a regular guest, and at the end it becomes a member of the household. Other rabbinic views are cited by Leibowitz (1981, 41–43). For example, Malbim understands the sense to be "sin lies at the door to accuse you." He equates "sin" with the evil inclination, man's baser instincts and passions and the bestial part of his nature. Rashi takes "sin couches at the door" to mean at the entrance to your grave is your sin. Finally, Biur contends that this is a vivid figure of speech which depicts iniquity outside a closed door waiting for an opportunity to enter. Of course, Gen 4:7 does *not* say that the entrance is closed. Biur's image anticipates the situation in Kafka's famous doorkeeper parable, which I discuss in Chapter 9, §8, below.

70.   The speaker in the *Republic* is Socrates. On the seeming absurdity of self-mastery, see *Resp.* 430e–431a. In *Leg.* 626e the speaker is Clinias, who adds that "a war against self exists within each of us" (Bury 1967, 11).

expose readers to the same epistemological limitations experienced by figures in the text, as they attempt to determine the character of others hidden in the recesses of their inner being. In these terms, the distinction between inside and outside signifies visibility and invisibility, and thereby the knowable and the unknowable.

The barrier between outside and inside does not affect Yahweh, a fact reiterated by biblical speakers, most often in terms of the bodily organs mentioned earlier. Thus, God can investigate people's disloyalty to him, for he knows the "secrets of the heart" (לב תעלמות; Ps 44:22). If the realm of the dead is "naked" and open to view before Yahweh, how much more is this the case with the hearts of humans (Prov 15:11; cf. Job 26:6). The life-breath of the human being is the lamp of Yahweh, searching out all the innermost parts, literally, all the "chambers of the belly" (כל־חדרי־בטן; Prov 20:27; cf. 20:30).[71]

Yahweh also examines and assays[72] the heart and the kidneys (Ps 7:10). It is Jeremiah who most often declares that God can see and test the heart and the kidneys (e.g. Jer 11:20; 20:12). On one occasion, Jeremiah declares that the heart is deceitful more than anything else and very weak, and asks: "who can know it?" (17:9). Yahweh answers for himself: "I Yahweh penetrate (חקר) the heart and test (בחן) the kidneys" (v. 10; cf. 1 Kgs 8:39). In other words, it is *only* Yahweh who can penetrate the truths hidden deep inside a human being. Many biblical speakers express their inability to fathom the depths of others in spatial terms, for example, when lamenting that "the inward thoughts of every man and the heart are deep" (עמק; Ps 64:7, a difficult verse). This inability makes them vulnerable to deception.[73] Fear of betrayal and being deceived can itself create a need to believe that people have reliable and knowable character traits, and simultaneously create the need for individuals who believe this to mask their own traits with deceit and practiced unpredictability.

A minority of voices in the Hebrew Bible are confident that humans can expose others' hidden nature. One verse in Proverbs concedes that "deep (עמקים) waters is counsel in the heart of a man," but goes on to

---

71. According to McKane (1970, 540, 547), the chambers of the belly are the locus of one's thoughts and motives, the place where the truth about a person is to be found. It is indicative of "the core of the personality." McKane interprets v. 27 as confidently asserting that "man has this inner light…the power of introspection by which he can examine the depths of his self and see clearly in Yahweh's light what is there."

72. The verb here is בחן; cf. Jer 17:10, discussed below. For more on God testing or assessing the human heart, see Chapter 8, §3, below.

73. This problem is expressed in many ways; see Lasine 1987; 1989a.

declare that "a man of insight will draw it out" (Prov 20:5). Other verses in Proverbs also express confidence that the hatred and wickedness some people hide with deceit will be laid open in public before the assembly (26:26; cf. Lasine 1989a, 72, 81 n. 16). Jeremiah is confident that his people, so long trained in doing evil, have become evil in nature and cannot change: "Can a Cushite change his skin, or a leopard his spots?" (13:23). One modern student of behavior does believe that people are capable of deep change, but even he remains skeptical about the frequency of such changes: "I used to feel quite hopeful of reconditioning even adult personalities… But with humans as lazy as they are about themselves…the zebra can as easily change his stripes as the adult his personality" (J. B. Watson 1928, 138; cf. Pervin 1994, 326). Both Jeremiah and Watson compare a person's inner nature with indelible *external* features, which are therefore visible and "readable" indicators of character. Unfortunately, many biblical speakers find that external signs, including skin and body language, are *not* reliable evidence of character.

I want to conclude this survey by examining two examples of the relationship between human epistemological limitations and topological space. The first is Ps 55. Here the speaker expresses his outrage over those whose words are smoother than cream, while inside their hearts are war (v. 22ab). His anger is matched by Homer's Achilles, who tells the wily Odysseus, "hateful to me as the gates of Hades is that man who hides one thing in his spirit (ἐνὶ φρεσίν) and says another" (*Il.* 9.311–12).[74] This feeling is shared by a number of biblical characters as well. The speaker in Ps 55 is especially distraught, because it was not an enemy who proves to be so untrustworthy, but a companion and friend (vv. 13–15), someone whose true character he would have had most reason to think he knew (cf., e.g., Mic 7:5–6 and Lasine 1989a, 74–75).

The dangerous discordance between outside and inside is expressed throughout the psalm. The speaker feels attacked by the anger of the

---

74. On the significance of Achilles' use of the term *phrenes* in this passage (the so-called embassy scene), see Sullivan 1988, 94. Worman emphasizes the dangers presented to ancient Greeks by figures such as Odysseus and Helen, who "could alter their visible characters at will" (2003, 196). Predictably, she cites Achilles' words to Odysseus in *Il.* 9.311–12; he "displays his wariness of Odysseus' type with a well-aimed proverb." Achilles' "use of the proverb indicates his awareness of how this character type operates: by a subtle set of associations that proceeds along deeply conventional lines…masking the speaker's attempts at coercion" (2003, 71). Stanford (1968, 18) points to ancient commentators who took the proverb as directed at Odysseus (see also Plato, *Hipp. min.* 365a–b). On Achilles' self-characterization here, and the way in which Plato's Hippias perceives Achilles' character in this scene, see Chapter 8 n. 35, below.

wicked (v. 4): "deep inside (בקרבי) my heart writhes and terrors assail
me. Fear and trembling invade me (יבא בי), and horror covers me over"
(ותכסני)" (vv. 5–6). His insides have been penetrated by his own
emotions and by those of his enemies outside. The root קרב appears
three more times in the psalm, when marking the location of the wicked.
The speaker begins by describing the walls surrounding the city and then
the wickedness and treachery in its inner precincts (בקרבה; vv. 11b,
12a), including the square (v. 12b). Evil is enclosed in the homes of
those who betrayed him, and in their inner depths (בקרבם; v. 16). If he
had not been fooled by the words of his friend, he could have hidden
from him (v. 13c). Instead, the friend's evil was hidden inside him.[75]

My second example is Job, whose words exhibit the mirroring of, and
tension between, internal and external spaces even more powerfully. His
experience of his situation recalls the accounts cited earlier from Snell,
Freud and Simmel. Job is also the open target of a great many forces
which impinge on him, and penetrate his very core. But unlike the individuals described by these authors, Job has no *Reizschutz* or *Schutzorgan*
with which to protect himself. His skin, the contact boundary between
himself and the outside, although hardly Freud's "baked-through crust,"
has indeed become black (Job 30:30), crusty (7:5),[76] and shriveled
(16:8).[77]

Unlike the situation in Ps 55, the anger and warlike aggression over-
whelming Job issues not from his human enemies but from God himself,
against whom there can be no shield against stimuli. In 6:4, Job claims
that the arrows of Shaddai have penetrated him (עמדי חצי שדי),[78] and his
spirit (רוח) must drink their poison. God's terrors are arrayed against
him in military fashion. In 16:9, Job talks about God's anger having torn

75. Kselman and Barré point out that one nuance of v. 16 "may be the hiddenness of the evil; it is 'in their homes' (i.e. is private, out of public view) and 'in their
hearts' (the seat of such hidden plotting). This nuance fits well with the theme of the
deceptive and false friend in vv. 13 and 22" (1998, 451).

76. On רגע meaning "crusty," see KBL 874. Clines (1989, 157; cf. 163) has
"grows firm"; BDB (921) has "harden."

77. This verse is very difficult. קמט appears only here and in 22:16, with the
meaning "seize." The usual translation "shriveled up" is justified by appeal to
rabbinic Hebrew. Targum has "and you have wounded me"; cf. Dhorme 1984, 233.

78. Dhorme (1984, 77) notes that עמדי, "with me," recurs often in Job with
different shades of meaning. It is parallel to בי, "in me," in 28:14, and Dhorme
believes that it is the meaning best suited here. LXX has "in my body," while Syr. has
"in my flesh." Driver and Gray (1977, 2:35) render "present with me," citing 9:35
for this "idiomatic usage." Habel (1985, 137) has "in me." Clines (1989, 171) cites
other passages featuring humans as targets of the archer god: Job 7:20; 16:12–13;
Deut 32:23, 42; Pss 7:13–14; 38:3; 64:8; Lam 2:4; 3:12–13; Ezek 5:16.

him. He continues, first, by describing God as a predatory animal seizing him by the neck and smashing him to bits (v. 12), piercing his kidneys deep inside him (יפלח כליותי; v. 13)[79] and spilling his bile on the ground. Military metaphors are also present in these verses: God sets up Job as his target (v. 12) and surrounds him with his archers (v. 13). After describing how his body has been penetrated, pierced, poisoned, pulverized, and had its insides spilled out, Job concludes his tirade by accusing God of having "breached" him, "breach after breach" (יפרצני פרץ על־פני־פרץ; v. 14; cf. פרץ in 30:14a), as though he were a city whose defensive walls were violently broken through by an attacking army.

The topological imagery intensifies further in ch. 19. Once again, Job feels his self to be a walled city, against which God has thrown up his siege works (v. 6b).[80] He is enclosed and his movements are blocked: "he has walled up my path and I cannot pass" (v. 8a). Job is a building which is being demolished[81] on every side (v. 10a). He concludes this part of his speech by returning to the idea of his being surrounded by a besieging army. This time, however, he expresses the defenselessness of his self, and the wildly disproportionate force of the attackers,[82] not by picturing himself as a walled city, but as a mere tent, against which God's surrounding troops are nonetheless building siege works[83] (v. 12). While in ch. 16 and elsewhere Job refers to the internal organs discussed earlier (heart, kidneys, gall bladder, innards [30:27]), in ch. 19 this language is absent. Is this because Job now views his self solely in terms of his defensive "walls," as though he had been hollowed out and only the contact boundary—the "casing" between inside and outside—remained?

79.   Dhorme (1984, 237) compares 16:12–13 with Lam 3:13: "he has pierced my kidneys with the sons of His quiver," although the verbs for "piercing" are different in the two cases. Cf. "kidneys" in Job 19:27. Clines (1989, 371) believes that we should take רביו as "his archers," with Jer 50:29, BDB, NJPS, NIV, Gordis and others, not as "arrows," as in LXX, Vg, Tg, NAB, Dhorme, and other versions.

80.   ומצודו עלי הקיף. Cf. נקף in Job 1:5 and Lam 3:5. On מצודו, Clines (1989, 428) notes that most connect it with ציד, "hunt," but the image of siegeworks is more appropriate in context (so Gordis, Habel, Whybray [1998], NJPS), a meaning that can be attested in Qoh 9:14. The usual word for siegeworks is מצורה.

81.   יתצני סביב. The verb נתץ is used figuratively of buildings being demolished, including houses. Dhorme (1984, 274) notes that "it is the person himself who is compared to the building that is destroyed," citing 16:14; cf. Clines 1989, 444.

82.   Cf. 7:12–20, where Job complains that God is treating him as though he were a sea (or Yam) or "dragon" (תנין), posing some kind of cosmic threat. In effect, Job accuses God of trying to kill a gnat with a nuclear weapon.

83.   Clines (1989, 445) notes that "Job is imaged as a city ringed by siege-troops who build a rampart up to his gate." The usual word for "rampart" or "mound" is סללה; here we have "they cast up their way" (ויסלו...דרכם). Cf. ויסלו in Job 30:12c.

While these are not the only cases in which Job describes himself (or is described) as enclosed, penetrated, and having his innards damaged, they are sufficient to indicate Job's experience of himself in topological space during his ordeal. A healthy organism (including a healthy human consciousness) requires steady and fluid intercourse between outside and inside through a permeable membrane or boundary. God has made this impossible for Job. Job is well aware of this, and it exacerbates his suffering tremendously. He knows that God can see and test his true character without having to rip him open to assess his "innards," his true character.

However, God is *not* always transparent to Job. Job implores God to help him understand what is going on and why. He never does learn that he has been the subject of a social psychological experiment, as I will discuss in my next chapter. The satan characterizes Job's situation up to this point in spatial terms: Yahweh has hedged Job in with possessions, which have "broken out," that is, spread out, into the land. He uses the same verb (פרץ) which Job himself uses later to describe Yahweh's army breaching his defensive walls. His situation is then turned inside out. Instead of being enclosed or "hedged in" (שכת; 1:10) by prosperity, he is exposed to the elements, like the naked and homeless poor whose exposure he portrays so powerfully in ch. 24 (see Lasine 1988, 34–37). Nevertheless, Job himself experiences his exposure as being "hedged in" (ויסך;[84] 3:23) by God in a very negative sense.

## 5. *Conclusion*

How, then, should we answer the initial question, "how different are they?" Some of the theorists cited earlier, as well as others in various disciplines, agree that some "fundamental factors in human experience" are universal and that while ancient literary works (such as Greek tragedies) are different from modern literature, their "human intelligibility" allows them to seem familiar to us (Halliwell 1990, 34–35; Pelling 1990, 254).[85] In addition, to the extent that situations and social

---

84. KBL derives ויסך from the Hiphil of סכך, while BDB (692) and many commentators posit a II סוך.

85. Halliwell contends that we *have to* presuppose certain fundamental factors in human experience or there will be no basis on which to identify and comprehend significant cultural traits and distinctions in the interpretation of character. Psychoanalyst Martin Stein (1969, 680) believes that it is impossible to conceive of a human being without character traits. In reference to the Homeric poems, B. Williams argues that we could not view Homer as speaking of human actions if we did not find in his characters' words a notion of intention, as well as beliefs, desires, and purposes, which seem constitutive of the notion of human action (1993, 33–34; cf.

figurations promote specific modes of self-experience and determine character, a supposedly "modern" self-structure like Elias's *homo clausus*, which grew out of the need for masking and duplicity in European court society, can be found in the ancient Court History of King David (see Lasine 2001, 9–15, 93–140 and below). However, the first biblical example of this type of personality is not a *homo clausus*, but a *serpens clausus* in the garden of Eden (see Lasine 2001, 167–75).

A more complex issue is whether biblical characters can or should be described as personality types, in the sense that modern psychologists describe and assess "real people." Later Elijah will provide us with an excellent test case. Brichto uses spatial metaphor to describe this complex figure, describing the prophet as "swelling" into a "three-dimensional" personality who invites us "to an ever deeper sounding" of his human "depths" (1992, 166). I will argue that Elijah is actually portrayed as a narcissistic personality in 1–2 Kings. Elijah's self-conception is also expressed through his movements in space, including his apparent ability to appear and disappear in space at will, his predilection for being alone, and his staging events so that others will serve as audiences before whom he can present his version of himself.

Finally, to view the figures in these ancient stories as fundamentally alien to us goes against the grain of biblical narrative rhetoric. Characters are presented to us as our "relatives," that is, our ancestors. The Hebrew Bible is the "family album" of the target audiences. At various points we are urged to identify totally with them, and to relive their experiences in the present of our reading, in order not to make the same mistakes they did (see Lasine 1989b). In other words, we are asked to take up residence in their "*moral* space."[86] This requires us to situate ourselves within the "frame" of the textual world. This is turn requires us to ask whether our

Breden 1982, 297). Church and Lonner (1998, 49) conclude that some of the best evidence for cross-cultural universality has been garnered in relation to the five-factor model of personality, the content and structure of values, some basic emotions and higher-order mood dimensions, although more corroborating evidence is needed. Palmer (1992, 235, 241) believes that the products of high culture are "universal" in the sense of showing certain constancies in human nature that different people can recognize. C. Taylor (1989, 111–12) grants that there is "some truth in the idea that people always are selves,…[and] have shared a very similar sense of 'me' and 'mine.'" Finally, Geertz concedes that "some conception of what a human individual is…is, so far as I can see, universal" (1983, 59).

86.   C. Taylor 1989, 28 (emphasis added). According to Taylor, "to know who you are is to be oriented in moral space, a space in which questions arise about what is good and bad,…what has meaning and importance for you and what is trivial and secondary."

judgments of characters and events are a function of our unexamined assumptions and prejudices, saying more about us than about the characters. Once again, the ethics of reading shows itself to be a crucial issue, not to be evaded.

Chapter 3

# WHEN SHOULD WE PSYCHOLOGIZE?
## EVALUATING CHARACTER IN REDACTED BIBLICAL TEXTS

> What we all admire...are works that are either consistent with themselves, and thus in some sense unified, or works that acknowledge their own inconsistencies and thus reflect a genuine encounter with recalcitrant materials.
>
> —Booth (1988, 193–94)

> "Inconsistencies," answered Imlac, "cannot both be right, but, imputed to man, they may both be true."
>
> —Samuel Johnson, *Rasselas* (1990, 33)

This chapter illustrates how the psychological and rhetorical perspectives described above can shed new light on the characterization of key biblical figures in specific narratives. In most of these cases, scholars have explained a character's seemingly inconsistent or contradictory behavior by postulating different levels of editorial activity, each of which projects a different image of that character. The interplay between character and situation is the central focus of my first example, Job 1–2. Character judgments have played a key role in speculation concerning the redactional history of the book in its present form. I will then turn to narratives involving prophets and kings. The characters of the prophets Moses and Elijah and the nature of their intertextual relationship have been the subject of intense study and debate for many centuries. The two kings I will discuss here, David and Zedekiah, are also related, in the sense that the former founds a royal dynasty and the latter is the last member of that dynasty to rule over Judah before it falls to the Babylonians. Job, David and Elijah are also among the most complex, "round" and elusive characters in the Bible. Other episodes in their careers will be discussed later in this study. While King Zedekiah is not as round a character as these three, his presentation in the book of Jeremiah is both complex and seemingly contradictory, prompting many hypotheses about the redaction history of these passages. For this reason, the varying presentations of Zedekiah and his fate will receive detailed attention in this chapter.

In the first epigraph, Wayne Booth asserts that we all admire either consistent works or works "that acknowledge their own inconsistencies." Leaving aside the riskiness of claiming to know what everyone admires, Booth's two categories would seem to include all works except those which are inconsistent without acknowledging it. Although some redaction critics seem to assume that many biblical texts fall into this last category, we should not exclude the possibility that some heavily redacted biblical texts may, in fact, be acknowledging their own inconsistencies, reflecting what Booth calls "a genuine encounter with recalcitrant materials." And when we assess the surprising actions taken by characters in these texts, we should keep in mind Imlac's observation in the second epigraph: inconsistencies in human behavior are at times "true" even when we feel that they are not "right," that is, logical.

## 1. *Character and Situation in Job 1–2*

Over the years a number of scholars have asked whether redactional activity has played a role in shaping the prologue to the book of Job. Specifically, many have suggested that the heavenly scenes in the prologue, or at least the sections involving the satan (*haśśatan*), are secondary.[1] More recent commentators have tended to explain perceived incongruities in the prologue and, most glaringly, the satan's absence in the rest of the book, without reference to redaction as an adequate solution.[2] However, their interpretations of the satan's actions and story-function still tend to over-attribute negative personality traits to this character.

In a sense, the entire book of Job is concerned with weighing Job's character by manipulating his situation.[3] Commentators usually assume that it is Job's "basic character" which is being weighed, if not the existence of *any* "true piety among human beings" (Whybray 1998, 33).

---

1. On the heavenly scenes as secondary, see Eissfeldt 1965, 157 and Pfeiffer 1941, 668–69, cited in Meier 1989, 191 n. 24. Meier notes that this theory is "generated by the adversary's absence from the epilogue and i 13–22, the suspended antecedent of the singular suffix pronouns in i 13, or the paradigm of related literature where the innocent sufferer's healing deity is the afflicting deity." On the satan being a secondary element, see, e.g., Whybray 1998, 12–14; Dell 1991, 12 n. 30, 200–203, and Dhorme 1984, lxxvi–lxxix.

2. For example, Brenner (1997, 309) suggests that the satan is not present at the end of the book because God admits that it is he who authors good and evil.

3. In Chapters 8 and 9 below, the metaphor of "weighing" in the book of Job is discussed together with Egyptian descriptions of the weighing of the heart during post-mortem judgment.

The satan's suggestion that Job has had good reason to serve God is usually taken to be a sign of the satan's bad character. Peake (1905, 59) and Rowley (1980, 9) are not alone in attributing heartlessness and malice to the satan's character, pointing either to the suggestions he makes to God or to his carrying out the trials. Gordis (1978, 19) reads "insolence and rebelliousness" into the simple notice that the satan stood in Yahweh's presence in Job 2:1. Dhorme (1984, lxxviii) assumes that it is the satan's "pleasure" to strike Job. Other scholars attribute to him "a total cynicism about human nature."[4] The satan "has lost all faith in human goodness" (Peake 1905, 59). In the satan's opinion, "there are no truly religious people in the world" (Reiss 2005, 257). According to these commentators, the satan believes that all piety is "spurious" (Whybray 1998, 31), motivated solely by "self-interest" (Reiss 2005, 257; cf. Clines 1989, 26).

Such attacks on the satan's character are based on the assumption that he is attacking Job's basic disposition, if not "human nature" in general (Terrien, in Clines 1989, 26). Is this assumption justified? In social psychological terms, God is acting as a dispositionist and "virtue ethicist" here. By twice taking up the satan's challenge, God seems to imply that Job's character traits are robust enough to withstand any changes in situation which might threaten to alter his behavior. The satan's objections are those of a "situationist." He is not denying that Job has possessed integrity in his life up to this point;[5] he is predicting that Job's attitudes and actions would change if his situation were radically altered. For him, it is hardly counter-intuitive that Job would show piety when prosperous. What he does consider counter-intuitive is that Job would retain his attitude toward God when an opposite situation would seem to call for an opposite response. Viewed in this light, the two heavenly scenes are describing a government-funded research protocol in attribution theory, foreshadowing Stanley Milgram's famous obedience experiments devised down on earth.[6]

Scholars like Good (1990, 198) believe that Job's acceptance of God's actions in the prologue show that his "basic character has not changed."[7]

---

4. Whybray 1998, 33, cf. 29; Gordis 1978, 2; Peake 1905, 59–60; Dell 1991, 30. Clines (1989, 20–21) argues that these condemnations go beyond the text, since readers do not yet know whether Job's piety is disinterested or not.

5. Nor is he necessarily impugning Job's motives for being pious, as Peake (1905, 60) assumes.

6. On the Milgram experiments, see Chapter 1 nn. 13, 15 and 38, above, and Chapter 4, below.

7. Commenting on Job 27:5, Good (1990, 287) remarks that "what Job calls his *tummah* is the bedrock of his assertion of his identity."

One could argue that even in the dialogues Job's failure to act precisely[8] as the satan predicted vindicates dispositionism and character ethics, at least in Job's case. Job and his friends also share a dispositionist perspective, in line with modern psychologists' descriptions of ordinary people as "lay dispositionists" or "intuitive folk psychologists."[9] They all assume that there are people who can reliably be labeled "wicked" or "righteous." And Job is not the only one who is certain which camp he belongs to. Elihu, for one, is equally convinced that *he* is תמים (36:4) and that *his* words emanate from the "uprightness of [his] heart" (ישר-לבי; 33:3).

Characters in other biblical books illustrate the same tendency. For example, David is convinced that his words and deeds are motivated by the "uprightness of his heart" (1 Chr 29:17; 1 Sam 24:12–16).[10] And when David cites the *mashal*, "from wicked men emanates wickedness" (מרשעים יצא רשע; 1 Sam 24:14), he is not only affirming virtue ethics but "lay dispositionism" as well.[11]

Biblical characters such as Job recognize the relation between their professed virtues and their actions. In his oath of clearance (Job 31), Job illustrates his תמה by citing his former actions, attitudes, and emotions. As Good (1990, 313) puts it, "Job depicts himself as the epitome of the ethical man…[describing] in detail just what it means, both in outward act and inward thought, to be *tam weyashar*." Viewed in terms of Job's many indictments of God for inattentiveness to social injustice, one could argue that Job's basic complaint in this regard is that he is no longer in a situation where he can exercise the virtues illustrated by his former actions.

Job's "integrity" is described as something that can be seized and be held on to (Job 2:3, 9; cf. 27:6), something that can be weighed (31:6) and turned away from (27:5). These metaphors describe integrity as though it were an object, or more precisely, Job's most treasured possession, something he *has*, rather than something he *is*. In Dhorme's rendering of 27:5, Job will not "renounce" or "disown" his integrity, "as though it did not belong to him" (1984, 381). And Whybray (1998, 133)

---

8. As is often noted, Job comes very close to cursing God, not only in cursing the day of his birth—and by implication, God's creation—in ch. 3, but by describing God's injustice and indifference to innocent suffering, and also by likening him to an attacking predatory beast or band of storm-troopers (Job 16:9, 12–14; 19:10–12; see Lasine 2001, 212–13, 239.

9. See, e.g., Choi et al., 1999, 47; Ross 1977, 174.

10. On 1 Chr 29:17, see Chapter 8, below.

11. In context, this means that David is affirming his own goodness, in contrast to Saul's wickedness; see Edelman 1991, 197.

notes that in the prologue, both Yahweh and Job's wife "had recognized [his integrity] as his inalienable characteristic." That Job is "blameless" (תם) and has integrity (תמה) is accepted not merely by Job (e.g. in Job 9:21; 27:5–6; 31:6), but by the narrator, by God, by Job's wife, and by Eliphaz.[12]

Carol Newsom has recently taken a "narrative character ethics" approach to Job 1–2. She concludes that the satan "is the narrative embodiment of a hermeneutic of suspicion," a "proto-Nietzschean figure" whose "clever genealogy of piety"—that is, his question "does Job fear God for nothing?"—is designed to "unmask" the "false consciousness of ideology."[13] Newsom concludes that chs. 1–2 are "a surprisingly philosophical little didactic tale" (2002, 125–26).

Newsom's heavily theoretical reading gives surprisingly little attention to the psychological issues at stake in this "tale." At one point she

12. Good includes Bildad, after noting that Bildad has used תם "ostensibly of Job" in 8:20 (Good 1990, 224–25). Moral psychologists and philosophers have many varying views of "integrity" as a virtue or "meta-virtue." Psychologist Blasi (2005, 90) defines integrity as "a person's serious concern for the unity of his or her subjective sense of self, as manifested in consistency with one's chosen commitments." He adds that this concept should be carefully distinguished from the more common "constructs of self-consistency" used by psychologists, including behavioral and trait consistency, cognitive and logical consistency and personality integration. Philosophers like Doris (2002, 18) point out that "integrity can figure in a life that is morally suspect or even morally reprehensible; the Nazi who cannot be bribed to spare Jews very arguably displays integrity." Cox et al. wisely conceive "integrity" in such a way as to exclude cases such as this. In addition to being "a kind of continual remaking of the self," it involves "a capacity to balance competing commitments and values and to take responsibility... Integrity is not a kind of moral purity. Nor is it a kind of wholeness or intactness...[or] a blindly steadfast devotion to one's convictions...The fanatic, the dogmatist, the sanctimonious moralizer are no more people of integrity than the capricious wanton" (2003, 41, 152).

13. In her *NIB* commentary on Job on 1:9, Newsom asserts that "the *satan* shifts the focus to the question of what motivates Job's behavior. This is not necessarily...merely a questioning of Job's sincerity... It is blessing itself that casts doubt on the very possibility of disinterested piety" (1996, 349). Like the commentators mentioned earlier, Newsom views the satan as focused on issues of character (e.g. "sincerity"), not situation. However, Newsom later insists that the characters in the prologue can *only* be understood as representing the values of an honor culture. In this light, the satan's question "besmirches God's honor" (1996, 361). She then asks whether "absolutizing" God's honor leads to "religious masochism" on the part of Job, and whether Job's integrity has "become such a fetish that he cannot recognize the perversity of blessing the one who destroys him for no reason" (1996, 361). On the moral dangers of absolutizing integrity as a value, see the preceding note.

does assert that the satan "perceives Job as one who may have a complex interiority…levels of motivation that are not so easily identified…[and] values that Job himself may not even be aware that he holds" (2002, 131). However, in terms of the social psychological issues I have just discussed, the opposite is more likely. That is, the satan's position is that situation trumps character, that turning Job's situation upside-down will make his mental complexities, motivations, and values irrelevant. The satan is not trying to "unmask" Job's convoluted character. If his question implies any "suspicion," it is that one can have character traits sufficiently robust to resist any and all external pressures.

Many dispositionally oriented Westerners who learn about the Milgram obedience experiments judge the so-called obedient subjects harshly, and consider the "defiant" subjects to be morally superior, if not heroic (see, e.g., Waller 2002, 105). This suggests a final question worthy of *haśśatan*: What does Job's obedience to a God who has blithely administered these "shocks" to him say about *Job's* moral character—*and* about God's?[14]

## 2. *Moses in Exodus 32 and Numbers 11*

The Moses narratives offer several examples of how "surprising" stories generate widely different explanations, depending on the expectations and assumptions of individual commentators and the theoretical paradigm which defines the scholarly groups to which they belong.[15] I will briefly discuss two cases, the second of which is particularly complex. Commentators like Houtman (2000, 618) and Toews (1993, 125) express surprise that in Exod 32 Moses initially remains calm when informed by God of the people's image-worship—calm enough to calm God's anger (vv. 7–8)—but then becomes angry himself after he descends and sees the calf and the dancing at the base of the mountain (vv. 15–19). In fact, they and others view this "sudden rage" as "incomprehensible" (Elias Auerbach 1975, 123) or contradictory (Hyatt 1980, 301, 307),[16] concluding that the angry Moses portrayed at the foot of the mountain "is entirely different than the one" who intervened with God on the summit

14. These uncomfortable questions are explored in Lasine 2001, 177–263.

15. As famously argued by Kuhn (1996, 23–24, 37), scholarly paradigms tend to limit the kinds of questions one can ask of a text by excluding those questions which the paradigm is not able to answer.

16. Gressmann (1913, 199 n. 4) argues that all of vv. 7–14 are to be regarded as a later, but relatively old, addition, because they "contradict" vv. 15–35. Gressmann also believes that 32:1–4a and 32:4b–6 contradict one another.

(Houtman 2000, 658). As Holzinger puts it, after vv. 7–8 the conversation in vv. 17–18 is "senseless" (quoted in Hahn 1981, 111).[17]

Some of the scholars[18] who find this surprising also assume (without textual evidence) that Moses is "caught by surprise" (Houtman 2000, 618) as well, as though he knew nothing about the apostasy and only later "discovers"[19] the sin. In effect, they preclude the possibility that Moses could hear the shocking news that God reported to him on the summit, intercede with God on Israel's behalf, and only become angry when he returned to the "scene of the crime," which was still in progress. Hahn (1981, 110–11) offers an alternate interpretation, suggesting that the text as it stands makes it seem as though Moses had not believed what Yahweh told him at the summit. Propp (2006, 557–58) wonders whether "at some earlier version of the text" Moses did not know what was going on even when he met Joshua on the way down the mountain and failed to inform him about the people's sin (v. 18). After all, Propp asks, "would he have appeased Yahweh had he fully appreciated the people's crime?" Is Moses "still in denial" (2006, 558)?

Other scholars do imagine it to be possible for one person to act as Moses does in the different situations reported in Exod 32. Reuss (quoted in Hahn 1981, 111 n. 64) and Cassuto (1967, 419) both point out that seeing something with one's own eyes has a greater impact than hearing about it at long distance. Benno Jacob agrees, asserting that the narrative communicates "an extraordinary psychological insight" (1992, 947).

Scholars like Hahn (1981, 111 n. 64) regard such explanations as harmonistic attempts to smooth out tension. Nevertheless, Christine Hayes has recently argued, in effect, that there is no psychological tension to be smoothed out. She contends that Moses' "outburst of anger" in vv. 19–20 is *not* "jarring and unmotivated." In a manner reminiscent of the Jewish commentators Cassuto and Jacob, she argues that when Moses is "confronted with the full vision of the people's folly, he, like God, is outraged and acts accordingly" (2004, 66).[20]

---

17. Cf. Toews 1993, 125: "Moses learns in two different ways about Israel's sin in vv. 7–8 and 15–20."

18. Houtman 2000, 618; cf. Hyatt 1980, 301; Hahn 1981, 110–11. Rarely do commentators say, more accurately, "I was surprised" rather than "*It is* surprising."

19. This is how Hayes describes the view of "many critical scholars." These scholars also believe that Exod 32 presents "two contradictory views of Moses," one in which he is "benign and patient," and one in which he is angry and only "grudgingly intercedes for them" (2004, 49–50).

20. Of course, Yahweh himself does *not* turn out to "act accordingly" at this point, due to Moses' intervention on the summit.

Unfortunately, Hayes vindicates the sense made by the present text by *over-psychologizing* Moses' behavior in the chapter. Following some rabbinic commentators, she contends that Yahweh actually makes two separate speeches in 32:7–10, with a pause of unspecified duration in between. She interprets the lack of any reported speech from Moses during this hypothetical pause as evidence of the prophet's psychological state: "Moses' failure to respond between God's two speeches suggests a kind of paralysis... Could Moses be anything but dumbstruck, shocked into inaction by the nightmarish news?" (2004, 55).[21] As usual when one asks whether a human response to a given situation "could be anything but" what the speaker assumes, the answer is "of course it could." According to Hayes, however, Moses is "roused" out of his initial "shock and then panic" by God's second speech, which makes Israel's survival depend upon him (2004, 56). Hayes's argument not only predicates a textual "silence" which may not exist, but fills in this imaginary blank with imaginary information about Moses' psyche. The resulting scenario is not anchored in the facts reported in Exod 32. Nor is it grounded in Moses' behavior in previous chapters, where he had had ample opportunity to expect this sort of apostasy from the people.

Hayes would have been on firmer ground if she had viewed Moses' behavior in Exod 32 in terms of social psychology. From this perspective, Moses' reported actions may be quite consistent, without our having to over-attribute emotions to him. Doris notes that we can plot certain situations in which people will predictably act in certain ways, even if they do not exhibit such "local traits" globally in all situations (Doris 2002, 25, 62–66, 116). Studies by Cervone and Shoda (1999, 21) also show that people exhibit "stable patterns of behavior variation." To investigate whether Moses is exhibiting such "cross-situational coherence" (Cervone 1999, 303), we would have to investigate whether there are any other situations in which Moses is faced with an angry Yahweh who wants to destroy his people and then reacts in a way similar to his behavior in Exod 32:7–14, in spite of being fully aware of their sin. The situation in Num 14 immediately springs to mind. Moses is fully aware of the magnitude of the people's sin in proposing a return to Egypt, but he intercedes on their behalf nonetheless.[22] Ultimately, of course, it is up

21. See, e.g., Leibowitz 1976, 563, 592–93; Cassuto 1967, 414–15. In contrast, Houtman (2000, 645) contends that explaining ויאמר יהוה by "pointing to the situation—Moses is dumbfounded; before he is able to say a word... YHWH again begins to speak...—seems artificial. Introduction of YHWH, by means of successive divine oracles, as one who is speaking is done more often."

22. The Pentateuch includes no other examples of situations in which Moses becomes destructively angry when encountering others who are engaging in sinful or

to each reader—with his/her particular set of assumptions and expectations—to decide whether any of these explanations can account for
Moses' behavior in this episode, and illuminate the dynamics of the text
in its present form.

Assessing Moses' behavior in Num 11 is much more problematic.
Once again Moses acts in a way which some scholars find surprising.
Milgrom (1992, 1153) is surprised by Moses' "all-too-human, flesh-and-
blood character" in Num 11. By this he means that Moses "betrays a
streak of self-doubt" (11:14), indulges in self-pity (11:11, 15), and begins
to doubt God (11:21–22). He is exhausted physically and psychologically, burnt out, worn down by his grueling task, and suffering from a
collapse. Chapters 11–20 record his steady decline.[23] Similarly, Sasson
(1990, 285) observes that "responsibility and duty…can destroy the self-
esteem of individuals" and concludes that in Num 11 Moses has been
called upon once too often to bear the brunt of a very difficult situation
and finally breaks down.

What does Moses do in this chapter to elicit such dire diagnoses?
Briefly, the people express disdain for their God-given manna. Moses
hears the people weeping. The narrator reports that Yahweh is enraged
and adds that "it"—the situation—is evil (רע) in Moses' eyes (11:10).
Moses complains to Yahweh that he has treated him "evilly" (הרעת;
11:11) by laying all the burden of the people on him, making him their
mother, nurse, and day-care provider. After all, they are Yahweh's kids,
not his.[24] Where is he supposed to find meat to feed all this people?
Moses then asks that Yahweh kill him if things are going to continue like
this, so he won't have to look upon his evil (ברעתי; v. 15). Yahweh
responds by saying that he will take from (or extend) the spirit (ואצלתי
מן־הרוח; v. 17) on Moses and put it on seventy elders who will help carry
the burden of the people. Later, Moses complains that not even whole

---

criminal behavior after he has already been informed about their behavior. If such
situations were reported, they would provide further evidence of cross-situational
coherence. Moses' anger in Exod 32 has made such a deep impression on many
generations of readers that we must be on guard not to attribute anger to him in
stories in which the narrator makes no mention of his emotions or motivations, such
as the account of Moses striking the Egyptian (Exod 2:11–14). In this instance, some
readers may simply assume that it is psychologically implausible for someone to
strike another person so forcefully without being angry. For other examples of
Moses' anger, see Exod 16:20; 32:22 (Aaron *fearing* that Moses is angry); Lev
10:16; Num 16:15, and 31:14.

23. Milgrom 1992, 1153; 1990, 85, 378.

24. Moses' statement implies this, rather than stating it explicitly.

flocks, herds, and all the fish of the sea would suffice for the people (Num 11:22).

Some commentators hesitate to take Moses' apparent doubting of God's power literally, and find ingenious ways of making this utterance fit their image of Moses as a heroic prophet. Rashi quotes Rabbi Shimon's cry, "Heaven forbid? Such a thought never occurred to that righteous man" (Davis and Rabinowitz 2004, 150). He interprets Moses to be saying that sheep and cattle should not be slaughtered so that (כדי) this great nation would be killed. In other words, Moses is actually interceding on behalf of the people here. Similarly, R. Gamliel argues that far from assuming that God lacked the power to provide meat for the people, Moses was saying that the people were insatiable: no matter how much meat you give them, it will not be enough for them (Rashi in Davis and Rabinowitz 2004, 151). Nevertheless, most scholars do believe that Moses is literally doubting God's ability to supply sufficient food, even after so many previous miracles. Suggesting that Moses has suffered a breakdown is one way of explaining doubts which seem very odd at this point, following as they do all the miracles Moses had witnessed from a front-row seat.

The commentators I have alluded to so far all read Num 11 as a unity in terms of characterization, or, at least as a text which has been "fused" into a "coherent composition" (Levine 1993, 327). Sommer offers the most detailed analysis of the chapter as a combination of sources. He argues that by bringing together two disparate stories, the redactor of Num 11 compels readers to contemplate several related motifs but bars them from achieving interpretive closure, adding that narrative coherence was not always a goal (1999, 602). He posits that the chapter is composed of two complete stories. Separating them out "renders many oddities in the text understandable, since the narrative disjunctions…are present only in the redacted text," while "each of the two strands…is free of the sudden shifts of topic and *non sequiturs*…" (1999, 608). In effect, Sommer is "liberating" two opposite stories from oddities and *non sequiturs* which only exist when one assumes that there is no plausible psychological explanation for Moses' behavior.

Each story Sommer isolates is univocal, two-dimensional and entirely readable. Unfortunately, the result is extremely reductive; in one story Moses is over-idealized and in the other he is the despicable *Doppelgänger* of the first. In the first, Moses is entirely positive, good-hearted, and loves the people (1999, 609, 611, 612 n. 27). In the other story about the people's grumbling, Moses delivers a long, verbose, rambling, angry tirade in which he exhibits a number of unpleasant personality traits. This Moses is petulant, bitter, self-centered, self-pitying, shirking, a snitch, an anti-prophet, and someone who feels contempt for the people and is punished for it (1999, 611–16).[25] While Sommer insists that the negative story does not "overpower" the positive one, he goes on to argue that this is indeed what happens, when, for example, in the redacted text even Moses' wish that all Yahweh's people were prophets (v. 29b) is used by Sommer as evidence that Moses *hates* the people (1999, 616–17).[26]

Sommer contends that readers are "compelled" and "forced" to read the chapter as he describes, and barred from achieving closure. But as I indicated earlier, many readers seem to have successfully resisted this compulsion. Some do so by accepting that Moses doubted God's ability to provide meat, and explaining this as caused by some kind of mental or physical breakdown. Others may believe that Moses has good reason for being fed up and frustrated at this point in his career, and recall that in this state of mind they themselves, as well as others, often say things which are irrational, melodramatic, stupid, or which otherwise go against their better knowledge. Once again, the kind of explanation an individual reader (or community of readers) will favor will ultimately depend on their "inch-rules," that is, on their expectations concerning what constitutes psychologically plausible behavior in specific situations, as well as what constitutes narrative coherence and what makes theological sense.

---

25.  Butler (1979, 9–15) claims that strong pre-existing "anti-Moses traditions" influenced the shape of other Moses stories. The goal of these traditions was "to show the true Moses as unqualified for any of Israel's positions of leadership" (1979, 14). Referring to Exod 2:11–14, Butler asserts that "this basic narrative pictures the guilt of Moses, the presumptuous pretender, interfering in a case in which he has no right to be involved. He acts furtively at each step, protecting his own interest. He is willing to slay both Egyptian and Hebrew in his desire for power and position" (1979, 10). The story of Moses saving Jethro's daughters is also said to be the result of a "basically anti-Moses" tradition. Why? Because the "girls do not respond properly to the hero. They ignore him." Butler even assumes that Moses is "passing himself off as an Egyptian" in this scene (1979, 11).

26.  Sommer is not the first to explain perceived inconsistencies in Moses' behavior by positing two opposed Moses-personalities. For example, Freud notes that while Moses is often described as imperious, hot-tempered and even violent, he is nevertheless said to be the most gentle and patient of all humans. Freud explains these "contradictions in Moses' characterization" by positing two separate Moses figures who have become fused together in the biblical text. One Moses is an Egyptian, an ambitious seignorial devotee of the new Aton religion, for whom the qualities of gentleness and patience would have been of little value. The other Moses is a Midianite priest who ministered to the bloodthirsty and uncanny volcano-god Yahweh; it is to the latter that the traits of gentleness and patience should perhaps be attributed (Freud 1950, 126, 131–33, 135, 141).

## 3. *Elijah in 1 Kings 19 and Other Passages*

Moses is not the only biblical prophet who has been accused of self-pity and diagnosed as suffering from "burn-out." These judgments have also been made about Elijah to a much greater degree, as I will discuss in Chapter 5. Most readers of 1–2 Kings come away with a firm impression of Elijah's character and his situation, although not all have the *same* impression. If some judge him to be egocentric, self-pitying, and petulant, others describe his personality to be so "distinct," "strong," and "unique" (Simon 1997, 224, 226),[27] that it "invite[s] us to an ever deeper sounding of [his] human depths" (Brichto 1992, 166).[28] Even commentators who ordinarily dismiss "psychologizing" as anachronistic, unnecessary, or "a serious exegetical mistake" do not hesitate to make definite judgments about the way the prophet's personality is depicted in 1 Kgs 19 (Nelson, 1987, 126; see Kissling 1996, 101).

Many critics find that explaining Elijah's behavior solely in terms of redaction eliminates interpretive headaches. For example, Keinänen simply states as a fact that the "moaning" Elijah's desire for death in 1 Kgs 19:4b "contradicts other emotions in the textual context" and "is not compatible" with v. 3, in which we are told that Elijah fled to save his life (2001, 142, 165–66). He does not ask whether the sudden turn-around in Elijah's mood might make psychological sense in terms of the specific personality exhibited by Elijah in 1–2 Kings, and the situations in which the prophet places himself in 1 Kgs 18–19. Commentators like G. Jones (1984, 327–28) find vv. 9–14 implausible in their present form, and therefore claim that one part of the passage or another is the "original kernel" to which has been attached interpolations and/or repeated elements.[29] De Vries observes that "psychologizing interpretations" have been hard put to explain Elijah's change of mood between 18:46 and 19:3. The good news is that this is not something which redaction critics

---

27. For Simon, the depiction of Elijah's personality is intended "to endow the signs and portents with full reality," so that "readers can hear the Lord's word through Elijah's ears" (1997, 224–26). From the portrayal of Elijah in the Bible, Rofé is certain that the historical Elijah also had a "unique personality" (1988a, 190). Cf. Reinhartz (1998, 148), who asserts that "personality traits have an impact on the ways in which [Elijah and others] enact their prophetic roles."

28. Brichto concludes that Elijah "seems to swell into a three-dimensional personality," in spite of the fact that he had begun by claiming that Elijah is "the embodiment of the prophet role more than a person" (1992, 166, 131).

29. Dumbrell (1986, 16) rightly objects to this practice, citing Alter's argument that "the relevant question…is not the fact of repetition as such, but the reason for it."

need to worry about: "but of course this question does not arise for those who recognize the original independence of these passages" (1985, 235).[30]

Marsha White takes a slightly different tack. She believes that the author's use of elements from the "Mosaic tradition" to legitimate Elijah is so "persistent," "incessant," and "unrelenting" that these elements cause "narrative difficulties," psychological "discordances" and "contradictions in mood" (1997, 4–6, 8, 11).[31] For White, interpretations which "resort to" psychologizing in an attempt to discern Elijah's motivation are wrongheaded and anachronistic, because narrative "coherence…[has been] sacrificed for a statement of prophetic authority" (1997, 4; cf. 7). Ironically, it is largely on the basis of unsupported *psychological* judgments about what constitutes "psychological discordance" that White, De Vries, Keinänen and others reject any attempt to provide a psychological explanation for Elijah's behavior.[32]

Recently, both Wagner and Meinhold have acknowledged the presence of different redactional layers in the narrative, but argued that this creates a "conceptual" and "literary" unity, rather than preventing such unity. Each suggests that the contradiction formed by Elijah's *"Lebensmüdigkeit"* immediately following his concern for *"Lebenserhaltung"* may be intentional, allowing the narrator to be able to take better account of the "multidimensional experience of reality" (Wagner 1996, 217; Meinhold 2002, 23). Wagner goes on to suggest that by reporting Jezebel's death threat against Elijah, and then quoting Elijah saying that it is the Israelites who want to kill him, the narrator is presenting a "bilinear" perspective which is better able to reproduce accurately the multiformity and the atmosphere of the situation and reconcile the tensions between vv. 3–4 and 10 and 14. He concludes that *both* Jezebel and Israel are in pursuit of Elijah (1996, 216–17, 222).

---

30.  For example, Keinänen (2001, 167) concludes that the "inconsistencies" he perceives in 1 Kgs 19 are the result of the author taking the "independent tradition" of Elijah's despair and placing it in the present location.

31.  White finds the main difficulty to be the motivation for Elijah's despair. Why would he want to die after his success at Carmel? If fear of Jezebel prompts this death wish, why would he flee for his life? If he wants to die, why does he eat and go on a forty-day journey which has a "purposeful goal." I address these questions in Chapter 5, below.

32.  Most scholars who emphasize the tension between the prophet's death wish and his preceding flight to save his life take at face value Elijah's accusations against his people in v. 10, and find his verbatim repetition of these charges in v. 14 as a sign of textual disorder. A common solution is to take the theophany in vv. 11–13a as an interpolation.

Wagner's attempt to take into account the complexities of our reality-concept is laudable. However, his demonstration of the stories' bilinearity and subsequent "depth of field" grants Elijah's own view of his situation equal reliability with the contrary information provided by the narrator throughout the Elijah narratives.[33] Later I will argue that Elijah's characterization of his situation here is highly *un*reliable.

The relationship between redaction and complex characterization must also be considered when we interpret other scenes in the Elijah narratives, especially those in which information is lacking which readers might reasonably expect to be given. If we limit ourselves to information directly reported by the narrator, all that Yahweh orders Elijah to do prior to Elijah's description of his own situation in ch. 19 (vv. 4 and 10) is to hide at Wadi Cherith (1 Kgs 17:2), go to Zarepthah (1 Kgs 17:9), and go show himself to Ahab, after which Yahweh will give rain (1 Kgs 18:1). We are also told that Yahweh hears Elijah's plea for the life of the widow's son (1 Kgs 17:22), and later at Mt. Carmel has fire fall from heaven, apparently in response to Elijah's call for an answer (1 Kgs 18:37). In addition, Yahweh's hand comes on Elijah in 1 Kgs 18:46, and an angel of Yahweh prepares Elijah for an unspecified journey in 1 Kgs 19:7, after which Elijah chooses to go to Horeb.

More frequent are cases in which Elijah acts without any mention of divine direction. In each instance, we must ask what the story tells us about Elijah's personality, in addition to whatever they might imply about the redaction of the narratives. For example, in 1 Kgs 17 Elijah announces a drought without our being told that Yahweh ordered him to do it, and without a reason being given for this privation to be inflicted on Israel. This has led some of the rabbis to suggest that the announcement was generated by an impulse of the prophet himself rather than being God's idea, so that God was more or less forced to back Elijah up.[34] This raises the question whether Elijah might be forcing God to

---

33. In spite of stressing the multi-dimensionality of reality, Wagner is less interested in establishing the biblical Elijah as a "realistic" coherent personality than as a kind of collective figure which Wagner describes as "almost…a 'corporate personality'" (1996, 222).

34. Later legends which link the consecutive verses 1 Kgs 16:34 and 17:1 also show God backing up Elijah. For example, when conversing with Elijah at the house of Ahab's grieving friend Hiel, Ahab cast doubt on the effectiveness of Joshua's curse of Jericho on the grounds that even a curse by Moses himself (in Deut 11:16–17) was not fulfilled. Thus provoked, Elijah uttered the prophecy now in 1 Kgs 17:1. Only *then* did Elijah pray to God, and have the "key of rain" given to him (*b. Sanh.* 113a; cf. *y. Sanh.* 10:2).

back up his plans and predictions in other episodes. Such a pattern of behavior would certainly tell us something about the prophet's personality. Later in 1 Kgs 17 Elijah responds to the desperate widow's accusations against him by uttering an accusatory plea to Yahweh, in order to persuade Yahweh to back him up by reviving the boy (v. 20). Similarly, Elijah calls for miraculous divine aid in the public setting of the Mt. Carmel contest with the Baal prophets (a contest not ordered by God in the first place!) and Yahweh is again forced to back Elijah up.[35] After the contest Elijah slaughters these prophets himself, again without a command from Yahweh.

At first glance, Elijah seems to have obediently accepted the ordinary limitations of a human emissary of Yahweh after the events at Horeb, as he quickly follows Yahweh's orders to condemn Ahab and later Ahaziah (1 Kgs 21 and 2 Kgs 1). However, even in these cases Elijah shows signs that his personality is influencing the ways in which he obeys. In 1 Kgs 21, after the judicial murder of Naboth, Yahweh directly orders Elijah to convey his words of condemnation to Ahab, but what Elijah actually says to Ahab adds to *and* subtracts from the message Yahweh had given him to deliver (vv. 18–24). Are the additions and subtractions explicable in terms of Elijah's personality, or only in terms of redactional activity? Elijah's words in vv. 20–22 differ strikingly from what Yahweh told Elijah to say. Yahweh had twice told Elijah to use the formula "thus says Yahweh," but instead Elijah uses the pronoun "I" four times *after* using "I" to refer unequivocally to himself, echoing Ahab ("I have found you"). This leads readers to take *all* five uses of "I" to refer to Elijah as agent, rather than as Elijah quoting Yahweh saying "I" of *him*self and what he, Yahweh, will do to Ahab. There are a number of other cases in biblical narrative in which Yahweh tells a prophet to relay a message which is to include the formula "Thus says Yahweh." This is the only case where the prophet not only fails to repeat the formula as directed, but continues to speak as though the words being relayed were his own

---

35. While I describe Elijah as controlling Yahweh's power in this scene, Conners describes Yahweh as using Elijah "to communicate divine power by bringing down fire on the sacrificial bull" (1997, 236; cf. Hauser 1990, 51–52). Other commentators compare Elijah's "bold" unauthorized initiative here with Moses' proposals to Pharaoh in the plague of frogs (on this see Chapter 5, below). In one midrashic tradition, Elijah (in 1 Kgs 18:36) is one of the three "prophets who asked that a miracle should be wrought for them, otherwise they would be declared as imposters" (Ginzberg 1968, 6.101 n. 571). The other two prophets are Moses (in Num 16:29) and Micaiah (in 1 Kgs 22:28).

and not Yahweh's.[36] In other words, Elijah identifies with his God, as he will do in later episodes.

Not only the form but the content of Elijah's speech to Ahab is radically different. Yahweh's few words were aimed solely and specifically at Ahab for his crimes against Naboth, and limited to predicting Ahab's blood being spilled and lapped by dogs at the same place where Naboth's blood was spilled (vv. 18–19). In contrast, Elijah indicts Ahab generally for doing evil in Yahweh's eyes, and declares that evil will be brought on all of Ahab's line, not merely on the king himself. Elijah uses language here which has become formulaic for readers of 1 Kings, repeating expressions already used in the indictments of Jeroboam and Baasha.[37] This could easily leave readers with the impression that these verses are statements by the narrator, but the narrator himself attributes these statements to Elijah.

The fact that vv. 20–22 are attributable in their entirety to Elijah is usually dismissed or left unmentioned by commentators. When it is acknowledged, it is usually explained in terms of redaction.[38] Cronauer (2003, 346) claims that the presentation of Elijah in this chapter is "uncharacteristically flat." He is "not the dynamic person" found in other

36. For example, Yahweh tells Moses to say "Thus says Yahweh" to Pharaoh (Exod 4:22) and Moses does so (Exod 5:1). In 2 Kgs 1:4 an angel of Yahweh tells Elijah to use the formula with Ahaziah's messengers, and we learn from the messengers in v. 6 that he did so. Later Elijah repeats this to the king himself (v. 16). There are indeed cases in which Yahweh tells a prophet to use the formula and the formula is not explicitly said to have been uttered. However, this is usually because the report of the prophet repeating the message is simply summarized with a notice that the prophet did as Yahweh commanded (e.g. Exod 7:17, 20; 2 Sam 7:5, 8, 17; 24:12, 13). In other cases the scene between prophet and king is simply skipped, although the sequel makes it clear that the message was indeed delivered (e.g. Exod 7:26; 8:16; 9:1, 13; 2 Kgs 20:5). Conversely, there are many instances in which Yahweh is not explicitly said to tell the prophet to use the formula and the prophet does so (e.g. 1 Kgs 11:31; 12:24; 13:2, 21; 2 Kgs 9:3). This occurs a number of times within 1 Kgs 17–2 Kgs 2, but usually with a prophet other than Elijah (e.g. 1 Kgs 20:13, 14, 28, 42; 22:11). These cases underscore the fact that Elijah is incorrect when he claims to be the only prophet of Yahweh left.

37. Compare 1 Kgs 21:19, 21–24 with 1 Kgs 14:10–11; 16:3–4.

38. See, most recently, Sweeney 2007a, 247–48, 251–52. At one point Sweeney's focus on redaction leads him to misrepresent 1 Kgs 21:27–29. He regards these verses as part of the "exilic edition," asserting on that basis that "Elijah's leniency toward Ahab in v. 27–29 provides the model for Huldah's declaration" that Jerusalem's fall will not come until after Josiah's death (2007a, 248). However, it is Yahweh, *not* Elijah, who is lenient toward Ahab in 1 Kgs 21:27–29. In fact, Elijah does not even inform Ahab of Yahweh's "leniency" toward him.

Elijah stories. As proof, he claims (inaccurately) that in 1 Kgs 21:17–20 Elijah "speaks only what God commands him to speak."[39] While Cronauer concedes that Elijah announces a long series of condemnations (including even vv. 23–26), he nevertheless dismisses vv. 20–26 by saying that all they contain "derives from the editor himself." As a result, he refuses to take seriously vv. 20–22 as Elijah's words and consequently does not take them as evidence of the way Elijah's personality is presented in the chapter.

Other scholars also fail to consider that vv. 20b–22 may function as part of the narrator's presentation of the prophet's personality.[40] Olley (1998, 43) comes closest to taking the given text seriously in this respect. He acknowledges that Elijah's words to Ahab are "quite different" from the message he had been given, and that Elijah speaks "uniquely, in narrative,…as YHWH without introduction ('I' in vv. 21–22)," elaborating the judgment on Ahab's household and Jezebel. However, his analysis of these peculiarities as evidence of Elijah's personality is limited to asking whether the prophet has "identified so wholeheartedly with the judgment" that he took it upon himself to embellish on Yahweh's behalf. I would go further, and suggest that Elijah is identifying with Yahweh himself, rather than with Yahweh's judgment—more specifically, that he is identifying with what he understands to be Yahweh's "jealousy."[41] We might also ask how *Ahab* would have heard the words quoted in vv. 20–22. Would *he* identify Elijah with Yahweh and his power? Would Elijah

---

39. Elijah does not repeat Yahweh's words in v. 20; see below. Other aspects of Cronauer's account are also inaccurate. He says that Elijah appears suddenly in ch. 21, as he had in 17:1, omitting that in 17:1 there is no mention of Yahweh sending him to the king, while in ch. 21 there is such a notice. He also claims that Elijah has a brief dialogue between relaying Yahweh's words and the editors' condemnations, when in fact the dialogue precedes any attempt by Elijah to relay Yahweh's message.

40. Brichto claims that v. 19 "gives God's words to Elijah, the very words that Elijah is to pronounce to Ahab," and that v. 20 "gives Ahab's answer to *those* words—but to Elijah" (1992, 278–79 n. 25; emphasis added). But it is difficult to see how Ahab's saying "Have you found me, my enemy?" in v. 20 constitutes Ahab's reply to *God's* words. Brichto assumes that the speaker of the words at the end of v. 20 is Elijah, while the speaker of the words beginning v. 21 is Yahweh, without offering support for this assumption. In contrast, Walsh (1996, 331) asserts that vv. 20b–22 are "clearly" Elijah's words. According to Nelson (1987, 143), "Elijah's words merge into God's at verse 21 and then into the narrator's by verse 25… The prophet, God, and the narrator all agree in a single Deuteronomistic chorus." Rofé (1988b, 94) contends that vv. 20β–26 is not a sequel to vv. 17–20a-bα; it is made up of Deuteronomistic stereotypes with no reference to the Naboth episode.

41. See Chapter 5 below on Elijah's "jealousy" in 1 Kgs 19.

want to create that impression in the king, as he had attempted to do with the people in ch. 18?

The following two verses (vv. 23–24) are also attributed to different speakers.[42] Verse 23 begins with an addition quoting Yahweh's alleged words about Jezebel. Here dogs are related to Jezebel's demise as well as to Ahab's.[43] Verse 24 continues the theme of dogs eating carcasses, although this time those eaten by dogs are members of Ahab's family who die in the city. The final clause adds that those who die in the country will be eaten by birds. The fact that only vv. 23–24 refer to the dogs mentioned in Yahweh's original instructions to Elijah would seem to increase the likelihood that Elijah is quoting these words to Ahab, rather than the narrator speaking in his own voice. At the same time, vv. 23–24 differ dramatically from Yahweh's words to Elijah. They make no mention of dogs lapping Ahab's blood, and they focus on Jezebel and Ahab's family rather than on Ahab himself. They also add the new element of being eaten by these animals. Because both of the expressions in vv. 23–24 are used together earlier in the stereotypical condemnation of Jeroboam in 14:10–11, readers are more likely to view vv. 21–24 as one unit, in which either Elijah or the narrator is quoting an apparently well-known formula of condemnation.[44]

In the final scene of the chapter we learn that Ahab "repents" after hearing Elijah's words of doom (1 Kgs 21:28–29). This prompts Yahweh to tell Elijah that he will defer Ahab's punishment to his son, but he is not said to command the prophet to inform Ahab of this reprieve. Nor does the narrator mention Ahab being so informed. Is this a redactional oversight or an expression of Yahweh's purpose in telling this only to Elijah? Yahweh makes a point of directing Elijah's attention to Ahab's humble submission to the Lord. Is Yahweh implying that this is an attitude which the self-willed prophet should himself adopt? Because

---

42. JPS and NJPS include vv. 23–24 in the quotation marks beginning in v. 20. In contrast, G. Jones (1984, 359) claims that vv. 21–22 do *not* continue Elijah's words, in spite of the fact that there is no narratorial notice marking a shift from Elijah as speaker to the alleged direct quotation of Yahweh's words (which, of course, differ from Yahweh's message recorded in v. 19). Jones does not believe that these verses continue Elijah's words because they "contain words which *would* more *naturally* be attributed to God" (emphasis added). He does not ask why those words are not attributed to God by the narrator.

43. If this is a notice by the narrator, it is appropriate to ask why it was not added to (or after) Yahweh's direct words to Elijah earlier.

44. Could it also be that vv. 21–22 are Elijah's personally couched threat to Ahab, while in vv. 23–24 Elijah is relaying Yahweh's threat to Jezebel and to Ahab's descendants?

Elijah is not instructed to inform Ahab that Yahweh has deferred bringing evil upon his dynasty because of his contrition, whatever message
Yahweh's words carry seems to be designed exclusively for Elijah
himself.

When we turn to Elijah's behavior in 2 Kgs 1, it becomes clear that
the situation mirrors 1 Kgs 18 in several ways. As in ch. 18, Yahweh
gives short instructions to Elijah, who then goes far beyond them when
he shows off his powers and authority from Yahweh and ultimately kills
large numbers of people. In both cases Elijah is in total control of the
situation.[45] In both stories fire from God plays a role. And just as Elijah is
afraid without good cause at the start of 1 Kgs 19, so in 2 Kgs 1 Elijah is
told by the angel not to be afraid at a time when Elijah again has no
reason to be afraid.[46] On the contrary, it is those who have to confront
Elijah who have good reason to be afraid. In fact, the third captain of
fifty never even relays a royal command for the prophet to come down.
His lengthy speech is restricted to asking for the life of his men and
himself, even referring to themselves as Elijah's servants.[47] The fact that
the captain has just expressed—at length—abject fear of Elijah makes the
angel's following statement to Elijah glaringly incongruous. Ironically,
the angel tells Elijah to descend on the one occasion when the captain
had *not* asked Elijah to do so. And later, after Elijah delivers the death
message personally to the king, we are not told of the king's reaction,
much less that he sought to harm or imprison the prophet, as the kings
did to prophet-figures in 1 Kgs 13 and 22. This reinforces the impression
that Elijah never was in danger, and therefore had no reason to fear, as
the angel of Yahweh implied he would.

If the angel had told Elijah not to be afraid the first time that the
soldiers approached, and had then sent the consuming fire without Elijah
ordering it himself, his assurance that Elijah need not be afraid would

45.   The people and the king obey all of Elijah's orders in ch. 18. He gives orders
in at least once in vv. 8, 19, 25, 27, 30, 34, 40, 41, 43, 44 (cf. v. 23). All are obeyed.
Moreover, ch. 18 leaves open the possibility that the contest of Carmel is Elijah's
own idea, rather than an event commissioned by Yahweh.

46.   In the conversations Elijah has with the first two captains, he repeats himself
verbatim, as he does with God in 1 Kgs 19, while the two captains differ in their
statements to Elijah. Some commentators believe that the king's words quoted by the
second captain are more curt and aggressive than those of the first one. If so, the
king now has good reason to be angry with Elijah, because it is reasonable to assume
that the king has learned why his first messengers failed to return. On Elijah's
unwarranted fear in 1 Kgs 19, see Chapter 5, below.

47.   The captain's pleas are entirely focused on Elijah himself, not on Elijah's
god.

hardly be remarkable. However, the fact that he says this to Elijah precisely when readers might not expect it, suggests that the resulting incongruity is by design. If so, its purpose could be to mock Elijah's earlier fearfulness and to remind readers of the incongruity between Elijah's ability to wield divine destructive power and his tendency to fear those whom he so easily defeats precisely because of those powers.

It is often said that Elijah is having Yahweh prove himself superior to Baal in bringing life or life-giving fertility in 1 Kgs 17–18.[48] The fire from Yahweh in ch. 18 could be part of such a demonstration. But it is difficult to see what similar purpose could be served by Elijah's evocation of fire from heaven in 2 Kgs 1, especially because the Baal who is explicitly mentioned in this chapter is not a God asked to bring rain, but a God who is to be asked for a medical prognosis. However, Elijah's order of "fire of God from heaven" (1:12; cf. v. 10) to destroy over one hundred more people does serve a function for Elijah *personally*, namely, to demonstrate his special status as a man of God ("If *I* [אני] am a man of God, let…") who has divine power at his disposal. In 1 Kgs 18, Elijah wanted the miracle to validate both Yahweh and himself; here the focus is only on his own power and authenticity,[49] a demonstration which he seems to feel necessary even though the first captain had himself affirmed that Elijah was a man of God, rather than casting any doubt on it (v. 9).

While indications that Elijah may be egocentric and self-promoting may not be as strong in 1 Kgs 21–2 Kgs 1 as they are in the Horeb episode, it is clear that any attempt to explain the gaps and seeming

48. According to Hauser (1990, 11), in order to make 1 Kgs 17–19 "an effective and convincing piece of drama, the writer allows death to pose numerous challenges to Yahweh's power, almost as if death were a personified force," like Mot. In ch. 19 "death works through Jezebel to deny Yahweh the services of his most powerful and successful prophet." In fact, death "gain[s] an overpowering hold on Elijah" (1990, 68, 80). To the extent that Hauser imposes a hypostatization and personification of death onto these narratives, his approach precludes viewing Elijah's attitudes toward death in personal psychological terms. In Hauser's reading, the presentation of Elijah's personality basically functions as a way to accomplish an ideological purpose. Specifically, the prophet's "assertiveness… is used to express the power and victory of Yahweh." This leads Hauser to blur the line between Yahweh and Elijah. For example, at times he asserts that Elijah killed the Baal prophets (1990, 22, 33, 53, 54, 57; cf. 80), while at other points he claims that Yahweh "used death" or "made death His tool" to do it (1990, 34, 76), that Israel/the people did it (1990, 34, 40, 68), that both Elijah and Israel did it (1990, 45; cf. 34), that Elijah "has them slain" (1990, 56), or that death "seized" the prophets (1990, 38).

49. However, Elijah does repeat God's words of self-validation to the king (2 Kgs 1:16; cf. v. 3).

incongruities in these passages should consider the possibility that these textual features may serve a function as characterization, instead of—or as well as—being indicators of redactional splicing. In Chapter 5 I will argue in detail that Elijah's surprising behavior throughout 1–2 Kings can be most fully (and "coherently") explained if we acknowledge that the prophet is being depicted as possessing what is now called a narcissistic personality.

## 4. *David in 2 Samuel 12:15–23*

If Elijah is a complex, controversial and elusive biblical prophet, the same is true for the biblical king David, as he is presented in 1–2 Samuel. Later in this work I will have occasion to discuss many aspects of David's personality and the ways in which readers evaluate his character. Here I will discuss only one scene in the Court History. In 2 Sam 12 David learns that the death sentence he had brought upon himself by his response to Nathan's parable would be transferred to his as yet unborn son. When the baby later becomes gravely ill, David fasts and lies on the earth while beseeching God for the child. After the baby dies, he gets up, washes, changes his clothing, worships in the temple, and eats.

Commentators like Schwally and Ackroyd find David's efforts "to save the child's life" to be inappropriate or incongruous in light of Nathan's unconditional prophecy. Schwally even describes David as "showing himself oblivious" to the prophet's pronouncement.[50] As a result, he, Ackroyd and others conclude that the "original sequel" to the end of 2 Sam 11 is v. 15 of ch. 12, not v. 1, thereby eliminating the perceived discordance. Other scholars interpret this story as indicating the presence of an admirable character trait possessed by David, such as strength of will or inner independence, unaffected by others' opinions.

In contrast, commentators like Hertzberg (1964, 316) argue that the explanation for David's conduct is "not to be sought in his own personality." Simon (1967, 219) agrees that David's actions should not be examined "in the light of the normal responses of a person," but adds that they should be examined in light of "the special destiny of this unique personality." Gerleman (1977, 137) contends that the episode is too indeterminate and ambiguous to serve as character portrayal, as the varying attempts at interpreting it show.[51] As mentioned earlier, other

---

50. Ackroyd 1977, 113; cf. Schwally in Simon 1967, 207–8; 1997, 127–29.

51. Fokkelman concludes the opposite: "we need not look for an interpretation; the text already offers it to us itself" (1981, 89). His optimism is based on two debatable assumptions: first, that the narrator's "interpretation" is necessarily reliable and

scholars believe that elusiveness and multivalence are actually the hall-marks of realistic characterization. Clearly, readers' differing concep-tions of character—and reality—play a role in how they will deal with stories like this one.

This narrative contains an element lacking in my previous examples, because here there is an audience *within* the text which reacts to David's behavior with surprise, if not shock. When the child is sick, the elders of the palace urge David to get up off the ground and eat. After the baby dies they are afraid to tell him, worrying that he will "do evil" (v. 18), usually taken to mean that he might do something desperate.[52] When David then foregoes all mourning procedures after learning of the death, his courtiers are baffled. David tells them that he had hoped Yahweh might change his mind and let the boy live, and now that he is dead, fasting will not bring him back.

The narrator does not tell us how they reacted to this explanation. According to Gerleman (1977, 138), the courtiers must have construed the existing situation differently from David, because they did not know the history behind it. In fact, they knew considerably *less* than *we readers* do about David's recent crimes and the curses pronounced by Nathan. That does not mean that all readers conversant with the Court History interpret David's words and actions in the same way. Hertzberg (1964, 316) believes that David acts as he does after the child's death because he recognizes "its deeper significance," namely, that his sins have now been expiated and he himself redeemed. He says nothing about the *other* curses hurled by Nathan which will continue to reverberate throughout David's personal life.[53] Simon (1967, 239) contends that David has "grasped the crux of his situation…in the intensifying of his dependence on God."[54] Such conclusions are apparently deduced from the two words

infallible, and second, that David's self-presentation is reliable. That this confidence in David's reliability is unwarranted will be demonstrated in Chapters 8 and 9, below.

52.  Hertzberg (1964, 315) believes that the courtiers feared a desperate act on the part of the king, perhaps even suicide. But is it possible that ועשה רעה in v. 18 alludes to David "doing evil" *to them*? Although this question might sound far-fetched, when other characters are later forced to inform David of a person's death, they have to be very careful how they broach the subject, or so David's courtiers assume. To David's "servants" we might compare Homer's Antilochus, who *correctly* anticipates Achilles' suicidal response to the substitute death of a loved one (*Il.* 18.32–34), after Achilles, like David, failed to go into battle himself.

53.  Hertzberg also ignores "Yahweh has transferred your sin (העביר חטאתך)" in v. 13. See McCarter 1984, 301.

54.  Fokkelman claims to know what David thinks "deep in his heart" and concludes that his reaction stems from "a deep feeling of factuality" (1981, 90–91).

David utters after Nathan concludes his curses (חטאתי ליהוה; v. 13). Other scholars fill in the blanks in ways which similarly reflect their understanding of biblical theology and their assumptions about David's character.

Unlike most commentators, Gerleman does not take David's words as reliable indicators of how the king actually views the situation. In fact, he thinks that the reply is a "pious" excuse designed to keep his servants in a state of ignorance, because the constraints of his situation prevent David from giving them an honest answer without giving away his secret. As long as David had to endure his expiation, disaster hung over his head—and Israel's (Gerleman 1977, 137–39).[55] Insofar as he stresses situational constraints Gerleman is not attributing David's supposedly dishonest answer to his character. Now, social psychologists point out that "people seek situations that will 'push' them in the same direction as do their own dispositions" (Gilbert and Malone 1995, 33). Consequently, "situations are largely of one's own making and are themselves describable as a characteristic of one's own personality" (Wachtel 1973, 330).[56] Not only is the situation in 2 Sam 12 of David's making, if we note all the other occasions on which David employs deception, we would have reason to ask whether deviousness is a defining trait of his character in such situations.

The courtiers' expectations about David's behavior were presumably based on the assumption that he was like themselves, that is, that he would act according to the conventional notion of appropriate behavior to which they would expect themselves to conform. One factor which is not thematized in the story is whether the courtiers know *more* about David's character[57] than we know or even more than the narrator knows or wants to tell. If we want to find an example of David being viewed in a very different light by a character who knew things about him from long experience—knowledge we cannot share—we need only recall Eliab's suspicious view of his brother's motives when David inquires

---

55.  Gerleman (1977, 139) then asks a thought-provoking question: "What would the child's recovery lead to?... It is difficult to shake off the impression that the narrator of the succession narrative, with his skeptical realism and his illusion-free knowledge of human nature, has consciously given his account an ironic secondary stress (*Nebenton*)."

56.  Similarly, Cervone and Shoda (1999, 4) assert that in a social-cognitive analysis of personality functioning, people select and shape their environments and give meaning to events by interpreting them according to their personal beliefs. However, at the same time, the sociocultural environment shapes self-views, knowledge mechanisms, and psychological tendencies.

57.  As opposed to knowing the specific facts which David is anxious to cover up.

about the prize package which was supposedly to be given to Goliath's slayer.[58]

Clearly, how a reader construes David's situation and his character will determine how she evaluates his conduct in these scenes. As is often the case in the Court History, possibilities are many and questions must remain. However, this complexity should not lead us to conclude that attempts to explain David's conduct in terms of his own personality are wrongheaded.

### 5. *Zedekiah in the Book of Jeremiah*

My final example here is Zedekiah, the last Davidic king to rule Judah. In Chapter 1 I mentioned that scholars sometimes explain perceived inconsistencies in characterization by assuming that coherence has been sacrificed on behalf of an ideological or other agenda. The widely varying portrayals and assessments of King Zedekiah in Kings, Chronicles, and Jeremiah are often explained by postulating a series of redactors with different ideological interests. By focusing almost exclusively on the contradictory predictions of the king's "fate," however, this strategy tends to downplay or exclude consideration of the ways in which Zedekiah's character is depicted, even in the chapters which contain the most detailed and nuanced presentations of the king.

For example, Applegate argues that the redactors of MT Jeremiah have deliberately "highlighted the tensions" in the available texts or traditions concerning Zedekiah in order to preserve a "debate" over the status and fate of the king (1998a, 138, 152; cf. 1998b, 304).[59] In a manner reminiscent of structuralist analysis,[60] Applegate views the "extremism" of the most negative and positive prophecies as "mitigating" or "mediating between" one another (1998a, 152; 1998b, 307). He also posits a "fuller" ideological debate about "the authority of the paradigm of response to

---

58. Of course, Eliab's opinion cannot be taken at face value; his judgment of David could be influenced by his own character and his perception of his relationship with his youngest brother. The fact that David's "innocent" response to Eliab (מה עשיתי) is repeated by him three times to others in 1 Samuel (20:1; 26:18; 29:8) lends a degree of credibility to Eliab's perspective; see further in Chapter 9, §6, below.

59. Applegate usually, but not always, places "debate" between quotation marks. At one point, he says that the text "*almost* takes on the character of a debate" over the fate of Judah (1998a, 139; emphasis added). Later he concedes that "'debate' may well be too formal a description" (1998a, 140).

60. See Lasine 1986, 62–68 on this idea of "mediation" and "undermining."

Yahweh's word determining one's fate."[61] Because Zedekiah is an ambiguous figure, the highlighted differences in the projections of Zedekiah's fate "undermine" and "subvert" this paradigm, which at some point the redactors found to be too "inflexible" (1998b, 302–4).[62]

A discussion of Zedekiah as an "ambiguous figure" might be expected to examine the ways in which the narrator characterizes the king. This would be particularly expectable if the "paradigm" under study involves the critical importance of an individual's decisions and actions for determining his or her fate (Applegate 1998a, 156–57), which raises the issue of divine justice toward individuals. Yet the closest Applegate comes to considering Zedekiah's characterization is when he asserts that the king "is portrayed as a man who fails to obey the prophetic words, but also as one who wants to obey but is constrained by circumstances" (1998b, 301). Specific cases in which Zedekiah desires to obey are not discussed; nor does Applegate ask whether *anyone* could have acted differently in such highly constraining circumstances. While he notes that Zedekiah views Jeremiah sympathetically at some points (1998b, 302), he does not ask whether the MT text prompts readers to regard *the king* sympathetically.[63] And if readers *are* being prompted to view Zedekiah's situation and good intentions as mitigating factors, how should they respond to the fact that Yahweh does not mitigate the horror and humiliation of Zedekiah's downfall (Jer 39:1–7; 52:4–11)?[64]

More recently, Pakkala has revisited the question of the differing forecasts of Zedekiah's fate and what they imply about the ideology of various redactors, although he focuses most on 2 Kgs 24–25 rather than on the book of Jeremiah. Pakkala finds the characterization of Zedekiah

61. Applegate 1998b, 307; cf. 1998a, 156–58; 1998b, 302–3.

62. On introducing flexibility into cultural categories, see Lasine 1986, 66–68.

63. Applegate (1998b, 302) agrees with R. Carroll's statement that "because Zedekiah oscillates between sympathy towards Jeremiah and inability to follow him (cf. 37.1f.), his fate at the hands of the Babylonians is uncertain in the tradition." But Zedekiah could sympathize with Jeremiah *and also* be unable to follow him for a number of reasons, including his situation. Or he could be acting sympathetically toward the prophet whenever his situation allows him to. Applegate does not ask whether Zedekiah's character or behavior "oscillates" in a consistent pattern when his situation changes. If it does, then his behavior cannot be considered ambivalent, ambiguous, or inconsistent. Applegate believes that Zedekiah is "problematic" for the redactors because he protects Jeremiah but "fails—for whatever reason—to obey the prophet" (1998b, 302).

64. On the brutal and humiliating nature of Zedekiah's fate, see Pakkala 2006, 445, 449. On the ways the horror is increased in later versions, see Stipp 1996, 636, 642.

in Jeremiah to be "confusing, and the picture...ambiguous" (2006, 445). For the most part, Pakkala explains the confusion and ambiguity solely in terms of the traditions' (if not the redactors') differing ideological investments in whether Zedekiah and his potential dynasty were legitimate or illegitimate. That is, he envisions a "dispute" between two royal lines behind the present text of the MT. Despite "massive editing by redactors influenced by the DtrH, the book of Jeremiah preserves 'some vestiges' of an alternative tradition that treats Zedekiah as the legitimate king whose line could provide heirs to David's throne" (2006, 452). In contrast to Applegate, Pakkala offers no reason why the redactors of MT Jeremiah did not remove the "vestiges" which contradicted their own view of characters and events.[65] This is particularly important because the relatively positive portrayal of Zedekiah and his fate in Jer 34:5; 37–38 constitutes more than a mere "vestige"; these passages include vivid portrayals of the king and his interaction with Jeremiah, as I will show in a moment.

Unlike the interpretations of Applegate and Pakkala, Stipp's study of redaction in the Zedekiah materials in Jeremiah (MT and LXX) emphasizes the ways in which the king's character is presented. The "remarkable variety of attitudes" toward Zedekiah is Stipp's primary evidence for determining the date and place of composition of each passage, as well as for speculating on the ideology and goals of the various redactors (1996, 627).[66] For Stipp, specific social and political needs have led each redactor to create a different coherent (but not necessarily round) portrait of the king's character, based on their changing "theological stance" and "the situation of the communities from which they wrote" (Stipp 1996, 628). He contends that it was the writers' need for meaning, self-definition and coherence that shaped these portraits of the king (1996, 648; cf. 643–44). His interpretation of the social and political dynamics prevalent in the exilic period allows him easily to identify different levels and periods of redaction: all relatively positive portrayals of Zedekiah must be earlier in composition than negative ones (1996, 628).

Stipp's attempt to uncover redactional activity by focusing on the "unlucky" (1996, 644) king's characterization is ingenious, but not without problems. For example, Stipp connects the relatively "sympathetic" and "favorable" portrayal of Zedekiah in Jer 37–38 to the ideological function of the pre-Deuteronomistic documents which formed the

---

65. For example, Pakkala (2006, 445–46) states that the author of Jer 32:4 was unaware of, or was consciously contradicting, the tradition that the king was blinded.

66. On the redaction of the book of Jeremiah, see Albertz (2003, 302–44) and Stulman (2005, 1).

basis of Jer 37–43 (1996, 632). For the authors of these documents, who worked during the early years after the fall of Judah, the main purpose of Jer 37:3–43:7 was "to encourage the deportees to adopt a cooperative attitude towards their Babylonian overlords" (1996, 629; cf. 632, 644). Because Zedekiah "had stepped down from the stage" there was "no need" for the authors to "denigrate" him or to "endow their portrait of Zedekiah with heavy distortion." Thus, the reason he receives a "fairly mild portrayal" is because he was "not the focus of the writers" (1996, 631–32, 646). Conversely, when later writers *did* begin to focus on the king, they reduced him to a "pawn," stripped him of "individual traits," and ultimately vilified him, gradually magnifying the horror of his fate (1996, 633).

In Stipp's reconstruction it is precisely the authors' *lack* of interest in the king which prompts them to create the most realistic, historically accurate, and complex characterization of Zedekiah, while their focus on the king generates flat, stereotyped depictions. Although this explanation may sound paradoxical, it is certainly cannot be excluded from consideration. However, ideological narrative which reduces characters to cardboard villains often defeats its own purpose, precisely because of its lack of realism and nuance (see Chapter 7, below). Stipp himself concedes that it is "the relatively nuanced portrayal" of Zedekiah in Jer 37–38 which "lends a degree of credibility to their authors' presentation of his conduct during the Babylonian siege" (1996, 645). In contrast, excessive stereotyping in ideological literature can undermine a story's credibility.

Stipp seems to assume that when a given character is evaluated negatively or positively by a writer,[67] the writer's *sole* criterion is how a given depiction of that character meets his own theological and ideological needs in the historical situation in which he and his "public" find themselves (1996, 644; cf. 628). Thus, the presumed "lack of a conspicuous bias" against Zedekiah in Jer 37–38 is conclusive evidence that "he was not the concern of these writers" (1996, 644). When Zedekiah is later shown to be evil, it is because he *had* to be made evil for the authors' purposes.[68] In a move typical of defenders of ideological writing, Stipp assumes that adding nuance in characterization would be

---

67. For example, through the choice of information to be included and through judgments made by the narrator and other characters, either directly or indirectly.

68. Cf. P. Ash's idea that when Jeroboam I is made evil it is because he *had* to be, since he was the dynasty's founder (1998, 22–23). Similarly, the rabbis depicted Jeroboam in ways which were a function of their own disputes (Aberbach and Smolar 1968, 127, 131–32).

counter-productive: "finer distinctions would only have complicated things." Therefore, "the portrayal of the king was *completely* determined by the Deuteronomistic view of his era" (1996, 647; emphasis added).[69]

Stipp does not consider the possibility that nuanced, round characterizations can also express an ideological stance, at times with more rhetorical power than flat caricatures of ideal and villainous characters. Just as importantly, even with his emphasis on characterization, Stipp does not examine Jer 37–38 closely enough to determine whether the depiction of Zedekiah here is actually as positive and ideologically irrelevant as he assumes. Stipp notes that "Zedekiah's fault was his inability to obey Yhwh's instructions in the face of the pressure exerted by those around him," but adds that "such a reproach is nowhere made explicit" (1996, 632). While his characterization is "less than flattering," the king is shown to be "weak rather than wicked." In labeling the king as weak and viewing this weakness as a mitigation, Stipp is in agreement with the vast majority of commentators. Before discussing whether the narratives in Jer 37–38 actually support these conclusions, I should note that the most fundamental problem with Stipp's approach is that he does not grapple with the question why the *final* redactors left the older depictions of Zedekiah's character intact, even though they are in tension with, or even contradictory to, the view of the king held by these redactors. This is an old and ongoing problem for redaction-historical studies.[70]

69.  Stipp does not entertain the possibility that Zedekiah's better "traits" are absent in these passages because the authors may have believed that only results count; intentions would then be irrelevant. On this issue, see Chapter 4, below.

70.  One example is Stipp's handling of Jer 34:5, which, as he notes, has been viewed as "puzzling," "strange," and "odd" by many scholars (1996, 636–37). Stipp reasonably asks, "could a blinded former king who was incarcerated until his death in a foreign country, who had witnessed the slaughter of his sons as his last sight of the world, and who, according to some (OG Jer 52:11), was subjected to the most degrading slog, really die *beshalom*, as 34:5 promises?" Stipp explains the presence of this positive oracle by speculating that it originally belonged to the most ancient level of traditions and became "severed from the original proviso attached to it" by "some quirk of tradition." If so, why wasn't this "quirk" corrected by the later redactors of the present ch. 34, whom Stipp believes are so hostile to Zedekiah? He cannot argue that the redactors felt obliged to retain old traditions with which they disagreed, because elsewhere he describes redactors making all sorts of radical changes in presumed older strands of Jeremiah. Stipp notes that this positive oracle was "dropped" (1996, 637) from the parallel passages in ch. 32; if it was dropped there, why not here? Stipp assumes that the creator of the "later" version in ch. 32 "had chap. 34 on his desk and rewrote it on purpose." How could the same redactor be so free with material in ch. 32 and so reverential in regard to ch. 34? If we view the prophecy of a peaceful royal death "intertextually" with Huldah's prophecy of

Compared to the widely varying reader assessments of characters like David and Elijah, readers who make dispositional attributions about Zedekiah in the book of Jeremiah have been relatively uniform in attributing to the king the same defining trait. Among biblical kings only Zedekiah surpasses Ahab in being consistently and emphatically labeled as weak by commentators.[71] While weakness can mean many things to many people, it always depends upon the context, that is, the "weak" person's situation. In the case of Zedekiah, readers are given a much narrower range of information about the king and his situation than is available in the narratives concerning the allegedly weak king Ahab. For example, we do not observe Zedekiah's interaction with his wife or wives, or see him in battle,[72] or witness the predicted "eye to eye" meeting with the Babylonian king (see Jer 32:4; 34:3; cf. 39:6–7), or even learn why he ordered a release of slaves (Jer 34:8–10). In fact, we see him only in variations of one complex situation, namely, that of a monarch who is hemmed in by pressure from nobles and court officials[73]

King Josiah's peaceful burial, a different rhetorical function of the verse in Jeremiah presents itself. Could the comparison prompt readers to compare Zedekiah with his father, who is told by a prophet that he will be buried *beshalom* (2 Kgs 22:20)? Both hear the prophecy of their own fate in conjunction with the announcement of doom for Judah (and, to that extent, for themselves, either as dying early or being taken to Babylon; Jer 34:2–3; 2 Kgs 22:16–19, respectively). Both are fathers whose sons have horrible fates. And neither can "see" the very end of Judah.

71. E.g. Polk 1984, 162; Stulman 2005, 306; McConville 1984, 267; Stipp 1996, 632; Holt 1999, 169. A. Diamond (1996, 330) contrasts the "weak figure" of Zedekiah in the MT with the hypothetical Hebrew version of 37:17–21 on which the Greek translation is assumed to be based. In the latter, the prophet "discerns in the king's private face a scheming Machiavellian." In Jeremiah's eyes, the king's request for an oracle is "motivated out of a quest for personal safety." The motive of *this* Zedekiah resembles that attributed to the MT Jeroboam by many commentators; see Chapter 6, below.

72. The flight of Zedekiah and his army from the Babylonians (2 Kgs 25:4–6; Jer 39:4–5; 52:7–9) do not qualify as a battle; contrast these accounts with the reports of Ahab's wars with the Arameans in 1 Kgs 20 and 22.

73. Although commentators tend to speak as though Zedekiah is opposed by a monolithic set of court officials, a variety of terms is used for different groups: סרסים, 34:7, 19; שרים, 34:10, 19, 21; 37:14, 15; 38:4, 17 [Babylonian], 18, 25, 27 [כל־השרים]; עבדים, 37:2, 18; היהודים etc., 38:19; אנשי שלמך, 38:22. Specific courtiers are also mentioned. Some, like Zephaniah son of a priest (21:1; 37:3), are sent by Zedekiah to Jeremiah and simply do the king's bidding. Others, like Pashhur son of Malchiah (21:1) and Jehucal (37:3), do the same on one occasion, but complain to Zedekiah about Jeremiah in another (38:1, 4). Others are shown to either aid (Ebed-Melech [איש סריס], 38:7) Zedekiah and Jeremiah, or to oppose them (Shephatiah, 38:1, 4; Gedaliah son of Pashhur, 38:1).

on the one hand and the prophet Jeremiah on the other—with his obligation to his Babylonian overlord always in the background.[74] As Elias might put it, Zedekiah is "enmeshed in a network of interdependencies."[75] In Jer 38:5 Zedekiah gives the nobles his perception of himself in this situation (or, at least, the way that he *wants the officials to think he views himself*[76]): "the king is unable to do anything against you" (כי־אין המלך יוכל אתכם דבר).[77]

Even though most commentators have found Zedekiah's behavior easily explicable by accepting his self-perception as weak, a few scholars find his actions to be much more surprising. Stulman finds it "surprising" and "unexpected" that Zedekiah listens to Jeremiah's pleas about his imprisonment and concludes that Zedekiah is a "strange and unpredictable character" (2005, 309, 312). Similarly, Roncace (2005, 74) finds it "somewhat surprising" that Zedekiah's response to Jeremiah's appeal for help in Jer 37 is to move the prophet to the court of the guard rather than to free him totally or send him back to Jonathan's prison (37:20–21). He also finds it "somewhat unexpected" that in ch. 38 the officials throw Jeremiah into a pit instead of killing him as they had proposed, after Zedekiah has made the "peculiar" (2005, 71) claim that he is powerless against them.

Similarly, R. Carroll is puzzled by the report of Zedekiah's release of slaves (34:8–10), due to "the absence of an editorial account of *why* Zedekiah should behave so out of character (in terms of the Jeremiah tradition)" (1986, 647). This "strange tale" raises many questions but provides no answers (1986, 646, 648). Stulman (2005, 288–89) has also found Zedekiah's role in this scene to be rather ambiguous and his motives puzzling.[78] However, many other scholars have no problem

---

74. Readers of the Bible get many different perspectives on this basic situation. In addition to 2 Kgs 25 and 2 Chr 36, there are several chapters in the book of Jeremiah as well as Ezek 17. The most "rounded" portrait is the one presented in Jeremiah.

75. Elias 2002, 128; see further in Lasine 2001, 3–4, 261.

76. As noted earlier, a character's self-presentation in the Hebrew Bible cannot always be taken at face value. For an extended discussion of such a case in the David narratives (2 Sam 3:39), see Chapter 8 below.

77. In the Hebrew of 38:5, Zedekiah hands over Jeremiah to the nobles, saying "For the king—he is not able to do anything against you." In the LXX, this part of the king's statement is changed so that it becomes the narrator's comment: "for the king was not able withstand them." According to R. Carroll (1986, 678), the "MT stresses the king's weakness, G the power of the princes."

78. Stulman (2004, 56) manages to lessen this ambiguity by characterizing it negatively as "ambivalent posturing."

coming up with explanations, by attributing various motives to the king. Many speculate that Zedekiah's aim was to "mobilize all the available forces" prior to the siege (Liverani 2005, 191), or to grant the slaves liberty so that their masters "would not have to feed them" (Miller and Hayes 1986, 414), or a mixture of these motives (Holladay 1989, 239).[79] Clearly, scholarly attempts to fill in the blank left by the narrator are guided by their assumptions about Zedekiah's character as depicted in the book as a whole.[80] Only on the basis of such assumptions can they know what is "in character" for the king and what is "out of character." On the other hand, many scholars follow the narrator in blaming the king as well as the nobles for the re-enslavement of the debtors (34:11–22), even though the narrator never states that Zedekiah played any role in the slaveholders' "turning" against the covenant they had made (v. 11).

*Is* Zedekiah's behavior strange, unpredictable, peculiar, puzzling and surprising, if we take into account all we know about his character and his situation? Both Stulman (2005, 312) and Roncace (2005, 6) assert that Zedekiah is "a 'round' character." For Stulman, "round" here means "lifelike and multidimensional," while for Roncace it is "complex and ambiguous." Yet Zedekiah's situation itself would seem to make his behavior highly predictable, when the nuances of the situation are calculated. Nevertheless, Stulman labels Zedekiah as weak, inept, flawed, vacillating, posturing, compromised, and exhibiting a failure of nerve.[81] Is *that* what he finds "lifelike" in Zedekiah's portrait? Holt (1995, 95) seems to think so. She contends that Zedekiah is the picture of a modern, indecisive man; for her, he is a lifelike group portrait of modern humans. Similarly, Stipp (1996, 632) describes the weak Zedekiah of chs. 37–38 as "full of struggles and fears," adding that "here the unfortunate king comes close to being a real-life character." Whatever these statements say about Zedekiah, they certainly paint a bleak portrait of modern human life.

Roncace differs from the majority of commentators by claiming that Zedekiah is "both weak and powerful" (2005, 104). He bases this assertion on my discussion of the king's paradoxical role in my book

---

79. R. Carroll (1986, 647) believes that these suggestions (as well as others) may be "rationalizing explanations [which] may be provided to make good the absence of an editorial account."

80. As noted by Stulman (2005, 288–89), some commentators believe that Zedekiah's motive is to placate Yahweh, while others assume that Zedekiah initially acts in good faith, motivated by genuine interest in the welfare of his fellow Israelites.

81. Stulman 2004, 56; 2005, 305–6, 311–12.

*Knowing Kings* (Lasine 2001), which focuses on the role of information management in the establishment and maintenance of royal power. Roncace believes that Zedekiah displays the "paradoxical nature of the king's position" *per se*, that is, "his simultaneous vulnerability and his strength and sagacity to manage the flow of information" (2005, 103–4; cf. 8). However, while all kings are interdependent in their relations with their nobles and the people, the situations of specific kings differ greatly in these respects. Any power which Zedekiah may exercise in Jeremiah 38 has more to do with the use of cunning by those in a weak position in order to protect themselves from the powerful than it does with a truly powerful king's control of the flow of information in his realm (see Lasine 2001, 90–91). In his review of Roncace's book, Sweeney asserts that "Zedekiah must use deception and manipulation to rule because he is not accepted as a legitimate authority" by his officers and people (2007b, 132). Although Sweeney makes this statement to rebut Roncace's view of Zedekiah's strength, it actually concedes Roncace's point that Zedekiah had the strength to rule thanks to his skills at information management and deception, in spite of his being installed by the Babylonians, and in spite of the fact that (in Sweeney's opinion) Jehoiachin was the "true king" in the eyes of all the officers and people.

The key question is whether Zedekiah's lack of decisive action indicates a basic character trait beyond the incapacity imposed on him by his situation. Would "strength" in this context mean remaining loyal to the Babylonian king and acting on Jeremiah's advice, running the risk of being overthrown or killed? Could anyone have done more in that situation?[82] And how would anyone feel after hearing such "mixed messages," that is, such contradictory predictions of one's fate, all emanating from the same formidable true prophet—especially those prophecies which are *not* conditional on the king's actions from that point on?

The MT of Jer 37–38 does indicate one way in which Zedekiah's character may have shaped his perception and handling of his situation. When the king tells those to whom he attributes power that he is powerless against them, Zedekiah is, in effect, acquiescing to their demand for Jeremiah to be put to death. But if Zedekiah really is as powerless as he says, how is he then able to save Jeremiah's life with impunity, as he had already done at the end of the preceding chapter (37:20–21)? Later he swears an oath to Yahweh not to leave Jeremiah in the hands of those

---

82. Would Judaean intellectuals bred in the atmosphere of royal courts and bureaucratic hierarchies find it difficult to consider that Zedekiah has been placed in an untenable no-win situation, like Jeroboam in 1 Kgs 11–12? On Jeroboam's impossible situation, see Chapter 6, below.

who want to kill him, that is, the same people against whom the king
claims to be powerless (38:16). And finally, Zedekiah seems to know
how to use verbal subterfuge to protect Jeremiah and himself from the
nobles after his secret *tête-à-tête* with the prophet (38:24–26; see Lasine
2001, 91). To this extent, Zedekiah's previous expression of his own
weakness seems disingenuous and/or a sign of moral weakness which is
*not* a function of his actual situation.

This, in turn, implies that the characterization of King Zedekiah in
Jer 37–38 may not be as positive and lenient as scholars like Stipp,
Applegate, and Pakkala assume. In fact, this analysis suggests that the
Zedekiah of Jer 37–38 may be a surprisingly elusive character. Not even
a close reading of the interplay between character and situation in Jer
37–38 allows us to make an unequivocal judgment that Zedekiah is as
weak as he claims to be, or as free from reproach as some commentators
claim him to be. To this extent, the portrayal of the king puts the responsibility on each reader to make a judgment about whether Zedekiah
should be viewed as a wicked king who is the immediate cause of the fall
of Judah, a pawn in the hands of conflicting interest groups, or a convenient scapegoat. In this way, the story calls upon readers to expose
their own assumptions, expectations, proclivities, and "ideologies" when
they evaluate the king, a process I will discuss more fully in Chapter 9,
below.


## 6. Conclusion

The stories of David and Elijah form part of the so-called Deuteronomistic History (the books of Joshua–2 Kings, also known as the "Former
Prophets"). Most of the characters and narratives I discuss below are also
located in the DtrH, particularly in the books of Kings. It is therefore
worth noting here that the concept of a "coherent" DtrH has been
challenged from several quarters in recent decades. Writing in the 2000
volume entitled *The Future of the Deuteronomistic History*, Van Seters
asks whether the DtrH can avoid "death by redaction," that is, whether
the notion of a single comprehensive DtrH can avoid "gradual dissolution" caused by redactional studies which "split it up into small fragments," each assigned to one of an increasing number of different
redactors (2000, 213–14, 222). More recently, Noll has gone so far as to
assert that the Former Prophets are a "recalcitrant hodgepodge of
narrative discontinuities." According to Noll, the final form of Kings is
particularly "baroque, a cacophony of dissonant sound"; Kings is the one
narrative in the Former Prophets that is utterly resistant to a coherent

sequential reading" (2007a, 344, 342; cf. 2007b, 66). As I discussed at the beginning of this chapter, Booth claims that "we" admire works which "reflect a genuine encounter with recalcitrant materials." He is not assuming that the result of such encounters is merely a "hodgepodge" which has failed to reveal any integration of these materials. The studies in this chapter have already shown that biblical narratives—including the Elijah narrative in 1–2 Kings—are only "utterly resistant" and "recalcitrant" toward attempts to impose alien notions of psychological and situational coherence or incoherence on them.

Redaction critics do in fact seek coherence when they analyze "blocks" of text, by separating out fragments which are viewed as "suspect" due to perceived inconsistencies involving ideology, plot, vocabulary, or incoherent behavior on the part of characters.[83] However, too often the standards of coherence which are employed prevent scholars from perceiving the most important kinds of coherence which *are* displayed by specific stories in their current form. Interpreters must ask how the overall structure of a narrative affects each of the pieces they isolate, as well as the relation of the pieces to one another. Equally important is the need to take seriously the possibility that stories may be entirely coherent even though one or more of the characters in a story behave in ways which seem at first glance to be inconsistent, or in which the narrator seems to be promoting different ideologies at different points.

In my next chapter I will make a more detailed examination of a narrative which has puzzled many commentators for many reasons. This is the story of the man of God from Judah and the old prophet of Bethel in 1 Kgs 13. Analyzing the role of characterization in this chapter might seem to be a daunting enterprise, considering the lack of information readers are given about the personalities, intentions, and motives of these two prophets. However, such an analysis is crucial for understanding the rhetoric of the story, the nature of its coherence, and its ethical implications.

---

83. Just within *The Future of the Deuteronomistic History*, Römer notes that the Göttingen school approach makes it "more and more difficult to see a coherent ideology in the DtrH" (2000, vii–viii), Knoppers asks whether "a block is a self-contained, coherent literary work or an edition that contains heterogeneous materials" (2000, 127), and Van Seters wants to reconstruct 1 Kgs 12:32 in order to make the "whole unit coherent with the one theme of the golden calf apostasy" (2000, 215). When Van Seters discovers an element that does not meet his expectations, it is said to be "suspect" or not to "fit."

# Part II

# PROPHETS AND PERSONALITY

Chapter 4

## PROPHECY WITHOUT PERSONALITY:
## LIONIZED PROPHETS AND THE POWER OF LYING
## IN 1 KINGS 13 AND 20

The gullible person believes every word
but the clever one considers his step.[1] (Prov 14:15)

A lazy person says "There is a lion outside—
in the middle of the square—I'll be killed." (Prov 22:13)

Commentators often point to the prevalence of prophetic activity and terminology in the books of Kings. At times biblical prophets are lionized for their ability to "interpret events from God's point of view" (Fretheim 1999, 3; cf. Auld 1984, 67, 73–78). Yet in 1 Kgs 13 and 20 we encounter prophets who mislead or lie to colleagues and others who are "gullible" or naïve[2] enough to "believe every word," as Prov 14:15 puts it. In each case, the one who has been misled is killed by a lion in fulfillment of a curse pronounced by the prophet who has misled them. Do these lying "true" prophets therefore represent "God's point of view"?[3] Does the way in which these stories are told allow readers to answer such ethical and theological questions?

---

1. The phrase "considers his steps" (יבין לאשרו) implies that the clever one understands the "going" or course of his life and therefore watches his step. Cf. the discussion of Job's "steps" (Job 31:4, 7 [אשרי], 37) in Chapter 8, below.

2. The Hebrew word for the "gullible" person (פתי) used in Prov 14:15 can also denote a simple or naïve individual.

3. 1 Kings also contains another example of a lying true prophet, Micaiah in 1 Kgs 22. In this instance Ahab's prophets truthfully deliver a false prophecy, a false prophecy which God purposely put into their mouths, according to the true prophet Micaiah, who has just lied when he delivered *his* first prophecy concerning the upcoming battle. See further in Chapter 7, below and Lasine 2004b, 75–76. For a defense of Micaiah's honesty, see Moberly 2003. On deceptive (and deceived) prophets, see, e.g., Jer 23:9–32; 28:1–17; Ezek 14:9.

Recently, some commentators have attempted to clarify the meaning of 1 Kgs 13 by claiming that the characters' intentions and personality traits are of no interest or importance.[4] Ironically, the lack of information on character intentions is said to reveal the *author's* intention, which is to communicate the absolute importance of radical obedience. For these scholars, the fact that "the narrative relentlessly refuses to deal in motivations" (Nelson 1987, 89) has caused "rampant misinterpretation of the story" (Simon 1997, 136). Readers should resist the temptation to explain the narrative by positing hypothetical intentions (Simon 1997, 122; Mead 1999, 199 n. 23). Some of these scholars attempt to bolster their argument by pointing to folklorists who claim that intentions are irrelevant for folktales (see, e.g., Gross 1979, 111). I will argue that the absence of explicitly stated intentions in these stories does *not* imply that the characters' intentions are irrelevant. On the contrary, such gaps can spur readers to think about the unspecified motivations, *and* to question a series of events in which intentions are not taken into account either by the narrator or by God, events which seem to turn ordinary notions of fairness upside down.

## 1. *Characters and Intentions*

Even a dog distinguishes between being stumbled over and being kicked.[5]
—Holmes (1881, 3)

As I noted in Chapter 1, dispositional attributions provide a useful "psychology of the stranger." We, as well as Jeroboam and the Bethel prophet, encounter the man of God in 1 Kgs 13 as a total stranger. What expectations do *we* bring with us when we are introduced to the man of God and his situation? What expectations *should* we have about prophetic behavior,[6] the obligation to practice blind obedience, and the

4. According to Gross, the old prophet's lie was "completely unmotivated" or "not of interest," the king's motives are not important, and the text pays no interest to the subjective level at which the man of God's innocence would come into play (1979, 118, 121, 123–24).

5. In 1 Sam 2:29, a man of God charges that Eli "kicked at" (תבעטו) Yahweh's sacrifices. In tandem with Holmes's statement, this raises a strange question: Can a dog intuit intention, but a god cannot? Eli himself had no intention to commit such a sin, and even rebukes his sons for having done so (1 Sam 2:23–25).

6. After the reign of Solomon God communicates to humans almost exclusively through prophets and men of God. This implies that the victims in 1 Kgs 13 and 20 could not simply assume that they would be able to ask God "directly" for confirmation of what others had told them, or that they could wait for God to contact them directly. Moreover, while Moses had anticipated the possibility of false

ability of humans to detect deception? The biblical focus on deception, disguise, trust, and epistemological anxiety[7] expresses an abiding concern with the difficulty and importance of making *correct* attributions about people's true character if one wants to survive. This is certainly the case in 1 Kgs 13. Equally important is one's ability is to detect when someone is manipulating a situation in order to cause others to make false attributions about their character.[8]

Even if the man of God turns out to be strongly constrained by his situation, that does *not* mean that his intentions are irrelevant. The strategy of excluding intentions fits in well with literary theories which question the importance of character in narrative, as I discussed in Chapter 1. However, critics like Breden (1982, 297) argue that questions of character motivation cannot be excluded from the folktale, let alone from narrative fiction or real life. Even biblicists who discount intentions have to admit that 1 Kgs 13 "raise[s] all sorts of questions about the inward thoughts of the prophet and man of God" (Mead 1999, 199, on vv. 11–19),[9] and "teases…the reader…into speculation" about motives (Nelson 1987, 86). Gross also seems to acknowledge this fact, but he discounts its importance by cautioning that "one should not place too much trust in the untrained reader" (1979, 128 n. 8).

prophets before he died (Deut 13:1–5; 18:20–22), we have not seen evidence of this prior to 1 Kgs 13. For all we know, the victims in 1 Kgs 13 and 20 were not familiar with this problem, making them especially vulnerable to such deception. On prophetic authority in general, see, e.g., Deut 18:19; Amos 3:7.

7.  For expressions of epistemological anxiety in the Bible and modern detective stories, including the fear of being deceived by others whose true character we are unable to fathom, see Lasine 1987, 248, 251–54.

8.  This is what the Gibeonites do to the Israelites in Josh 9, and it is what Elijah attempts to do to God, and to us, in 1 Kgs 19 (see Chapter 5, below).

9.  Mead (1999, 199–200) argues that our only "glimpse into the heart of a character in the story" is the narrator's statement "he lied to him." (In the MT this is the report of a reliable narrator; many scholars omit the statement as a gloss, although Mead retains it.) Mead rejects Eynikel's attempt to use 2 Kgs 23 to establish the old prophet's motivation for lying, because this view "relies on a knowledge of the characters' inward thoughts, which is beyond the reader's purview" (1999, 198 n. 19). Mead's argument is problematic. First, the statement "he lied to him" hardly constitutes a glimpse into the heart. We are not told *why* the old Bethel prophet lied. Second, a character's motivation involves more than his or her "inward thoughts." We need to take the character's situation into account (including the character's perception of her or his own situation). And of course, an individual's motivation involves factors which may not be registered in their conscious thoughts. The personality type of the character may also have to be considered, as I will show in relation to Elijah in my next chapter.

Of course, different "trained" readers also fill in the blanks in very different ways.[10] For D. Marcus (1995, 83), the man of God is being ridiculed; he is so easily fooled by the old prophet that "the" reader is shocked. De Vries (1985, 174) views the inspired man of God as stupid, wayward and disobedient. For Van Seters (1999, 229), the man is *not* disobedient; he is merely stupid. Simon sees him both as trusting, naïve, and subjectively innocent, and as "acting the pious fool" (1997, 142, 147; cf. Crenshaw 1971, 62[11]). Reis (1994, 377) takes issue with exegetes who give "commiserative evaluations" of the man of God which stress his ingenuousness, innocence, or unwariness. In her reading, the man is "a guileful, acquisitive schemer" who has an "intense longing" to accept the old prophet's invitation[12] in order to "defect" to Bethel, a longing of which the old prophet is somehow aware (1994, 382). In other words, the prophet perceives that the man of God's "no" really means "yes." He's asking for it![13] The old prophet, on the other hand, finds favor with God because of his self-abasement, courage, charity, and "penitence." In spite of 2 Kgs 23:17–18, Reis concludes that it is the merits of the old prophet which "safeguard the joint sepulcher," not the man of God's presence in the grave (1994, 385–86).

Most commentators take a much less sympathetic view of the old prophet. If Reis demonizes the man of God, Josephus does the same to the Bethel prophet, calling him "a wicked old man" and "false prophet" who deceives Jeroboam and urges him to commit impious acts (*Ant.* 8.236, 245). In a similar vein, Barth (1955, 36) calls the old prophet "this true satan of the story." D. Marcus (1995, 86, 87–88 n. 70) believes that the old prophet may have had "purely selfish reasons" for wanting to be

10.   Much of this has to do with differing reader attitudes toward what constitutes obedience, both in general and specifically in relation to God. Readers also differ in how confident they feel about their own ability to detect deception. Readers are also affected, to varying degrees, by prevailing cultural attitudes about these issues, as well as by their own upbringing.

11.   Crenshaw (1971, 62) describes the man's naïve trust as directed only to fellow prophets: "a simple faith in the truthfulness of others in the profession of prophecy."

12.   U. Simon (1997, 142) also contrasts v. 8 and v. 16, asserting that the man of God now tells the old prophet "that he would very much like to accept his invitation but is forbidden to do so." But the man of God says no such thing. Simon later has to admit that the man of God "declines, in the same terms [he used with Jeroboam], the almost identical invitation extended by the old prophet" (1997, 147).

13.   Reis concedes that the old prophet lies, but adds that "he can excuse his lie with the rationalization that the man of God is ready to be enticed, desires it, and certainly, by his cupidity, deserves it. Perhaps the old prophet would not have attempted deceit had the man of God shown constancy" (1994, 383).

buried with the man of God. However, he also acknowledges other scholarly views, for example, that the old prophet was merely telling a "white lie" in order to persuade the foreigner to accept his hospitality,[14] or that he was testing the man of God in order to test the validity of the word of Yahweh (J. Gray 1970, 322) or to "undermine" the word of Yahweh (Simon 1997, 141). Still other scholars argue that the prophet is motivated by "narrow patriotism" (Walsh 1989, 360) or by the desire to protect Bethel and its cult (Provan 1995, 114; cf. Fretheim 1999, 79) or the city tombs (Simon 1997, 141).

Interpreters such as Nelson, Gross, and Mead, who assume that intentions are irrelevant in 1 Kgs 13, also believe that attempts to find moral and religious messages in the story are misdirected, because "there is really no moral enigma" (Nelson 1987, 89).[15] In so doing, they ignore or dismiss the fact that many readers have found the story to be morally and theologically problematic, if not disturbing. After all, the man of God's unknowing disobedience brings about his death, while the intentional lie of the Bethel prophet goes unpunished. In fact, the man of God ends up providing burial insurance for the old prophet when Josiah arrives, as the man of God had predicted.

## 2. Der Gottesmann ohne Eigenschaften: *Obedience and Vulnerability to Deceit*

> And all of a sudden Ulrich had to admit to himself with a smile…that…
> he was, after all, a character, even without having one.
> —Musil, *Der Mann ohne Eigenschaften* (1978b, 150)

What, then, *can* be said about the characters of the protagonists and how their characters are related to the notion of obedience to God projected by 1 Kgs 13? Whether they consider the story to be a parable, a negative example of an obedience legend, a composite of two originally independent prophetic legends, a midrash, or a "didactic" tale,[16] many

---

14. See, e.g., Rofé, who argues that the old man had "good intentions" for telling his "simple…crude, common lie about the angel" (1974, 162; 1988a, 181). Rofé believes that the old man "did not merit punishment" thanks to good intentions (1974, 162). Noth (1968, 306) contends that readers should not attach too much importance to details like the old prophet's lie.

15. Gross (1979, 110) claims that his method is to focus on the "immanent value system of the text itself," and not to "impose" moral and theological value categories on the text.

16. Parable: Rofé 1974, 158; 1988a, 173; Van Winkle 1989, 36–37, 42; negative obedience legend: Coats 1982, 66; a composite of prophetic legends: Würthwein

commentators agree that "the narrative is a lesson in obedience" (Nelson 1987, 89). Nelson claims that "God's commands have an unconditional claim to external obedience," so that "any subjective feeling of guilt or innocence or any pleading of good intentions are ultimately beside the point" (1987, 89; cf. Gross 1979, 124). Sweeney judges the man as having "betrayed his G-d—even if he was deceived" (2007b, 181). Rofé's description of the lesson (1988a, 181) is quite Ignatian: "the Man of God owes his Master blind obedience, total subjugation of will and self-abnegation." Coats (1982, 67) believes that the man has instead *chosen* to be disobedient: he knew the commandment and heard the "alternative" from the old prophet, and then chose his fate. But if the man of God believed the old prophet's statement that the *new* command also came from God, he did *not* choose between these two "alternatives"; he was obeying the new divine command which had replaced the original one.

Even those who concede that the man remains obedient tend to fault him for his inability to recognize deceit. While De Vries and Van Seters simply assume that he is stupid,[17] others attempt to show *why* he should have known better. For Simon (1997, 142), the fact that the old prophet comes from the direction of Bethel and asks for the man of God's identity should have alerted him. Werlitz (2001, 118) argues that the man of God "should—indeed, must—have been able to expose the lie of the Bethel prophet," because his orders instruct him to refrain from anything which could serve to legitimate Bethel as a cult center." In fact, "the behavior that was required of him should have been obvious even without the explicit instructions." Rofé (1974, 162) asserts that he "easily could have recognized his partner's blatant lie" by considering the old prophet's appeal to an angel as authority. Instead, the man falls "into the snare of heresy, a belief in angels." Van Winkle finds Rofé's solution to be inadequate; he correctly finds nothing objectionable in the use of angels as intermediaries of divine messages (1989, 39; cf. Crenshaw 1971, 44). We might add that the old prophet would have been a very poor deceiver to choose a lie which would not sound convincing to his dupe. Van Winkle might also have pointed out that vv. 1–2 and 9 do not specify *how* the man of God received the *initial* command; for all we know, that too could have been delivered by an emissary of

1985, 168; cf. Long 1984, 150; midrash: Montgomery and Gehman 1951, 41, 260; cf. Klopfenstein 1966, 646; didactic narrative: Gross 1979, 125; Long 1984, 150, 152.

17. Admittedly, the man of God is not as savvy about detecting prophetic false-hoods as is Ahab when Micaiah lies to him in 1 Kgs 22:15.

Yahweh.[18] Rofé (1988a, 178 n. 113) asks a key question about how divine instructions are communicated to prophets: "was it ever really forbidden for prophets to believe their colleagues?" He notes that Gersonides points to Gen 22 in this regard, a scene in which an angel commands Abraham to disregard an order previously given to him directly by God.

For De Vries (1985, 174), "once properly interpreted," the clearest test for determining whether to listen to one who presumes to speak for God is radical obedience.[19] Van Winkle rejects this criterion, because Yahweh is free to change his mind.[20] He believes that the man "should have recognized the [old prophet's] assurance to be false, since it encouraged him to violate the commandment of God" (1989, 38, 40). But the "satanic" old prophet, unlike the serpent in Gen 3, does *not* explicitly encourage the man to violate any divine command.[21] By conceding that Yahweh sometimes changes his mind in 1 Kgs 21 and other passages, Van Winkle acknowledges that the old prophet's lie was plausible. He fails to distinguish between Yahweh replacing one of his orders with a new contradictory order, and Yahweh using a prophet to encourage disobedience to his original order.

Scholars who criticize the man of God do so for two mutually exclusive reasons: inadequately blind obedience and failure to exercise his own judgment. However, the man consistently obeys what is presented to him as an authoritative command.[22] He is not described as someone

18.    All we know about the transmission of the initial command to the man of God is the man's cryptic statement to the king that he was commanded "in the word of Yahweh" (*bidbar Yahweh*; v. 9), and the narrator's report in vv. 1–2 that the man came from Judah *bidbar Yahweh* and cried against the altar *bidbar Yahweh*. On the possible meanings of this expression, see below. Similarly, readers are not told by whose authority or by what means Elijah came to view himself as "standing before Yahweh" as his spokesperson when Elijah first appears in 1 Kgs 17:1.

19.    De Vries (1985, 174) argues that it was not enough for the man of God to demonstrate his spiritual power by healing the king; "it had to be demonstrated by a tenacity in such 'little things' as not eating, not drinking, not returning by the same road." De Vries assumes that the man thought the prohibitions to be trivial and initially refused the king merely out of "naïve obedience." He had not yet been given the "sorest test." De Vries goes far beyond the text when he concludes that the man's "obedience was not carried out simply because Yahweh had said so."

20.    See, e.g., Exod 32:14 and 2 Kgs 20:1–6.

21.    Conversely, the serpent does not say that he has been sent by an angel of God to tell the humans to eat the formerly forbidden fruit.

22.    As an example of "self-destructive obedience," Tarnow (2000, 111) points to first officers in aircraft who feel unable to challenge foolish orders given them by

who is unwilling to question the authority of the old prophet or who is deliberating whether the new order is just as authoritative as the original order. For such descriptions to be appropriate, readers would have to be given access to his subjective deliberations, as was the case when we were told of Jeroboam's intentions for fabricating his golden calves (1 Kgs 12:26–27; see Chapter 6, below). Such information is lacking for the man of God. In fact, the narrator gives no information about his reaction to the prophet's second invitation. We are merely told that he went along. In other words, there is no narratorial notice saying "he believed him" to go along with the earlier "he lied to him." Nevertheless, the very fact that the man of God is unquestioning has certainly spurred many readers to question his motivation for accepting.

To the extent that the man of God might exhibit blind, unquestioning obedience, he is in what Stanley Milgram calls "the agentic state." As I mentioned earlier, Milgram is the researcher who performed the famous experiments requiring subjects to administer painful shocks to "learners" in obedience to the orders of an authority figure. He describes the agentic state as a condition in which "the individual no longer views himself as responsible for his own actions but defines himself as an instrument for carrying out the wishes of others" (1974, 134; cf. 143–48). Milgram's subjects felt responsible to the authority directing them but felt no responsibility for the *content* of the actions that the authority prescribed" (Collins and Ma 2000, 69). When films of Milgram's experiments were observed by Westerners, they underestimated the strength of the social situation in which the subjects were placed, even though the film emphasized situational factors (Collins and Ma 2000, 68).[23] Highly constrained subjects were assumed to be lightly constrained. From this point of view, readers who criticize the man of God may do so because they think he acted as though he were lightly constrained by the initial divine command when he should have been highly constrained by it. Although

older, more experienced captains, who are defined as the ultimate authority in the cabin. Such obedience has been estimated to cause twenty-five per cent of all plane crashes. In 1 Kgs 13 there is no evidence that the man of God considers the older prophet's request to be foolish, and, of course, in 1 Kgs 13 the older prophet is *not* destroyed, as are the foolish older captains in Tarnow's example. For a different perspective on "illogical" self-destructive behavior, see the discussion of the scorpion and frog fable, below.

23.   Cf. Gilbert and Malone 1995, 24, 27; Ross and Nisbett 1991, 132. This was not the case with Russian observers, who interpreted the teacher's behavior in terms of the situation, not the personality of the individual who was playing the teacher role.

Milgram makes no reference to monastic metaphors, his characterization of the obedient person as an "instrument" recalls Ignatius's famous description of the obedient person allowing himself to be directed in the manner of a corpse or an old man's stick (*Constitutions* VI.547; Ganss 1991, 303–4). Such obedience requires the sacrifice of one's understanding and judgment in order to make the superior's will and thoughts one's own, blindly[24] carrying out the superior's commands.[25]

According to Simon (1997, 147), the repeated invitations and refusals show that while the man of God's ability to withstand enticement had not weakened, he is "powerless against deceit." He was required "to apply his best judgment to distinguish between truth and falsehood," but failed. But how could he "apply his best judgment" if being obedient requires that he surrender his own judgment? In other words, blind obedience *itself* may cause his failure, not "weak judgment" (Simon 1997, 147), stupidity, or disobedience.

One might object that the man is simply too trusting or gullible. In his study of the psychology of deceit, Ford notes that there are socially acceptable standards for seeking out the truth: "if an individual is too accepting and unquestioning of information, we call that person gullible or unsophisticated" (1996, 197). Is that the case here? One key aspect of the man of God's obedient behavior is his passivity and seeming obliviousness. Just as he failed to question the old prophet about his second invitation, he is not said to have reacted in any way to the prophet's pronouncement of his unhappy future.[26] In Cogan's view he is "unresponsive"; he receives the word "with equanimity" and proceeds to finish his meal (2000, 371). U. Simon agrees that v. 23a implies the

24. See, e.g., *Spiritual Exercises* 365: "To keep ourselves right in all things, we ought to hold fast to this principle: What I see as white, I will believe to be black if the hierarchical Church thus determines it" (Ganss 1991, 213; cf. 486 n. 63). The official declaration is that the subject must renounce (*abnegando*) his own judgment and act blindly (*quadam caeca obedientia*).

25. In two letters on this type of obedience (January 14, 1548 and March 26, 1553), Ignatius cites 1 Sam 15 to illustrate his point. God was not pleased with Saul's non-obligatory sacrifice after the victory over the Amalekites, because he had earlier disobeyed the LORD's commandment to him through the prophet Samuel (see Young 1959, 160–61, 289).

26. Eynikel (1990, 231) notes that Jeroboam does not react to the altar's destruction. Although this might be another example of the kind of subjective obliviousness exhibited by the man of God, Eynikel believes that the author is intentionally presenting the king in a "grotesque" manner, in order to show that he is only interested in his own welfare. This goes far beyond what we can know about the intentions of both the author and the character Jeroboam; see further in Chapter 6, below.

man kept eating "as if nothing untoward had occurred" (1997, 143). However, he finds this too astonishing and implausible to be the case, because "the story provides no psychological justification for such brazen behavior."[27]

There is no evidence to suggest that the man of God's seeming obliviousness to the dire message has anything to do with brazenness, guilt feelings, *or* calm acceptance of his coming punishment.[28] He does not even yell "You tricked me!" to the old prophet. On the other hand, the oracle might have reduced *anyone* to a state of stunned *aporia*. After all, if the old prophet's new message of doom is true, then he had lied earlier. But if he was *not* lying before, then this new oracle must be a lie. In other words, if the prophet was a liar, he is now telling the truth, and if he was telling the truth, he is now a liar. Shades of the Cretan liar paradox! Can *anything* a liar says be trusted? No wonder the man of God has nothing to say!

One thing is clear: the narrator is again withholding access to the man of God's subjectivity, presenting readers with what we might call "a man of God without qualities," an agent of Yahweh who lacks will, judgment, and spontaneity. His passivity is reinforced by the fact that the old prophet saddles the donkey (v. 23) on which he rides to his doom. It is as though he is dead already. He is as silent as Alcestis, when she returns from the grave in Euripides' play (*Alc.* 1143–48). In fact, he is not quoted as saying *anything* after v. 17, that is, after the old prophet lies to him. Long before Ignatius, St. Francis had also illustrated true obedience by referring to a corpse, noting that it does not protest when it is cast aside (Bonaventure 1978, 232). And once he is killed by the lion, the man of God who had exhibited unprotesting "corpselike" obedience is

27. Simon evades the problem by concluding that the preposition אחרי must not be a temporal indicator after all (1997, 144, 304 n. 31). He thinks it has "a circumstantial meaning" as in Gen 13:14; 41:39 etc. It should be noted that in 1 Kgs 13 nothing in the old prophet's words implies that the man of God's death would follow *immediately*.

28. Cf. the other occasions where no response is recorded by the narrator when one might expect to hear a reply from those who have just been given a doom oracle or blessing. For example, within 1 Kgs 11–14 alone, Solomon is not said to respond when God condemns him in 1 Kgs 11:11–13, there is no response by Jeroboam after Ahijah announces both doom for Solomon and elevation to kingship for Jeroboam in 1 Kgs 11:31–39, and no response is mentioned when Jeroboam's wife hears the long and grisly oracle of doom against her sick son and her husband's entire line in 1 Kgs 14:6–16. And since there is no report of Jeroboam's wife actually delivering Ahijah's message of horror to her husband, there is no mention of Jeroboam's response to this doom oracle (1 Kgs 14:17–18).

repeatedly referred to as a "corpse" (or, carcass)[29]—ten times—until the old prophet calls him "my brother" (v. 30) and "man of God" (v. 31).

As is often noted, the style of 1 Kgs 13 is extremely redundant. The man of God's formulaically repeated speeches about food and water, coupled with his lack of personality and spontaneity, give him a mechanical aspect, much like the similarly obedient but doomed Balaam.[30] If there is an element of satire in 1 Kgs 13, as D. Marcus (1995, 73) suggests, it stems from this incongruous mechanical obliviousness, which is so well described by Bergson (1959, 450–51, 475–76). The mechanical aspect also accords with the man of God's style of obedience. Nietzsche includes "punctual unconscious obedience" among the examples of "mechanical activity" which allow people to escape pain through being "disciplined to impersonality" and forgetting of one's self (1999, 382).

The story of the mechanically obedient Balaam resembles that of the man of God in a number of respects. Just as the old prophet intercepts the man of God in the way, so does the angel intercept Balaam in the way. But in 1 Kgs 13 the intercepting angel (that is, the old prophet allegedly carrying an angelic message) does more than check the traveler's driver's license and let him off with a warning, as is the case in Num 22. Balaam would have turned back if the angel had told him to; in fact, he offers to do so. The man of God in 1 Kgs 13 *is* told to go back and he does. In Num 22:22 the angel of God comes "as a satan" (לשטן) to Balaam, and Barth (understandably) calls the old prophet in 1 Kgs 13 the "true satan" of the story. The man of God refuses a king's offer and then a fellow prophet's offer, until the old prophet lies to him saying that God has authorized him to accept. Likewise, Balaam initially refuses an offer by a king, and then accepts after God gives a different order. The wording of Balaam's refusal is so similar to the language used by the man of God that the verse in Kings seems to be rhetorically designed to have readers recall Balaam's story (Num 22:18; 1 Kgs 13:8).

In Balaam's case, his ass is *not* more obedient than he is, merely more perceptive—literally. The ass is actually less obedient, because it disobeys its master Balaam in order to adapt to the new situation of which

---

29. Hebrew נבלה; Vg. *cadaver*. The Hebrew word refers to animal carcasses in a number of passages, particularly in Leviticus and Ezekiel. It refers to human corpses when used in Deuteronomy–2 Kings, Jeremiah, and Isaiah.

30. Angel's recent comparison between Balaam and the man of God is weakened by his assumption that both figures were "unfaithful" to God and therefore "blameworthy" and deserving of "Divine chastisement" (2005, 33). In line with his assumption, Angel predicates negative intentions, thoughts, and emotions to both characters which go far beyond the text. The resulting interpretation serves to justify the violent deaths of both figures.

Balaam himself remains unaware. When Balaam is finally allowed to know what is going on, he does not have the self-assertive impulse (or *chutzpah*) to say to the angel, "Make up your mind; do you want me to go or not?!" In the same way, the man of God could have inquired of God, asking "can I eat or can't I?" The second order addressed to the man of God by the prophet in 1 Kgs 13 also resembles the later order given to Balaam by the divine messenger on the road (Num 22:35), in that the second command contradicts the first. Balaam, for one, is ready to obey both orders, and he, like the man of God, accepts without question that the later order also derives from God.

While the story of a prophet killed by a lion in 1 Kgs 20 does not include the element of mechanical obliviousness, it is a mirror image of the earlier story about the lionized prophet in several important ways.[31] In 1 Kgs 13, the old prophet *does not* inform the man of God that his invitation does not issue from Yahweh. In 1 Kgs 20, the son of the prophets does not inform his colleague that his request[32] to be beaten *does* come from Yahweh (vv. 35–36). Only after the colleague refuses this bizarre, unexplained request does the prophet inform him that he has not obeyed Yahweh's word. The narrator had previously informed *readers* that the request was "in the word of Yahweh" (בדבר יהוה; 1 Kgs 20:35), but the victim is not told. This crucial fact is obscured by readers like Gross, who says that the colleague is characterized as disobedient to Yahweh "on his own accord" (1979, 116, 118). Nelson (1987, 135) is closer to the mark when he observes that "the reluctant prophet is set up just as Ahab will be!"[33]

The parallels in language and plot between 1 Kgs 13 and 20 invite readers to reconsider what the man of God should have done when the old prophet announced permission from God to eat with him. If we assume that the man of God was disobedient because he believed that the old prophet was really conveying God's instructions, we would be forced to conclude that the companion in 1 Kgs 20 did the *right* thing when he refused the request of the "son of the prophets." Similarly, we would be forced to conclude that the man of God should *not* have listened to the old prophet's *second* oracle announcing the man's demise, even though we readers are told it is truly from God. In my experience, many students

---

31. Ironically, while lions are expected to act instinctually—that is, without conscious intentions in the human sense—the lion in 1 Kgs 13 acts against instinct by not attacking the ass, in a way which accords with *Yahweh's* intentions.

32. That is, the addition of נא to the imperative הכיני makes the statement a request or "polite command."

33. On Ahab being held responsible for violation of a holy war ban about which he had not been informed—in this very chapter—see Chapter 7, below.

who read the two stories together tend to fault the colleague in ch. 20 for *not* doing exactly what they fault the man of God *for* doing, namely, listening to a prophet. Some also fault the colleague for not asking the son of the prophets *why* he wanted to be struck, and criticize the man of God for not checking with Yahweh directly before accepting, through prayer or some other means. Another common suggestion is that he should have done what Van Winkle (1989, 40–42) also criticizes the man for not doing, namely, consulting an advance copy of the DtrH to discover that it is unprecedented for an invitation to be offered by one prophet on angelic authority to another prophet.[34]

If to be uncritically accepting of information is to be gullible, the man of God is just as vulnerable to deceit as Dante's "failed prophet" Virgil (Hollander 1989, 3–9), when Dante and his poet-tour guide encounter the demons of fraud in the *Inferno*.[35] As Carugati (1998, 298) puts it, Virgil is altogether unprepared to face the resourceful malice of the devils who inhabit part of Dante's hell. If the man of God in 1 Kgs 13 is "powerless against deceit" (Simon 1997, 147), Virgil uncritically accepts lies told him by the sly demons, while the ordinary man Dante is much more wary and street-smart (*Inf.* 21.127–33; cf. 23.10–21). Later events prove Dante correct, and Virgil looks quite foolish. Like the man of God, Dante's Virgil has often been called "naïve."[36] Raffa (1995, 279–80) calls Virgil "hopelessly ingenuous," adding that he seems "oblivious to the danger" presented by the demons. And if the man of God has been called stupid,[37] Virgil has been accused of carelessness and incompetence (Falvo 1988; Carugati 1998, 298). For many Dante scholars, Virgil's gullibility exhibits the failure of Reason, or the limitations of classical humanism and "philosophical wisdom," although they believe that the root cause of his naïveté is the fact that "the unbaptized Virgil has no access to any conception of diabolic evil" (Ellis 1998, 291; cf. Ryan 1982, 22; Carugati 1998, 299), an explanation that I will examine further below.

---

34. In any case, the fact that there may be no other examples of a prophet communicating a changed divine order to another prophet/man of God in the Hebrew Bible does not mean that it is impossible for God to use this means of communicating.

35. On Virgil's reputation in the Middle Ages as either a *vates* or "a *propheta nescius*, an unwitting prophet capable of error," see Barolini 1998, 279–84.

36. Carugati 1998, 298; Raffa 1995, 279; Ryan 1982, 22.

37. While the man of God knows what will happen in the distant future with Josiah, he has no insight into what is going on at present, when the old prophet lies to him. In Dante, the ability to see the future but be ignorant of the present resembles the condition of the dead (*Inf.* 10.97–108), whose ranks the man of God will soon join.

Earlier I noted why the Garden of Eden story is an incomplete parallel to the man of God's situation.[38] A more exact analogy can be found in the story of David and the priest Ahimelech in 1 Sam 21–22.[39] Just as the old prophet lies by saying Yahweh sent him, David lies by saying that Saul sent him. And like the old prophet, David ends up well in spite of being deceitful—or, more accurately, *because* he was deceitful.[40] Similarly, the priest and the man of God both trust liars with fatal results. To my knowledge, no commentator has called Ahimelech stupid or disobedient to his king for being tricked. Ahimelech and the man of God remain loyal to those to whom they believe they owe their loyalty. They uncritically trust those whom they assume share the same loyalties, and as a result are duped into becoming disloyal to those they serve. They seem to take for granted that their colleagues will respect the admonition contained in Lev 19:11: "You shall not…deal falsely (תכחשו) or lie, a man to his fellow" (cf. כחש in 1 Kgs 13:18).

### 3. *Lying, Success, and the Social Functions of Deceit*

"And now I'm going to tell you about a scorpion. This scorpion wanted to cross a river. So he asked the frog to carry him. 'No,' said the frog, 'no thank you. If I let you on my back you may sting me and the sting of a scorpion is death.' 'Now where, asked the scorpion, is the logic of that?'— for scorpions always try to be logical—'If I sting you you will die. I will drown.' So the frog was convinced and allowed the scorpion on his back. But, just in the middle of the river he felt a terrible pain and realized that, after all, the scorpion had stung him. 'Logic!' cried the dying frog, as he

38. However, at least one Dante scholar believes that the demons' deceptive speech to Virgil mixes falsehood and truth in a way which "evokes the crafty speech of Satan [*sic*] in the Garden of Eden" (Falvo, online).

39. Rofé (1988a, 181 and 181 n. 118) asserts that falsehoods such as David's lie to Ahimelech are not in themselves sins. David's deception is merely one of the Bible's many examples of "small lies told for accepted reasons." My rejection of such excuses for David's behavior is explained in Chapters 8 and 9, below. On the Ahimelech episode, see Lasine 2001, 39–50.

40. For further discussion, see Lasine 2001, 47–50. It is also worth noting that in 1 Sam 22:22 David does not say that he is to blame for the deaths of Ahimelech and the other priests because he deceived the innocent priest. Rather, he claims that he is to blame because he had seen Doeg at Nob and knew that Doeg would inform Saul about David's presence there. Of course, David's way of wording his responsibility may be tailored specifically for the ears of Abiathar, not only because Abiathar is the son of the priest whose death David has just caused, but because Abiathar has with him the ephod, a cult object which David later uses to contact Yahweh (1 Sam 23:6, 9; 30:7).

started under, bearing the scorpion down with him. There is no logic in this.' 'I know,' said the scorpion, 'but I can't help it, it's my character.' Let's drink to character!"

—Orson Welles, *Mr. Arkadin* (film; 1955)[41]

Surrendering one's will and judgment in order to be obedient leaves one open to be deceived by those who retain their self-will and take the risk to improvise, lie, and redefine their roles, like the old Bethel prophet. It is he who successfully negotiates his way through the ominous, God-driven and dangerous world presented in 1 Kgs 13. Falsity and deception have "survival value" (see Steiner 1975, 224). According to Nietzsche, the fact "that lies are necessary in order to live is itself part of the terrifying and questionable character of existence" (1964e, 576).[42] If lying helps individuals like the old prophet to survive, scholars like Ford (1996, 282) and Gilsenan (1976, 191)[43] argue that the social prohibition of deceit preserves the self-interests of power structures which demand truth from others but do not willingly reciprocate. Prohibitions against lying serve "the system of power and control in a society" (Gilsenen 1976, 191).[44] The same social function is served by equating disobedience with sin. Fromm (1975, 234–35) asserts that "obedience is perhaps the most deeply ingrained trait" in all hierarchically structured societies.

Studies of 1 Kgs 13 rarely consider the cultural significance of lying, obedience, *or* discounting intentions. Nevertheless, when Gross declares that the "intentions of the actors are of no account," and that it is not important if the man of God acts in good faith or not (1979, 122–23), he is describing something similar to the "results-culture" of ancient Greece. Adkins asserts that the function of a results-culture is to maintain the prosperity and stability of the city-state (1973, 61). While "the

41. In most versions of the scorpion–frog fable, such as that related in the film *The Crying Game* (1992), the scorpion's final words are "I can't help it, it's [in] my nature." In *Mr. Arkadin*, the problems of knowing others' true "character" and determining how situations affect behavior are basic to the plot of the entire film. The mention of "logic" in Welles's version of the fable seems to be unique to *Mr. Arkadin*, although the word points to a major question in all versions: Why do people unreasonably act against their own self-interest?

42. In Nietzsche's opinion (1964d, 606), the powerful always lie: "the intellect, as a means for the preservation of the individual, unfolds its main powers in dissimulation (*Verstellung*)."

43. Gilsenan (1976, 191–92) notes that lying often manifests itself to us socially as an attribution of a specific intention to the actor, whether or not such an intention "in fact" existed.

44. On the role played by dissimulation and information management by those in power, see Lasine 2001, 51–71, 127–40.

individual can and does have intentions...[externally] what is important is the result" (Adkins 1970, 42; cf. 1965, 49). And if only results count, "it is not worthwhile to distinguish a moral error from a mistake...a disastrous result is shameful (*aischron*),...whatever the cause" (Adkins 1970, 43, 44).[45] Good intentions have no value unless crowned with success. Adkins (1970, 44) cites Odysseus as one example of a self-controlled, strong-willed, enduring, successful "Homeric man." Yet Odysseus's survival in both Homeric epics *also* depends upon his prodigious Athena-like skills as a liar and deceiver.[46]

Admittedly, there are also cases in the Bible where only results count. Among these are cases of so-called objective guilt. As von Rad puts it, sins which can affect the community are viewed only in terms of "actual performance and initially without any regard [to] personal motivations... or intention" (1962, 267). He points to the "subjectively guiltless sinners" Abimelech (in Gen 20) and Jonathan (in 1 Sam 14) as examples. Earlier, when discussing the "material" and "impersonal" component of the biblical concept of holiness, von Rad also cites Uzzah, who was killed by God after he touched the ark, to steady it (2 Sam 6:6–7).[47] One rabbinic tradition claims that "God smote [Uzzah]...for his error [because] an error in learning *amounts to* intentional sin [or presumption]."[48] However, the situations of the man of God and the prophet's colleague are too different from those of Uzzah and Abimelech for the parallel to further illuminate these prophetic stories.

Instead let me return to the partial parallel between the man of God and Dante's Virgil. Earlier I mentioned Dante's notion that full awareness of the dangers presented by "diabolic evil" is only available to baptized Christians. This concept obviously has no place in 1 Kgs 13, read as part of the Jewish Bible. However, the same issues concerning

---

45.  Adkins is referring to Homeric society. Gouldner (1965, 82) differentiates between a shame culture or "action morality" and a guilt culture or "intention reality."

46.  See, e.g., Stanford, 1968, 19–24. Odysseus remained the "archetypal" liar even in later antiquity; see, e.g., Juvenal 15.13–26; Lucian, "The True History" and Chapter 2, n. 74 above.

47.  The narrator states that Uzzah took hold of the ark *because* the oxen stumbled (כי שמטו הבקר).

48.  *Midrash Rabbah*, Num 21.12, citing *Pirqe Avoth* 4.13; emphasis added. *Avoth* 4.13 reads: ששגגת למוד עולה זדון. Blackman (1985, 71) translates "an error in study [or teaching; of the Law] is accounted presumptuous transgression"; Travers Herford (1962, 111) has: "be cautious in teaching; for error in teaching may amount to intentional sin." On the role of holiness in the Uzzah episode, including David's response to Uzzah's death, see Lasine 2010, 41 n. 31.

human character and vulnerability to deceit are raised by Dante's presentation of the naïve Virgil and the depiction of the trusting man of God in Kings. In *The Inferno*, Virgil becomes fully aware that he has been duped by the demons when one of the damned, Friar Catalano, informs him that a bridge which a demon had told Virgil was intact was actually broken (*Inf.* 23.133–35). Virgil realizes that the demon had given "an ill account of the business" (23.140; Sinclair 1961, 289), whereupon Catalano alludes to John 8:44, when he says that once in Bologna he heard people discussing the devil's sins, including that the devil is a liar and the father of lies (23.142–45). The full form of this controversial[49] verse states that the devil is a liar and father of lies, so when he tells a lie, he does so "out of his own" (ἐκ τῶν ἰδίων; Vg. *ex propriis*), usually understood to mean "according to his own nature," "character" or "characteristics."[50] In the context of the *Divine Comedy*, Dante is implying that Virgil is incapable of detecting the true "character" of demonic evil.

In 1 Kgs 13 it is the old prophet who is the "demonic" liar, although readers have no way of ascertaining whether he is a "habitual liar," or has a basic personality trait of deceptiveness. However, we *do* know that the old man uses a time-honored strategy when lying to the man of God. Hankiss (1980, 106, 111) points out that confidence artists ("con men") try to establish a connection with their victim (the "mark"); this may be something shared in the past, a common friend, or similar tastes and values. The old prophet uses their common professional status as prophets as his connection (גם־אני נביא כמוך; v. 18).

Even if the man of God's character does tend to be too trusting of strangers and their plausible lies, is he as constitutionally incapable of detecting a lie as Dante imagines Virgil to be? Is the man of God's failure the result of prematurely attributing a disposition of trustworthiness to the old man, based on the old man's self-presentation as a prophet? In other words, is the man's downfall that he evaluates this "stranger" using "naïve lay dispositionism" (Ross and Nisbett 1991, 119;

---

49. The controversy concerns its claim that Jews are the children of the devil; see the next two notes.

50. "Character" is the ESV rendering. Barrett (1978, 349) understands the phrase to mean "of his own substance or characteristics." R. Brown renders this part of the verse "when he tells a lie, he speaks his native language" (1966, 353), noting that v. 44 is pervaded by "the stress on the devil's essential nature" (1966, 364). Bultmann contends that "a man like this speaks ἐκ τῶν ἰδίων, i.e., like the rest of the family, in the way they have learnt from their father," referring to the "constant behavior" of the Devil's child (1971, 319). In other words, the consistent behavior of the Jews reveals their lying disposition, which they either share by nature with their father or learned from him.

cf. 120–25, 139, 143)? To address this question it is helpful to ponder the implications of the fable told in the epigraph to this section. In all the many versions of this story, the scorpion convinces the frog to carry him across a river by arguing that if the scorpion stung the frog in the water, the scorpion himself would die as well as the frog. When the scorpion nevertheless stings the frog and both are about to die, the frog asks the scorpion why he did such a thing. The scorpion answers that it was his "nature" or "character" to do so, usually adding "I couldn't help it."

A number of messages can be derived from this tale, many of which touch on the role of character and situation in behavior. Readers who view the story from the frog's perspective have reason to conclude that people always act according to their character, so that we must expect a scorpion to act like a scorpion even when it is against the scorpion's self-interest—and even his survival—to do so. However, the frog's fatal error is not that he made an incorrect attribution about the scorpion's character. Rather, the scorpion led him to assume incorrectly that the situation of being in a river, in danger of drowning, would play a stronger role in determining the scorpion's behavior than would his character. The fable is therefore radically dispositionist. For frogs, the lesson is never to expect a scorpion to do anything other than act according to his basic character, which is to sting. For scorpions, one lesson is that their professed character can be used as an excuse for any destructive acts they might commit; they "can't help" acting like scorpions. They cannot fight their own nature, even in situations in which acting according to character means their own death.

The psychological premises of the fable imply that it is absolutely crucial for frogs like us to ignore the conclusions of the social psychologists who conclude that situations usually trump character in determining behavior. To bowdlerize Heraclitus, the scorpion's character was destiny, not just for himself but for the frog. The fable also underscores the critical importance of correctly identifying others by their essential nature. After all, in our life-world not all scorpions look like scorpions. The man of God in 1 Kgs 13 certainly failed to detect the deceptive intent of the old prophet ("he lied to him"; v. 19), although, as we have seen, in this case the old "scorpion's" deception turned out to be in his own self-interest, not against it. In contrast, both the frog in the fable and Dante's Virgil have little excuse for failing to detect the "causal" role of their destroyer's character. The frog knows that he is confronted by a scorpion who looks like a scorpion and Virgil believes a demon whom he knows to be a demon, and who actually looks and acts like a demon.

If the essential nature of the devil is to lie, as John 8:44 insists, we, like the man of God, must hope to be able to detect scorpions and "black angels" (*Inf.* 23.131) who do *not* appear as such. Admittedly, over the centuries people have allayed their epistemological anxiety by identifying others as being unmistakably "of the devil," say, on the basis of their Jewish noses and names and the horns they attempt to conceal by wearing skullcaps on their heads.[51] The man of God had a much more difficult task, because his demonic "scorpion" looked and acted as a true prophet when he told his lie, and is then actually allowed by God to function as a true prophet in condemning to death the man he had deceived.

As I noted in Chapter 1, some social psychologists contend that our dispositionist assumptions often function adequately as we negotiate our social world, and when they do not, the consequences are rarely very serious. But the stories of the frog and the man of God from Judah show that the consequences of making an incorrect attribution, or miscalculating the role of situation in behavior, can indeed be fatal.

### 4. *Moral and Theological Implications: Is Character Destiny?*

*Ēthos anthrōpō daimōn.*

—Heraclitus (Fr. 119)

In one sense, the deceitful prophet manages to use Yahweh's power to turn a public disaster into a personal triumph. Benzinger asserts that the story reflects "a rather mechanistic concept of Prophetism" (quoted in Lemke 1976, 303). Klopfenstein (1966, 647, 657) and Gray go further, arguing that the Bethel prophet is operating from a "primitive mechanical view of the...word of God" in order to nullify the oracle against the altar and thereby "frustrate" God's purpose (J. Gray 1970, 321). If so, while the old prophet fails at nullifying the oracle, he succeeds in redirecting divine power against the very man who had just wielded it.

When the old prophet dooms the man for disobedience (vv. 21–22), he makes it clear that in this case only results mattered to God. If 1 Kgs 13 does present us with a results-culture, there is indeed a basis for saying that a moralistic assessment of these events is wrong-headed. However, there would *also* be a basis for saying that the quick-witted and deceitful old prophet is the character whom readers should admire. The failure of the man of God would be shameful, regardless of his intention. In this

---

51. On the role of specific New Testament texts in Christian demonizing of the Jews throughout history, see, e.g., Trachtenberg 1943, 20–21 and Felsenstein 1995, 33–37, 84.

scenario, the supposed "didactic purpose" (Gross 1979, 125) of the story would *not* be to demonstrate the necessity of radical obedience, but to demonstrate that such obedience can fail miserably at protecting one from the dangers of deceit. It would also convey the lesson that deceit and versatility are keys to insuring survival and success, even when that involves putting divine powers to one's own selfish use. A number of stories in earlier biblical books also demonstrate the value of self-assertion, risk, and improvisation—as well as the value of lying—over passive obedience. Significantly, many of these deceivers are God's favorite patriarchs and matriarchs. It is the gullible victims—including Isaac, Esau, and King Abimelech—who lose or come out second-best. The survivors and the big winners tend to be the ones who deceive and manipulate others in order to gain what they want without being punished—even though the Bible is filled with calls to obey, warnings about disobedience, and cautions against the dangers of smooth words and false facades.

In 1 Kgs 13, the man of God is the great loser. As Van Dorp puts it, he is "the victim of his own obedience" (quoted in Eynikel 1990, 234). Or, to borrow a metaphor from St. Ignatius, this obedient man has sacrificed his will and offered himself as a "holocaust" to his Creator through the hands of his ministers (Young 1959, 290). Lack of information on the man of God's intentions actually makes the moral problem posed by the story *more* pressing, not less, because it implies that his violation of his original orders cannot be explained away as the result of an immoral character or disordered personality.[52]

Does the story tempt readers to judge the man of God negatively because this would allow them to deny that an innocent person can fall prey to a deceptive situation with divine complicity? If so, it would not be the only situation in the Hebrew Bible which has led many readers to interpret a character's fatal action in a comforting manner, by basing their interpretation of that action on another character's reaction to it.

---

52. Todorov (1990, 45) points out that "not every 'character' [in a story]…is a character." For Todorov, "characters" without character are those "without content," who are "identified without being described." As soon as "psychological determinism surfaces, the 'character' is transformed into a character; he acts in a given way *because* he is timid, weak, courageous, and so forth" (1990, 45). In the case of the man of God from Judah, we do not find evidence of character traits being causes. He is not a "person" in the sense of being what Heider calls a "causal origin" (see Chapter 1, above). Todorov's notion of psychological determinism is problematic. As noted by Cohan (1990, 128–36), to imagine a character is not necessarily to "read" that character as a determinate stable predictable self which conforms to the needs of bourgeois society or has a character which "causes" its actions.

In Gen 9, for example, it is Noah who reacts with a curse to Ham's ambiguously described action, prompting readers to ascribe all sorts of heinous crimes to Ham (and, sadly, to his supposed descendants).[53] In 1 Kgs 13 the character who reacts with a curse is Yahweh. In such cases, prior expectations can lead readers to invent a criminal disposition to fit the punishment, rather than the other way around.

Although motives are left unexpressed for the human characters, the sevenfold mention of the phrase *bidbar Yahweh* ("in the word of Yahweh") reminds readers that some kind of divine influence drives the action. This rare phrase appears almost exclusively in the two stories of prophets killed by lions. Montgomery and Gehman (1951, 263) note that the "cryptic character of the expression" is reflected in the variety of ways it has been translated: "in the word," "through the word," "with the word," "at the command," "moved by," "on the strength of divine inspiration," "invested with the word," "by the word," and "through the power of."[54] Because of its vagueness and rarity, the expression does not exclude the possibility that instructions given *bidbar Yahweh* were *also* delivered by angels or prophets.

In 1 Kgs 20, the colleague is held accountable even though he had not been told that the prophet's request is *bidbar Yahweh*. Accountability here means being ripped apart by a lion. If this penalty is a case where "only results count," it is so disproportionate to the colleague's "offense" as to be incompatible with *any* idea of justice, whether human or divine, ancient or modern. In 1 Kgs 13, the repeated[55] use of the expression *bidbar Yahweh* underlines the ambiguity concerning Yahweh's possible role in the man of God's unhappy fate. Yahweh does not intervene to warn his obedient emissary; he only intervenes to destroy him for his unwitting error.[56] The fact that Yahweh uses the lying prophet to relay

---

53. In the most despicable version of this tradition, this refers to people of African descent. On the so-called Hamitic myth, see, e.g., Evans 1980.

54. Examples of all these renderings are given in Montgomery and Gehman 1051, 263. Würthwein (1985, 166) translates "at Yahweh's behest (*Geheiß*)."

55. Montgomery and Gehman (1951, 263) find the expression to be "rather overworked." In Würthwein's view (1985, 169), it is "consistently superfluous or even annoying."

56. And, as the sequel to the story shows, the old prophet goes on to take over the role of the man of God when he affirms the man's previous oracle against Jeroboam (v. 32). While 1 Kgs 13 and 20:35–36 may constitute some kind of "object lesson" for readers of the Hebrew Bible, they are not said to serve that purpose for the people of Israel in world of the stories. There is no evidence that the old prophet ever informed the people as a whole—or King Jeroboam—about the unknowing disobedience of the man of God, or the reason why he was subsequently killed by a lion which did not eat either his carcass or the donkey.

his message of doom to the victim, and never punishes the liar, effectively constitutes a choice of the old prophet over the man of God. However, this choice should not be construed as a sign that the old prophet had good motives or that he is repentant. Neither should it be construed as evidence that the man of God had bad motives or that he is a gullible moron. Rather, it should be construed as illustrating who is most likely to survive in this dangerous and deceptive story-world.

Chapter 5

PROPHECY, PERSONALITY, AND DEATH:
PSYCHOLOGIZING ELIJAH

1. *Describing Elijah's Personality*

Such is the biblical portrait of Elijah: tough, fierce, and cruel, irascible,
inflexible, monolithic... A man of extremes, he rejects weaknesses and
compromises. His severity and rigor are legendary; he hardly ever smiles.
More than a person, he is destiny.
—Wiesel (1981, 40–41)

If the man of God from Judah in 1 Kgs 13 is presented as though he were
devoid of personality, the opposite is the case with the next "man of
God" we encounter four chapters later.[1] By the time most readers have
been informed of Elijah's exploits in 1 Kgs 17–19, they have formed a
definite impression of the prophet's personality. According to Jobling
(1986, 88), it is the context supplied by the Horeb episode which "makes
a real character of [Elijah], a 'personality' subject to changes." However,
as I mentioned in Chapter 3, not all readers gain the same impression of
his personality. Many commentators judge Elijah to be egocentric, self-
pitying, arrogant, petulant, or truculent.[2] Others argue that his "distinct,"
"strong," and "unique" personality is simply "an instrument for imple-
menting his mission" (Simon 1997, 224, 226).[3] In a sense, Wiesel

1. 1 Kgs 17:18, 24; cf. 2 Kgs 1:10–13.
2. Egotistic/egocentric: Provan 1995, 148; Lockwood 2004, 52; cf. R. Gregory
1990, 103; Walsh 1996, 273. In an overcautious understatement, Kissling (1996,
123) suggests that "Elijah might be...perhaps even slightly egocentric." Self-pitying:
B. Robinson, 1991, 531; Wiseman 1993, 171; Fretheim 1999, 111. Arrogant: B.
Robinson 1991, 535. Truculent: R. Gregory 1990, 124; Uffenheimer 1999, 337.
Petulant: Lockwood 2004, 53; Clark 1893, 328, 354–55.
3. Cf. Reinhartz (1998, 148), who notes that "human interactions and personality
traits have an impact on the ways in which they enact their prophetic roles." From
the portrayal of Elijah in the Bible, Rofé is also certain that the historical Elijah also
had a "unique personality" (1988a, 190). Clark (1893, 9) calls Elijah "the most
unique" of all Old Testament prophets.

combines these perspectives. In his reading, Elijah possesses many significant and revealing "traits" (1981, 40), but these traits point to the fact that he is "more than a person"; he is unsmiling "destiny."

At Horeb Elijah actually thematizes his own personality and selfhood. As mentioned earlier, some social psychologists believe that at times people seek situations that push them in the same direction as do their own dispositions, so that their situations are largely of their own making. In 1 Kgs 19, Elijah gives God (and us) his reading of both his situation and his character, including the charge that the murderous Israelites seek to kill him, and his belief that jealousy for Yahweh is his defining trait. Whether he intends it or not,[4] his behavior here follows a Mosaic script: after Jezebel sends a message to Elijah announcing that he will suffer the same fate as the Baal prophets who died at his hand, Elijah flees into the wilderness, asks God to take his life, and then proceeds to Horeb, apparently by his own choice.[5] Is God convinced by Elijah's version of events and his self-portrait?[6] Should *we* be convinced? Or does the narrator present Elijah as the type of person—and the type of prophet—who *needs* to convince others that he is a unique and special individual?

The answers to these questions depend upon how readers construe Elijah's situation at Horeb in relation to the preceding stories,[7] and what

---

4. On the notion that Elijah may be consciously patterning his life after Moses', see B. Robinson 1991, 519 and n. 22 below.

5. On the question whether Elijah chooses his own destination, Cogan (2000, 452) goes beyond the text when he states that "Elijah knew to continue on to Horeb," even though "no direct command had been given." The same is true of Provan's impression that Elijah "seems to know what the angel means" (1995, 145). Provan would have to know what *the angel* means before he could be in a position to say that Elijah knows what the angel means, and the narrator does not allow us to know this, although many (e.g. Fretheim 1999, 109) assume the angel is alluding to a trip to Horeb, since Elijah proceeds to go there. Walsh (1996, 270) is closer to the mark when he concludes that the narrator "leaves room to question whether the road to Horeb is the 'way' Elijah is supposed to be following. In the next scene we shall learn that it is not."

6. Obadiah seems to think that Elijah's defining trait is his elusiveness (see 1 Kgs 18:12 and Lasine 2001, 85–88).

7. Concerning 1 Kgs 17, Ska (1990, 72) points to the narrator's use of "external focalization" and concludes that here Elijah "seems to lack any emotional life." In fact, Elijah "is always the same, imperturbable." Leaving aside counterevidence like the perturbed Elijah's prayer in 17:20, the fact that the narrator refrains from giving us direct access to Elijah's thoughts, emotions, and perceptions does not mean that readers will necessarily conclude that the prophet "lacks any emotional life," especially if they are already familiar with Elijah's behavior in later chapters. On Elijah's personality in 1 Kgs 17, see Lasine 2004a.

disposition they attribute to him. In Chapter 3 I discussed the psychological judgments made by redaction critics who attempt to deal with Elijah's behavior in this passage. It quickly became clear that if we seek to make an accurate assessment of the biblical Elijah, we must trace the interplay of character and situation in these narratives. In fact, we must do more, because this prophet is being presented to us as a specific *type* of personality, a type well known to psychologists of personality and, in its extreme and dysfunctional forms, to psychotherapists.

Some commentators on 1 Kgs 19 do more than make evaluative judgments about Elijah's personality. These scholars diagnose Elijah as suffering from a mental disorder, such as "generalized depression" (Nelson 1987, 126), manic depression (Wiseman 1993, 171), paranoia (Jobling 1986, 88), prophetic or "ministerial" burnout,[8] a "mid-life crisis" (Conners 1997, 236–37), a "messianic complex" (B. Robinson 1991, 528; cf. Conners 1997, 237), or the hopelessness and "selective abstraction" of a depressed introvert who is engaging in distorted, maladaptive thinking (Howell and Howell 2008, 3–4).[9] For these scholars, Elijah presents *symptoms* such as excessive sleeping, loss of appetite, suicidal urges, distorted perceptions, feelings of loneliness, inability to cope, and "psychomotoric retardation" (Kruger 2005).[10] And even though

---

8. Nelson, 1987, 122, 129, Seow 1999, 145, Conners 1997, 236–37, and Lockwood 2004, 51. According to Brenninkmeijer et al. (2001, 879), the "core symptom" of burnout is emotional exhaustion. Depression is more strongly related to a reduced sense of superiority and perceived loss of status than to emotional exhaustion. Burntout individuals are "still 'in the battle' for attaining status," while depressed people have given up. Burnt-out people are more able "to enjoy things" than depressives, rarely report thoughts of suicide, have a more realistic feeling of guilt if they feel guilty, and often have difficulty falling asleep (2001, 874). The Elijah of 1–2 Kings does not present the specific symptoms of burnout. And to the extent that Brenninkmeijer is correct in asserting that depressed people "do not seem to enhance themselves by derogating other people" (2001, 874), Elijah behaves like the opposite of a depressed person in most of 1–2 Kings, including 1 Kgs 19.

9. The Howells (2008, 3) claim that Elijah qualifies as an introvert according to the Meyers-Briggs Type Indicator and that Yahweh's responses to the prophet illustrate the strategy of a cognitive therapist giving the patient Elijah "homework assignments" and refuting his distortions of reality, thereby providing directive "cognitive restructuring" (2008, 5–6). On Meyers-Briggs, see Paul 2004, 111–22 and Chapter 9 n. 77, below.

10. Kruger contends that Elijah crouching with his face between his knees in 1 Kgs 18:42 signifies depression and implies psychomotoric retardation. He links the "body language" of the depressed person with "limited, slow and exhausted" movements. Yet Elijah runs approximately seventeen miles immediately after this (admittedly with the "hand of God upon him"; 1 Kgs 18:46). With Kruger, compare

Lockwood (2004, 51) accuses other scholars of resorting to "pop psychology commonplaces" in order to "shore up" their fixed positions regarding Elijah's behavior, he does the same thing when describing Elijah as depressed and "suffering a massive dose of burnout."

Even though "psychologizing" is a fact of reading as well as a fact of life, to "diagnose" Elijah, trading in DTR for *DSM*, would require us to exceed the level of precision attained by "naïve lay dispositionism" when people "psychologize in the wild," as some psychologists and philosophers rather snobbishly describe our normal practice (Doris 2002, 97; cf. Choi et al. 1999, 47). Of course, many scholars make dispositional attributions about Elijah's personality without invoking diagnostic categories. One group describes Elijah as being "plagued by his own ego and exaggerated importance," and as displaying "hubris."[11] In B. Robinson's reading, Elijah is a "tetchy and arrogant prima donna of a prophet" (1991, 535).[12]

Similar appraisals of Elijah's personality were also made by some of the rabbis. For example, Elijah is accused of slandering God's servants, the children of Israel. Citing 1 Kgs 19:14, God is portrayed as chiding Elijah: "'Is it My covenant or thy covenant?... My altars or thy altars?'... 'They are My prophets; what concern is it of thine?'"[13] In a sense, Elijah is upstaging God, that is, over-identifying with father Yahweh—or, at least, with *his* image of Yahweh. In the process, he has forgotten that God has other children besides himself, children for whom the prophet should have interceded. One rabbinic tradition relates that in spite of God consoling him and granting him a theophany in spite of his complaints (1 Kgs 19:11–12), Elijah remained in the same mood even

Lockwood 2004, 51, who describes Elijah's victory in ch. 18 as "energy-sapping." Kruger does not provide support for his assumption that Elijah is depressed *prior* to Jezebel's threatening message.

11. R. Gregory1990, 102–3, 124; cf. Walsh 1996, 273; B. Robinson 1991, 528; Olley 1998, 48; Lockwood 2004, 58.

12. Could one reason for such vehement denunciations be a suspicious attitude toward self-centeredness and self-love in a culture which, since late biblical times, has made selfless humility into a cardinal virtue (e.g. Phil 2:3–4; see Briggs 2010, 64–65)? On the ethical implications of self-abasement when judging others, see Chapter 9, §9, below. On the history of attitudes toward humility, see, most recently, Button 2005, 840–46. Kohut (1972, 364) notes that the Western value system which extols altruism and disparages egotism and self-concern may have given the term "narcissism" a slightly pejorative connotation and made it difficult for the notion of a healthy form of narcissism to be accepted. Also see Nietzsche on the human "will to self-belittlement" (*Selbstverkleinerung*; 1999, 404). Nietzsche bitterly denounces humility as a virtue created by "slave morality."

13. *Midrash Rabbah*, Song of Songs, I. 6. 1; M. Simon 1939, 56.

after God waited for three hours, hoping that the prophet would calm down and seek mercy for Israel![14] Elijah stubbornly refuses to acknowledge anything other than his own perspective, seemingly acting Jonah-like in his childish persistence.[15] When Elijah repeats his complaint verbatim after the theophany, it is almost as though he is cueing God to return to the script that he wants God to follow. The story must go his own way or no way.

Although none of these interpreters uses the term, the excessive self-concern and desire to be unique and superior which they attribute to the prophet are potential indicators of what psychologists now call a narcissistic personality.[16] That is, 1 Kgs 17–19, 21 and 2 Kgs 1–2 portray a literary character who acts in a way which many readers would take to be narcissistic.[17] In what follows I will show that readers who view Elijah in this fashion have a good deal of psychological theory and observation to support them. In fact, a rigorous examination of the dynamics of narcissistic personality functioning can illuminate many aspects of Elijah's behavior throughout 1 Kgs 17–2 Kgs 2, including those features of the Horeb episode which seem most inconsistent, such as the prophet's wish to die immediately after his flight from death.

14. See, e.g., *Tanna Debe Eliyyahu, Zuta* 8, 186 (Braude and Kapstein 1981, 397); cf. Wiener 1978, 49.

15. In rabbinic times, the rain-producing wonder-working Honi was probably viewed "as a type of Elijah" (Urbach 1987, 574; see *b. Ta'an.* 19a–23a), and he too is often portrayed as a "special,…spoiled child in the heavenly household" (Neusner 1981, 318).

16. "Narcissism" as a pathology is *not* synonymous with extreme self-love. Rather, it should be equated with "painful and chronic shortage of self-love and endless efforts to substitute love with external admiration" (Švrakić 1990, 192). For a history of the ways in which the word "narcissism" has been used within psychoanalysis and psychiatry, see, e.g. A. Cooper 1986. On the many meanings of the term within the body of Freud's work, see Baranger 1991, 109–11. My application of the overdetermined and overused term "narcissism" to the biblical Elijah might seem inappropriate, since Elijah, as we know him, is a literary character, not a living person (except, perhaps, during the Pesach *seder*!). However, as I discussed in Chapter 1, we make judgments about literary personages and real people in very similar ways. On the legitimacy of applying such concepts to characters in ancient literature, see Chapter 2, above and Lasine 2001, 197 n. 9.

17. And if Elijah's desire to die is driven by his inability to maintain a grandiose self-image, that would be another indicator. In addition, narcissists tend to imagine the world "as being devoid of food and love," filled with "dangerous, sadistically frustrating, and revengeful objects," and to imagine *themselves* as "hungry wolves out to kill, eat and survive" (Kernberg 1985, 276, 311; cf. Lasine 2001, 207–8). Does the hostility Elijah perceives around him, and the mass violence he inflicts on others, imply that he too views his world in this fashion?

Admittedly, a number of scholars attempt to "vindicate" Elijah as a reliable, if not ideal, prophet-figure, even in 1 Kgs 19. In order to do so, they go to great lengths to defend the accuracy of Elijah's charges against the Israelites in 19:10, thereby explaining why Elijah fled so soon after the great victory on Carmel and asked to die.[18] For example, U. Simon contends that Yahweh adopts all of the postulates on which Elijah's complaint is based. In fact, it is on the basis of Elijah's charges that "Yahweh proclaims almost total annihilation," after which Israel will be left with only the seven thousand most righteous (1997, 214–15).[19] Moreover, Elijah's claim that the Israelites killed Yahweh's prophets "refers to" Jezebel killing the prophets in 18:13 (1997, 206). Simon believes that when Ahab tells Jezebel about Elijah's killing of the prophets in 19:1, it is a sign of "the king's recidivism." He then suggests that both Elijah and the narrator see the king as "the embodiment of the collective personality of the people." This allows Simon to conclude that there was a "rapid dissipation" of the experience of the miracle on Carmel, which, in turn, explains Elijah's "bitter disappointment" and subsequent despair (1997, 207).

Brichto also attempts to justify Elijah's charges against the Israelites by equating the royal couple with the people. He describes the picture given of Ahab, Jezebel, and Baal as "hyperbole,"[20] reasoning that if "Jezebel and the Baal prophets served but as a metaphor for pagan influence, it is Israel that has breached its covenant with God" (1992, 138–39, 142). This hyperbole "*must* serve to explain why a prophet made invulnerable by an omnipotent God has decided to throw in his hand" (1992, 143; emphasis added). By reading the story metaphorically in order to justify the factual validity of Elijah's charges, Brichto has no need to interpret Elijah's desire to die in terms of his personality. Brichto also justifies Elijah's claim that he is the only prophet left by assuming that "every last one" of the hundred prophets saved by Obadiah "was hunted down or driven out save for Elijah" (1992, 131), even though this is nowhere stated in the books of Kings and is contradicted by the activity of other individual prophets of Yahweh in 1 Kgs 20 and 22 and large groups of such prophets in 2 Kgs 2.[21]

---

18.   De Vries takes for granted that Elijah's charges in v. 10 are true, adding that he repeats himself in v. 14 simply because "that complaint remains true" (1985, 237).

19.   Using the remainder of 1–2 Kings as historical evidence, U. Simon also argues that "ancient readers" knew that Elijah was "right on the mark" with his charges, which were "quickly verified on the national level" (1997, 208).

20.   Other scholars also detect "hyperbole" in Elijah's speeches; see, e.g., Dumbrell 1986, 16; J. Gray 1970, 410; Fretheim 1999, 109.

21.   See 1 Kgs 20:13, 28, 35–42; 22:6–28; 2 Kgs 2:3, 5, 7, 15–18.

Scholars vindicate Elijah in other ways as well. For example, J. Clark (1893, 354) defends Elijah's claim to be alone by asserting that he had not been informed about the existence of the seven thousand righteous until the conversation on Horeb. Other commentators focus exclusively on the theophany report in vv. 11–12, ignoring Elijah's behavior in the remainder of the chapter, in order to view Elijah's revelation as a new high point in the religion of Israel, far exceeding the experience of Moses. The most extreme form of this position is put forward by Masson, who claims that the formula קול דממה דקה ("voice of sheer silence") defines the very essence of God through a concrete experience. This experience is "mystical," akin to nirvana and Böhme's *Ungrund*. Elijah's experience involves the abandonment of the banal self or ego (2001, 120–23). Masson believes that Elijah's "apophatic revelation" prevails over and "demolishes" Moses' revelation at Sinai (2001, 123, 130). In fact, Elijah may be the key personage of the Bible (2001, 131). U. Simon also compares Elijah and Moses in ways flattering to Elijah. He believes that Elijah's ability to go without food and drink on the long trek to Horeb, with its Mosaic associations, "constitutes a triumphant answer" to Elijah's assertion that he is no better than his fathers. In fact, it persuades Elijah "through personal experience, that he is on a par with Moses" in his capacity to serve as Yahweh's messenger (1997, 204). It must be added, however, that nowhere does Elijah express any awareness of his experiences being Moses-like,[22] let alone any indication that he himself is persuaded that he is on a par with Moses.

Ultimately, how readers will judge Elijah's personality will depend on a number of factors. Differences of opinion will result from the extent to which various readers assume that prophets and "men of God" are by definition positive figures, and that their words are necessarily reliable and truthful. Readers who operate on this assumption and encounter reports of behavior which would seem to have negative implications may attempt to retain their positive view of Elijah by reducing the cognitive dissonance between the narrated negative facts and their own positive beliefs, usually by changing the facts to fit the theory.[23] In addition, the views of different readers will vary according to the amount of credibility they grant to other characters in the story-world who express opinions about Elijah's character (e.g. the widow in 1 Kgs 17:24 and Ahab in

---

22. Nevertheless, some scholars do assume that the character Elijah is consciously emulating Moses. For example, to Dumbrell "it seems clear that [Elijah] had hoped to reduplicate in his own experience the Mosaic experience at Sinai" (1986, 16).

23. On cognitive dissonance and the reading process, see Chapter 9, §3, below.

1 Kgs 18:17; 21:20). The fact that God favors Elijah with power over life and death (1 Kgs 17:22) and later grants him immortality through translation (2 Kgs 2:11)[24] may also lead readers to give Elijah the benefit of the doubt when they encounter seemingly negative information about him.

The fact that the Elijah narratives are bracketed by several tales of unreliable and untruthful prophets of Yahweh may also influence readers' assessments of Elijah's reliability. The story of Micaiah in 1 Kgs 22 most dramatically undermines Elijah's claim to be the only prophet left. When Ahab tells Jehoshaphat that another prophet is available, one whom the king has always hated, readers familiar with the preceding chapters naturally expect Ahab to name Elijah, but he does not; in fact, Elijah is not mentioned in the entire chapter. It is Micaiah whom Ahab names as his habitual *bête noire* (22:8). Ahab refers to a long-term relationship between himself and Micaiah, characterized by Micaiah predicting only evil for the king. Another determinant of reader opinion is the extent to which readers find that contextual evidence supports Elijah's view of Israel's sin, particularly the evidence represented by the narrator's (and Yahweh's) repeated statements that the people were continually led into sin by their idolatrous kings.[25] Finally, the ways in which readers go about judging people as self-absorbed or heroic in their ordinary lives— and the ways in which those views are influenced by their own self-absorption and their assumptions about their own heroic potential—may also influence how they evaluate a character like Elijah.

## 2. *1 Kings 19:1–14*

> God said to him, "What are you doing here, Elijah?" [1 Kgs 19:9] And he said, "I have been very zealous…" [1 Kgs 19:10]. God said to him: "You are always being zealous! You were zealous at Shittim about forbidden sexual unions, as it says, 'Phinehas the son of Eleazar, [son of Aaron the priest, has turned back my wrath from the people of Israel],' and here you are being zealous again." (*Pirqe R. El.* 29; Kugel 1998, 814)

At first glance, the exchanges between Elijah and Yahweh (and Yahweh's emissaries) in 1 Kgs 19:4–18 seem characterized by indirection. That is, it is not immediately clear how the statements and actions of each

---

24. On the issue of whether Elijah's translation is a reward from God or a way of frustrating the prophet's desire to die, see Lasine, "Translating Death: Elijah's Ascension in Comparative Perspective," presented at the 2003 international meeting of the SBL in Cambridge, England.

25. In the six chapters which immediately precede the Elijah narratives, examples include 1 Kgs 11:33; 12:30; 14:15–16, 22–24; 15:26, 30, 34; 16:2, 13, 19, and 25.

responds to what the other has said or done. For example, after Elijah asks God to take his life (v. 4), an angel (or messenger; מלאך) tells him to rise and eat (v. 5). Is this a life-affirming reply to Elijah's request, or a divine action taken independently of Elijah's words? In v. 7 an angel/ messenger of Yahweh tells Elijah the same thing, adding that "the way is too much for you" (כי רב ממך הדרך). To what "way" or "road" (דרך) is the angel referring and in what sense is it "too much" (רב)?[26] Does the "way" denote wherever Elijah might choose to flee? Or is it referring to an unexplained journey which God has in store for Elijah, perhaps as an alternative to granting the prophet's wish for death? Does the angel already know that Elijah will go all the way south to Horeb? Does Elijah himself know that, at this point? And after Elijah reaches Horeb, why does God ask him what he is doing there? Why does God repeat the same question after Elijah has already answered the first time, and why does Elijah then repeat his answer verbatim?

This open-endedness leaves it up to readers to explain for themselves the nature and meanings of these interactions, by using evidence from the preceding and following Elijah narratives, and perhaps by drawing conclusions from the parallels between Elijah's situation and that of Moses, when Moses asks God to kill him if his situation does not improve (Num 11:15).[27]

How should we assess the reasons which Elijah gives for making his request? Immediately after his flight from Jezebel, Elijah implores God to do the very thing which he had just prevented the queen from doing: taking his life. His initial reason is that he is "no better than my fathers." This phrase is unique in the Bible. In Gen 47:9 the aged patriarch Jacob voices a complaint which is both similar to, and the opposite of, Elijah's. Like Elijah, Jacob compares himself with his fathers, but rather than doing so in order to justify a wish for his life to be shortened, Jacob complains because he has not lived as long as did his fathers. Elijah's reason for wanting God to take his life has been understood in various ways by commentators, depending upon how they understand the reference to "my fathers." Some take "my fathers" to refer to other humans in general (e.g. Cogan 2000, 451). Others point to the possibility that Elijah may be specifically alluding to earlier prophets (G. Jones 1984, 330; Seow 1999, 140). Simon (1997, 202, 222) contends that the reference is

26. Cf. רב, usually translated "enough" rather than "too much," in v. 4.

27. For a comparison between Elijah's wish to die and similar desires by other prophets, including Moses, see Lasine, "Take My Life, Please! A New Look at Stories about Prophets who Desire Death," presented at the 2006 international meeting of the SBL in Edinburgh, Scotland.

to Elijah's own ancestors, "undoubtedly meaning that…he ought to have stayed in his ancestral home in Gilead and followed in his forefathers' course." Uffenheimer (1999, 407) believes that Elijah is surely alluding to "the Israelites who perished in the same wilderness," and that the miracle granted him confirms that he is in fact "better than them." Lockwood goes even further. His Elijah *still* regards himself as superior to the patriarchs and prior prophets, and is "crudely manipulating the Lord to give him the chance to prove that he's still the best of the bunch" (2004, 52–54).

The key question is why being no better than his fathers should make Elijah want to die. Here responses generally take two forms. Some find a positive motive for the prophet's desire to die: Elijah is exhibiting devotion to his ancestors (Josephus, *Ant.* 8.348–49; cf. Feldman 1994, 72), or simple acceptance of his mortality, or recognition that he is no better off than his ancestors (Provan 1995, 148; cf. Seow 1999, 140). Others suggest that Elijah knows that he has been less successful than prophets like Samuel (J. Clark 1893, 328–30).[28] Sasson simply translates v. 4b as "I am not as good as my ancestors" (1990, 284). Still others take Elijah's apparently sudden realization that he is not better than his fathers to mean that up to now he *had* "ranked himself above the first fathers of his faith" (Auld 1986, 123) or had been "the bearer of a special relationship" with Yahweh (Cogan 2000, 451)—in short, that he is "egocentric,… [thinking] himself much better than his ancestors," only to be "reduced to the self-loathing of the high achiever who thinks he has failed" (Provan 1995, 148). Is this indeed a case of wounded narcissism, as Provan implies? Elijah does not explain himself further at this point.

When Elijah finally makes his way to Horeb God asks him "why are you here?" In answer Elijah presents himself to God as a victim. He acts as though his flight from Jezebel has been tantamount to being expelled by his community, even though he had brought his audience around to affirming Yahweh (and presumably himself) unanimously at Mt. Carmel (1 Kgs 18:39; cf. v. 36). He insists again and again that "I, I alone, am left, and they seek my life" (19:10, 14; cf. 18:22). He tries to convince Yahweh that he inhabits a hostile world in which his own people seek to kill him. Yahweh isn't buying it. For one thing, he reminds Elijah about the seven thousand who did not bend their knee to Baal (19:18). We shouldn't buy it either. We know about the hundred prophets whom Obadiah saved from Ahab and Jezebel, and we know that Elijah knows,

---

28. Clarke believes that Elijah had already been informed that he was going to be translated; therefore, when he asks to die he means that he does not deserve to be translated, since predecessors such as Samuel and Moses had not been translated.

because Obadiah told him (18:13; cf. v. 4). Chapters 20 and 22 drive the point home by showing other prophets who act loyally and courageously on Yahweh's behalf.

In his complaint Elijah characterizes himself as having been "extremely jealous" (קנאתי קנא) for Yahweh (v. 10).[29] The prevailing metaphor in reference to divine jealousy (*qin'â*) in the Hebrew Bible is that felt by a husband (Yahweh) concerning his unfaithful wife (Israel). There are three cases in which a human (one priest, one prophet, and one king) are jealous for Yahweh. In Num 25, wife Israel has "yoked itself to" Baal, and Phineas acts just as some husbands do when they catch their wives in bed with another man: he kills both the unfaithful spouse (in this case, the Israelite male Zimri) and the "lover" (the Midianite Cozbi, who is presumably a follower of Baal Peor).[30] In this episode, Yahweh himself says that Phineas was jealous for him. More precisely, Yahweh uses language which highlights the element of identification: "he was jealous with my jealousy among them (בקנאו את־קנאתי בתוכם)…so that I did not consume the children of Israel in my jealousy" (Num 25:11; cf. v. 13).

Because of the previous use of the term with Phineas, readers have naturally focused on Elijah's act of slaughtering four hundred and fifty Baal prophets as the parade example of Elijah's extreme jealousy for Yahweh. Because of their shared "zeal" and links with immortality, rabbinic texts like *Pirqe Rabbi Eleazar* actually equate Elijah and Phineas.[31]

---

29. In a number of biblical stories a character (including Yahweh) notices another's sad or angry mood and inquires about it, with the intention of drawing the moody person out and helping him (see Chapter 7, below). Does the fact that Yahweh does *not* act as helper when Elijah is depressed indicate a significant deviation from this pattern? In contrast, two chapters later Yahweh not only notices what he takes to be Ahab's repentant mood, but decides to reward Ahab for it. Or is Yahweh attempting to draw out Elijah by twice asking "what are you doing *here*?," as he had earlier drawn out Cain by asking "why has your face fallen?"

30. Milgrom (1990, 217, 477–78) points to the fact that Phineas's victims are an Israelite chieftain and a Midianite princess, and makes the ingenious suggestion that Phineas is beginning to carry out God's original command to Moses in v. 4, which calls for all "heads of the people" to be impaled in public. But when Moses conveys God's command to the "judges" of Israel he changes it from execution of leaders to slaying of guilty individuals. This would seem to imply that if Phineas were aware of any divine order it would be Moses' version. However, from Phineas's reported actions and words it is more likely that his action is impulsive and approved of by Yahweh only after the fact.

31. Later in this work, Rabbi Eliezer is quoted as saying, "He [God] called the name of Phineas like the name of Elijah" (47; see Friedlander 1965, 371). On the tradition that Phineas never died, but instead reappeared later as Elijah, see Kugel 1998, 813.

And like Phineas, Elijah kills on Yahweh's behalf without being told to do so by Yahweh. Many commentators also compare Elijah's slaughter with Moses' command to the Levites to massacre their friends and relatives at Mt. Sinai, although there are significant differences between the two situations (Exod 32:27–28; 1 Kgs 18:40).[32]

In 2 Kgs 10 it is again the human who characterizes himself as jealous for Yahweh. This time it is King Jehu, who invites the Rechabites to come along and see his jealousy for Yahweh (v. 16). Once again this jealousy consists of killing people, this time the remnants of the royal family which had sponsored Baal worship. In this instance, a "son of the prophets" tells the new king that Yahweh has commissioned him to kill the house of Ahab (2 Kgs 9:6–10). Jehu and the narrator both repeat that the king does so in fulfillment of Elijah's words back in 1 Kgs 21 (2 Kgs 9:36; 10:10, 17). However, like the others, Jehu goes on to kill without being told to do so by Yahweh (2 Kgs 10:18–28). His zeal is so similar to that of Elijah that Jehu has been dubbed "Elijah in royal robes" (Fretheim 1999, 172) and described as a king who "speaks like some avatar of Elijah" (Long 1991, 121).[33]

In all of these cases, jealousy for Yahweh seems to include identifying not only with Yahweh's emotion of outrage against his unfaithful spouse, but identifying with Yahweh's tendency to kill humans when jealousy drives him to do so (e.g. Deut 29:19; 32:16, 21; Ezek 16:38).[34] In terms of the relationship between Elijah and Moses, it is notable that the only time that Moses mentions being "jealous," it is in telling Joshua *not* to do be jealous for his sake (Num 11:29). Moses does not jealously guard his status as the only prophet, as Elijah seems to do.

32. Another example of the perceived similarity is the fact that the contest at Mt. Carmel is the *haftorah* to the Torah portion כי תשא, which includes the story of the golden calf. However, in most Jewish traditions the *haftorah* ends at 1 Kgs 18:39, thereby omitting the account of Elijah's butchering (וישחטם) of his defeated rivals. Differences between the situations in Exod 32 and 1 Kgs 18 include the fact that while Elijah single-handedly kills all the Baal prophets, Moses is not said to personally participate in the slaying of his fellow Levites. Moreover, Moses claims that the order for the massacre emanates from Yahweh ("thus says Yahweh the God of Israel"; Exod 32:27), while Elijah's action is reported without any reference to God, even from Elijah himself. Elsewhere I have argued that the Levite slaughter should be viewed as a voluntary sacrifice rather than as a punishment of the guilty (Lasine 1994, 206–14).

33. Long is referring to in 2 Kgs 9:22–23. Later, Long notes that Jehu is "shaded…in Elijah's colors as a severe prophet-destroyer" (1991, 138).

34. In 1 Kgs 14:22, Judah's sins under Rehoboam arouse God's jealousy. Although no immediate lethal punishment is mentioned, in the next verses the narrator reports Shishak's invasion of Jerusalem.

In 1 Kgs 19:10, Elijah continues with a scathing attack on the infidelity of the Israelites, culminating with the accusation that they have killed Yahweh's prophets and are seeking to do the same thing to him. Elijah's statement that "they" seek to kill him certainly constitutes a reply to Yahweh's specific question, "why are you *here*?" However, Elijah does not say what he wants Yahweh to do about his claim that he is being pursued, unless we assume that his request to die voiced many days earlier in v. 4 is still in effect. In that case, Elijah would be wanting Yahweh to take his life rather than having Jezebel or the Israelites do so. In short, by itself v. 10 is a report of the prophet informing Yahweh about the sins of his own people, beginning with a very general statement and ending with the charge that they desire to kill him. In Elijah's eyes, the situation is a case of all against one, just as it was on Mt. Carmel (1 Kgs 18:22).

Readers have indeed been informed that Elijah's life is being sought. However, it is the Sidonian Jezebel, *not* the Israelites, who seek to kill him.[35] His charge against the Israelites and his omission of any complaint about Ahab and Jezebel are equally problematic. One cannot simply dismiss these problems by claiming that the king and queen represent the entire nation. In 18:18 Elijah had already accused Ahab and his father's house for "troubling" Israel, by abandoning the commandments of Yahweh and following הבעלים. Yet in 19:10, not only do Ahab and Jezebel go unmentioned; so do the Baalim and Asherah. The prophets of Baal are also ignored, including the fact that Elijah has killed all four hundred and fifty of them after prompting all the Israelites to affirm their loyalty to Yahweh. Clearly, the *Mekilta* is correct to view Elijah's attitude toward his people and his accusations as his personal reaction to events, rather than a report which accurately reflects the facts presented by the narrator of Kings.[36]

35. There is no textual basis for assuming that Jezebel had put "a price on his head" (Wiesel 1981, 49), or even that the people had been informed that Elijah was a wanted man. If that *were* the case, it certainly would give Elijah reason to fear his fellow citizens.

36. The *Mekilta* takes Elijah's declaration that he has been very jealous for the Lord as evidence that he "insists upon the honor due the Father" but not "the son" Israel (*Pisha* I, 88–99; Lauterbach 1933a, 9). Commenting on this passage, Kadushin (1969, 53–54) claims that this citation of 19:10 is designed to show that the entire verse is not prophecy but Elijah's own words, "his own personal attitude," an attitude which leads God to dismiss him in 19:15–16. In Rom 11:2–4, Paul cites Elijah's appeal to (or pleading with) God "against Israel" in this verse, adding the divine answer that God has kept for himself seven thousand who have not bowed to Baal.

The same can be said for Elijah's charge that the Israelites have "thrown down" (הרסו) Yahweh's altars (1 Kgs 19:14). This accusation is usually validated by referring to the destroyed (ההרוס) altar on Carmel repaired by Elijah (1 Kgs 18:30). Several factors complicate this solution. For one, in 18:31–32 Elijah builds a new altar, rather than repairing an old one. For another, the Carmel mountain range may have marked the border between Israel and Tyre during this period (H. Thompson 1992, 875), raising the question whether the altar repaired in 18:30 was for Yahweh, and, if so, whether this was an appropriate cult site, especially in terms of the cult regulations in Deut 12. Some find the same question raised by 18:38, in which Yahweh's action destroys the altar more completely than when Elijah "healed" it (וירפא) in v. 30 (see Cogan 2000, 444).

Commentators deal with these problems in a number of ways. G. Jones (1984, 318) suggests that neither the Phoenician nor the Israelite sanctuaries here were in regular use, so that "a certain amount of rebuilding was necessary." This implies that the altar mentioned in 18:30 cannot be used to validate Elijah's charge in 19:10, unless one wants to stretch the meaning of הרס to include damage from disuse rather than active destruction.[37] Hauser (1990, 47) says that the use of הרס indicates that it is not simply a matter of the altar's having fallen into disrepair through lack of use; it has been deliberately destroyed.[38] Cogan (2000, 442) believes that 18:30 assumes that the altar has been "destroyed as a result of Jezebel's hounding of YHWH's cult," pointing to 19:10 for corroboration. This would also exonerate the Israelite people from Elijah's charge, because, as noted above, there is no evidence that the people as a whole actively pursued their queen's policies. Walsh also sees 18:10 as implying "*royal* persecution of Yahwism" (1996, 250; emphasis added). A bit later he notes that the narrator depicts the people in general as having "no difficulty worshiping both gods simultaneously." If this is the case, it would seem to be against the people's own interest to destroy

---

This implies that Elijah's charges are largely true. Commentators on Rom 11 such as Fitzmyer (1993, 604–5) tend to share Paul's opinion that Elijah has "become an object of the Israelites' scorn because of his allegiance to Yahweh," even though 1 Kgs 18 shows that the opposite is the case. Morrison (1997, 122) argues that in the *Tg. J.* version of 1 Kgs 18:21 Elijah is interceding "with God for the people," when in 1 Kgs 19 (and Rom 11) he is speaking *against* the people.

37. This verb is also used to denote tearing or throwing down an altar in Judg 6:25; cf. Ezek 16:39.

38. Hauser cites 1 Kgs 19:10, 14 for support, but elsewhere he makes it clear that he considers Elijah to be unreliable in his statements there.

either a Yahwistic *or* a Baal altar. Once again, Elijah has traduced his people by indicting them for royal practices, without ever mentioning the royals Ahab or Jezebel.[39]

What does the fact that Elijah repeats himself verbatim in v. 14 say about what he had attempted to convey in v. 10? Elijah's repeated answer to Yahweh's repeated question may well imply that the divine demonstration with fire, wind, quake, and silent sound simply did not address Elijah's concerns. This of course depends upon how readers take vv. 11–12, assuming that they do not simply dismiss these verses as a secondary interpolation (see, e.g., Keinänen 2001, 155; Würthwein 1984, 229). Traditionally, Yahweh's words and actions are taken as a way of showing Elijah that Yahweh transcends phenomena like fire.[40] The sound of thin silence is then taken as a sublime (if not mystical) experience in which Elijah is allowed to share, and through which he loses his "banal ego," as Masson puts it (2001, 123). On the other hand, there is no hint that Elijah had wrongly assumed that Yahweh was "in" the fire sent in ch. 18. Nor did Elijah's words in 19:10 ask God anything about his cosmic mastery. Was Yahweh simply attempting to intimidate Elijah into silence and submissiveness with this demonstration, in the manner he will employ with Job? If so, the palpable silence described in v. 12 would simply be the calm following all the noise of the wind, quake, and fire. Elijah's covering himself with his cloak would then be nothing more than a means of self-protection.[41]

---

39. Provan (1995, 141–42) neatly ties together vv. 30 and 38 by speculating that the authors of Kings would not want readers to view Elijah's restoring of the altar negatively, since idolatry is a more serious problem than "high places," and "any worship of the LORD is better than worship of Baal." Once the rebuilt altar has "served its purpose," Yahweh simply "removes" it (i.e. destroys it) in v. 38. In other words, it was the lesser of two evils at the time. When the greater evil was removed, the lesser could also be removed.

40. Volz (1924, 35–36) argues that Yahweh is attempting to teach his "demonic prophet" that he should no longer use "demonic weapons" like the sword, as he had in slaughtering the Baal prophets, because Yahweh "no longer wants to be the wild, destructive god of Sinai." From this point on, prophets should only act with the word, the "weapon of the spirit" (1924, 38). Volz believes that Elijah mirrors Yahweh's demonic traits.

41. Predictably, opinions differ as to the significance of Elijah covering his face with his cloak. Some scholars think that Elijah is hiding from, or "blunting the force" of, the divine presence (Cogan 2000, 453; Long 1984, 201; cf. Nelson 1987, 125). For Provan (1995, 146), this implies a kind psychological denial on Elijah's part. For Wiener (1978, 26), it signifies humility and complete passivity of the ego, while for Nelson (1987, 125), it could be a sign of guilt.

However one understands Elijah's repetition of his charges in v. 14, it does evoke a different answer from Yahweh in vv. 15–18. This answer is indeed relevant to the concerns twice voiced by Elijah. Elijah is given specific instructions of what to do next in the battle against rival gods and any Israelites who have been unfaithful to him.[42] As mentioned earlier, Yahweh also responds to Elijah's feeling of aloneness by pointing to the seven thousand who have not (or will not) go over to Baal. Yet Elijah does not end up accomplishing any of the three tasks which Yahweh now gives him, although some scholars take his gesture of throwing his cloak over Elisha (v. 19) to be equivalent to anointing him. Many commentators believe that Yahweh's order for Elijah to anoint Elisha as prophet "in your room" means that Yahweh is dismissing Elijah and replacing him with Elisha (תחתיך; i.e. "in your place"; v. 16). If so, given the depiction of Elijah's personality in the rest of 1 Kgs 19, it is hardly surprising that Elijah seems to treat his successor in a brusque, dismissive manner in the following scene (on this, see Lasine 2011b, 24).

### 3. *Narcissism and Death in 1 Kings 19*

Moses' invitation to Pharaoh to "have this triumph over me"…is an unauthorized venture, and has been compared to Elijah's bold venture of a test between the Lord and Baal… Just as Elijah prays that God acquiesce in his initiative and show thereby that "I am your servant and have done all these things in accord with your command," so…Moses assures Pharaoh that it will be "as he ordered" and proceeds to cry to God.
—M. Greenberg (1969, 155)

You can teach your god to follow behind you like a dog.
—*Pessimistic Dialogue Between Master and Servant*, line 60

In jealousy there is more self-love than love.
—La Rochefoucauld, *Maximes*, #324 (1950, 293)

By focusing on the relationship between narcissism, jealousy, and death, we may be able to answer some of the most puzzling questions raised by Elijah's behavior in 1 Kgs 19. What kind of person would want to die so soon after a great victory, and immediately after he has fled precisely in

---

42. Conners (1997, 237) thinks the voice charges him to continue his heroic mission, now that he has "let go of his society-sensitive ego and his need for approval from others." Hauser (1990, 81) argues that in ch. 19 Yahweh is making repeated attempts to get Elijah to resume his role as Yahweh's advocate. When Elijah continues to be consumed with the prospect of his own death in v. 14, Yahweh directs him to anoint others.

order to *save* his life? Why would he apparently view himself as a failure[43] and experience such great despair at precisely this point, especially since the contest on Carmel was his own idea, maneuvering God to "acquiesce in his initiative"? What kind of person would seek to prove himself in the eyes of others, and at the same time dismiss all others as disloyal or pronounce them dead? Why would he lament his aloneness, and yet seek to be alone and apart from others? As I discussed in Chapter 3, some scholars avoid such questions by explaining what White (1997, 6) calls Elijah's psychological "discordances" and "contradictions in mood" in terms of redactional activity. Before adopting that strategy we need to ask whether Elijah possesses the type of personality for which such behaviors are neither discordant nor contradictory.

Whether critics evaluate Elijah positively or negatively, they tend to agree that Elijah believes himself to be a failure. When ch. 19 begins, Elijah has just achieved great success. Yet shortly thereafter he claims that he is no better than his fathers and wants to die. As I mentioned earlier, Provan (1995, 148) views Elijah as "reduced to the self-loathing of the high achiever who thinks he has failed." His reference to the failed high achiever recalls what Tartakoff (1966) has dubbed "the Nobel Prize Complex," namely, the feeling of being singled out for special recognition and entitlement. Elijah's desire to die does not come because success makes him feel guilty over having surpassed his fathers, like the people Freud calls those who are "wrecked by success" (*die am Erfolge scheitern*; 1946a, 370).[44] People who exhibit the "Nobel Prize Complex" feel like failures no matter how much success they have attained, because they are judging success according to grandiose infantile notions of omnipotence and secretly feel that they are shameful frauds.

Elijah's desire to die does not arise because enjoying popular support makes him feel guilty. Nor is anything said about his success being temporary, that is, about the people reverting back to "hopping from branch to branch" between Yahweh and Baal (1 Kgs 18:21). Yet Elijah becomes deathly afraid after Jezebel's announcement of her intention to kill him. In ch. 17 Elijah hides not because he is said to be afraid but because Yahweh tells him to; no reason is given. Yahweh even protects

---

43. From 1 Kgs 19:10, 14 commentators often assume that Elijah expected himself (or that God tacitly expected him) to make the nation universally and exclusively loyal to Yahweh through activity generated by his characteristic "jealousy" for Yahweh. However, there is no evidence that Yahweh commissioned Elijah to perform any such task.

44. These people may fail at the new position they have attained, if not suffer more severe consequences.

Elijah's life by arranging for him to be fed in both 1 Kgs 17 and 1 Kgs 19. Moreover, Jezebel and Ahab do not constitute any greater threat to Elijah in ch. 19 than they had in ch. 18, but the royal pair did not have this effect on the prophet on the earlier occasion. So why does Jezebel's new threat in ch. 19 suddenly lead Elijah to panic when his inflated self-image is punctured?

Elijah's fear[45] seems to indicate a growing awareness of vulnerability, in spite of the aura of invincibility surrounding his masterful behavior in ch. 18. While Elijah is in one sense an outsider, he has also exerted total control over the ultimate insiders, the king, and his courtier Obadiah, as well as over the people and the prophets of Baal. He may even have had Yahweh "follow behind him like a dog," by maneuvering Yahweh to "acquiesce" in the prophet's "initiatives."[46] It is only Jezebel who refuses to submit.[47] Elijah is acting as though he needs *unanimous* submission if he is to go on living. Apparently the one dissenting voice of Jezebel issuing hollow threats[48] is enough to prevent Elijah's grandiose self-image from being reflected in the world, transforming his success into an experience of total failure. It is then that he presents himself to God as a sole survivor and victim, a supposedly isolated and abandoned victim who, in reality, had recently made four hundred and fifty Baal prophets *his* victims, by single-handedly slaughtering them with the assistance of the same people he now claims are disloyal and out to kill him (1 Kgs 18:40; 19:10, 14).

According to Tartakoff (1966, 237–38), adults who suffer from the "Nobel Prize Complex" are hypersensitive to minor disappointments, because "the corrective effect of reality confrontation on fantasy has been lacking" due to their "special fate." That is, they have not had to confront their limitations. With people whose apparent self-absorption and grandiosity mask feelings of inadequacy and helplessness, even a seemingly minor disappointment of expectation can lead to feelings of

---

45. 1 Kgs 19:3 reads "afraid" (וַיִּרָא) in most ancient versions, and "saw" (וַיַּרְא) in the SC. Most modern commentators prefer the former reading.

46. On this aspect of 1 Kgs 18, see Chapter 3, above.

47. On the other hand, Elijah does not raise the subject of Jezebel's threat with Yahweh, which one would expect if it were the queen who had caused Elijah's fright and flight (see Cogan 2000, 456).

48. As pointed out by Walsh (1996, 265–66) and Cogan (2000, 451), by sending a messenger to threaten Elijah verbally, Jezebel is, in effect, warning the prophet that he should flee. After all, she could have dispatched the messenger to assassinate the prophet, as did Saul when he sent "messengers" to David in order to kill him. The only reason that David escapes is because Michal warns him and helps him to flee in order to save his life (1 Sam 19:11).

failure, despair and mortification severe enough to lead to suicide (Reich 1973, 301). If such a narcissistically vulnerable person views himself as having an enemy, that adversary will be seen by him "as a *flaw in a narcissistically perceived reality*...whose mere independence or otherness is an offense" (Kohut 1972, 386 [original emphasis]). Elijah's adversary Jezebel is an independent "other" in precisely this sense.

Kohut observes that when such "absolutarian expectations" and perceived failure are viewed as irremediable and despair leads to suicide, the suicide is not an expression of guilt "but a remedial act—the wish to wipe out the unbearable sense of mortification and nameless shame imposed by the ultimate recognition of a failure of all-encompassing magnitude" (1972, 386; 1977, 241). And to the extent that Elijah identifies with Yahweh's feeling that Israel has been unfaithful to him, his sense of mortification and failure would be even greater.

La Rochefoucauld's intuition that jealousy is linked to self-love is supported by recent psychological research. Investigators like Berke (1988, 74) have demonstrated a link between romantic jealousy, envy, and narcissism, beginning with the "narcissistic wound" suffered by a betrayed spouse.[49] While cultures differ in how they define the situations which call forth the complex of feelings, thoughts, and actions they call jealousy (see White and Mullen 1989, 9–13), there is ample information within the Hebrew Bible—particularly in the prophets—to establish the similarity between Yahweh's experience of Israel's infidelity and the experience of romantic jealousy in modern Western cultures. Psychologists have shown that envy of the other whom the wife prefers often leads the jealous husband to deflate and denigrate both the wife and her lover.[50] Elijah certainly engages in deflation and denigration of Baal and his prophets—*and* Israel—at Carmel.[51]

49. See White and Mullen (1989, 21) for references to scholars who discuss "the 'narcissistic wound' inherent in jealousy." Vauhkonen's study notes the frequency of narcissistic characters in cases of pathological jealousy (1968, 119). Vauhkonen concludes that narcissistic characters need to regard their spouses as worthless and unfaithful so as to inflate their own vulnerable self-esteem.

50. Berke (1988, 71) notes that envious and narcissistic persons initially differ because the envier attacks the problem by deflating others, while the narcissist inflates himself; however, "their thinking, feelings, and actions run along convergent tracks... Like the envier, the narcissist looks upon others with an eye that puffs them up and squashes them flat as soon as he perceives qualities or features better than his own. In such cases "the quality of hurt...seeks discharge by omnipotent self-inflation and other-denigration" (1988, 74).

51. Of course, speakers like Moses denigrate Israel without their own narcissism or jealousy playing a direct role, as in Deut 9:4–7, 24. While Elijah is usually

According to Berke (1988, 76–77), when envy, jealousy, and narcissism converge, the result is not only rage but a preference for death over life, specifically, "auto-annihilation."[52] This may seem counterintuitive, considering that on the most elemental level "the idea of death...is extremely painful to our self-esteem" (Rank 1989, 70). Rank notes that "primitive narcissism feels itself primarily threatened by the ineluctable destruction of the self" (1989, 70, 83). In fact, on the most elemental level narcissism is an attempt to overcome death. Odd as it may seem, it is for this very reason that the "narcissistic attitude" is associated with the "strange paradox of the suicide who voluntarily seeks death in order to free himself of the intolerable thanatophobia." What torments such people is the conscious idea of their eternal "inability to return, an idea from which release is only possible in death" (1989, 77–78).

From this perspective there are two possible—and seemingly opposite—"remedies" for Elijah's perceived plight: what has been called the "negative narcissism" of death (A. Green 1983, 278) and translation to heaven as the unending equivalent of the seemingly godlike invulnerability he had enjoyed earlier—an equivalent which *also* grants him a unique ability to "return" (see 1 Kgs 18:10–12; 2 Kgs 2:11; Mal 3:23–24).

In Chapter 2 I mentioned Geller's assertion that the new biblical awareness of "the perceiving individual self" is "born of prophetic experience" (1996, 179). Whatever one thinks about this general claim, we *can* say that on Mt. Horeb the prophet Elijah describes how he experiences *his* individual self. On the other hand, the fact that many commentators have found Elijah's characterization to be inconsistent, if not incoherent, might lead one to conclude that this ancient character supports the literary theorists who claim that the notion of a coherent self is an illusion. In fact, Elijah has been described in terms which are quite similar to the way critics like Cixous (1974, 384) portray the "I," once the "myth of 'character'" has been exposed. If Elijah is viewed by Obadiah and the sons of the prophet as elusive and always able to escape

---

supposed to be depressed at Horeb, people who are depressed (but not narcissistic) tend to derogate others *less* than people who are not depressed, at least in modern Western culture. Non-depressives tend to recall more negative information about others (Kuiper and MacDonald 1982, 223, 227, 236–38; cf. Brenninkmeijer et al. 2001, 874). On the operations of the "negativity bias," see Chapter 9, §2, below.

52. As noted by Walcot (1978, 1), both sociologists and laymen find it difficult to distinguish between "jealousy" and "envy." Walcot cites George Crabb in nineteenth-century *English Synonymes*: "we are jealous of what is our own; we are envious at seeing another have that which it wants for itself." Walcot finds this distinction to be "hardly valid nowadays." On envy, see Lasine 1989a, 70–72.

capture, Cixous's "insubordinable 'I'" is engaged in a "permanent escapade"; in fact, "the 'personnage' is...that which escapes and leads somewhere else" (1974, 387–88).

In contrast, the *personality* of the biblical Elijah is not at all elusive, once we recognize that he is being presented to readers as narcissistic. In addition, his presentation further undermines the assumption that the words of Yahweh's prophets are necessarily reliable, an assumption which had already been called into question by the story of the man of God from Judah and the old prophet of Bethel. If Elijah really is being presented as a narcissist, his statements—and even some of his actions in chs. 18–19—may be motivated by a need to maintain a certain image of himself, even at the expense of the people for whom he, as a prophet, is supposed to be the intercessor. As mentioned earlier, one rabbinic tradition faults Elijah for not interceding on behalf of the people at Horeb as had Moses. Lack of interest in the welfare and feelings of others is just one of a number of story elements (and interpretive choices by readers) which might lead one to view the jealous Elijah as egocentric and self-pitying, if not narcissistic.

### 4. *Narcissism, Death, and Immortality in the Elijah Narratives as a Whole*

[As a child] I used to brood over the stories of Enoch and Elijah, and almost to persuade myself that, whatever might become of others, I should be translated, in something of the same way, to heaven.
—Wordsworth (1947, 463)

Enoch was [nine-year-old Seryozha Karenin's] favorite character in the whole of the Old Testament... He did not believe that people he loved could die, and more especially that he himself would die... [H]e had been told everyone died... But Enoch had not died, so not everybody died. "But why shouldn't anyone deserve the same in God's sight and be taken alive to heaven?" thought Seryozha. The bad ones, those, that is, whom Seryozha did not love, might die, but the good ones might all be like Enoch.
—Tolstoy, *Anna Karenina* (2002, 609–10)

What draws the reader to a novel is the hope of warming his shivering life with a death he reads about.
—Benjamin (2002, 156)

According to Meinhold (2002, 25–26), there are two climactic points in the Elijah narratives, the theophany at Horeb and the ascension report. Each climax focuses on one of the two "remedies" for Elijah's distress which I mentioned earlier: God-assisted suicide or God-assisted immortality. Rather than giving Elijah what he asks for in 1 Kgs 19:4, God gives him immortality through translation.

In the ancient Mediterranean world only "a few special favorites of the gods" evade death through translation, at times irrespective of merit (Rohde 1966, 1.61; cf. 2.536–39). Is Elijah a favorite of Yahweh in this sense? Does his ascension show that he actually *is* "better than his fathers," after all (1 Kgs 19:4)? At first glance, the apparently numinous end of his life would seem to put to rest any questions concerning Elijah's specialness to Yahweh; his ascension is obviously a remedy for his plight, if not a reward. Yet some commentators resist this conclusion, arguing that Yahweh had dismissed Elijah at Horeb,[53] and that Elijah's ascension is the ultimate sign of this dismissal rather than a special boon.[54] After all, Yahweh assigns several new tasks to Elijah at Horeb and then ends his earthly life before he attempts to accomplish most of them.

Modern readers who encounter the account of Elijah's (and Enoch's) translations often view this outcome so positively that they desire it for themselves. In his notes on the "Immortality Ode" from which my first epigraph is taken, Wordsworth remarks that "nothing was more difficult for me in childhood than to admit the notion of death as a state applicable to my own being." He attributes his "difficulty" not to the unconscious in Freud's sense, but to "a sense of the indomitableness of the Spirit within me" (1947, 463). Writing during World War I, Freud remarks that because our unconscious "behaves as if immortal," heroism becomes possible. Heroism returns us to infantile feelings of invulnerability: "war constrains us once more to be heroes who cannot believe in

---

53. For examples of modern commentators who adopt this view, see Cogan 2000, 457 n. 3. One rabbinic example is in *Mek. Pisḥa*, I, 99–100 (Lauterbach 1933, 9; cf. Kadushin 1969, 53–54). According to Fretheim (1999, 111), God allows Elijah to "state his self-pity" and then "recommissions him to his vocation."

54. Elsewhere I have compared the account of Elijah's ascension in 2 Kgs 2 to reports concerning other ancient wonder-workers, including some who have also resuscitated dead individuals, and were later translated instead of dying a normal human death. That analysis showed that the personality of the biblical Elijah has a surprising amount in common with these remarkable and otherwise very different literary figures, including indicators of narcissism. Lasine, "Translating Death" (n. 24 above). For a study of Elijah's resuscitation of the widow's son in relation to similar examples of reanimating the dead by other ancient—and modern—wonder-working healers, see Lasine 2004a. A narcissistic personality also turns out to be characteristic of a surprising number of these healers, as different as they may seem in other respects.

their own death" (1946b, 354). To clarify his point, he quotes a character in a work by Anzengruber who recommends that one tell oneself: "nothing can happen to *you*" (Anzengruber 1980, 59; Freud 1946b, 351).[55] For Freud, the feeling that "nothing can happen to me" is less an "intimation of immortality" than it is the expression of our unconscious attitude. Regardless of their origin, Wordsworth's intimations of immortality serve a vital function. As he puts it in his essay "On Epitaphs," "if the impression and sense of death were not... counterbalanced, such a hollowness would pervade the whole system of things, such a want of correspondence and consistency, a disproportion so astounding betwixt means and ends, that there could be no repose, no joy" (1974, 52).[56]

In these statements, Wordsworth seems to approach Seale's characterization of an existentialist viewpoint: "facing up to our mortality seems to result in...no room [being] left for the care people can feel for others... The vision of life as nothing more than a flight from death seems impossibly bleak" (Seale 1998, 58). Paraphrasing Voltaire, Wordsworth is implying that if there were no intimations of immortality, we would have to invent them.[57] In a sense, parents *do* invent these feelings, by treating their child as "His Majesty the Baby," a being "not...subject to illness, death, renunciation of enjoyment, or restrictions on his own will" (Freud 1946c, 157–58). The parents' purpose is to rediscover their lost narcissism through their child by giving the child feelings of omnipotence, invulnerability, and immortality.[58]

---

55. *Es kann dir nix g'scheh'n.* To avoid confusion, I should note that all English translations of the two essays in which Freud quotes this line render it "Nothing can happen to *me*," not "to *you*," even though Anzengruber wrote "*dir*," not "*mir*." In an earlier essay, Freud had observed that this same aura of invulnerability characterizes heroes in literature.

56. Similarly, in Book 8 of *The Prelude*, Wordsworth notes that we are "all led to knowledge." He then asks, "were it otherwise, and we found evil fast as we find good in our first years, or think that it is found, how could the innocent heart bear up and live?" (8.441–46; quotations from *The Prelude* are taken from the 1805 version [Wordsworth 1979]).

57. Earlier in *The Prelude*, Wordsworth relates that he told a prophecy to the open fields and poetic numbers came spontaneously to him, clothing his spirit in priestly robes, "thus singled out, as it might seem, for holy services" (1.62–63). While the allusion here is to priesthood, elsewhere in *The Prelude* Wordsworth stresses the affinity between the poet and the prophet (e.g. 12.301–5). Wordsworth's childhood belief that he might share the fate of the biblical prophet Elijah also expresses a desire to be singled out. See further in Lasine 2005.

58. For discussion and critique of this notion, see Lasine 2001, 4–9, 25, 202–4, 231–33, 237.

In two wartime papers written for lay audiences, Freud listed three blows to human narcissism, delivered, in turn, by Copernicus, Darwin, and Freud himself. All three reveal that we—our conscious selves—are not at the "center," either in the universe as a whole, within the natural world, or within our individual internal worlds (Freud 1947, 6–12; 1963, 284–85). However, one can argue that death is the ultimate blow to human narcissism, insofar as it annihilates all worlds, by annihilating our ability to experience them. My death is the ultimate blow to my narcissism.

According to Freud's earlier essay on narcissism, His Majesty the Baby should really be again the center and core of creation. He will fulfill the wish-dream to become a hero in place of the father. The ultimate benefit of this procedure involves the transcendence of death (Freud 1946c, 158). The life-story of the child is to function for the parents in the same way that a popular novel functions for its readers. In a 1908 essay, Freud had described the hero of popular novels as the center of interest, protected by the author with a special providence (1941, 219). If the hero is left seriously wounded and bleeding at the end of a chapter, he will be cared for with the utmost concern and on the way to recovery at the beginning of the next. The feeling of security which accompanies the hero through his dangerous destinies in these "ego-centric narratives" is the same as that with which a real hero plunges into the water to save a drowning person. It is the feeling that "Nothing can happen to you," the same line which Freud later quotes in his wartime essay on death.[59] This invulnerability of the fictional hero betrays the presence of "His Majesty the Ego/Self [*das Ich*]," the hero of all day-dreams as it is all novels (1941, 219–20).[60]

---

59. See above on Freud's use of this quotation in his 1915 essay on death (Freud 1946b). It is worth noting that the statement only means that *death* cannot happen to me. Many painful things happen to the *Steinklopferhanns*, the speaker of this line in Anzengruber's "*Die Kreuzelschreiber.*" Nor are Freud's wounded and bleeding heroes of the novels "invulnerable." They simply have not *died*.

60. In an earlier essay Freud observes that "being present as an interested spectator at a spectacle or play does for adults what play does for children, whose hesitant hope of being able to do what grown-up people do are in that way gratified" (1953b, 305). Freud imagines audience members in this situation to believe that "nothing can happen to me" in a very different sense: "the spectator is a person who…has long been obliged to damp down, or rather displace, his ambition to stand in his own person at the hub of world affairs; he longs to feel and to act and to arrange things according to this desires—in short, to be a hero. And the playwright and actor enable him to do this by allowing him *to identify himself* with a hero."

Like His Majesty the Self and the hero of the novel, His Majesty the Baby[61] is invulnerable and protected by a special providence. The charmed life the parents envision for their heroic baby grants them a vicarious immortality as they "read" their child's continuing life story. From this perspective, reading novels and living through one's children serve the same function as telling stories served for Shahrazad in the *Arabian Nights*, namely, postponing one's own death. And even if the hero in the novel does die,[62] readers who identify with the hero nevertheless live on in their extratextual worlds, following the continuing events in the novel as though they were present at their own funeral in a dream. As Nell puts it, whether a reader witnesses the hero's death or his "literal or figurative apotheosis," the story affirms the reader's personal survival (2002, 23).[63]

When Wordsworth recalled his childhood musings on Elijah, he frankly admitted having thought that "whatever might become of others, *I* should be translated" (emphasis added). Tolstoy's child-character Seryozha has the same feeling when musing on Enoch.[64] One psychiatrist

61. The phrase "His Majesty the Baby" is used by Freud in English, probably because the phrase had been used as the title of more than one work of art; see Plotz 2001, 25.

62. If Freud, Benjamin, and Nell talk about readers as surviving the death of characters in fiction, Schopenhauer (1960, 139) talks about a reflective individual being like an actor who finishes his scene, takes his place among the audience-members, and placidly looks on at whatever may transpire, even if it is "the preparation for his own death (in the play)." The faculty which allows this detachment for Schopenhauer is reason and calm deliberation, not imagination (see further in Lasine 1977, 97–107).

63. Nell believes that this is the case whether the text is a folktale, formulaic fiction, or an "unflinchingly mimetic narrative" (2002, 18, 23). Cf. Bettelheim (1976, 8–11) on the way that fairy and folk tales serve to dissipate children's fear of death. In the epigraph to this section Benjamin claims that narrative offers a reader "the hope of warming his shivering life with a death he reads about." He is referring specifically to novels, in contrast to earlier storytelling. Benjamin says that for modern readers of the novel, only death gives us the meaning of our life. In the words of Camus' character Clamence, only when one is dead does one become a "definitive case" (see further in Chapter 9, §1, below). In this sense, the prophet Elijah *never* becomes a definitive case.

64. While Dahood believes that the speakers in Pss 16:10 and 49:16 (Heb.) also hold the firm conviction that "God will take him to himself, just as he took Enoch and Elijah" (1966, 301; cf. 91), Liess (2004, 20–25) and others have shown that his interpretation has little support. In any case, there is no evidence in either psalm that the speaker believes him- or herself to be the only one who will receive this rare gift from God; in fact, the two psalms are probably not referring to translation or any other form of immortality in these verses; see, e.g., Goldingay 2001, 77–79.

calls this maneuver the method of "self-exception": "making use of... irrational optimism...we except ourselves from the common laws of mortality whilst readily acknowledging them as far as others are concerned" (Geiringer 1952, 179).[65] As I will discuss below, Geiringer's observation leads to the question whether the issue is not simply accepting others' deaths, but *needing* others to die in order to feel truly alive.

Wordsworth contends that one who dismisses the sense of immortality as childish ignorance must inhabit a world which is forlorn, hollow, cold, and loveless (1974, 50–52). Elijah describes himself as inhabiting such a forlorn and hostile world. He rages at others, mocks them, orders them around, uses them, discards them, or kills them, until he flees from the world and wants to die. Narcissistically wounded people inhabit a world of this sort, or create it for themselves by their objectification of others and isolation. Or perhaps I am confusing cause and effect. It may be that some children undertake the narcissistic immortality project in order to find safety in such a hostile and forlorn world. Narcissism can then be understood as a defensive response to the experience of abandonment, or, as Winnicott puts it, the death that happened and was not experienced.[66]

From his government's point of view, Elijah is a hostile and scornful "troublemaker" (1 Kgs 18:17). At first glance, he is repeatedly in danger of death, not only from starvation twice in ch. 17 and by his claim of being persecuted by his own people in ch. 19, but also by what he seems to view as the threat presented by Ahaziah's men in 2 Kgs 1:15. Viewed in terms of His Majesty the Baby, however, the life of the hero Elijah follows the pattern of the parental wish-dream and Freud's fictional heroes. A "special providence" watches over Elijah, and the laws of nature are suspended for the prophet, just as they are for His Majesty the Baby. In fact, Elijah even exhibits godlike qualities. He has acted as a divinely empowered paramedic to return the widow's son to life. He has proved invulnerable to the dangers posed by Jezebel and Ahab. His mysterious disappearances imply that he has mastered the divine art of becoming invisible.[67] He is never said to be ill or grow old. This contrasts sharply with the prophets who appear just before him, namely, the old prophet from Bethel (1 Kgs 13:11, 25, 29) and Ahijah (1 Kgs 14:4), as well as the great prophets of earlier times, Moses and Samuel (Deut 31:2; 34:7; 1 Sam 8:1, 5; 12:2; 28:14).

65. Geiringer adds, "'It can't happen to me yet'—a less blatant form of this doctrine—is well suited to the young" (1952, 179).

66. Winnicott 1965, 145; see further in Lasine 2001, 207–8, 208 n. 25.

67. On invisibility, omnipotence, invulnerability, and immortality as qualities associated with the ideal king as well as with gods, see Lasine 2001, 5–15, 18–28.

In addition, the fact that God grants him the boon of translation seems, at the very least, to show a unique degree of divine favor toward the man thus chosen, in spite of the fact that there is no report of Yahweh originally "choosing" him, that is, commissioning him as a prophet. In fact, by his translation Elijah has achieved the ultimate divine trait of immortality. Put another way, Yahweh has lent Elijah traits and powers which uniquely mirror his own. We possess no information about the birth, parentage, or childhood of either Yahweh or Elijah. Neither has a spouse. And of course, neither dies. In addition, both insist upon being the only one of their kind, both hide themselves and both are consistently elusive (e.g. Isa 45:15). Elijah enhances this aura of divinity by identifying strongly with the emotions experienced by his divine father, and by acting as Yahweh's agent on the basis of those emulated emotions. For Volz, actions such as the "gruesome bloodbath" of the Baal prophets' slaughter and the "furious and uncanny" immolation of Ahaziah's messengers show that Elijah is "completely the image [*Abbild*] of his demonic God" (1924, 24).

We might ask some unanswerable questions at this juncture: Did most or all actual readers of and listeners to the story in ancient Israel believe that Elijah was *really* able to do what no one in the Bible had ever done before, that is, resuscitate a dead person? Would they believe that he was *really* translated? Or did some both believe and not believe, in the sense that Veyne describes Greek attitudes toward myths (1988, 83–93; cf. xi)? If they shared the view of some modern scholars (and some of the rabbis) that Elijah is self-absorbed and narcissistic, they might certainly have been tempted to view Elijah's special fate with suspicion; in modern terms, these acts smack too much of a wish-fulfillment fantasy. Or, if one accepts that Elijah really did enjoy such God-given powers and such a godlike fate, would they have concluded that Elijah *deserved* such unique gifts? And if they did *not* view him as deserving, would they conclude that Elijah is simply Yahweh's favorite, irrespective of merit?

Canetti's portrait of the "survivor" may be helpful here. Canetti also describes the life of a unique individual toward whom "the higher powers are favorably disposed," although here uniqueness is achieved only through the death of others:

> it is important that the survivor is *alone*... One not only wants to be there always, one wants to be there when others are no longer there... [I]t is as though the battle were fought so that he could survive... It is a feeling of chosenness among many... In some way one feels oneself to be *better*, simply because one is still there. (1980, 249–50)

Like Canetti's survivor, Elijah seems to have considered himself "better" than his fathers. Moreover, he not only sees and feels himself as alone, but arranges a kind of "battle" in which he alone challenges four hundred and fifty opponents and personally slaughters every one of them, just as he later demonstrates that he is a "man of God" by killing over one hundred more men (2 Kgs 1:9–12). Seale (1998, 58) compares the feeling of being alone in the world caused by "facing up to our mortality" to "that which is achieved by killing everyone"; is this how Elijah deals with *his* feelings of aloneness?[68]

Two scholarly characterizations of Elijah's personality point to another aspect of the prophet's behavior. Trible (1994, 171, 178) stresses the fact that Elijah's "identity depends not upon others but comes through his own speech... As Elijah first appeared, so he disappears, mysteriously unconnected to human relationships." B. Robinson (1991, 517) contends that Elijah "has always seen himself as *sui generis* and cannot live with the realization that has come upon him during his flight that he is as other men." These observations suggest that Elijah might have embarked upon what Becker calls the "*causa-sui* project." Becker (1973, 36, 120–21) claims that the child wants to conquer death by becoming the father of himself. He describes the "genius" as someone who "repeats the narcissistic inflation of the child; he lives the fantasy of the control of life and death... [His] uniqueness also cuts off his roots... [H]e doesn't seem to have traceable debts to the qualities of others... He is truly without a family, the father of himself" (1973, 109). To abandon the *causa-sui* project is to continue to "melt oneself trustingly into the father, or...the Great Father in the sky." The result of abandoning the project is that "your destiny is no longer your own; you are the eternal child making your way in the world of the elders" (1973, 116).

Now Elijah's "Great Father in the sky" is a god who demands that his human creations remain "eternal children" in the sense described by Becker. This is especially true of the children he makes his "special treasure" (Exod 19:4–5; cf. Deut 7:6–8), namely, the children of Israel and specific individuals like Job.[69] The Israelites and Job know what it is like to inhabit a hostile and deadly world where even total submission to the holy Great Father is no guarantee of safety.[70] This raises again the

68. On the narcissistic fantasy of killing everyone and being the sole survivor in Homer's *Iliad*, the book of Isaiah, and the records of Ramesses II, see Lasine, 2001, 239–53.

69. On Yahweh's narcissistic "parenting style," see Lasine 2001, 177–89, 208–14; 2002.

70. On the dangers of being the subjects, spouse, and scion of this holy divine king, husband, and father, see Lasine 2010, 48–53, 56–57.

question of Yahweh's attitude toward Elijah and Elijah's self-promoting project. In the world of the books of Kings, Yahweh certainly seems to appreciate it when his children are submissive and self-effacing, like the repentant Ahab in 1 Kgs 21:28–29. Insofar as Yahweh is a manipulative and domineering parent, Elijah's self-assertion can be viewed in a much more positive light, namely, as an attempt to liberate himself from a life of eternal childhood.

Ironically, the means Elijah uses to achieve autonomy involve acting like the Great Father. As we have discovered, the God before whom Elijah "stands" (1 Kgs 17:1; 18:15) is very similar to himself in both "life-style" and personality—including their shared trait of jealousy. Elijah is jealous for Yahweh, the "jealous god" whose very name is "Jealous."[71] Elijah is also jealous for Elijah. The dissolution of differences between human and divine in their relationship leads to Elijah preempting, if not upstaging, God.[72] To the extent that their lack of difference might lead to conflict between them, the chance increases that Elijah's ascension is a way for Yahweh to prevent the prophet from continuing to emulate his jealous wrath. In effect, Yahweh reasserts the difference between himself and his prophet by reducing their similarity to a single shared trait: immortality.

If we were in a position to counsel the young Wordsworth and Karenin, perhaps we should point out to them that Elijah, the one person who was definitely translated in the Hebrew Bible,[73] may have eluded death because he had never lived a fully human life. If Benjamin is correct that death gives modern life its meaning, modern readers may conclude that the fate of the ancient character Elijah precludes the possibility that his time on earth could ever achieve meaning as a *human* life. This may be the price one has to pay for a ticket to ride on a whirlwind to heaven.

71. קנא שמו אל קנא הוא; Exod 34:14. On the different ways in which the personality of Elijah's successor Elisha mirrors that of Yahweh, see Lasine, forthcoming.

72. For cases in which Elijah may be forcing God to back up his plans and predictions, see Chapter 3, above.

73. Commentators disagree about whether the verb לקח in Gen 5:24 indicates that Enoch was translated. Some of the rabbis (see, e.g., *Gen. Rab.* 25.1), as well as some modern scholars, believe that Yahweh "taking" Enoch means little more than he died. Others, like VanderKam (1984, 33), contend that לקח is "employed to describe removal to the divine presence" in relation to Elijah (2 Kgs 2:9, 10), if not Enoch as well.

# Part III

# CHARACTERIZING KINGS

Chapter 6

REASSESSING THE CHARACTER OF CONDEMNED KINGS:
NEW PERSPECTIVES ON JEROBOAM AND JEHORAM

1. *Judging Jeroboam's Character*

a. *Reading and Misreading Jeroboam's Intentions*

> Must church-government…be conformable and pliant to civil, that is
> arbitrary, and chiefly conversant about the visible and external part of
> man? This is the very maxim that moulded the calves of Bethel and of
> Dan; this was the quintessence of Jeroboam's policy, he made religion
> conform to his politic interests.
>
> —John Milton (1889, 79)

> Jeroboam,…preferring the policies of the world before the service and
> honour of God,…erected two golden calves.
>
> —Walter Raleigh (1829, 297)

In my previous study of Jeroboam's intentions (Lasine 1992), I noted
that readers who are familiar with the golden calf story in Exod 32 have
good reason to be surprised by Jeroboam's actions in 1 Kgs 12. In fact,
when they discover that Jeroboam sought to attract pious Yahwists by
reenacting the apostasy at Sinai—complete with the blasphemous declaration "Behold/These are your gods, O Israel, which brought you up out
of the land of Egypt" (1 Kgs 12:28/Exod 32:4)—they might well share
the astonishment of R. Judah bar Pazzi when he compared the people's
giving up their gold for Aaron's calf with their later giving of gold for
the Tabernacle and exclaimed: "Shall we read and not be startled and
confounded (נבעת)?"[1] In short, readers of the text as it stands[2] could
reasonably conclude that the king must be a self-destructive fool, even
though nothing in his previously reported behavior would lead one to
believe him capable of such folly. Some biblical commentators are
equally unsure what to make of Jeroboam's strategy. While most believe

---

1. See *y. Seqal.* 1.1.45d; see Exod 35:21–29.
2. That is, as "the ideal narrative audience" would read the story, to use
Rabinowitz's terminology. See n. 74 below.

that they know the intentions of the authors and editors who contributed to the portrait of Jeroboam now in 1 Kings,[3] many are less certain about the "original intention" of the character Jeroboam (Seow 1999, 104), what he "thinks he is doing with his calves" (Provan 1995, 112),[4] and his motivation for inviting the man of God from Judah to his house (Walsh 1996, 180).

So how *are* we to assess the situation and character of the king as he is depicted in 1 Kgs 12, whether from a psychological, historical, *or* literary-intertextual point of view? Like Elijah (1 Kgs 18:22; 19:10, 14) and Zedekiah (Jer 38:5), Jeroboam expresses his reading of his situation in directly quoted speech (1 Kgs 12:26–27), although in this case the narrator is quoting thoughts, not voiced words.[5] What all three express includes a perceived threat to their lives. Modern scholars tend to evaluate Jeroboam's motives here in the same way as Sir Walter Raleigh, John Milton, and Hugo Grotius[6] did in the sixteenth and seventeenth centuries.[7] Seow (1999, 103–4) and Würthwein (1985, 162–63) claim

---

3.  Historians are well aware that, on one level, only an insane person would seek to court loyal followers of Yahweh by introducing golden calves with the same blasphemous declaration made by the calf worshippers at Sinai, if those followers were familiar with the events at Sinai as they are reported in Exod 32. For this reason, many conclude that the literary Jeroboam of 1 Kgs 12 is a victim of "polemical distortion" (Cross 1973, 73), and propose as a realistic alternative that the presumably sane historical Jeroboam was appealing to a tradition of acceptable Yahwistic calf symbolism known to his followers in the north, a tradition which the author of Kings is attempting to obscure. See further in Lasine 1992, 135–39.

4.  Some scholars speculate that the historical Jeroboam may have caused the people to confuse Yahweh with Baal when he made the calves, "however excellent [his] intentions may have been" (Kennedy 1901, 342; cf. Jenks 1977, 103). It is usually assumed that Jeroboam himself was aware that the calves simply represented a pedestal for the divine presence, although this distinction would have been lost on ordinary worshippers. Only Jeroboam and "people of a more refined religious sensitivity" could appreciate the difference (de Vaux 1971, 102–3; cf. Noth 1960, 233; Nelson 1987, 81).

5.  On the use of quotation to expose the self-will and self-deception of idolaters throughout the Hebrew Bible, see Lasine 1992, 139–42.

6.  Sheehan (2006, 45) notes that Grotius offered the "typically laconic comment" that "princes are accustomed to twisting sacred matters to their end," but declared it God's will that Jeroboam, like the Pharaoh, "might be hardened more and more in his idolatry." Among seventeenth-century Catholic theologians, Jacque-Bénigne Bousset (1990, 201) concludes that Jeroboam erected his calves "only by pure policy" (*par une pure politique*).

7.  Kugel (2007, 525) briefly discusses the use of the phrase "sin of Jeroboam" in Protestant–Catholic polemics since the Reformation. For Catholics, the real Jeroboam was Luther, who rended the unity of the Church with results which were

that from this quotation readers gather that Jeroboam's "interests" and "motives" were "purely political and selfish" and "egoistic," and "had nothing to do with faith in the Lord."[8] For Van Seters (1983, 313), Jeroboam is motivated by "weakness and political expediency." Sweeney (2007b, 176) calls him a "cynical monarch interested in his own hold on power."[9] Carasik contends that Jeroboam's establishment of the calves "is not grounded in religious intentions, *as he pretends*"; his "internal thoughts…reveal that his motives are grounded not in faith but in realpolitik" (2000, 229; emphasis added).[10] And Pakkala concludes that "the

---

just as disastrous as the consequences of Jeroboam's secession. The Protestant rebuttal stressed that the sin of Jeroboam was bowing down to statues, not secession. Kugel hears a "faint echo" of early Protestant apologetic in today's scholarly insistence that Jeroboam's secession was only natural and that his calves were not really idolatrous. (Of course, in the Hebrew Bible the secession is not merely "natural," in the sense of politically necessary, but also "supernatural," in the sense that Yahweh mandated it as a way of punishing the house of David for Solomon's idolatry.) Cf. Levenson, who notes "the curious tendency of scholars to invert the canonical judgment by treating Israel as normative and Judah as deviant," claiming that it "owes much to an unreflective identification of Israel with Protestantism, and Judah, with its inviolable monarchy, centralized authority, and high liturgy, with Roman Catholicism" (1985, 203–4 n. 21).

8. Würthwein adds that this is only true of the deuteronomistic historian's tendentious portrait of the king, since it is implausible that the historical Jeroboam would have stated his fears so openly to anyone. Würthwein apparently assumes that Jeroboam is speaking "out loud" to others in these verses. To whom, Würthwein asks, would Jeroboam have presented his fears so openly (1985, 162)? However, as discussed below, many commentators believe that vv. 26–27 put "words into Jeroboam's mind that must have been close to actuality" (De Vries 1985, 162; cf. Talmon 1958, 50). Toews (1993, 35) points to Jeroboam thinking of the people turning again "to their lord" Rehoboam and comments, "surely Jeroboam would not have thought in this way, and no patriotic author from the Israelite State would have presented him in this way."

9. In a book which employs biblical stories as a tool in psychotherapy and counseling, Schwartz and Kaplan cite Jeroboam as a character "undone by ambition," claiming that his "new nonbiblical religion was initiated solely to support his own ambition for power." They judge Jeroboam to be guilty of "arrogance" and "moral weakness" (2004, 155–56).

10. Carasik (2000, 229) interprets the narrator as having Jeroboam secretly reason "that the ritual connection to Jerusalem will make his own partial usurpation of the Davidic kingship untenable… [N]arratively 1 Kgs 13:1–6 confront[s] Jeroboam in public with the illegitimacy that he had acknowledged in his private thoughts." In the context of 1 Kgs 11–12, however, it is difficult to imagine Jeroboam considering himself to be illegitimate when Yahweh has just granted him kingship through the prophet Ahijah and told him that his "usurpation" is actually divine punishment for Solomon's apostasy.

history writer wanted to show the reader that this challenge was illegitimate, *for* it was based on political interests and selfish motives: by
making the calves Jeroboam *only* wanted to protect his own life and his
new kingdom" (2002, 88; emphasis added). In this reading, the root
cause of Jeroboam's sin is his character, as it is revealed through his
actions, or, more precisely, as he appears when one attributes to the king
the character trait of selfishness in order to explain his actions.[11] From
that perspective, Jeroboam's character becomes his destiny.

A number of other scholars go even further, judging Jeroboam to
be self-willed, self-serving, ungrateful, recalcitrant, and obdurate. For
some, he is the possessor of a "wayward heart," characterized by "inner
insecurity" and an "inability to trust."[12] Many interpret Jeroboam's concern for his safety as indicating fear,[13] a fear which to some "rings
hollow" (Cohn 1985, 30) or "hardly ring[s] true" (Walsh 1996, 172).
According to Pakkala, Jeroboam's fear indicates that "an editor wanted
to give the impression that Jeroboam was…a coward, a significant insult
in any Semitic culture" (2008, 504).

Others have a totally opposite impression of the king, viewing him as
a "truly religious" monarch who acted with "commendable," "inborn"
piety (Danelius 1967, 102),[14] and whose "original nature" as a "second
Moses" emerges "despite…hostile curtaining" by "Davidic historiogra-
phers" (Zakovitch 1991, 87, 97). Many commentators believe that when
Jeroboam made his calves and installed them in Bethel and Dan, he did
so "with the best and most sincere of intentions and commendable
piety."[15] Whether they condemn the king or condone his behavior,

11. Pakkala leaves one key factor unmentioned: by protecting his life and the
kingdom, Jeroboam is acting in a way which helps to fulfill Yahweh's intentions for
the new king, as reported to him by Ahijah. Pakkala calls the Ahijah passage a
"prophetic legend" (2002, 87), but he does not take into account this part of the
narrative when he assesses the character or situation of Jeroboam in the final edition,
represented by the MT. See further in n. 29 below.

12. Cohn 1985, 31; Provan 1995, 109; Fretheim 1999, 75; Walsh 1996, 172–73;
cf. Knoppers (1994, 64) on Jeroboam's character in 1 Kgs 13.

13. Walsh 1996, 172; Fretheim 1999, 75; Cohn 1985, 30; Toews 1993, 35;
Schwartz and Kaplan 2004, 156.

14. Danelius (1967, 102) leans heavily on Jewish midrashic traditions in her
"proof" of Jeroboam's religious motives.

15. Morgenstern 1948, 485; cf. De Vries 1985, 162; Jenks 1977, 103. Aaron has
also been said to have had "good intentions" when he made his calf (Janzen 1990,
605). That explains why he "could declare in all sincerity, after making the image,
that the next day would be a 'festival to the Lord'" (Sarna 1986, 217). Even the
people who had demanded "a god" from Aaron "intended nothing more than an
appropriate object emblematic of the divine presence" (Sarna 1986, 217).

however, scholars often leave it unclear whether they are referring to the historical Jeroboam, the king as he is depicted in the various individual strata of the text which they have isolated,[16] or the king as he is portrayed in the text as it stands, taken as an organic whole.

I would suggest that the condemnations of Jeroboam's character are examples of our tendency to over-attribute dispositional traits and underestimate others' situational constraints. It is not surprising that commentators tend to emphasize character attribution here, since they are led to do so by the narrator's and the prophet Ahijah's indictments of the king.

Suleiman (1983, 183–84) points out that in modern ideological narrative "the events and characters' various functions...are redundant with the interpretive commentary made about them by an omniscient narrator...or by a 'correct interpreter' within the story." If the commentary "precedes (i.e. announces) the event, then the latter confirms the commentary and constitutes a 'proof' of its validity"; if the commentary follows the event or happens simultaneously, then "the commentary 'fixes' the events' meaning by eliminating other interpretations." In the Jeroboam narrative the blanket condemnations by the narrator and the "correct interpreter" Ahijah would seem to resist being "fixed," because they are in tension with the positive information about the king's character both have offered in chs. 11–12.[17] On the other hand, the "negativity

16.   There is wide agreement that 1 Kgs 12:26–28, if not most of 1 Kgs 1–14, is a polemic written from a Judean or "sarcastic Jerusalemite point of view" (Toews 1993, 37), in line with the standards set in Deuteronomy. There is also a substantial consensus that the polemic contains anachronistic and unhistorical elements, such as the notion that Deuteronom[ist]ic cult reform standards would have been known and operative in the tenth century, particularly those involving the magnetic attraction of Jerusalem as the only site at which to worship Yahweh in fully developed pilgrimage festivals. Also cited as anachronistic is the idea that Jeroboam's worship of Yahweh through calf images was innovative and syncretistic; see, e.g., Horn and McCarter 1999, 134; Cogan 2000, 361–62; P. Ash 1998, 24; Hoffmann 1980, 64; Ahlström 1993, 554. The view that Jeroboam's thoughts are represented in unhistorical fashion is also common, as noted above.

17.   Knoppers (1994, 7, 15) argues that the presentation of Jeroboam is entirely positive before 1 Kgs 12:26–32 and entirely negative thereafter. He does not consider how the information provided in the first half of the story will affect readers when they encounter the negative reports later, in spite of the fact that most readers do read stories holistically, if not harmonistically. For empirical studies of the reading process, see Chapter 9, below. According to Amit (2006, 77), the Deuteronomistic author/editor could not ignore that events mingled good and evil, and dealt with that fact by separating reigns into good and evil periods. She cites Jeroboam as someone who fails from the start, arguing that the author makes no attempt to show a process of development or enter into the king's personal life. Instead, all actions

bias" leads people—including readers—to judge an individual's total character negatively on the basis of one negative report, in spite of having been acquainted with a good deal of positive information about that individual.[18] The negativity bias would act as a catalyst in the process described by Suleiman, so that, in this instance, the concluding commentaries by Ahijah and the narrator in 1 Kgs 13–14 "fix" the meanings of Jeroboam's actions, eliminating all other interpretations, at least for readers who do not resist this bias.

The fact that the narrator of 1 Kgs 11–12 also reports other information about Jeroboam's position and personal history indicates a more complex situation with less obvious implications about his character. The narrator describes the future king as the son of a widow[19] who became a man of worth or power (גבור חיל), an industrious young man את־הנער (כי־עשה) מלאכה who was promoted to a position of authority by Solomon on the basis of merit (1 Kgs 11:28). Even though he was put in charge of the "burden" (סבל; 11:28)[20] of labor for the Joseph tribes, he is well-liked enough among those workers to be chosen by them to be their king instead of Rehoboam (1 Kgs 12:20).[21] Most importantly, he is chosen by Yahweh to rule the new Northern Kingdom, which means that the "rebellion" he leads is in accord with Yahweh's plan to punish the house of David.[22] Finally, elements in his early life associate him with the

are evaluated by a strict regulatory code. However, this still leaves the question whether all the information reported by the narrator in 1 Kgs 11–14 is chosen according to the same "regulatory code" as the narrator's explicit blanket condemnations.

18.  On the negativity bias, see Chapter 9, §2, below.

19.  In the Hebrew Bible, widows who have not remarried and who are not said to be supported by their family or clan, are often described as being among the poorest and most vulnerable people in the society (see, e.g., Exod 22:21; Deut 14:29; 24:17, 18; 1 Kgs 17:17–24; 2 Kgs 4:1–7; Job 24:3; 31:16). For another talented and successful son of a widow (Hiram the bronzeworker), see 1 Kgs 7:13–14.

20.  Because the term employed here is סבל and not מס (the term used in 1 Kgs 5:27; 9:21), many commentators conclude that this "burden" refers to temporary portage work, probably conducted by members of the northern tribes; see, e.g., Mulder 1998, 584–85.

21.  Würthwein (1985,163) argues that it is unjustifiable to take Jeroboam's quoted thoughts as historical, since, as a proponent of the people's will to freedom from exploitation by the Davidic dynasty, he is not a usurper who needs to fear that his people will turn against him.

22.  Many redaction critics view the Ahijah pericope as interrupting or replacing an original account of Jeroboam's rebellion (e.g. Mulder 1998, 580–81; G. Jones 1984, 232). Some view it as a "typical prophetic legend" (Sweeney 2007b, 160). In the present text, however, this section presents a full and adequate account of the reasons for Jeroboam's actions, when viewed together with the earlier rejection of

Moses who fled from the tyrannical Pharaoh (in this case, Pharaoh-like Solomon)[23] and the David who, according to Abner, has the opportunity to rule over all that his heart desires.[24] These scenes also dissociate Jeroboam from the rejected king Saul, for whom the tearing of a prophet's[25] robe symbolizes the loss of a kingdom, not the acquisition of a new kingdom.[26]

As for Jeroboam being concerned with his survival, suffice it to say that it would be quite difficult for him to function in the capacity in which Yahweh had placed him if he were assassinated. That leaves the accusation that Jeroboam lacks trust that God's promise for his kingship would protect him, apparently without any effort on his part. By this standard, biblical leaders like Abraham, Moses, Joshua, and David would all have to be characterized as distrustful. It is worth noting that four of the other figures I discuss in this book (Moses, Elijah, Zedekiah, and David) *also* read their situations as implying they might be killed at one point or another, and none of *these* is condemned by exegetes for basing their course of action on what Cohn (1985, 30) and Brueggemann (2000, 160) both call Jeroboam's "pragmatic" concerns.[27]

The Jeroboam of 1 Kgs 12 has good "pragmatic" reason to doubt both the people's continuing loyalty and Yahweh's continuing favor, especially if one takes into account the lessons about mass psychology and leadership raised by the intertextual links with both Exod 32 and the Saul narrative.[28] Thus, to the extent that Jeroboam's motives *do* appear

Solomon by Yahweh and the Israelites' rejection of Rehoboam for threatening to increase the oppressions which his father had inflicted upon them.

23. 1 Kgs 11:40; cf. Exod 2:15; 4:19.

24. 1 Kgs 11:37; cf. 2 Sam 3:21. As Leuchter (2006, 52) puts it, "Jeroboam is introduced as a charismatic and industrious leader" in the mold of young David. As Solomon promotes Jeroboam, so had Saul promoted David. Moreover, "the covenant pronounced by Ahijah…essentially mirrors those pronounced by Nathan in 2 Samuel 7." In other words, "Jeroboam, the anti-David in the Deuteronomistic universe, is initially presented in a Davidic mold."

25. A minority (e.g. Cogan 2000, 339) hold that it is Jeroboam's new robe which is torn.

26. For Nelson (1987, 71) the positive information in 1 Kgs 11:26, 28 "lures" readers into positively identifying with Jeroboam, adding that readers "naturally" identify with Jeroboam here. Nelson seems to be using "identify" in the weak sense of "view positively." On the strong sense of the term, and how some authors prompt readers to identify with a character and then "break the spell of identification," see Chapter 9, §5 and §8, below.

27. For Moses, see Exod 17:4; for Elijah, see 1 Kgs 19:2–3, 10, 14; for Zedekiah, see Jer 38:19; for David, see 1 Sam 21:10–12; 23:26; cf. 30:6.

28. On the parallels between Saul and Jeroboam, see section 1b, below.

reasonable—given the situation sketched in the narrative—there is cause to qualify Boshoff's claim that the polemical depiction of Jeroboam as wicked king *par excellence* is successful (2000, 26).[29] The fact that the final redactors left intact the positive notices and intertextual allusions in 1 Kgs 11 would also seem to reduce the effectiveness of 1 Kgs 11–12 as a tendentious portrait of a king whose character and intentions are fundamentally and exclusively evil.[30]

As I mentioned in Chapter 3, social psychologists point out that people seek situations that will "push" them in the same direction as do their own dispositions, so that "situations are largely of one's own making." 1 Kings 11–14 raises the question whether Yahweh put Jeroboam into a no-win situation of *Yahweh's* own making. After all, how could the new Northern king establish a viable independent state with the necessary royal sanctuaries within its borders without breaking the laws of centralization announced in Deuteronomy?[31] If Solomon put his father's enemy Shimei in a position where he would in effect commit suicide by leaving Jerusalem and crossing the Kidron to retrieve his runaway slaves (1 Kgs 2:36–46), Deuteronomy–Kings implies that Yahweh puts Jeroboam in a

29.   Pakkala implies that the polemic is unsuccessful in the sense that the final form leads "many readers" and "some scholars" to be "misguided" about the original idea conveyed by the story (2002, 88). Pakkala contends that for the first "history writer," Jeroboam's sin primarily involved the location of his cult; this writer had no "major interest in the calves as such" (2002, 89). For the history writer, the problem was Jeroboam's desire to provide the people with an alternative to the Jerusalem temple, not apostasy from Yahweh. It was the "nomistic" and other late editors who held Jeroboam guilty of apostasy and took *that* as the main reason for the destruction (2002, 87–88). For Pakkala, a "misguided" interpretation results from giving too much weight to the nomistic editors' perspective, even though he believes that "the main idea" of the passage was *not* "disturbed" by them (2002, 86). However, the fact remains that "many readers"—if not most—focus on the ideas expressed in the text as it stands, rather than searching for the writer's "original idea." Pakkala underestimates the rhetorical power of the present text, particularly in terms of the messages conveyed by the intertextual links between 1 Kgs 11–12, the Moses and Saul narratives, and the nexus comprised by Exod 32–Judg 18–1 Kgs 12.

30.   Other strategies employed by the narrator tend to inhibit reader sympathy for the king's plight. For example, the narrator includes no response from Jeroboam or his wife after the doom oracle of Ahijah in 1 Kgs 14, let alone a response which could be construed as penitent, in the way that Yahweh construes Ahab's response to Elijah's condemnation as penitent in 1 Kgs 21:29. Similarly, in 1 Kgs 13 we are not even informed whether Jeroboam learns all the details concerning the fate of the man of God from Judah to which readers are privy, let alone how Jeroboam might have reacted to that news if he were informed of it.

31.   Cf. Würthwein 1985, 163; Cogan 2000, 363; Hoffmann 1980, 64; Ahlström 1993, 550–55.

position where he has to commit a kind of "ritual suicide" by transgressing ritual laws in order to keep his people from crossing the southern border and returning to Jerusalem. Put differently, while it is indeed possible to argue that the Jeroboam of 1 Kgs 11–12 has good intentions, one can do so only if one is willing to question the intentions of the character Yahweh.

Jeroboam's situation doesn't merely trump his character after he is made king by Ahijah, and then again by his people. It makes his character *irrelevant*, since he is heavily constrained to act as he does in order to fulfill the mission given to him by Yahweh. The reports beginning with 1 Kgs 12:26 do not show readers Jeroboam's "true" character, or imply that his character has changed from what it had been earlier. Rather, the new information shows that the new king has an accurate view of the situation into which Yahweh has placed him. In terms of the demands of his role as an ancient Near Eastern monarch and the double-bind position into which he has been placed, Jeroboam's actions are sagacious. However, in terms of the historically unrealistic[32] standards of royal behavior by which the king is evaluated by the narrator and Ahijah, the king's response is deplorable and destructive, especially when the story is read together with its parallel in Exod 32 (see Lasine 1992, 133–35, 143–45).

b. *Redaction and Coherence in 1 Kings 11–14*
Redaction critics have attempted to explain perceived discordances in the MT of 1 Kgs 11–14 in a variety of ways. Scholars like Van Seters (2000, 214–16; 1983, 313–14) and Knoppers (1994, 250, 253) contend that the themes of centralization and idolatry are both part of the Deuteronomistic history. For van Seters, the post-Deuteronomistic component is the emphasis on Jeroboam's altars in 1 Kgs 12:33–13:33. For Pakkala (2002, 87), the characterization of Jeroboam's sin as idolatry is the product of the "nomistic...post history writer editors," not the earlier "history writer" who stresses the violation of cult centralization and who, unlike the later nomistic editors, views Jeroboam's sin as the main reason for the destruction of the Northern Kingdom.[33] Whether we are convinced by

32.   That is, standards which any educated audience familiar with ancient Near Eastern royal practice would deem unrealistic, not just modern readers who recognize the anachronistic nature of the polemic.

33.   Like many other scholars, Pakkala (2002, 88) believes that "the Deuteronomistic history writer did not accuse Jeroboam of apostasy from Yahweh... the history writer regarded Jeroboam's cult as that of Yahweh." The main offense of the passage is revealed by the strongly Jerusalemite perspective: Jeroboam poses a serious challenge to Jerusalem and its temple. The nomists clearly show less interest in the temple than does the history writer.

any of these arguments or prefer one of the scenarios mentioned earlier,[34] if we then conclude that our task is complete, we are implying that the present form of 1 Kgs 11–14 is an unintegrated combination of competing authorial interests and ideologies.

Approaching the present text as a coherent integral unit, as readers naturally attempt to do when they encounter a new text, requires taking seriously the features which are positive to Jeroboam. Even scholars who take these elements as evidence that there was an originally laudatory Northern version of Jeroboam's reign must ask why a final editor who was antipathic to Jeroboam did not demonize the king. After all, Manasseh is demonized in 2 Kgs 21 by listing only Manasseh's evil acts, omitting any positive information about him, and providing no basis for readers to identify with, and perhaps sympathize with, him (see Lasine 1993, 163–65, 173–77). While the authors of Kings did not employ this strategy with Jeroboam, the Chronicler does tend to make Jeroboam a "flat" villain who did not "retain strength" (עצר כח) after losing territory to Judah, and who died after being struck by Yahweh (2 Chr 13:19–20).[35]

The fact that positive information on Jeroboam is present in the MT of Kings implies that the king is *not* being "lampooned" and "satirized as a cartoon villain" (Hayes 2004, 92).[36] If he *is* being satirized, we must ask what kind of satire this might be. Is the king being lampooned in the way that Jon Stewart's *Daily Show* reported on "Barack Hussein Obama" during the 2008 American Presidential campaign, calling Obama an elitist follower of a fanatical Christian preacher and, at the same time, an Arab Moslem who "pals around with domestic terrorists"? This kind of satire relies on the audience knowing full well that these statements are both self-contradictory and ridiculous, and that the target of the satire is not the show's intended audience but those who take these absurd allegations as gospel truth. If the supposed satire in 1 Kgs 12 were of this kind, it would imply a reading audience capable of noting the variety of

---

34. See Knoppers (1994) for a review of scholarly speculation concerning pro- and anti-Judean and pro-Shechem and anti-Bethel elements in the narrative.

35. One might also ask why the final redactors left the identity of Jeroboam's root sin unspecified, if they could do so in a way which supported their interests and ideology. The fact that several condemned actions coexist and interact in the final text indicates that Jeroboam's religious failure is more of a "sindrome," a cluster of interrelated elements, than it is a matter of labeling one of a number of possible sins as the essential transgression, which is then dubbed Jeroboam's "original sin."

36. This is how Hayes characterizes the conclusions I reached in my earlier paper on the golden calf narratives (Lasine 1992). Knoppers (1994, 37) claims that the "mode" of 1 Kgs 12:26–33 is "caricature"; this caricature "portrays Jeroboam's *cultus* as a sham."

seemingly conflicting information about Jeroboam's character in 1 Kgs 11–14, and realizing that the narrator is "winking" at them, letting them know that he knows that they know that the king wasn't "really" that foolish, even if they accepted the judgment that the king's behavior resulted in eventual catastrophe for the nation. If this were the case, it means that the complex present form of 1 Kgs 11–14 exhibits an effective rhetorical design targeted for a sophisticated audience capable of recognizing its ironic elements[37]—and perhaps also capable of recognizing that Jeroboam's apparently out-of-character actions in ch. 12 are caused by the exigencies of his situation, not by his character.

However, 1 Kgs 12 could be misrepresenting Jeroboam in a very different way, namely, the way in which Rupert Murdoch's Fox News Network claims to report Obama's activities reliably in a "fair and balanced" fashion. In this case, blatant and shameless lies are cynically designed to be taken flatly as truth by a very different target audience. If *this* is the kind of critique directed against Jeroboam in 1 Kgs 12, the audience envisioned by the authors would be as stupid as the Fox viewers who fervently believe that Obama is in fact a dangerous Moslem Arab terrorist-lover. Our analysis of Kings suggests that the Jeroboam narratives were *not* produced for the Fox Network.

In the last analysis, 1 Kgs 11–14 implies that it is the king's God-created situation which renders his personal character irrelevant to his fate. To this extent, the king's position reinforces the parallel with Saul established by the robe-tearing symbolism. Saul and Jeroboam are the only founders[38] of a new "kingdom of Israel." In both cases, the king's character is overwhelmed by the constraints of the situations into which God has placed him.[39] While Saul is "turned"[40] into "another man" with

37. For more on the sophisticated target audience of the Jeroboam narratives, see Lasine 1992, 137–39.

38. P. Ash (1998, 17) contends that "Jeroboam became the *Unheilsherrscher* because of the Deuteronomist's…ideological notion that the fate of a kingdom or dynasty was determined by the behavior of its founder."

39. Saul is in an impossible situation in two senses: Samuel functions as Saul's anointer and introducer, if not mentor, but Samuel harbors *ressentiment* at being rejected as leader in favor of a king, and does what he can to undermine Saul's position and make the people feel guilty for requesting a king in the first place. Later Yahweh puts Saul in a situation that could drive anyone crazy, by anointing a second "sole ruler" (mon-arch) when the first is still on the throne, a second king who is more self-confident, charismatic, and is moved by the kind of spirit which Yahweh has removed from Saul and replaced with an evil spirit. One might also argue that God initially put Saul in an untenable position because of Saul's diffidence, and perhaps the low self-image which Samuel attributes to Saul in 1 Sam 15:17.

40. The verb in both verses is הפך: ויהפך־לו אלהים לב אחר ... ונהפכת לאיש אחר.

"another heart" by Yahweh (1 Sam 10:6, 9) after he is anointed, there is no evidence that Jeroboam's character underwent a radical change when he was drafted into kingship, whether caused by divine influence or the corrupting influence of royal power.[41] If Jeroboam was an industrious גבור חיל before, he remains one; the fact that he has good reason to fear assassination by the Israelites implies that his personality has not suddenly sprouted traits such as timorousness, cynicism, and insecurity, or that he has been revealed to be a habitually distrustful person. Rather, it shows that Jeroboam had no need to consult advance copies of Thucydides, Le Bon, or Freud to understand the potential fickleness of people in groups and their tendency to scapegoat their leaders.[42] It was sufficient that the king was intimately familiar with the biblical treatise on the dangers of mass psychology in Exodus–Numbers, or at least the key chapter, Exod 32.

According to scholars like Noll, all of 1–2 Kings is a "baroque... cacophony of dissonant sound,...utterly resistant to a coherent sequential reading."[43] To Noll's generalization we must reply: if it ain't baroque, don't fix it. That is, there is no reason to dismantle and reconstruct pieces of a text on the grounds that it is psychologically or narratively incoherent if the text is not in fact incoherent—or even if ordinary readers do not *perceive it as* incoherent thanks to the effectiveness of its rhetorical design. Our analyses of Jeroboam and other characters in Samuel and Kings indicate that the conceptual chaos in these books is not as complete as Noll would have it, depending, of course, on how we choose to define "coherence." It remains to be seen whether further evidence of such psychological and narrative coherence can be found in the biblical reports concerning kings like Jehoram and Ahab.

## 2. *Being Sane in Insane Places:*
### *Evaluating Jehoram's Character in Besieged Samaria*

Assessing King Jehoram's behavior in the story of the cannibal mothers (2 Kgs 6:24–33) presents an unusual challenge, due to the bizarre situation in which the king finds himself. As I discussed in my previous essay on this episode (Lasine 1991), readers of the exilic and post-exilic periods

---

41.  If Saul becomes another man by divine action, redaction critics talk about Jeroboam as though he became a man with a different character after both Yahweh and the people gift him with the new kingdom.

42.  On the views of Thucydides, Le Bon, and Freud concerning mass psychology, see Lasine 1992, 151 n. 16.

43.  Noll 2007b, 344, 342; see further in Chapter 3, above.

would not be totally surprised by the thought of parental cannibalism, which is threatened, or reported to have occurred, during sieges reported in five other books of the Hebrew Bible, and which is one of the curses mentioned in eighth- and seventh-century Assyrian treaties. At the same time, this story includes some unique elements which are surprising even in the biblical context. Foremost among these is the complainant's callousness and her utter obliviousness to the fact that she has committed an abominable crime. When she approaches the king her sole concern is with the injustice she believes she has suffered because the other woman reneged on an agreement. She states all this publicly and even acts as though she assumes the king will share her view of the situation. Her inattentiveness to the way others might view her deed shows that she lacks the public emotion of shame, which makes possible orderly social relations (see Gilmore 1982, 198; Gouldner 1965, 85–86).

In order to evaluate the king's response to the mother's plea we must first seek to understand his nightmarish and highly "constraining" situation. Accounts of parental and social cannibalism in the Hebrew Bible and Assyrian treaties indicate that this behavior serves as the most violent symbol of a society characterized by lack of trust, disruption of family ties, and advancement at others' expense (Lasine 1991, 29–37). Ancient Greek sources describe cannibalism during siege, ritual cannibalism, and maternal cannibalism as a divine punishment.[44] Reference to social cannibalism can be found as early as the eighth century, when Hesiod implies that humans would eat each other if Zeus had not given them law and justice (*Works and Days* 276–79). In the modern European world, cannibalism was rampant in besieged Leningrad during World War II (M. Jones 2008, 4–5, 215–19, 242–44). Some of the women who were tried for eating parts of their husbands or children "openly admitted" their actions. Of course, the vast majority of mothers did not resort to such acts, in spite of their dreadful plight.

While scholars like Shemesh (2008, 6 n. 13) believe that 2 Kgs 6 does not condemn the mothers for eating their children,[45] I will argue that the

---

44. For example, Thucydides (2.70) reports cases of cannibalism caused by starvation during the siege of Potidaea. Suggestions of ritual cannibalism accompany some accounts of Dionysiac *omophagia* (see Dodds 1960, xviii–xix, xxvi, 224); for more evidence on cannibalism in ancient Greece and modern tribal societies, see Lasine 1991, 34–35.

45. Brueggemann (2000, 356) claims that the statement of the cannibal mother "reflects the kind of desperate concern for survival in the Jewish death camps, wherein for some the aim of survival overrode all that might be called moral." This analogy is inappropriate, if not downright offensive. Besides the obvious fact that these were *Nazi* death camps, not "Jewish" ones, Brueggemann makes innocent

story invites readers to condemn the mothers, the God who put them into this horrific situation, *and* the prophet who had to be pushed by Jehoram to intervene on the victims' behalf. King Jehoram, on the other hand, is presented sympathetically in this extreme situation, as well as in other reports of his interaction with Elisha, the man of God who is consistently ill-disposed toward the king. In terms of the ethics of reading, those who identify with the desperate ruler of besieged Samaria will be led to question a divine justice devoid of maternal compassion which punishes the guilty by inverting human nature itself.

a. *Is Jehoram Acting Sane in an Insane Place?*
This section title alludes to psychologist David Rosenhan's controversial study of diagnostic labeling in mental institutions. As both he and his critics are aware, even medical staff can make attribution errors when evaluating the interplay between situation and disposition among patients. Rosenhan and his other "pseudopatients" claimed that they had had hallucinations and were admitted. Once inside, they acted "normal" but were nevertheless labeled as schizophrenics in remission, in almost all cases. Leaving aside the flaws in Rosenhan's experimental design, the fundamental question is clear: What constitutes sane behavior in an insane environment—in our case, the besieged Samaria in which maternal cannibalism takes place?[46] Rosenhan's critics argue that the experiment did not adequately take into account the fact that it is *not* normal for a normal person to act "normal" if he or she finds themselves institutionalized, leading to a debate about what would constitute normal behavior for sane people in such a situation.[47]

victims in the camps (both Jewish *and* non-Jewish) analogous to a woman who eats her own child and acts self-righteous about it. He offers no examples of camp inmates murdering and eating one another, including their own children; nor does he offer any other specific examples of camp behavior which "overrode *all* that was moral." If Brueggemann had compared the mothers at Leningrad who ate their children during the Nazi siege to the women of 2 Kgs 6, he would have been able to acknowledge that these cannibal mothers are *both* victims *and* perpetrators of a heinous crime.

46.	Films from *Love Crazy* (1941) to *Le roi de Coeur* (1966) and *One Flew over the Cuckoo's Nest* (1975) also deal with the theme of being labeled "incorrectly" in an insane environment where the staff has strong expectations and assumptions. In his response to his critics, Rosenhan (1975, 472) mentions a different film, Frederick Wiseman's disturbing and long-banned 1967 documentary called *Titicut Follies*, about conditions in a Massachusetts state mental hospital.

47.	See, e.g., Millon 1975, 457; Rosenhan 1975, 471–72; cf. Weiner 1975, 435–36.

The "insane" setting of 2 Kgs 6:24–33 is a starving besieged city. Should readers of 2 Kgs 6 envision the situation of Jehoram and the complainant mother in a "realistic" fashion, as though the Samaria of 2 Kgs 6 were modern Leningrad? Should we condemn their behavior *without* taking into account their extreme situation? It is unlikely that this tale of cannibalism is present simply to indicate the fulfillment of a treaty curse. Both the cannibalism curse in Deut 28:53–57 and the story in 2 Kgs 6:24–33 are embellished with vivid detail and reports of human behavior, much more than required if these were merely formulaic notices of curse fulfillment. Moses had also predicted insanity as one of the curses; individuals will be driven mad by the sights they will see (Deut 28:34; cf. v. 28). Is Jehoram on the verge of madness from what he has seen and heard in 2 Kgs 6?

Against this background, the question is whether Jehoram's reaction to the cannibal mother's request is actually expectable and logical, rather than a sign of dispositional flaws like distrust in God, weakness, or inherited evil from his mother Jezebel, as Provan (1995, 200–201) implies. Given that Jehoram knows the miraculous power Elisha is capable of wielding, and the fact that Elisha has apparently done nothing to alleviate the present situation, is it really surprising that Jehoram holds the prophet responsible and wishes for his death? Does *he* view the cannibalism as the fulfillment of a treaty curse? Of course, if one has already labeled Jehoram an apostate, idolater, or evil scion of Jezebel, as do some commentators, one would be predisposed to view his angry call for Elisha's death to be caused by the king's depraved character. Readers who make this judgment will be less likely to sympathize and identify with his situation, and less apt to consider that Jehoram might view his situation in the same way that they themselves might have done, aware as they are of the announced curses for disloyalty to Yahweh.

If the king is indeed motivated by a sense of social responsibility, can one conclude that the story is constructed so that readers will identify with the king at this point and sympathize with his response, even if they do not agree with it? Is Jehoram attempting to enact the role of the just king, as Solomon is assumed to have done in the case of the harlot mothers? According to Würthwein (1984, 311–12), the king's sackcloth indicates that he has attempted to elicit God's help. Würthwein asks how the king could have made a judicial decision in a case such as this; a gesture of horrified agitation could be his only answer. He concludes that the king is depicted sympathetically, insofar as he is presented as contrite. Similarly, Bergen (1999, 137) argues that the king's confessional reply to the mother "opens the possibility of the king as a sympathetic figure."[48] Other commentators stress how seriously the king takes his role as the representative or embodiment of the people (e.g. J. Gray 1970, 523; G. Jones 1984, 433), although they may point out that the king's desperate commitment to this role leads to attempted murder (e.g. Nelson 1987, 189). Rofé (1988a, 65) believes that the king is "an ideal figure in comparison with the people," even if he seems flawed and weak when compared to the prophet." According to Hobbs (1985, 74–75), while Jehoram is presented as "something of a fool" and "excited babbler" in the first part of 2 Kgs 6, in our story he "emerges…as a man of sympathy who wears mourning dress (v. 29)," and whose anger at Elisha is "understandable." Finally, Fretheim (1999, 159) concludes that the king's "remorse" is "probably sincere" from the fact that Jehoram's sackcloth was inadvertently revealed.[49]

Other scholars are much more suspicious about Jehoram's character and motives. Some claim that the story shows the king's faithlessness or lack of sincerity (J. Robinson 1976, 65; Šanda 1912: 55). Provan views the king's anger at Elisha as "arrogant" (1995, 185). LaBarbera also condemns the king, not so much for lack of faith, insincerity or humility as for lack of power and wisdom. He contends that the story has the function of ridiculing the king by showing that he is ineffective and that his "wisdom is non-existent" (1984, 647). Put simply, LaBarbera's charge is that the story condemns the king for not being Solomon, whose godlike judicial wisdom is (on the one occasion we hear about) supremely effective.

Reading 2 Kgs 6:24–33 in light of Solomon's judgment highlights the predicament of the king in besieged Samaria.[50] Solomon was able to demonstrate that a judge with godlike wisdom can use his knowledge of maternal nature to reveal the truth in a difficult case by exposing the true

48.  Bergen (1999, 139) contends that within the world of the story the people "esteem" Jehoram for his private suffering before Yahweh and that "for readers, the king is viewed briefly through the eyes of his adoring subjects." However, nothing in the story indicates that the people esteemed or adored the king. All we know is that one woman, a cannibal, vainly sought the king's judicial intervention. Focalization, which would allow us to see the king "through the eyes" of his subjects, is not employed in the story.

49.  We might ask why Fretheim reads the king's mourning clothing as indicating "remorse" rather than empathy or compassion—and why he would question the king's "sincerity" in the first place. On the ways in which commentators have judged Mephibosheth's mourning apparel and sincerity in 2 Sam 19, see Lasine 1989b.

50.  See Lasine 1989a for a detailed comparison between 1 Kgs 3:16–28 and 2 Kgs 6:24–33. Pyper (1993, 25–30) takes issue with my interpretation of the intertextual linkages between these two narratives. For my response to Pyper's arguments, see Lasine 1993.

characters of the disputants, or at least that one cannot hide the truth of one's acts and thoughts from this fear-inspiring panoptic king. Taken at face value, the judgment story carries the comforting message that human nature is stable and predictable. In contrast, the king in Samaria is approached by a woman whose behavior turns upside down all expectations concerning maternal nature. Far from exposing the mother's nature, the king can only expose the sackcloth he wears under his clothes, revealing that he has been in a state of constant mourning for his people. His despair is entirely appropriate. The fact that he proceeds to order Elisha's execution might seem to be anything but appropriate. According to G. Jones (1984, 433), the king's antagonism toward Elisha is "out of character with the rest of the narrative, which does not mention king's lack of faith in God."[51]

I would argue that the king's lethal vow does *not* signal a change in his character when it is viewed in terms of his previous relations with Elisha. We are introduced to this king in 2 Kgs 3, when Jehoram heads a "coalition of the willing" in putting down the rebellious vassal, Mesha of Moab. As in 1 Kgs 22, Jehoshaphat of Judah and his army contribute to the war effort led by the king of Israel. This suggests a parallel between Ahab in the earlier narrative and his son Jehoram in 2 Kgs 3. However, the parallel is in part contrastive; it is not simply a case of "like father, like son." For one thing, here the conflict is not initiated by the Israelite king. In 1 Kgs 22 Jehoram's father Ahab had headed a military expedition to recover territory earlier lost to a rival power; here the Moabite king responds to Ahab's death in that expedition by taking military action, "rebelling" against his vassalage to Israel (2 Kgs 3:5).

For another thing, the narrator himself points out a key difference between father and son in relation to religious practice. The narrator's mixed assessments of Jehoram in 2 Kgs 3:2–3 can be read in many ways.[52] Verse 2 does not exclude the possibility that Jehoram is unlike his parents in ways besides having removed the Baal pillar.[53] Jehoram

---

51. Referring to vv. 27 and 33 of 2 Kgs 6, Nelson writes that the "character of the king's faith resembles what the narrator has already presented in 3:13. He does not doubt God's power so much as God's good will" (1987, 188). On whether Jehoram has good reason to doubt God's good will toward him, see below.

52. Long obscures this fact by attributing to the narrator the unmixed contempt for Jehoram which is actually expressed only by Elisha. It is Elisha, not the narrator, who "hints" that "Jehoram's purposes have within them some vestige of father and mother" (1991, 43).

53. Is רק in 2 Kgs 3:2 drawing attention to the extenuation which follows? If so, it contrasts with the appearance of רק in 1 Kgs 3:2, which is followed by the negative news that Solomon's people sacrificed in the high places.

never shows signs of worshipping other gods than Yahweh,[54] and is never criticized by Elisha for worship of alien deities *or* for ministering to Jeroboam's calf cult. Readers who view Jeroboam as a king who is constrained by an impossible political situation might hesitate to assess Jehoram's character negatively simply on the grounds that he did not abolish the calf sin (v. 3).[55]

These considerations have not prevented many commentators from adopting Elisha's unrelievedly negative view of Jehoram, calling the king a self-pitying "idolater" and selfish "apostate" who followed in his parent's evil footsteps and may have even consulted their pagan prophets.[56] In addition, the king is often criticized for not consulting Yahweh immediately concerning the upcoming battle against Moab.[57] However, the "good" Judean king Jehoshaphat does not say anything about doing this either, until *after* the expedition is underway and experiencing difficulties. Jehoram then assumes that God is punishing them (v. 10). Significantly, Jehoram's framework for understanding his situation is entirely in terms of Yahweh as author of the circumstances, not any alien god.[58] In 1 Kgs 22 Jehoshaphat had wanted to consult a prophet of

54.  This is conceded by Montgomery and Gehman (1951, 360), who nevertheless view Jehoram as having "defected from Yahweh." Is their judgment influenced by Elisha's view of Jehoram? This seems to be the case with Provan's and Long's views of Jehoram in this scene; see nn. 58 and 60 below.

55.  After all, the narrator had earlier claimed that Ahab was worse than Jeroboam (1 Kgs 16:30–33), and inappropriately "pagan" means of worshipping Yahweh is not an issue in the Ahab narratives. And for readers who are already familiar with 2 Kgs 9–10, the fact that Jehu is rewarded in spite of leaving Jeroboam's calves intact might further discount the importance of 2 Kgs 3:3 as an indicator of Jehoram's bad character.

56.  Krummacher (1870, 77, 244) calls Jehoram a selfish and despicable "apostate" and Hobbs (1985, 36) refers to the king's "apostate character."

57.  E.g. G. Jones (1984, 395), who, on the basis of Elisha's negative view of the king, suggests that Jehoram may have already consulted the prophets of his parents before setting out on his campaign; contrast Fretheim 1999, 142.

58.  Provan (1995, 182) questions "how seriously we are meant to take" Jehoram's recognition of "the Lord's hand in what has happened," since these words issue from "the lips of an idolater." The only way Provan could have reached this judgment is by uncritically adopting Elisha's attitude, since 2 Kgs 3–9 do *not* show Jehoram to be an "idolater." Provan then further diminishes Jehoram by claiming that "his is certainly not a 'faith' that leads to pious behavior," apparently forgetting that the same could be said of the faith of many "positive" biblical characters, most dramatically, King David. In contrast, Nelson (1987, 166) affirms the logic of Jehoram's reading of Yahweh's intentions here, noting that "in light of 1 Kgs 22, the reader knows that [God bringing out Israel to defeat them] is not an unlikely scenario." Nevertheless, Nelson considers Jehoram's "brand of faith" to be "pecu-

Yahweh before going to battle. In 2 Kgs 3 neither king is said to consider this possibility, leaving the silence to be interpreted in several possible ways. Only after Jehoram voices his interpretation of Yahweh wanting their defeat does Jehoshaphat suggest that a prophet be consulted. This scene does show readers an ongoing trait of Jehoram's character, which is consistently displayed later when he feels defeated or at a loss and a prophet proves to be the solution for the king's problem. In 2 Kgs 6:31, 33 Jehoram himself assumes that Elisha is the solution and condemns the man of God for having done nothing to help. Jehoram is consistently depicted as easily panicked and depressed, impulsive in jumping to conclusions,[59] and consistently in need of rescue or at least good advice.

All this is qualitatively different from the behavior of a monarch who is consistently apostate and evil.[60] Readers may therefore be surprised when Elisha begins by telling Jehoram to consult the prophets of his parents Ahab and Jezebel (2 Kgs 3:13), especially since we have been told that Jehoram dismantled a Baal pillar. Jehoram responds by denying this charge and repeats his pessimistic assessment that Yahweh has doomed the expedition. To this Elisha responds by extending his previous insult to Jehoram, saying that he would not even look at Jehoram if Jehoshaphat were not there (v. 14). Jehoram then recedes into the background until ch. 5.[61] The impressions of Jehoram's character which readers may take away from 2 Kgs 3 will depend in large part on whether they adopt Elisha's unequivocally negative judgments of the king or heed the narrator's mixed assessment which is reflected in the king's reported behavior in this chapter.

Clearly, Jehoram is consistently presented as a king who, while not very perceptive or intelligent, is at least aware of the limitations of his

---

liar." Long trivializes Jehoram's lament in v. 10 by dismissing it as a case of "self-pity" which shows the king at his "most lame." For Long, this is part of a narratorial strategy designed to "deny sympathy to Jehoram" (Long 1991, 41, 43, 47).

59.  Just as Jehoram incorrectly assumes that the cannibal mother is going to ask him for food and wine in ch. 6, in 5:7 he wrongly assumes that the Aramean king is seeking an occasion against him. Later, he responds to the lepers' report of the abandoned enemy camp by wrongly assuming that it is part of an enemy trap (7:12).

60.  Long (1991, 41) also criticizes Jehoram because it is a servant who suggests Elisha to Jehoshaphat (v. 11). However, the verse leaves open the possibility that *neither* king knew that Elisha was present with the army; it is not the norm for prophets to travel to war, as commentators often remind us. In contrast to Ahab in 1 Kgs 22, Jehoram has no objection to consulting this prophet of Yahweh. Even the king of Edom goes along to consult Elisha!

61.  This does not prevent commentators like Hobbs (1985, 34, 38) from blaming Jehoram for the odd, less than complete, conclusion of this battle in 2 Kgs 3:27.

power, and as a person who is saved by the power of Elisha.[62] Within ch. 6 Elisha has helped Jehoram against the king of Aram (vv. 9–10) and afflicted enemy soldiers with blindness (v. 18). The king shows his dependence on and respect for Elisha after the latter miracle by asking the prophet (whom he calls "my father") whether he should smite the soldiers (v. 21).

Elisha has already demonstrated that he can invoke divine power to help the king. In 2 Kgs 5:6 Jehoram receives a letter from the king of Aram asking him to cure the leprous Naaman. The king responds to the letter in the same way that he responds to the petition of the cannibal mother. In both cases he tears his clothes and despairs because he is not God and therefore does not have the power to help (5:7; 6:27, 30).[63] In ch. 5 Elisha sends to the king asking him why he has torn his clothes and telling the king to send Naaman to him, so he will know that there is a prophet[64] in Israel (v. 8). Thus, Elisha himself leads Jehoram to expect that the prophet can end the king's predicament through the use of God's power.[65]

This is precisely the situation in 2 Kgs 6:24–33. The king begins by declaring that only Yahweh can help and then curses the man of God, whom he has every reason to believe *could* help.[66] According to

62.   The story in ch. 3 follows the same basic pattern as chs. 5–7: the king despairs because he feels powerless in a crisis and Elisha is presented as the solution to the problem (3:10–12).

63.   After the initial response, the situations do differ. In 1 Kgs 5 the king's problem is that he fails to recognize that Elisha can help, while in ch. 6 his problem centers on his recognition that Elisha could help but has failed to do so. If Jehoram is a vassal of the Aramean king in the Naaman story, as asserted by Pitard (1987, 124), readers may be invited to compare Jehoram's reaction to the Aramean king's letter with Ahab's earlier reaction to a request made by his Aramean overlord in 1 Kgs 20. In the earlier story, the request was clearly unreasonable and Ahab's response should be viewed as laudable (see Chapter 7, below). Readers who view the two stories together might therefore have an extra incentive to sympathize with the vassal Jehoram's perplexity over a request which he has reason to view as unreasonable or provocative.

64.   Interestingly, Elisha does *not* say "that there is a *God* in Israel," even though Jehoram had just asked "Am I *God*, to kill and make alive?" (5:7). In contrast, Elijah promotes both Yahweh and himself on Mt. Carmel (1 Kgs 18:36). On Elisha's habit of self-promotion, see Lasine forthcoming.

65.   For a detailed analysis of Elisha's characterization in the Naaman narrative, see Lasine 2011b, 9–15, 23–25.

66.   Contrast Stinespring's comment on 6:31: "For some unknown reason, the king blamed Elisha, although in vv. 8–23 king and prophet were on the best of terms" (in May and Metzger 1977, 463; emphasis added). See Schweizer 1974, 316, for similar remarks by other commentators.

Josephus, Jehoram's initial wrath is due to the fact that Elisha did not ask God to give them a way out (*Ant.* 9.67). This interpretation is supported by Jehoram's final statement at Elisha's door, to the effect that the evil is from Yahweh and that there is no longer any reason to wait for Yahweh's intervention (6:33), apparently because everything is already so topsy-turvy that it is too late for help. Josephus interprets the king's statement as indicating that he has repented of his wrath against the prophet, but is still reproaching Elisha for not having asked God for deliverance and "for looking on so indifferently while they were being destroyed" (*Ant.* 9.70). Indeed, it is only after the king's confrontation with Elisha in 6:33 that the prophet takes action, predicting an end to the siege and famine (7:1). Insofar as the king responds to perceived disorder and violence with urgency rather than simply looking on with indifference, he resembles biblical heroes like Moses and Job[67] more than his father Ahab.

b. *Yahweh's Character and the Ethics of Reading 2 Kings 6:24–33*
According to Geertz, humans cannot deal with chaos, "a tumult of events which lack not just interpretations but interpretability" (1973, 99–100). Chaos threatens when we are at the limits of our analytic capacities, our endurance, and our sense of intractable ethical paradox. Hanson (1987, 488–91) has analyzed the ways in which these three human vulnerabilities—bafflement, suffering and ethical paradox—are registered in biblical texts written in the wake of the fall of Jerusalem and the destruction of the Temple. Hanson notes that while apocalyptic and millenarian tendencies might have been expected among oppressed peasants in the early postexilic situation, the ruling elite also exhibited this response to the recent calamity, a calamity which shook the fundamental conceptual foundations which had sustained the society (1987, 492). In the same way, 2 Kgs 6:24–33 expresses a sense of bafflement over ethical paradoxes stemming from a recognition that the society's fundamental conception of human nature may be inadequate, and that what makes it inadequate is Yahweh's readiness to turn human nature upside-down.

This view does not require that the story was composed in response to a social crisis precipitated by an actual famine in besieged Samaria around 850 B.C.E., analogous to the crisis following the later siege and fall of Jerusalem. Evidence for such an event at that time is lacking.[68]

67. Ironically, in one rabbinic tradition it is Job who is charged with indifference to the violence inflicted on innocent sufferers. As one of Pharaoh's counselors when the Israelites were oppressed in Egypt, Job remained silent, justifying the suffering which he himself later undergoes in the Bible (e.g. *b. Sanh.* 109a).

68. "Kuenen was the first to state the obvious: 'In the reign of that king [Jehoram], Israel was not in the condition described to us in 2 Kgs 6:24–7.26' [*sic:*

Nor can one simply assume that the narrative contains "historical remi-niscences"[69] of siege cannibalism for which an exact date cannot be determined. Similarly, one cannot assume that it was composed after the fall of Jerusalem and retrojected to a time and place distant enough to allow contemplation of a painful crisis, as Greek tragedies dealt with recent military and social disasters by depicting them as having occurred in distant times and places.[70] The fact that cannibalism and other world-upside down[71] metaphors are used to express violent social distrust and rivalry at various points of biblical history implies that a social break-down capable of shaking the foundations of a culture's reality-concept can occur during any period of social stress, without the catalyst of a famine or a military disaster.

Another aspect of the biblical reality-concept concerns motherly love. 2 Kings 6:24–33 undermines ordinary assumptions about human nature by showing that one cannot rely on mothers to act with compassion or jealousy. Maternal nature becomes unpredictable—and therefore baf-fling—when God allows people to turn things upside-down, or when he turns things upside-down for them as a punishment. In Isa 49:15 Yahweh asks, "Can a woman forget her sucking child, that she should not have compassion (מרחם) on the son of her womb?" He then answers, "Yes, these may forget, yet I will not forget thee." The poet of Lam 4:10 makes it clear that even mothers who are "full of compassion (רחמניות)" can boil and eat their children during a famine caused by siege, not just mothers like the complainant of 2 Kgs 6, who has no compassion what-soever for her son and no remorse for her deed.

However, both Lam 4 and 2 Kgs 6 can be viewed as calling into question the nature of God as well as the nature of the mothers. They suggest that God too can "forget" his motherly[72] compassion for his

read 20]" (Cogan and Tadmor 1988, 84). Like many other commentators (e.g. G. Jones 1984, 430–32), Cogan and Tadmor believe that "a siege of Samaria of the proportions described…is hard to imagine before the reign of Jehu" (1988, 84).

69. MacLean 1962b, 972; Ottosson 1974, 238; cf. Whitelam 1979, 182–83.

70. Thus, while Sophocles' *Oedipus Tyrannus* takes place in pre-Trojan War Thebes, the play's characters, setting, and plot reflect conditions in Athens follow-ing the great plague of 430–429 B.C.E. This tendency to view contemporary problems obliquely is also illustrated by Herodotus's story about audience response to Phrynichus's play on the loss of Miletus (*Hist.* 6.20). After the audience burst into tears, the author was fined a thousand drachmae for reminding them of this painful disaster, and a law was passed forbidding anyone from putting the play on the stage again.

71. On this *topos*, see Lasine 1991, 35–40.

72. On the metaphorical connections between רחם ("womb") and God's רחמים ("compassion"), see Trible 1978, 31–59.

children in spite of his declaration in Isa 49:15. This impression is reinforced by the earlier mention of maternal cannibalism in Lam 2:20, which occurs near the end of a moving account of the results of Yahweh's retribution. The poet repeatedly states that this retribution was administered without pity (לא חמל; 2:2, 17, 21; cf. 3:43).[73] Mintz (1984, 31) asserts that the passage actually makes "God responsible for cannibalism as well as for priest and prophet murder." In 2 Kgs 6:24–33, Jehoram's reaction to cannibalism among Yahweh's people expresses both his bafflement and his awareness of ethical paradox. His response implies that he believes in a compassionate God who could turn things right side up again, although, paradoxically, he and his agent Elisha have not chosen to react with compassion.

If one is to draw any final conclusion about audience response to this pericope, one must consider not only the baffling problems with which it is concerned but the way in which its narrative rhetoric raises the issue of the ethics of reading. Are readers being led to condemn Jehoram as well as the cannibal mother and to accept Elisha's passivity and God's mode of punishment? Or is the audience to affirm Jehoram's desperate response and to question Elisha's behavior, if not his character? Is the audience also being invited to question the fairness of divine punishment, in spite of the fact that the DtrH is generally assumed to reflect prophetic interests, to be theologically opposed to the northern kings, and to be based on a schema of divine retribution? The king acts as the audience's surrogate in the story, prompting readers to witness the narrated events from his perspective and to share his helplessness.[74] Whether readers choose to identify with the king or to condemn him, the story as a whole challenges its audience to acknowledge that God can not only turn creation back into chaos, but turn creation upside-down with all its structure intact, in a way that is even more threatening because it is still

---

73. Similarly, Isaiah's description of a society in which no man spares or pities (לא יחמלו) his brother and every one eats the other's flesh (9:18–19) is preceded by the declaration that Yahweh will not have compassion (לא ירחם) even on the orphans and widows among the people (9:16).

74. When readers make ethical judgments about characters they do so in their capacity as members of the "narrative audience," which pretends to believe in the existence of the people and events about which the narrator is speaking (Rabinowitz 1977, 127–29). According to Rabinowitz's "rules of snap moral judgment" (1987, 84–93), readers begin by assuming that physical appearance reveals character, and judge fictional personages by the way those personages judge other characters in the story. By these standards, Jehoram's exposed sackcloth undergarment and his implied judgment of the cannibal mother would lead the narrative audience to judge him favorably.

"orderly," although the order is now perverse and uncanny. The complainant, whose crime was so perverse, proceeds to play by the rules of the old right-side-up world by presenting her grievance according to judicial custom.[75] The king, on the other hand, refuses to play along, responding instead to the woman's inhumanity.

The king's response to Elisha suggests that the prophet's position may be inhumane in another sense. If a prophet "sees the world with the eyes of God" (Heschel 1969, 212), human moral agents cannot afford to "see as God sees" (Job 10:4) when such sight implies indifference to those suffering down on earth (see Lasine 1988, 30–37). A number of biblical passages imply that humans must intervene with urgency, like the prophet Moses and the prophet-like Job,[76] when their fellows are hunting and devouring one another and their children. 2 Kings 3–7 demonstrates that Jehoram views Elisha as a human being with unlimited power from God. If he views God as a deity who feels maternal compassion for his children, it is easy to understand why Jehoram would have expected Elisha to intervene immediately to set things right, and why he would have held the man of God responsible for allowing heinous crimes to occur, crimes so contrary to human nature that neither he nor any other just king could "solve" them.

75. As Cogan and Tadmor put it (1988, 79), "the proceedings follow formal rules of address"; cf. 2 Kgs 6:26 and 2 Sam 14:4–5. Whitelam (1979, 182) also notes the appearance of "formal judicial language" in the passage. He discusses the story as though it were an incomplete account of a legal case which may or may not be historical (1979, 183).

76. Exod 2:11–12 (cf. Isa 59:15–16) and Job 24:1–12; 29:17. See Lasine 1988, 36–37, 47.

Chapter 7

# KINGS WICKED AND WEAK: THE CHARACTERIZATION OF AHAB IN COMPARATIVE PERSPECTIVE

## 1. *Introduction: Flat Statements About Round Characters*

Ahab is "the epitome of Israel's sin," a "paradigm" of the bad king, and the arch idolater.[1] In the Naboth affair, he is not only a vicious, ruthless tyrant, but a weakling whose wife views him as such.[2] He is incapable of resisting his queen's machinations; to her, he is not "man enough."[3] He is a weak "hen-pecked husband" who has been "emasculated" and "depraved" by his "sexy, seductive" Baal-worshipping wife.[4] He lacks "moral fiber," and in his dealings with Ben Hadad he is an "international weakling."[5]

So say the vast majority of commentators. Rarely have so many flat statements been made about such a round character. There *are* dissenting voices, although fewer than is normally the case with important biblical personages. Yeivin (1979, 139) contends that the stories "reflect

1. Brenneman 2000, 95; cf. Patrick and Scult 1990, 69; Horn and McCarter 1999, 141; Waldman 1988, 41.
2. Uffenheimer 1999, 326, 337; Rofé 1988b, 91; De Vries 1985, 257. On Ahab as weak and lacking in moral fiber, also see Simon 1997, 199; Waldman 1988, 44, 47 and *b. Sanh.* 39b. According to Brichto (1992, 278 n. 19) Ahab also displays "whimsicality" in this episode, wanting Naboth's vineyard only to "convert it into a…pleasure park…for royalty's ease."
3. Uffenheimer 1999, 396, 412; cf. Brenneman 2000, 90. Uffenheimer (1999, 396–97) goes so far as to charge that Ahab is not "man enough" to confess his sin to Elijah "as David did to Nathan." However, David, the rich man in Nathan's parable, is *not* "man enough" to confess his sins *until* he has been directly identified as "the man" by Nathan *and* heard the list of curses that are in store for him because of those sins (see further in Chapter 9, §6, below).
4. Appler 2000, 30; 1999, 60; Holt 1995, 96. Holt seems to view Ahab's weakness vis-à-vis Jezebel through the lens of Rev 2:20.
5. U. Simon 1997, 199; Miller and Hayes 1986, 252, 262; cf. Pitard 1987, 116.

a positive image of Ahab as a wise ruler and a man of agreeable disposition."[6] In 1 Kgs 20, Brichto finds Ahab to be a "brave and capable"
warrior who displays selflessness matched by concern for his subjects,
"manly firmness," "regal restraint," generosity, mercy, forgiveness, and
peaceableness (1992, 170, 174, 179). Uffenheimer (1999, 322) praises
"Ahab's calm, firm behavior" and "cool and calculated moderation," as
well as his role as a hero, leading his people to war. And for Avigad
(1993, 1303), Ahab possessed "the vision of a great builder."

In this chapter I will examine these judgments of Ahab by comparing
the way he is presented in 1 Kgs 16–22 with Herodotus's *logoi* concerning Periander and Homer's portrayal of Agamemnon. Periander has also
been described as an "archetypal tyrant," "bloodthirsty, suspicious,
without feeling…[or] a single redeeming feature in his character" (Ferrill
1978, 396; Pearson 1954, 142).[7] For these interpreters, he is set "in the
worst possible light" (Andrewes 1956, 45). And like Ahab, Homer's
Agamemnon has been called weak, vacillating, easily depressed and at
times deluded, as well as often anxious and unfair.[8] Other commentators
view Agamemnon as both weak *and* wicked. For them, he is "a selfish,
craven, ignoble, contemptible villain" (Basett, in Griffin 1980, 73 n. 41)
or "a nasty piece of work" who "behaves like a rat" (Taplin 1990, 65).[9]

---

6. At the same time, Yeivin concedes that Ahab was probably weak in relation to
Jezebel.

7. In Andrewes's formulation, Periander "was execrated by posterity as the type
of the wicked tyrant" (1956, 43; cf. 51). Aristotle notes that Periander is said to have
instituted many of the measures whereby tyrants ensured their safety (*Pol.* 1313a36-
b32); for a discussion of these measures, see Lasine 2001, 100–101. Plato's Socrates
attributes to Periander (or "some other rich person who thought he had great power")
the saying that it is just to benefit friends and harm enemies (*Resp.* 336a). Romm
contends that Herodotus is working with "the Asian autocrat," a character type
which is "clearly fixed by tradition"; however, Romm also notes the "remarkable"
*differences* in the ways in which these autocrats "wield power or subdue their
enemies" (1998, 158; cf. V. Gray 1996, 364).

8. Redfield 1975, 93; Griffin and Hammond 1998, 67. Others view him as
stumbling helplessly "against his own limits" (Whitman 1965, 161–62) or suffering
from "a profound personal insecurity" (Donlan 1971, 111; cf. N. Greenberg 1993,
198). Whitman believes that this weakness "win[s] him some measure of compassion"; Homer, whose "sense of character is always profound," has created in
Agamemnon "a consummate masterpiece" who functions as "the opposite of
Achilleus, the nadir of the heroic assumption" (1965, 162).

9. Similarly, Kirk (1985, 56) remarks that his threats against Chryses are "typical
of Agamemnon at his nastiest." Whitman (1965, 162–63) describes him as a
"magnificently dressed incompetence" whose prowess is marred "by a savagery
which is the product of a deep uncertainty and fear."

If a minority of commentators view the biblical Ahab positively, the same is true in respect to Periander and Agamemnon. Herodotus includes a number of Periander's positive actions in various portions of his history. Even Aristotle concedes that Periander was moderate in some respects; he "raised no taxes,...was neither unjust nor insolent, [and] hated wickedness."[10] And Jaeger (1965, 226–27) concludes that Periander, one of the "seven wise men" of Hellas in some traditions, is undoubtedly "the greatest of the tyrants" in Greece. Similarly, Edmund Spenser contends that Homer "ensampled the good governour" in the person of Agamemnon (quoted in Taplin 1990, 81). Much earlier, Philostratus's *revenant* Protesilaos says that "Agamemnon was experienced in the arts of war,...inferior to none...in combat, and fulfilled all the duties of a king; ...was persuaded by whatever insight someone else had,...[and] looked majestic" (*On Heroes* 29.1–2; Maclean and Aitken 2002, 46). Even Redfield tempers his sharp criticisms of Homer's Agamemnon by adding that he is not a "bad man"; he is devoted to his brother Menelaos and displays considerable personal courage. Redfield concludes that Agamemnon's problem is that "he occupies a social role which is too big for him" (1975, 93). In other words, his character is unable to cope with the constraints of his situation as king.

Redfield is not the only modern commentator who acknowledges both positive *and* negative aspects in one of these rulers. In the cases of Ahab and Periander, perceived discordances are sometimes explained by referring to information about their achievements known from other sources. For Ahab, the most startling silence concerns the king's major role in the coalition which opposed the forces of Shalmaneser III at Qarqar in 853 B.C.E., according to the Assyrian king's so-called Monolith Inscription (*ANET* 279). In addition, there exists ample archaeological evidence of ambitious building projects during Ahab's reign (see, e.g., Ahlström, 1993, 582–85). In his regnal summary for Ahab, the narrator of Kings merely hints at such achievements by referring readers to the unknown book of the chronicles of the kings of Israel for "the rest of the acts of Ahab, and all that he did, and the ivory house which he built, and all the cities that he built" (1 Kgs 22:39). Similarly, Herodotus makes no mention of Periander building the Peloponnese's largest temple, an artificial harbor, or the *diolkos* built to transport vessels across the isthmus (see Salmon 1984, 134, 136–37; 1997, 66).[11]

---

10.   Aristotle, fragment F611.20; Dillon and Garland 1994, 39.

11.   Lavelle (1994, n.p.) notes that even though Periander's "depravity" was part of a hostile tradition, a cenotaph remained in Corinth apparently through the Classical period, marking his grave there.

Other commentators suggest that some of the unflattering stories reflect later opinion or did not originally refer to these kings at all;[12] some conclude that the stories are legendary or mythical rather than historically reliable.[13] Brichto (1992, 181–82) finds the positive and negative information about Ahab to be irreconcilable in terms of unity of character. His solution is that 1 Kgs 20 and 22, which present a positive picture of Ahab, are concerned with prophetic activity, not historical precision about Ahab (1992, 168, 184–85). In a similar manner, Pearson (1954, 142) explains Herodotus's seemingly inconsistent characterization of Periander by asserting that popular opinion, prejudice, and gossip have no regard for consistency in characterization; he is disappointed that Herodotus could not go further than "what people are saying" in his historical setting. And while Salmon agrees that the ambiguous tradition concerning Periander means that conflicting views were held of him during his lifetime,[14] he suggests that the description of Periander as warlike may rely more on what was believed of the typical tyrant than on what was known about the historical Periander (1984, 198, 222).

Seemingly contradictory behavior on the part of characters like Homer's Agamemnon is sometimes explained as a pathology, such as "manic depression" or paranoia.[15] We have found the same to be true of

12.  For example, many scholars conclude that the depiction of a weak Israel and defeated Ahab implied by 1 Kgs 20 and 22 do "not fit the period or personage of Ahab" (Pitard 1987, 119). They believe that these reports originally referred to events during the later reign of Jehoahaz (e.g. Miller 1966, 442) or Joash (e.g. Pitard 1987, 124). Similarly, Salmon (1997, 62) believes that "the baggage of later interpretation" has led to overly negative assessments of Periander's rule. He finds it to be "most unlikely that favourable stories about tyrants were invented."

13.  For example, Sourvinou-Inwood (1991, 283 n. 123) concludes that the story of Periander and his son Lycophron (*Hist.* 3.48, 50–53) is composed of mythical schemata and has no historical kernel at all (contrast Boedeker 2002, 114). Salmon (1984, 198) finds Herodotus's stories concerning Periander to have "a variety of probable origins," but "it is doubtful whether all the stories are to be rejected." On the Arion story, see the sources cited by Harrison (2000, 76 n. 35). Aly (1929, 93) contends that "up to the end of the Samian stories, only the great Periander-*Novelle* [the Lycophron tale] drops out of history... Whenever Herodotus deals with Periander he is a genuine *logopoios*."

14.  According to Hart, "*every* piece of information about Periander is a logos, a popular tale of the type that tends to attach itself to powerful personalities of the moderately recent past" (quoted in V. Gray 1996, 362 n. 3; emphasis added).

15.  Griffin (1980, 72 n. 39) notes Gundert's reference to "the inner insecurity" of Agamemnon's nature, adding that this is "much nearer the truth" than the view of Kirk, who speaks of "veering attitudes to Agamemnon, who is presented now as a great and admirable leader, now as a manic depressive" (Kirk 1962, 265). Zanker (1994, 6) points to Agamemnon's speech when his brother Menelaos is wounded,

scholarly opinion concerning the biblical prophet Elijah. Homeric scholars also employ another strategy we have encountered when biblicists explain the inconsistent behavior of characters like Elijah as the result of editorial splicing of sources from different traditions and times. For example, because the speech Agamemnon delivers when his brother is wounded combines self-confident and defeatist moods, many nineteenth-century scholars cut out one of the moods to restore simplicity (*Il.* 4.155–82; see Griffin 1980, 71–72). While redaction history, textual corruption, and ideological imperatives are all used to explain perceived incoherence, these maneuvers are once again based on *psychological* judgments about what constitutes realistically consistent behavior, whether this is acknowledged by the commentator or not.

Is Ahab really a "flat" or "stock" character who can be dismissed as a "type" or adequately pegged with a label such as "wicked" or "weak"? If so, why would the biblical authors give mixed signals about a king who is so strenuously condemned by the seemingly reliable narrator? To answer this question, we must first ask whether it is possible to show a character in action, quote his speech, and still convincingly portray that person as a totally flat villain. Suleiman (1983, 206–7) cites cases in which a strongly negative character "comes alive before our eyes." She notes that the narrative is "obliged to report" the character's words in order to condemn them. But "if it reports them…with sufficient detail and precision…these words can acquire an authentic tone that will counteract the condemnation they are supposed to provoke."[16]

So should the author of an ideological narrative "play it safe" by consistently portraying a negative character as a one-dimensional, consistently evil villain? Suleiman (1983, 194) believes that this strategy is likely to fail. She points out that readers may "rebel…against a meaning whose communication is all too clear," that is, when a narrative is "excessively" redundant and therefore too predictable. Allowing a few contradictory voices into a *roman à these* "leave[s] certain openings open. Paradoxically, it may be these very openings that make a reader 'swallow' the thesis" (1983, 183).

noting that it "vividly characterizes the manic-depressive ruler." Donlan believes that Agamemnon is "frightened and insecure" throughout Book 2, and "begins to display the paranoid tendencies that mark his character" (1971, 111; cf. 112).

16.   On the other hand, if the narrative "makes no explicit affirmations but lets its truths 'speak for itself' it leaves the door open to misunderstanding" (Suleiman, 1983, 223–24). Somehow the author of an ideological narrative must steer clear of these two extremes in order to succeed in propounding the intended message. On readers who identify with negative characters and resist the narrative rhetoric designed to condemn them, see Chapter 9, §5 below.

In short, allowing a supposedly wicked character to speak and be viewed in contradictory ways could *either* lead readers to conclude that the character is too complex or sympathetic to be scorned as a cardboard villain *or* make readers rely on, if not "swallow," the narrator's wholly negative appraisal of that character. What does 1 Kgs 16–22 lead us to conclude about the biblical Ahab?

## 2. *Ahab and Periander as Wicked:*
### *Character, Situation, and Context*

To answer this question we must look at the larger context of the Ahab narratives. Readers of the Hebrew Bible and Herodotus are invited to evaluate the conduct of kings according to standards set forth elsewhere within the work. In the Bible, these include speeches given by Moses in Deut 17:14–20 and Samuel in 1 Sam 8:11–17. In Herodotus, speeches delivered by the Persian Otanes and the Corinthian Socles help to form what Dewald calls "the despotic template" (2003, 28). Such texts create expectations in readers.[17] While Moses and Samuel focus solely on actions, Otanes discusses the monarch's actions *and* his disposition. The king will turn upside down ancestral customs, rape women, and kill men without trial. His defining character traits are *hubris* and envy. Otanes' emphasis is actually on the king's situation rather than his disposition. He claims that one could take the best man on earth and put him into the position of monarch, and he would have thoughts unlike his normal ones, and presumably end up acting in this manner.

---

17. Moses' speech is simple and straightforward: the king *is not* to have any intercourse with Egypt or multiply wealth, horses, or wives "for himself," and he *is* to make a copy of the law for himself to consult for guidance. In contrast, Samuel describes the king as a quintessential "taker" who will force citizens to work for him, will take their land and ten per cent of their income, and ultimately make them his servants. After hearing Samuel's harangue readers are prepared for the first king, Saul, to exhibit all the covetous behavior Samuel has outlined. But he does not. It is the next two kings who do so, particularly Solomon, both before and after Yahweh has blessed him with incomparable wisdom. Solomon fits the template even better than Ahab, not only in terms of his actions as king but in the *way* that his story is told. The narrator "says too much" about Solomon's opulence and too little about opposition to his policies. Moreover, there is too little access to his feelings, interactions with others, and appearance for him to "come alive" (see Lasine 2001, 127–40). Thus, in context, Samuel's speech raises the question whether biblical narrators set up stereotypes only to show them to be inadequate to the realities of human behavior. For more on the speeches by Moses, Samuel, and Otanes and their relation to biblical kingship, see Lasine 2001, 148–51.

Plato's brother Glaucon makes a similar claim about tyranny in the *Republic* (359b). Glaucon proposes to give the power of invisibility to both a just and an unjust man, so that they can commit the misdeeds of a tyrant with impunity. They would both end up acting the same, says Glaucon. In other words, the situation would be more powerful than their basic character. As Seaford (2003, 97) points out, the defining traits of a tyrant "are not just defects of character but instruments of power." To that extent, the tyrant's situation calls for him to act impiously, distrustfully and greedily in order to maintain his position. While Dewald claims that "in personality the autocrat is full of hubris and envy," she too implies that Socles' approach is fundamentally situationist as well: "It is *not* an intrinsically evil personality that makes the tyrant and the tyrannical family bad… [S]omething in the nature of autocratic imperialism prevents despots from taking seriously their own fallibility and mortality and also the real dynamics motivating others" (2003, 29, 30–31, 35). Elsewhere I have argued that this "something" is not merely a function of the structure of "autocratic imperialism," but the structure of leaders' narcissistic personalities and their situations "on the ground" as well (Lasine 2001, 1–28).

Moses' speech assumes that it *is* possible for a king to avoid *hubris* by following the dictates of the *torah*, while Samuel's self-serving diatribe against kingship in 1 Sam 8 is similar in perspective to the views of Herodotus's Otanes. In fact, if the biblical stories of David and Solomon had been available to the Otanes depicted by Herodotus, we might expect him to jump at the opportunity to use their careers to prove his point.

Socles' long speech employs a different strategy. Although he begins with a general indictment of monarchy, accusing it of turning the world upside-down through injustice and violence, he quickly moves to a series of specific anecdotes about Cypselus and his son Periander, not all of which seem to illustrate his assertions. Not surprisingly, scholars have found this tactic "puzzling." After all, by describing Periander's actions, quoting his words, and reporting his emotions, Herodotus has previously risked the danger of "saying too much" and making Periander "come alive," in Suleiman's sense. In addition, many commentators on Herodotus believe that if Socles' purpose is to condemn tyranny "he has made a mess of it,"[18] by including anecdotes about Periander's father Cypselus which might lead his listeners to identify with the tyrant.

---

18. This is Johnson's description of the majority view. Romm (1998, 122) points out that Socles does not make the kind of logical or theoretical argument against tyranny that Otanes did. Socles bypasses the most historically relevant facts about the tyranny, focusing instead on the necrophilia.

D. Johnson (2001, 3) notes that scholars tend to employ three[19] strategies to explain the puzzling aspects of Socles' speech: detecting conflicting sources or traditions, detecting the ways in which Herodotus's
presumed ideological stance on tyranny has affected his telling of the
story, and attempting to determine how the speech has been tailored
for Herodotus's own target audience. All of these procedures are analogous to techniques employed by biblical scholars who are dealing with
puzzling inconsistencies Johnson himself employs what he calls a
"contextual" approach, seeking first to determine the functions of the
stories in their present context before having recourse to these other
strategies—in essence, the same approach I have adopted throughout this
book in relation to the portrayal of character. Johnson concludes that
Socles' most pressing goal is to offer "an emotionally powerful [but
indirect] account which will goad the allies into acting on their preexist-
ing beliefs about tyranny" (2001, 6). I would add that Herodotus's
inclusion of Periander's actions, words, and emotions is one reason why
the speech is so "emotionally powerful."

Do the words and actions of Ahab and Periander conform to the
patterns of monarchical and tyrannical behavior etched in these tem-
plates?[20] At first glance, it would seem that both *do* act according to type:

19.  Moles (2007, 245–46) has discovered no fewer than nine different categories
of scholarly response to this speech. Pelling (2006, 107) points to another cause of
puzzlement, namely, that Socles talks only of the "internal impact of a tyrant," while
the Spartans' point was the "external threat of Athens to other states, including
Corinth." And if Herodotus's own audience knows that Athens later oppresses
Corinth as a result of Corinth remaining non-tyrannical, this would cast doubt on
Socles' wisdom, especially because it is the tyrant Hippias who correctly understands
the oracles which predicted that terrible things would be done by the Athenians
against the Lacedaemonians, only to have his warnings ignored in favor of Socles'
rhetoric (*Hist.* 5.90–94).

20.  Dewald believes that, on the whole, Herodotus's anecdotes about Periander
are not structured around the traits that Otanes uses to define a despotic ruler (2003,
43; contrast Forsdyke 2002, 544; Seaford 2003, 96–98). Otanes lists unaccount-
ability as a tyrannical trait, but in a sense Periander's son Lycophron does hold his
father to account. Overturning established ancestral customs and forcing women
would seem to be illustrated by Periander's necrophilia with his wife's corpse
and his stripping of the Corinthian women. However, I have already noted more
positive interpretations of the latter act. If Herodotus wanted to depict Periander
as an archetypal tyrant-villain he could also have gone into more detail about his
killing of Melissa. In fact, Melissa's ghost does not complain about being killed by
her husband or about the necrophilia; her grievance is that she lacks clothing.
Periander himself represents his wife's death as a misfortune (συμφορά), made
greater only by his own responsibility (*Hist.* 3.52.4; see Harrison 2000, 52 n. 54).

Ahab and Jezebel kill a man and his sons to gain his property and Jezebel attempts to cut off prophets of Yahweh, while Periander follows a fellow-tyrant's advice to cut down his most prominent citizens and has the women of Corinth take off their finest clothes in public to burn for his dead wife—after having killed her and slept with her corpse. And because the biblical authors and Herodotus omit or downplay some of the greatest achievements of these kings, they seem even more typically tyrannical.

At the same time, the book of 1 Kings shows Ahab being docile and obedient with Elijah, standing up to an unreasonable Aramean overlord, leading his men to victory in battle, and apparently repenting after being condemned to death. Similarly, Herodotus introduces and ends his reports on Periander with stories about his loyalty to a very close guest-friend[21] and acknowledges that Periander was invited to act as mediator in an international dispute.[22] In addition, he is shown exercising judicial wisdom[23] and displaying patience and compassion toward a rebellious son.[24] Even Periander's stripping women of their clothes to offer to his

Some later traditions portray his killing of Melissa as accidental (or based on his being misled by concubines' false testimony against his wife). Admittedly, other traditions accuse Periander of an act of *flagitia*, committing incest with his mother Krateia (see Parthenius, in Lightfoot 1999, 341–43; cf. Diogenes Laertius 1.96). Still other sources describe the incest as the final result of a deception perpetrated by his sexually abusive mother. As for the tyrannical habit of executing men without trial, Herodotus's Periander did *not* convict and execute Arion until he had a chance to hear both sides of the story. Finally, in the example of Periander wanting to castrate the boys, Herodotus informs us that the king's motive is vengeance for what the narrator calls an act of reckless folly against him by the Corcyreans (*Hist.* 3.50).

21. This guest-friend is Thrasybulus, despot of Miletus; *Hist.* 1.20; cf. 5.92.

22. Herodotus reports that Periander was chosen as the political arbiter between the Mytileneans and the Athenians, and succeeded in this role (*Hist.* 5.95).

23. I am referring to Periander's relations with the great musician Arion, who is forced to jump overboard from a ship whose crew wants to steal his wealth. Arion is miraculously saved and transported to Corinth by a dolphin (*Hist.* 1.23–24). Periander does not believe Arion's incredible story and holds him under guard. However, rather than executing the musician, the king waits until the sailors accused by Arion arrive and tests them by inquiry (ἱστορέεσθαι; see V. Gray 2001, 14–16), thereby displaying royal wisdom. In other words, he withholds a decision until both parties are heard from, unlike David in his haphazard handling of the Mephi-bosheth/Ziba dispute (2 Sam 16:1–3; 19:24–30; see Lasine 1989b). The fact that Periander holds Arion under guard rather than having him killed also recalls Ahab holding Micaiah under guard rather than having him killed for his hated (and not necessarily truthful) oracles (1 Kgs 22:26–28).

24. Periander's son Lycophron is told by his maternal grandfather that Periander had killed Lycophon's mother Melissa. Lycophron then refuses to talk to his father,

dead wife, and his "lopping heads," have been viewed as metaphorical (or even literal) ways of referring to actions by the tyrant which can be interpreted favorably, namely, his enactment of sumptuary laws (Aristotle F611.20) and his measures to ensure equality by cutting off the power of the unpopular elite (see Salmon 1997, 60, 63, 65).[25]

In the case of Ahab, it is the Naboth's vineyard story which, more than any other, leads readers to view the king as wicked and/or weak.[26] Yet, as noted by Walsh (1996, 321), the conversation between Ahab and Jezebel suggests complex relationships between the royal couple. This implies that there are depths in the character of Ahab which go beyond what is reported in Kings. The same possibility is suggested when the king later asks Micaiah, "How many times have I made you swear to speak to me only the truth?" (1 Kgs 22:15; cf. v. 8). This question is especially striking for readers of 1 Kgs 22, who suddenly learn that the king has a long history of discord with a prophet other than Elijah, the prophet whom they would naturally have expected Ahab to name here.

One thing we *are* told in 1 Kgs 21 is that Ahab goes to bed and refuses to eat after Naboth turns down his offer, leaving many modern readers with the impression that the king is pouting like a child. Freedman, however, believes that Ahab is manipulating the manipulative Jezebel (quoted in Cogan 2000, 485 n. 3). In other words, he's counting on Jezebel viewing him as frustrated and immobilized so that she will take action. Freedman contends that Jezebel could not have used Ahab's

---

at first giving no reason. Significantly, though Periander gets very angry (περιθύμως ἔχων) he does not kill his son. Instead, he drives Lycophron out of his house and threatens anyone who might want to aid him (*Hist.* 3.50–51). Later, when Periander sees his son starving and unwashed, his anger abates and he takes pity on him but he cannot convince Lycophron to let go of his anger (*Hist.* 3.52). According to V. Gray, the fact that the son remains in "unrelenting opposition" to his father after Periander displays pity for him "highlights the greater capacity of the father for human feeling." Gray concludes that the contrast of father and son is more important to Herodotus than any stereotype" (1996, 369, 371, 376). Similarly, Dewald (2003, 44) concludes that Herodotus has chosen not to organize this story "around the motif of tyrannical family violence and transgressive excess"; rather, "what the narrative vividly depicts…is paternal forbearance and frustration."

25. In his earlier treatment of Periander, Salmon interpreted the stripping of the women less as an illustration of serious sumptuary legislation than as an expression of Periander's fashion sense: "it is difficult to resist the conclusion that this is a telling perversion of the tyrant's attempts to prevent rich Corinthian women from wearing what he thought showy" (1984, 200).

26. On the effects of Ahab's reported mood (1 Kgs 21:4; cf. 20:43) on readers' assessments of his character, see below.

name signet without his permission and knowledge. Smith (1998, 156) also assumes that Ahab is waiting for Jezebel "to come and ask him what is wrong," but she interprets this as weakness on his part, not cunning manipulation. Freedman's scenario has a royal male waiting in bed to manipulate a woman. This recalls Amnon waiting in bed to manipulate (and ultimately violate) Tamar. Smith's Ahab is more reminiscent of a child "working" its parent. The Ahab envisioned by Freedman is both wicked and wily. Brenneman (2000, 90) also refers to Ahab as "wily" in a general way, without explanation. Citing 1 Kgs 21:20, Abarbanel (quoted in Cogan 2000, 485) understands Elijah to be accusing Ahab of pretending "not to recognize and not to know a thing." If Freedman's surmise is correct, Ahab has slyness in common with Dewald's view of Periander. She points out that Socles also presents Periander as a trickster figure who, "though violent, principally shows the fierce cleverness in pursuit of particular objectives that we find in many other talented individuals" in Herodotus (2003, 44).

One wonders if Freedman would extend his interpretation of Ahab's behavior to the end of ch. 21, after the king has been condemned to die once again, this time by Elijah. Yahweh views the king as humbling himself before him, but Ahab is silent. Could Ahab be attempting to manipulate God? The LXX removes any room for doubt by adding that he "was pierced[27] before the Lord, and he went weeping" (3 Kgdms 20:27).[28] Walsh (1996, 335) believes that the apparent discrepancy between the image of a humble, contrite Ahab and the narrator's preceding condemnation of Ahab as an incomparable evildoer is never clearly resolved.[29]

---

27. In vv. 27 and 29 κατενύγη is used metaphorically to indicate being "stabbed" or "pricked" with contrition or sorrow.

28. On v. 27, see Gooding 1964, 272–77. The LXX is much more explicit about the meaning of Ahab's dress and actions. In this version, Ahab tore his garments and put on sackcloth when Jezebel first told him of Naboth's death (20:16). According to Brenneman (2000, 92), "the LXX preserves a tradition in which Ahab is seen as more impotent than depraved. In contrast, the MT vilifies Ahab relentlessly." See Gooding for detailed examination of how "the LXX depicts a not-so-bad-after-all Ahab, more weak than wicked, who is grieved at Jezebel's crimes and is quick to repent of his misdeeds" (1964, 272).

29. Or is this behavior merely another indication that he is disposed toward depression, rather than being truly contrite? While the king tears his garments and puts on sackcloth, the fact that he does not eat and lays down is reminiscent of his earlier behavior in v. 4, when he was depressed but showed no sign of contrition. And when he walks around now, he does so gently, or subdued (v. 29). Is Yahweh drawing a hopeful conclusion from the king's dress and behavior or looking into his

Some classical scholars find similar unresolved discrepancies in Herodotus's portrait of Periander. Dewald provides a way for such perceived discrepancies to be explained. She points out that the "larger thematic patterns about monarchical autocracy…produce a strongly negative pattern of despotism and what *it* does to people and institutions" (2003, 26; emphasis added). In contrast, the "foregrounded portraits of individuals in specific stories show the tyrant to be "acting out of a desire to obtain some particular objective through whatever means are realistically available," given the constraints of external circumstances (2003, 41–42). Thus, *within* the individual *logoi* Periander remains a round character whose feelings and actions do not always conform to the template, a character who is *not* always viewed as wicked by those with whom he interacts, and who shows himself capable of changing.[30]

### 3. *Ahab and Agamemnon as Weak Kings*

Do Ahab's actions also go beyond the despotic template when he copes with "the constraints of external circumstances"? Contrasting the weakness of Ahab and Homer's Agamemnon will help to answer this question. The most striking parallel between the two does not involve an obvious display of weakness. Each is asked to consult a prophet by a subordinate king with whom they are engaged in a military enterprise. When Jehoshaphat asks for a prophet of Yahweh to be consulted prior to going to battle, Ahab mentions Micaiah, adding "I hate him, for he does not prophesy good concerning me, but only evil" (1 Kgs 22:8). In the first book of the *Iliad*, Achilles calls an assembly and asks for a prophet or priest to be consulted, because a plague has been afflicting the army. After the prophet Kalchas makes his pronouncement, King Agamemnon calls Kalchas an "evil prophet, never yet have you once told me a good

heart? Or does the end of this story illustrate Prov 25:3 ("the heart of kings is impenetrable")?

30. In some traditions, Periander's disposition *is* changed, both by the constraints of his situation as tyrant and by events during his youth. According to Parthenius (n. 20, above), Periander was originally reasonable and had a mild disposition until he was traumatized by his mother's sexual abuse, including her tricking him into incest. Even Herodotus's Socles concedes that at the beginning of his reign Periander was gentler (ἠπιώτερος) than his predecessor had been. It was the actions he had to take to consolidate power which caused him to become more bloodthirsty (μιαιφονώ-τερος; *Hist.* 5.92ά). Later, Plutarch suggests that one can successfully resist those constraints. In the "Dinner of the Seven Wise Men" Thales implies that Periander is "recovering" from having been born into the situation of a tyrant (147c; Babbitt 1956, 354–55).

thing, always the evil things are dear to your heart (φρεσὶ) to prophesy" (1.106–7).[31]

The narrator of 1 Kgs 22 does not inform readers about Ahab's history with Micaiah, but in the case of Agamemnon we do hear of good things which Kalchas has done for the coalition.[32] Later sources add that Kalchas had earlier told Agamemnon that he must sacrifice his beloved daughter Iphigenia, raising the question whether ancient hearers of the *Iliad* would recall this earlier tragic event when they are informed of Agamemnon's present hostility toward Kalchas.[33] In short, both 1 Kgs 22 and Book 1 of the *Iliad* describe a king who expresses his hatred for the prophet whose assistance has been requested by a subordinate, saying that the prophet only prophesies evil concerning him, never good. And in neither case is the king able to prevent the hated prophet from speaking one more "evil" word against him.[34]

31. Whereas Ahab calls for Micaiah at Jehoshaphat's repeated request (1 Kgs 22:9), Kalchas speaks up on his own after Achilles makes his initial call for prophetic assistance (*Il.* 1.68–83), without Agamemnon having responded to Achilles' request. However, before the seer risks naming Agamemnon as the cause of the crisis, he asks Achilles for protection from the son of Atreus, "who now claims to be the best of the Achaeans" (*Il.* 1.91). While Kalchas states that Achilles had "urged *me* to declare" the cause of the problem, Achilles had *not* in fact named Kalchas. Rather, he had suggested asking "*some* prophet or holy man or dream interpreter" (*Il.* 1.74, 62; emphasis added). Given the need for discretion in this tense diplomatic situation, it seems likely that Achilles does have Kalchas in mind, not merely because he is present, but because Homer goes on to introduce Kalchas as "by far the best of the diviners by birds, who knows everything past and future (*Il.* 1.69–70).

32. Homer tells us that Kalchas had used his prophetic powers to guide the Greek ships to Troy (*Il.* 1.71–72) and later Odysseus reminds the Achaeans of Kalchas's earlier prophecy at Aulis, which forecast victory in the tenth year of the war (*Il.* 2.323–30).

33. Perhaps the most powerful and disturbing report of the sacrifice is that given by the chorus in Aeschylus's play *Agamemnon* (184–247). According to Taplin (1990, 80 n. 20), even in the ancient period it was suggested that Agamemnon's abuse of Kalchas looks back to Iphigenia's sacrifice, which is not directly alluded to in the *Iliad*. And Geddes (1998, 192) points out that when Agamemnon accuses Kalchas of always prophesying ill for him, the scholiasts remember the incident at Aulis. But since Homer says nothing about this event, hearers may not be expected to take Agamemnon's accusation against the seer as a factual statement about Kalchas's past behavior. If so, the audience may be expected to take the king's statement as the kind of thing people say when they are very angry, and do not intend their outbursts to be taken literally.

34. Launderville (2003, 195–98) summarizes and compares the two passages at some length. However, his discussion focuses on explaining the passages in terms of historical and cultural practice, not the interplay between character and situation in

While both Ahab and Agamemnon have been described as weak and vacillating in other contexts (e.g. MacLean 1962a, 63; Redfield 1975, 93), the two differ considerably in *how* they manifest weakness. As I noted earlier in reference to King Zedekiah, weakness can mean many things to many people, but it always depends upon the context, that is, the "weak" person's situation. For example, Periander resolves not to show any weakness toward his disaffected son.[35] What *he* means by this is "softness," that is, leniency toward his child. Saul confesses his inability to resist pressure from the people when he tells Samuel that he feared the people and listened to their voice, rather than fulfilling his God-given mission of restraining the people (1 Sam 15:24; cf. 9:17). And we have already seen that King Zedekiah admits to weakness when he tells the princes that he is unable to do anything to stop them from harming Jeremiah (Jer 38:5). And of course Samson loses his physical strength when he can no longer resist Delilah's constant prodding and plotting.

What do readers mean when they call Ahab and Agamemnon weak? On some occasions, each has been viewed as a foil for another, stronger character. In Agamemnon's case this is Achilles, while in Ahab's it is both Elijah—another prophet whom Ahab considers to be a "troubler" and his "enemy"[36]—and his wife Jezebel. Yet we would be mistaken to view Ahab as weak in his relationship with Jezebel in the same sense that Samson has been seen as weak in his relations with Delilah. The queen does not repeatedly pressure Ahab to kill Naboth (*or* Elijah), as Delilah does with her lover. Nor does Ahab confess that he is powerless to resist his wife, as Zedekiah later claims to be in relation to his princes (Jer 38:5). Admittedly, the narrator claims that Jezebel "incited"[37] Ahab, but

determining behavior. Thus, Launderville suggests that in seeking a second opinion Jehoshaphat "may have been following his own practice in Judah," and concludes that these examples of a king hating a critical prophet "clearly has features that are not confined to a specific culture" (2003, 197). While this conclusion is hardly surprising, Launderville adds the helpful observation that Agamemnon did not request another prophet "to give a second opinion." We can add that no other king who is present during Agamemnon's confrontation with Kalchas suggests consulting another prophet either, including Agamemnon's brother Menelaos.

35.  Once Periander finds out what the problem is, he is resolved not to show any weakness or softness (μαλακὸν; *Hist.* 3.51). It is unclear whether his concern is not to appear weak to the public, to his son, and/or to himself. Later in Herodotus's narrative, Cyrus declares that "soft lands breed soft men" (*Hist.* 9.122). With the metaphorical meanings of Gr. μαλακός, cf. Heb. רך and the discussion in Chapter 8, below.

36.  See 1 Kgs 18:17; 21:20.

37.  1 Kgs 21:25.The verb used by the narrator (סות) also appears in Job 2:3, where Yahweh claims that the satan incited him to move against his servant Job for

this primarily refers to matters of religious policy, not the abuse of citizen rights and judicial corruption which are exemplified by the murder of Naboth and his sons.

Nor does the narrator tell us that Ahab lacked the determination simply to take Naboth's vineyard from him by force, or that he successfully resisted the impulse to do so. Habel agrees that one need not read the account as "primarily an example of royal greed." Habel views Ahab as "apparently caught between the ideal of the strong monarch, who takes whatever lands are needed to promote the wealth of the palace, and the ideal of the just monarch, who upholds the rights of the peasant" (1995, 29, 30). When confronted with a strong peasant who insists upon the principles of "peasant ideology," Ahab is "unable to assume the role of the strong king."[38]

In Agamemnon's case, weakness includes vacillation and stubbornness. He is irresolute: on three different occasions he despairs of ever winning the war against Troy and gives up.[39] In contrast, when we are told about Ahab in battle, where he is not burdened with the presence of Elijah or Jezebel, he never falls into despair. This is true even when Ben-Hadad has surrounded his capital and when his death in battle has been

---

no reason, and 2 Sam 24:1, where Yahweh incites David to commit a sin (see Lasine 2001, 180–81). In these cases, however, there is no implication that God or David is weak, although Yahweh's words could certainly be interpreted as implying that he regrets having been talked into acting against Job (on 2 Sam 24, see Chapter 9, §3, below).

38. The way in which Ahab apparently remembers Naboth's words in 1 Kgs 21:4, and the way he quotes Naboth's words to Jezebel in v. 6, have been interpreted in various ways. The one element common to both verses is Naboth saying "I will not give to you." Could it be that Ahab takes this personally, as though Naboth had said, "I won't sell *you* my vineyard"? Josephus adds an interpretive account of Ahab's intense reaction to Naboth's refusal of the king's generous offer, which, in this reading, was made after Ahab has explained to Naboth why he wants the property: "the king, who was aggrieved, as if at an insult,…would neither bathe nor take food; and when his wife Jezebelē inquired why he grieved…he told her of Naboth's contrariness (σκαιότητα) and how, in spite of his having used mild words toward him, hardly in keeping with the royal authority, he had been insulted…" (*Ant.* 8.355–56; Thackeray and Marcus 1977, 763–65). For Rofé, the situation involves a clash between traditional society and a kind of plutocracy. Ahab does not seem to understand Naboth's social-religious reasons for refusing (1988b, 91). Seow (1999, 156) observes that "Israelite laws stipulate that ancestral estates should remain within the family or the clan; these rights are generally inalienable (Num 27:8–11; 36:1–12)." Thus, it is "not merely for sentimental reasons" that Naboth wants to hold on to the land.

39. *Il.* 2.139–41 (meant only as a "test" of his men); 9.26–28; 14.74–81.

forecast by Micaiah (1 Kgs 20:7–11; 22:26–27). When the priest Chryses tells Agamemnon that he must return his prize of war, the priest's daughter, in exchange for ransom and all the army encourage him to do so, the king is not pleased in his heart (θυμῷ) and simply ignores his soldiers' opinion (*Il.* 1.22–25). Agamemnon's weakness here is not akin to Saul, who is unable to resist being influenced by his soldiers' opinion.[40] On the contrary: Agamemnon's insecurity about his position and worth lead him to become obdurate and self-defeating. He is "hard," but in this context hardness is hardly a sign of strength.[41]

In one important sense, Agamemnon and Ahab *are* analogous: in order to understand their actions, one must take into account the social, political and religious constraints of their situations. If Ahab is involved in upholding the principle of royal authority over land against "peasant ideology" in the Naboth affair, Wilson (2002, 37) argues that Agamemnon is caught between "two different ideological models for determining social hierarchies and leadership" in the *Iliad*. Leader of the largest contingent, Agamemnon's authority comes from his position as sceptered king within a "fixed" system of ranking, while Achilles challenges his authority on the basis of the "fluid *timē*-based system" according to which Achilles is preeminent (2002, 5).[42] Wilson contends that

---

40.   On a later occasion, Agamemnon, like Saul, is unable to restrain his soldiers (*Il.* 2.54–110). For Saul's mission from Yahweh to "restrain" (יצר) the people, see 1 Sam 9:17. Agamemnon also lacks *self*-restraint. Wilson (2002, 43) points out that the priest and the army petition Agamemnon to act with restraint in Book 1. Instead, Agamemnon sends Chryses away harshly, threatens him, and disregards the will of the army, actions which "are figured negatively in the narrative as lack of restraint."

41.   Kirk's comments on Agamemnon illustrate the difficulty of deciding between explanations in terms of redaction and psychological insight: "it is far more likely that the character of Agamemnon in the *Iliad* is an amalgam of attitudes…and actual descriptions…that existed in earlier poems…imperfectly sorted and assembled" (1985, xviii; cf. 71–72, 122, 124–25). Kirk points to "the incomprehensible reactions to the testing-motif by various of the parties involved in the action." At the same time, he concedes that apparent discrepancies can be explained to some extent as psychological subtleties (1985, 71–72). While Kirk uses some of the same criteria of consistency as the "Analysts," he does not share their confidence in the idea of the finished product being "an accumulation of fixed versions conjoined with each other by an improbably incompetent literate co-ordinator" (1985, 120). Cf. Sandmel's critique of biblical redaction theories which assume that the final editors were "mindless" (1972, 34; see Chapter 3, above).

42.   Wilson (2002, 9–10) points out that the "the Homeric term *apoina* denotes 'ransom,' and *poinē* 'reparation' and 'revenge' alike." Achilles feels he is owed *poinē* for Briseis, but Agamemnon offers *apoina*.

Agamemnon's "exasperation" with Achilles "makes sense *only*" from this perspective (2002, 59; emphasis added).[43]

Although Wilson is ready to admit that "there may be value in exploring the psychology of Homer's characters," she believes that "one cannot do so apart from the sociocultural background of Homeric society" (2002, 5). Other Homerists *do* focus primarily on Agamemnon's psychology, but not without taking into account the workings of Homeric society as well. Donlan believes that critics have underestimated the complexity of Agamemnon's personality because they have seen him principally as a foil to Achilles (1971, 109). Donlan argues that the linear quality of epic style produces an accumulation of personality-detail, so that in succeeding episodes established patterns of behavior are presupposed and new traits of character may be added economically. He concludes that Homer's completed portrait of Agamemnon is "psychologically coherent," and that the king develops during the course of the epic (1971, 109, 115).

### 4. *Conclusion: Judging Ahab's Character*

When all is said and done, is the biblical Ahab also a "psychologically coherent" character who cannot be completely characterized by calling him wicked or weak? To decide, we should first examine the two occasions on which Ahab is said to be "sullen and irritated" (סר וזעף; 1 Kgs 20:43; 21:4). The scene with Jezebel recalls a number of occasions in the Bible where a character's bad mood is noticed by another person who inquires about it and offers help. Elkanah questions his distressed wife Hannah, who, like Ahab, refuses to eat (1 Sam 1:8, 10).[44] The imprisoned Joseph views his fellow prisoners, the royal baker and cupbearer, as זעפים ("dejected" or "out of humor"), as was Ahab (Gen 40:6). Like Jezebel, Joseph directly asks the moody persons about it and offers to help remove the cause of their faces being sad (פניכם רעים; 40:7–8). A similar sequence of events occurs when King Artaxerxes interprets the expression on Nehemiah's face as indicative of "sadness of heart" (רע לב) and asks him about it (Neh 2:2–3), and when Jonadab asks

---

43. We must still ask whether the character Agamemnon views his situation in the way that Wilson suggests, i.e., whether he feels that his rights within this "system" are being abused, or whether he feels himself to be *personally* abused—or are the personal and the political inextricably conjoined in Agamemnon's view of himself?

44. Hannah's husband Elkanah views her heart as "grieved" (ירע לבבך; v. 8), and the narrator tells us that she was in "bitterness of soul/life" (מרת נפש; v. 10).

Amnon why he looks haggard or leaner every morning and offers a
solution to Amnon's dilemma (2 Sam 13:4–5). Finally, Yahweh himself
asks Cain and Jonah about their bad moods and attempts to fix the
problem (Gen 4:6–7; Jon 4:4–11).[45]

In these other cases, commentators rarely characterize the moody persons as weak, perhaps because their mood can be adequately explained
by their situation. Does *Ahab* have any justification for his mood on the
occasions when *he* becomes "sullen and irritated"? In the first episode,
Ahab is condemned to death just after he has extracted major concessions from Ben Hadad, after defeating the forces of the Aramean king yet
again. The death sentence is uttered by the pummeled prophet who
quotes Yahweh's judgment: "because you have released from your hand
'the man of my ban' (איש חרמי), your life will be substituted for his life,
and your people for his people" (1 Kgs 20:42; see Chapter 4, above).
However, the unnamed prophet (or prophets) and man of God who
previously delivered Yahweh's words to Ahab prior to the battles against
Aram had said nothing at all about any holy war against the Arameans or
their king (20:13–14, 22, 28). In any case, Aram does not occupy the
territory which once required the army of Israel to evict or exterminate
its inhabitants, and it has not committed any act against Israel which led
Yahweh to declare a *ḥērem* against them, as he had against the Amalekites. The situation reported at the beginning of 1 Kgs 20 is that of an
overlord making unreasonable, if not outrageous, demands of a vassal,
who, with the assent of his country's elders, refuses to comply. Ahab
would therefore have ample reason to view the battered prophet's doom
oracle as unjustified.

Nevertheless, commentators are at best reluctant to acknowledge the
lack of foundation for the prophet's condemnation of Ahab in the present
text of 1 Kgs 20. While Nelson (1987, 136) concedes that "on the surface
of things" neither Ahab nor readers "knew nothing about this application
of the ban to Ben-hadad," he immediately adds that "on another level,
both king and reader should have known about this ban all along… That
this was holy war has been obvious since verse 13. The reader should
have remembered the analogous story of Saul and Agag." I would
suggest that readers who view 1 Kgs 20 together with 1 Sam 15 "should
know" that this analogy is misleading. Unlike Ahab, Saul *was* told by a

---

45. In most of these cases, the setting is in a royal court, and the helper is a
present or future courtier/advisor to the king or the human (or divine) king himself.
In the case of Jonah, it is not said that Yahweh notices Jonah's face or body language (as implied with Cain in Gen 4), other than Jonah's action of plopping down
east of the city.

prophet that he was to engage in a holy war. In addition, readers have known that Amalek was under the ban since Deut 25:17–19. In contrast, readers familiar with the holy war laws in Deut 20 and the accounts of previous diplomatic relations between Aram and Israel are likely to find the notion of a ban against Ben-Hadad to be quite surprising.[46]

Provan (1995, 114) attempts to make Ahab's situation analogous to Joshua's. He cites Josh 7:25 and, like Nelson, comments that "Ahab should have read the past in the present." In contrast, Cogan (2000, 467) correctly notes that the collapse of Jericho's walls (Josh 6:20) is a "less than apt" analogy. There is no cultic ceremony prior to the taking of Aphek and the victory is not attributed to Yahweh's fight for Israel. Cogan adds that at Jericho the Israelites slaughtered the inhabitants, but here the Aramean soldiers died under the rubble.[47] Clearly, if 1 Kgs 20 is prompting readers to recall Josh 6–7 or 1 Sam 15, it is doing so contrastively, just as Judg 20 alludes to Josh 8 in order to highlight the insanity of the Israelites' anti-holy war against their brother tribe Benjamin (see Lasine 1984b, 48–50).

In 1 Kgs 22, Ahab is shown to be analogous to another biblical character who may be naïve, but is neither wicked nor weak: the man of God from Judah in 1 Kgs 13. That story has already alerted us to the fatal consequences of being lied to by a prophet. There, the old prophet lies to the man of God from Judah; here Yahweh lies to King Ahab, both through Ahab's court prophet Zedekiah and Yahweh's "true" prophet Micaiah (1 Kgs 22:11–12, 15). In the earlier story, the formerly lying prophet predicts the man's inevitable demise apart from his family tomb. In 1 Kgs 22 the formerly lying Micaiah prophesies Ahab's death in battle (1 Kgs 22:22, 28). Unlike the man of God, however, Ahab is eventually buried in his home town (v. 37).

In spite of the fact that Micaiah has an apparently long history of prophesying "evil" for Ahab,[48] the king neither tortures nor kills him. He

46. Nelson (1987, 137) asserts that "the law of the ban is unambiguous (Deut 20:16–18)," but he is citing a part of the holy war laws which applies specifically to extermination of the tribes who had been occupying the heart of the promised land prior to the Israelite invasion. It is the law in Deut 20:13 which is actually relevant here, at least to some extent. This rule of engagement deals with suzerain–vassal relations between Israel and nations "far away" from the heart of the promised land, with Israel in the role of suzerain.

47. Cogan (2000, 470) notes that the reference to *ḥērem* in 1 Kgs 20:42 is the latest one in the narratives concerning the monarchic period. Brichto's conclusion on Ahab's condemnation in 1 Kgs 20 is more blunt; he believes that the king is convicted on "flimsy" and "illogical" grounds (1992, 176–77, 179).

48. This history is consistent enough for Ahab to be able immediately to recognize that Micaiah's initial victory prediction is insincere.

merely has the prophet held under guard until it can be determined whether his prophecy of doom proves correct.[49] Although Ahab's going into battle despite Micaiah's prophecy may seem to be foolish, it could also be viewed as a sign of bravery, in the same way that King Saul can be viewed as brave for going to battle after hearing the prophet Samuel predict that he and his three sons would die on the battlefield.[50] Of course, the fact that Ahab disguises himself when he goes into battle, and makes his vassal Jehoshaphat the target for enemy snipers, does not seem very brave (1 Kgs 22:30, 32–33). However, this strategy *can* be viewed as prudent in light of the fact that Ben Hadad does indeed plan to target the Israelite king in the battle (v. 31; cf. 2 Sam 17:2–3). Finally, the significance of Ahab remaining propped up in the chariot after being wounded can also be interpreted in opposing ways. For some it is an unequivocally heroic act (e.g. Holt 1995, 91; Montgomery and Gehman 1951, 336, 341) while for others it is either a matter of "subterfuge" or deception by Ahab or his soldiers (De Vries 1985, 269; Fretheim 1999, 125), or simply a necessity due to the fact that his chariot was, in effect, stuck in traffic (J. Gray 1970, 455; Würthwein 1984, 256).

Clearly, when we examine Ahab's behavior in all of 1 Kgs 16–22 in terms of his situation and "external constraints," a consistent pattern emerges: Ahab acts resolutely in situations involving foreign powers, and when left to himself he makes no attempt to murder those who become his "troublers," namely, Elijah, Naboth, and Micaiah. Both his weakness and his wickedness are concentrated in situations involving religious policy, especially when he is caught between the opposing religious zealots Elijah and Jezebel. Thus, there is no basis for the claim that Ahab's behavior is "irreconcilable in terms of unity of character" due to a lack of interest in "historical precision" on the part of the author

---

49. The narrator adds that Micaiah is to be given לחם לחץ ומים לחץ, usually rendered as "scant" bread and water, or bread and water "of oppression/affliction." Meier (2009, 186–87) points out that "bread and water is precisely what the prophet would have expected whether jailed or otherwise," citing 1 Kgs 13:9, 17, 18 and 18:4, as well as in Ezek 4:9–17. We might add that this pattern underscores the sumptuousness of Elijah's raven-served diet of meat and bread twice daily, eaten together with fresh water from the *wadi*, even if the waiter bringing the food is an unclean bird (1 Kgs 17:6).

50. Ahab's action in ch. 22 is even more multivalent in the LXX, which reverses the order of MT chs. 20 and 21. In the Greek, Ahab goes into battle after hearing the doom oracle of the bandaged prophet *and* Micaiah's dire prophecy. This could be taken as even more foolish or more brave than in the MT, in which the battle report follows the news that Yahweh has transferred the doom declared by Elijah to Ahab's son, due to what Yahweh views as the king's contrite behavior.

(Brichto 1992, 168, 181–85), or as the result of editors having transferred events from another monarch's reign to Ahab's. Nor can the characterization of Ahab be summed up with simple labels such as "wicked" or "weak," just as Herodotus's Periander and Homer's Agamemnon cannot be reduced to a flat "despotic template." Of course, whether a given reader will accept the narrator's strongly negative judgment on Ahab, or conclude that he is too complex and sympathetic to warrant a blanket condemnation, may ultimately depend upon that reader's character, situation, and style of reading.

Part IV

CHARACTER AND THE ETHICS OF READING THE BIBLE

Chapter 8

# THE WITNESSING HEART: SELF-EVALUATION IN THE STORIES OF JOB AND KING DAVID

## 1. *Self-evaluation and Self-betrayal in the* Book of the Dead *and the Book of Job*

O my heart which I had from my mother! O my heart of my different ages! Do not stand up as a witness against me,…in the tribunal, do not be hostile to me in the presence of the Keeper of the Balance [Anubis],…Do not tell lies about me. (*Book of Going Forth by Day* 30B[1])

In the Egyptian *Book of the Dead*, the deceased asks his heart not to "lie" when testifying against him at the final judgment. This raises intriguing questions: Has the dead person committed actual crimes that he wishes to conceal or does his heart have some motive for inventing such sins? Is this an ancient way of expressing a more universal fear of betraying oneself in a critical situation, that is, fear of what Poe calls "the imp of the perverse"? Does the speaker actually believe that he could fool the

---

1.  Faulkner and Goelet 1998, 24–25. This text is more popularly known as the Egyptian *Book of the Dead* (*BD*). The heart is weighed against a feather, which represents Maat (*mȝ't*). "Maat" denotes proper behavior, order, harmony, justice, and truth; in Allen's formulation, it "means essentially the ways things ought to be" (2000, 115). If the scales balance, the person has lived a just and proper life. The person is then pronounced *mȝ' ḥrw*, "true of voice," or justified (e.g. *BD* Spell 125). As Brownlee points out, "the verb 'weigh' is here not concerned with *how much* the heart weighs, but with whether the scales *balance*" (1977, 43). Allen notes that the judgment is always successful (2000, 317; cf. 95). In Homer's *Iliad*, Zeus "weighs" the fate or death of an individual or group on his golden fate-scales (*Il.* 8.69–74; 16.658 [ἱρὰ τάλαντα; "holy scales"]; 22.209–13). However, these instances of "*kerostasia*," as well as the later examples of soul-weighing (*psychostasia*) in late archaic and classical Greek art, do not represent a testing or judgment concerning an individual's moral character, but an "eternal affirmation of destiny" (Vermeule 1979, 76; cf. 160–61).

gods with the aid of this spell and hide his sins (or at least keep his bad deeds from being added to the "heap"[2] of his actions during life)? Or does he think that his *heart* could fool the gods by making false allegations against him? Are the speaker's pleas an illustration of what Assmann (2005a, 102–4) calls the Egyptians' fear of dissociation between self and heart, and the resulting loss of self-control?

Egyptologists answer these questions in different ways. According to Pinch (1995, 155–56), this spell "allows the deceased to evade a guilty verdict by preventing his heart from owning up to crimes."[3] This implies that the heart would be confessing the truth about real crimes, not lying by making false allegations. Similarly, Brandon (1958, 123) asserts that "at this judgment the very secrets of their hearts would be revealed," implying that the "secrets" are true, not fabrications which the heart may reveal in order to sabotage the self during the judgment.[4] While Goelet affirms this interpretation, he also leaves open the possibility that the heart could utter a malicious lie: "the apparent intent of the text was to prevent the heart from blurting out the sins which the deceased had committed on earth, *but at the same time* to dissuade the heart from telling falsehoods" (Faulkner and Goelet, 1998, 155; emphasis added). He admits that "it is unclear why the heart would wish to sabotage the dead," but goes on to attribute this wish to the fact that "the afterworld was a place where the irrational was a commonplace occurrence," just as it is "our irrational subconscious that leads us to blurt out hidden feelings in slips of the tongue."[5]

2. On this metaphor, see Chapter 9, §1, below.

3. Most commentators conclude that "if the heart was heavy with sin, it would weigh more than the symbol of *maat*" (Pinch 1995, 155). Assmann imagines that "with every lie, the pan in which his heart lay would have sunk" (2005a, 75). Pinch believes that "the point is probably not that the Egyptians felt that they were unworthy of passing the judgment, but that the denizens of the underworld could not be relied on to do justice." She notes that in funerary literature, demons controlled by the high gods seem to threaten both innocent and guilty dead people. Similarly, referring to the vignette accompanying spell 30 in the *BD*, Assmann (2005a, 123) observes that Ani's posture makes it "obvious" that while he recites the spell he has no real confidence in its power to change the verdict of the scales.

4. In spell 105 of the *BD* the speaker concedes that he has spoken "evil phrases" and done "evil impurity" (Faulkner and Goelet 1998, 112), but assures his *ka* that "nothing has been imputed to" him, because of an amulet he possesses. Cf. spell 30A: "say not against me, 'He actually did it' according to what I have done" (Assmann 2005a, 103; cf. Faulkner and Goelet 1998, 103).

5. Explaining the impulse of the deceased's heart as an example of a Freudian parapraxis may recall Poe's imp of the perverse, but it can tell us little about the

Others understand this scene in terms of the loss of self-control. In J. Taylor's formulation (2001, 37), the heart is temporarily out of the deceased's control during the weighing, prompting the fear that it might reveal "something" detrimental to its owner. According to Assmann (2005a, 104), in Egypt "to be a person meant to be able to exercise self-control. But this control was lost when the heart, the *ba*, or some other aspect of the person was dissociated from the self." In this situation, "all depended on the heart's not deviating from the mouth and thus from the speaking 'I'" (2005a, 102). In this formulation, the emphasis is on inconsistency between mouth and heart, rather than on the action being "lied about." As I discussed in Chapter 2, for Homer's Achilles such discord between mouth and heart is "as hateful as the gates of Hades."

Some scholars come close to viewing the fear of the deceased as a sign of a guilty conscience. Brandon suggests that the Egyptians "came almost to hypostatising the heart" as an independent internal witness to the nature of his deeds, comparable to the "Christian idea of conscience" (1958, 122; cf. Laver 1972, 182). Leaving aside the question whether this idea is exclusively Christian, Brandon is not the only Egyptologist to view the Egyptian concept of the heart in terms of "conscience." Earlier I noted Assmann's contention that at one phase of development in Egyptian history the heart functions as a social "superego" which is identified with the divine voice, coming very close to our idea of the conscience. During this phase, the authority demanding self-control is the internalized voice of the community and tradition, whose interests are best served when individuals suppress their spontaneous feelings and drives.

The idea of the heart denoting "conscience" is also familiar from the Hebrew Bible. David is clearly feeling the pangs of conscience and remorse when his "heart smites him" after he has humiliated King Saul by cutting off the hem of his garment when the king was in a compromising situation (1 Sam 24:5; cf. 2 Sam 24:10). And commentators routinely take Job's statement in Job 27:5–6 as a declaration that his "conscience is clear" (Habel 1985, 381):[6] "Far be it from me that I should say you are right; until I die I will not put away my integrity from me. My righteousness I hold fast, and will not let it go; My heart shall not reproach from my days."[7]

meaning of this ancient text until we can affirm the validity of Freudian psychodynamics *and* demonstrate that these dynamics were operative among individuals in ancient Egypt—at least, as these individuals were imagined to act in the Egyptian afterlife. On this fundamental problem, see Chapter 2, above.

6. Cf., e.g., Rowley 1980, 175; Driver and Gray 1977, 226.

7. Habel (1985, 376), following Gordis, understands יחרף not in its ordinary sense of "reproach" here, but rather as to "blaspheme"; Good (1990, 121) prefers

Now, Prov 21:2 cautions us that "every way of a man is right in his eyes, but Yahweh weighs the hearts (ותכן לבות יהוה)."[8] This implies that we can be wrong about the rightness of our actions and intentions, if not that we are *often* wrong.[9] While Yahweh considers Job to be unique in his piety and loyalty (Job 1:8; 2:3), Job may also be unique in terms of the accuracy of his appraisal of his own "rightness."

Job is so certain that he possesses integrity and is righteous (e.g. 6:29; 9:21; 31:4–6, 37) that he can confidently ask to be "weighed on scales of righteousness" (ישקלני במאזני צדק) so that God may know his integrity (31:6).[10] Other passages show that Job is aware that God *already* knows his innocence.[11] In fact, Job not only has accurate knowledge about his own heart, but knowledge of the secrets which *God* "hides" in *his* heart as well (10:13; cf. 10:7; 23:10).[12] As Habel puts it, Job knows what is "not the case with himself" (9:35) and what *is* the case with God (10:13b).[13]

---

"taunt." The phrase "from my days" (מימי) is usually taken to mean "all [or any] of my days," although Gordis (1978, 288) understands the literal meaning to be "from the days of my birth"; on the grammatical difficulties, see Clines 2006, 642–43.

8.  There are three references to God weighing or assessing hearts or spirits in Proverbs (16:2; 21:2; 24:12). The verb for "weighing" (תכן) is the same in all three verses, and appears in this form (Qal participle) only in these instances. It is not the verb used in Job 31:6, however; there the verb is שקל. McKane (1970, 243) renders Prov 21:2 "but it is Yahweh who weighs up motives." However, in Prov 16:2 he translates תכן as "adjusted to standard," adding that "Yahweh's appraisal of motives is normative, and there is no echo of the mythological representation of judgment associated with Thoth" (1970, 496).

9.  It is possible that our "way" (דרך) may denote both our behavior and our intentions in choosing one path over another on the basis of our character.

10. On the concept of integrity, both in general and in the book of Job, see Chapter 3 n. 12, above.

11. Whybray (1998, 133) believes that Job is "ironically pretending" that "the God who 'numbers his steps' (v. 4) is unaware [of it]." Is it possible that the deceased in *BD* is engaging in pretense when he worries about his heart being able to fool the gods about his facticity or his character?

12. The friends also speak as if they know God's thoughts and attitudes, for example when they assume that God views his creation (the heavens, his "holy ones," angels, the sun and moon and humans) as impure or worse (Job 4:17–19; 15:14–16; 25:4–6; cf. Lasine 1988, 30–38). God becomes angry at the friends for their statements about him, for their views were "incorrect," unlike Job's (Job 42:7–8). This raises the question whether the harsh accusations Job makes about divine injustice are also viewed by God as "correct."

13. Habel (1985, 199): "What Job knows to be 'the case with you' (v. 13b) in the way God operates, stands in contrast with what Job knows is not 'the case with me' (9:35)."

Even though Job believes that God knows his innocence, he nevertheless expresses a fear which is quite similar to the worry expressed by the speaker of spell 30B in the *Book of the Dead*. In that text, the speaker fears that his heart may incriminate him by uttering lies or exposing secret sins. Job fears that he too would incriminate himself in a hearing before God, but for different reasons. He isn't worried about his heart telling lies about sins he didn't commit; his friend Eliphaz has already done *that* in ch. 22. However, while he insists that his heart will not "reproach" all his days, he also accuses God of having made his heart "soft" or "weak" (הרך לבי; 23:16) and fearful. Job fears that God might confront him in a stormy, angry fashion, intimidating him so much that he would act guilty and be unable to speak in his own defense.[14] The fact that God has shriveled up his body even makes his appearance into a "witness" against him (16:8). "Clothed" by disease and distress, he fears being misjudged, although for reasons different from the misjudged "clothed" souls in Plato's *Gorgias*.[15] All these factors militate against Job being able to be weighed in "just scales"—except by readers, for we have known from the outset that Job is being "tried" only in the sense of a "clinical trial" or social-psychological experiment (see Chapter 3, above).

Thus, both we and God know Job to be unique and incomparable. But what about the many other biblical characters who insist that they too are righteous or that they possess laudable character traits, including the characters who are put into situations where they are forced to explain and justify themselves? In these cases readers do not have the luxury of being given access to a prologue in heaven, where God himself vouches for the integrity of the human in question. There are many examples of such situations. In the following sections I will consider several representative types, and then turn to an extended discussion of David's self-presentation as "soft" and weak in 2 Sam 3.

14. See Job 9:2–20, 28–35; 13:21, 25–27; 23:14.

15. In that case, judges were misled by the "clothing" of beautiful bodies, ancestry, and wealth. In contrast, the formerly wealthy Job fears misjudgment due to his withered body, if not his impoverished condition. In Plato, correct judgment requires that both the person judged and the judge be dead. Job, on the other hand, wants to be judged fairly while he is still "in the flesh" (Job 19:26–27); he has no hope of an afterlife which might include judgment in scales of righteousness (see, e.g., Job 14:1–12).

## 2. *Varieties of Self-Evaluation in the Hebrew Bible*

| | |
|---|---|
| I am today soft/weak (רך) | 2 Sam 3:39 |
| You made my heart soft/weak (הרך לבי) | Job 23:16 |
| They are too hard (קשים) for me | 2 Sam 3:39 |
| He is hard (קשה) and evil in his practices | 1 Sam 25:3 |
| I am not able to do anything against you | Jer 38:5 |
| You are little in your own eyes | 1 Sam 15:17 |
| Come see my jealousy for Yahweh | 2 Kgs 10:16 |
| He became jealous with my jealousy among them | Num 25:11 |
| I did this in the uprightness of my heart | 1 Chr 29:17 |
| You are upright…and good in my eyes | 1 Sam 29:6 |
| The uprightness of my heart are my words | Job 33:3 |
| Who…is as trustworthy as [he] | 1 Sam 22:14 |
| I know your impudence and the evil of your heart | 1 Sam 17:28 |
| You love those who hate you | 2 Sam 19:7 |

According to their self-characterizations, David, Zedekiah, and Job are weak, David and Elihu[16] are upright of heart, and Jehu and Phineas share Yahweh's self-declared trait of jealousy.[17] According to others' characterizations of them, Joab and his brothers are hard, Nabal is both hard and evil, Saul lacks self-esteem, and David is either upright, good, and trustworthy, or impudent, evil-hearted and emotionally skewed. Of course, all these trait attributions are made in specific situations, for specific reasons, to specific interlocutors. Like "real" people, these literary characters may attempt to reframe the situations in which they are involved by characterizing themselves in a specific way, prompting their fellow characters to view them in terms of their self-interested construal of themselves and their shared situation.[18]

In some cases, biblical figures are prompted or forced to characterize themselves, for example, when they are presented the so-called

16. Few commentators are quick to accept Elihu's claim that his words reflect the uprightness of *his* heart (ישר־לבי אמרי ;Job 33:3); see, e.g., Hoffman 1996, 141; Rowley 1980, 210.

17. For Yahweh's self-description as "jealous," see, e.g., Exod 20:5; Deut 5:9. In Exod 34:14, Yahweh names himself "Jealous" (כי יהוה קנא שמו). Hertz (1960, 366) understands "name" here to mean "character"; Houtman (2000, 722) renders "jealous by nature."

18. For example, when speaking to Eliab, Ahimelech, Jonathan, Saul, and Achish, David presents himself as innocent and innocuous, often by exclaiming either "what have I done now?," "wasn't it just a word?," or both; see 1 Sam 17:29; 20:1; 26:18; and 29:8. Boecker (1964, 31–34) and others refer to such questions as the "appeasement formula" (*Beschwichtigungsformel*).

accusation formula (*Beschuldigungsformel* or *Anklageformel*), "what is this you have done?"[19] This question, as well as questions like "why did you do such-and-such?," are often demanding the motives and causes of a person's behavior, not just facts of what occurred.[20] This is particularly the case when the questioner considers the behavior to have been foolish or sinful (e.g. 1 Sam 15:19), or when he or she suspects the person's motives or sincerity for acting in an apparently positive fashion (e.g. 2 Sam 16:17). When God is the one asking "what have you done?," he already knows what occurred; he is both accusing and drawing out the person questioned, so that they explain the reasons for their actions. In many cases, they answer by attributing dispositional traits to themselves and others.

In other cases, characters will attribute motives to others for their own reasons. Examples include the serpent imputing motives to God in Gen 3, Joab interpreting Abner's actions in 2 Sam 3:25, and Ziba predicating a traitorous motive to Mephibosheth in 2 Sam 16:3. Their attributions imply that they have no epistemological limitations when it comes to knowing the true character of the people they are judging, even though other biblical passages insist that only Yahweh knows the hearts and kidneys of all humans (e.g. 1 Kgs 8:39; see Chapter 2, above). In 2 Sam 3, Joab encourages David to accept his negative view of Abner's motives by introducing it with the phrase "You know Abner…" In other words, "you know Abner's true character just as well as I do, and we both know that a person's actions should be interpreted in terms of their character." Since Abner is treacherous by nature, his proposal to David must also be treacherous.

On occasion biblical personages will, in effect, stake their life on the accuracy of their self-knowledge by uttering "*ḥālîlāh lî*" (חלילה לי), a

---

19. E.g. Gen 3:13; 4:10; 12:18; 26:10; 29:25 etc. On this accusatory question or "summons," see Boecker 1964, 26–31. Job claims that God is not accountable in this way: "who can say to him, 'what are you doing?'" (9:12). On the genre of "juridical parable," see Simon 1997, 112–18. While Simon (1997, 298 n. 61) takes my discussion of the melodramatic aspects of Nathan's story (Lasine 1984a) to mean that I do not consider it to be a juridical parable, this is not the case.

20. For example, in Gen 20:9–10 King Abimelech asks Abraham three מה questions. He begins by asking "what have you done to us?" and then demands that Abraham explain what led him to do things that ought not to have been done. In 1 Sam 17:28 Eliab asks David why he is there at the battlefront, and then goes on to answer his own question with an explanation in terms of David's dispositional traits. On God asking Elijah (twice!) why he is there at Mt. Horeb in 1 Kgs 19, and Elijah's revealing repeated response, see Chapter 5, above. On Joseph asking his brother Judah "what is this deed that you have done?" (Gen 44:15), see n. 23 below.

self-imprecation[21] which is usually translated "far be it from me," and less often "I'll be damned" or "it would be a desecration for me/you."[22] As Habel (1985, 380) puts it in relation to Job 27:7, the formula implies "that it would be tantamount to sacrilege not to speak the truth of the declaration involved. Others who invoke the formula include Judah, Samuel, Ahimelech, David, Joab, and Yahweh himself.[23]

The interrogation of Ahimelech by Saul illustrates several aspects of a forced self-characterization situation. The king asks Ahimelech a "why" question, but one which shows that he has already decided that the priest has committed conspiracy against him (1 Sam 22:13). Ahimelech responds by stating his belief that David is a trustworthy and honorable servant of the king. Far be it from me, says Ahimelech, to withhold aid from such a man, adding that Saul should not impute anything to him (אל־ישם דבר ב־), since he knew nothing about David rising up against the king. Here חלילה לי occurs in a context where the speaker is pleading for his interrogator not to attribute (ישם ב־) a false negative character trait to him, in this case, the trait of disloyalty (22:13–15).

As in the other cases of self-imprecation mentioned above, Ahimelech is claiming that he is not the sort of person who would do the kind of thing or have the sort of bad intentions that have been attributed to him. In other words, these speakers claim to know the sort of person they are, and that their sort of person would never do or think such things. It would be against their character. Of course, readers are not obliged to agree with them. Samuel's use of חלילה לי in 1 Sam 12 follows his oath

21. According to KBL (301–2), I חלילה denotes a profane, abominable, unthinkable thing. Tawil (2005, 92) disagrees with KBL, BDB and *DCH*, arguing that there are not three or four different roots with the letters חלל, but one root from which all these different senses stem.

22. Fokkelman (1990, 305) calls it "a cursing word" in 2 Sam 23:17/1 Chr 11:19. McCarter (1984, 487, 491) follows the LXX and translates the phrase "I'll be damned, Yahweh" in 2 Sam 23:17. Hamilton (1995, 16, 16 n. 8) chooses "it would be a desecration" in Gen 18:25 on the grounds that the usual "far be it from you" misses the force of the verb חלל; cf. Milgrom 1976, 86–89 and 87 n. 306.

23. In Gen 44:17 the disguised Joseph asks his brothers "what is this deed that you have done?" after his silver cup has been found in Benjamin's sack. In his reply, Judah denies having done the deed using חלילה לי (v. 17). Samuel employs the expression after his self-presentation during his oath of clearance when leaving office (1 Sam 12:23). David employs the formula twice, when denying that he would put forth his hand against Yahweh's anointed (1 Sam 24:7; 26:11). Joab also uses the expression twice, when assuring the wise woman that he does not intend to destroy her town because of Sheba's rebellion (2 Sam 20:20). In 1 Sam 2:30 a man of God attributes the use of the phrase to Yahweh in his curse against the house of Eli. On Ahimelech, see below and Lasine 2001, 39–50.

of clearance when leaving office, a speech in which he gives a self-serving and distorted[24] account of events leading up to the inauguration of the monarchy. In 1 Sam 24 and 26 David uses the formula to express his abhorrence at the idea of raising his hand against Yahweh's anointed. What this says about *his* character will depend on how a given reader understands his motive; after all, it is in David's own interest to avoid setting a precedent for assassinating anointed leaders, since David is himself Yahweh's anointed. And while Joab may be sincere in negotiating with the wise woman in 2 Sam 20, he has often employed deception; in fact, he did so earlier in this very chapter (20:8–10).

Given the ambiguities associated with the personalities of these characters, Ahimelech stands out as extraordinarily candid and honest. Yet he is the one who ends up dead as a result of his testimony. In other words, the only one whose self-imprecation "may I be damned if..." is fulfilled may be the one who least deserves it, something which would hardly surprise the self-consciously blameless Job, who himself utters חלילה לי at one point (Job 27:5).

In other situations, the speaker will claim to know someone else with certainty, using the expression "far be it from you/so-and-so." Elihu refers to God this way in Job 34:10, as does Abraham twice in Gen 18:25 ("far be it from you...to kill the righteous with the wicked...far be it from you..."). As noted earlier, the degree to which Elihu's knowledge of God's character is accurate is open to debate. And Job, for one, challenges Abraham's assumption that it is *against* Yahweh's character to sweep away the righteous with the guilty so that both are counted the same (see, e.g., Job 9:22; 12:16–25; 21:1–26).

---

24. Samuel begins in vv. 1–3 by denying that he himself committed a series of offenses, including bribery (עשק); he refers to himself (with "I" or "me") twelve times in just these three verses. In v. 2, he mentions that "my sons are with you," conveniently omitting that *they* have taken bribes (שחד) and perverted justice—which is precisely the reason why the people asked for a king to replace the sons who "do not walk in [their father's] ways" (1 Sam 8:3, 5). 1 Sam 8 makes no mention of Samuel attempting to stop his sons' abuse of power or initiating other reforms which might have cleaned up his corrupt regime. Samuel goes on to relate a revisionist history of what led the people to ask for a king, omitting entirely the actual cause, namely, his sinful sons. Instead he claims that the people demanded a king when the Ammonite king Nahash came against "you" (12:12). According to 1 Sam 11, however, Nahash came against only the town of Jabesh-gilead and did so *after* the people's request for a king, and *after* Samuel himself had introduced King Saul to the people (10:24–25).

## 3. *David's Self-presentation as Soft and Weak in 2 Samuel 3*

As mentioned above, David attributes character traits to himself both in 2 Samuel and 1 Chronicles. In 1 Chr 29:17 David declares that God examines the heart (בחן לבב)[25] and has pleasure in uprightness. He then adds, "I, in the uprightness of my heart (אני בישר לבבי) have..." Like Job, David takes his knowledge of his own moral character as complete and accurate, and uses it as the motive for the action he goes on to relate. However, he is not challenging God to check his heart according to God's standards, as does Job; rather, he seems to assume that his standards and God's are identical. "Heart" is the key term in David's speech; he mentions the heart five times in vv. 17–19 alone.[26]

In the story of Abner's assassination (2 Sam 3) David describes himself "soft" (or "weak"). Should we take this declaration at face value? To answer this question we need to focus on the sociologist Goffman's question, "what is it that's going on here?" (1974, 8). David is a master of "impression management," that is, the ability to frame situations so that others will view him according to the character he wants to project at that time.[27] For example, David presents himself to Ahimelech as a trustworthy servant of Saul on an urgent secret mission from his king. Later in the same chapter David stages the first of two performances for King Achish, playing the role of a madman (1 Sam 21:14). In ch. 27 he casts himself as a loyal vassal of the Philistines who has been attacking Achish's enemies (vv. 8–12). In both cases Achish is convinced by David's acting ability. Could David also be engaging in impression management in 2 Sam 3, even though here the narrator stresses David's ignorance of "what it is that has been going on"?

---

25. The verb בחן is used for examining or testing the heart (or the kidneys or a person) more often than verbs meaning "to weigh" (in reference to the heart, see, e.g., Jer 12:3; Ps 17:3, 10). However, in Chronicles it appears only here, as does the word "uprightness" (see Braun 1986, 282).

26. It also echoes David's earlier admonition to Solomon to serve God with a whole heart (1 Chr 28:9; cf. 29:9), because Yahweh searches (or "seeks") all hearts and has insight into all the intent of the thoughts (וכל־יצר מחשבות מבין; cf. Gen 6:5; 1 Chr 29:18). Braun (1986, 275) notes the Chronicler's "emphasis upon the necessity for actions to flow from a perfect, undivided heart."

27. David's mastery of impression management may have started as early as the Goliath episode, if one reason that David declined Saul's armor is because he was counting on his youthful, attractive appearance and lack of armor and sword to make Goliath underestimate him.

When attempting to describe what *is* going on in 2 Sam 3, commentators sometimes slide back and forth between the story-world and "history," between believing David's version of what is happening and being skeptical of it, or between thinking that the narrator is portraying David positively or that he is undermining that positive image by "protesting too much" when he insists on David's ignorance (see Lasine 2001, 111). Within the story, it is David's behavior after Abner's death which convinces the people that the king knew nothing about what Joab was up to (2 Sam 3:37). Then, addressing his servants, David uses self-characterization to explain why he has not taken punitive action against Joab: "And *I* today am soft and weak, though anointed king, and these men, the sons of Zeruiah, are too hard for me. May Yahweh reward the evildoer according to his wickedness" (3:39). Has David remembered the lesson which Abigail taught him earlier, namely, to leave vengeance to God? If so, his lament "should Abner die as a *nābāl* dies?" (3:33) is particularly a propos, considering that Joab and the man named Nabal are two of the very few individuals whose dispositions are described as קשה ("hard" or "severe") in the Bible. Of course, Abigail's point was that David should abstain from private revenge, while here David claims to have a pragmatic reason for not exercising his authority as just king.

Commentators like Fokkelman (1990, 117) accept without hesitation David's self-characterization and the sincerity of his behavior following Abner's death: the "tough guys," David's nephews, are "too much for him"; David's "makeup" does not involve his taking into account the worst that could happen.[28] Fokkelman knows David's true character and the thoughts and actions which are impossible for a person of that character. However, his use of the term "makeup" to describe David's disposition recalls the theatrical meaning of the word, and points to another possibility, namely, that David's public performance at the funeral and his self-description to his courtiers are part of a staged performance.

Schley attempts to explain David's behavior toward his sister's sons by viewing Joab and Abishai according to two "archetypes": "as a historical figure, Abishai is one of David's staunchest supporters. As a

---

28. Fokkelman (1990, 117) "imagines" that Zeruiah's sons make David conscious that "for him there is no way back out of the hard reality of war and politics." They "give him the shivers" at the idea he too could be bumped off due to "a certain amount of naivety" on his part. In other words, in order to accept the narrator's insistence on David's ignorance of what was afoot, Fokkelman must attribute a degree of naïveté to David which hardly accords with what has been reported about David's actions in 1 Sam 16–2 Sam 2.

literary figure, he and Joab provide a violent foil for the self-renunciatory David" (1992a, 25–26).[29] This attempt to reduce ambiguity by separating out historical and literary elements precludes the possibility that Joab and Abishai are both foils for David *and* his staunchest supporters within the story world. If David orchestrated the series of events leading up to and following the murder without Joab's voluntary participation, he was able to do so because he was aware of the ways in which situation and character affect one another. It is difficult to imagine that David would not have realized that by bringing Abner into the picture Joab would be concerned over the security of his position,[30] quite apart from any worries Joab might have that Abner was spying (2 Sam 3:25). In other words, if David knew the characters of both Joab and Abner, including their characters in their professional role as generals, he would know how to set up a situation which would lead Joab to act precisely as he did. In this way, David would not only avoid having to kill Abner himself, but could "honestly" claim that he knew nothing about it at the time.

Could these events—as depicted—have taken place *with* Joab's voluntary participation, or was Joab probably "framed," as Halpern (2001, 83) contends? McKenzie (2000, 121) believes that it is "logical" to assume that Joab is acting on David's orders. He does not say whether this includes Joab agreeing to play the role of David's "foil" or fall guy. Are we to imagine that the harangue Joab delivers to David in 3:24–25 was scripted by the king "for show," the way that Joab later scripts the speech of the wise woman to David? There is no evidence of such contrivance in the text. Whether or not the author is writing an apology which calls for Joab and Abishai to be made foils for David, within the story it is David himself who makes his nephews his foils, when he publicly condemns Joab and Abishai and contrasts his softness with their hardness.

---

29. Schley argues that it is the juxtaposition of these two perspectives that allows the author to place the blame for the bloodshed during David's reign onto these nephews. He notes that in 2 Sam 16, the impression created is that the sons of Zeruiah are "ruthless men of blood" (1992a, 25). If Schley is correct, this is quite ironic, since Shimei says exactly this about their uncle David in the same chapter. Schley concludes that David emerges as the Wisdom tradition's paradigm of the righteous man who leaves vengeance to God, and Joab and Abishai are the paradigmatic violent men. In contrast, Fokkelman (1990, 119) contends that David's failure to take effective action against Joab "has a serious backlash on the moral stature of David himself."

30. Many factors indicate that David would be well aware of the consequences of the situation he was setting up; see my discussion in Lasine 2001, 108–13 and Bodner's comments on that discussion (Bodner 2005, 54–56).

Is it in fact possible to determine from the story whether David directed this series of performances with such subtlety? One way is to ask whether his behavior in this chapter is situationally consistent with his self-description. Is David really "weak" in the sense that kings Zedekiah and Ahab have been viewed as weak in their specific situations? Certainly one *could* say that the reason David doesn't punish Joab is that he really is too weak, or that it is because of his weakness that he couldn't do without Joab's help in the future. On the other hand, David is strong enough to order Joab to endure humiliation without Joab objecting or resisting at all. Of course, this could also indicate that David and Joab are colluding together, as McKenzie and others suggest. However, if this were the case it would be unnecessary for David to covertly maneuver Joab into killing Abner so that David could grant himself absolute deniability.[31] When all is said and done, there are no clear examples of "collusion" between David and Joab in Samuel–Kings, other than during the cover-up following the Bathsheba affair.[32]

Josephus's version of these events (*Ant.* 7.31–45) is instructive here. Josephus believes that Joab killed Abner because he feared for his position as commander; the vengeance for Asahel was just a cover story. For Josephus, the moral of the story is that such powerful men should be kept apart. This statement implies that David failed to realize that these strong men would clash if they met, resulting in one doing away with the other. At the same time, Josephus's David is aware of the need for the public to perceive him as uninvolved; otherwise, he would be seen to be violating his promises to Abner. Josephus also notes David's elaborate funeral for Abner, adding "all the others rejoiced that he was of so kind and gentle (χρηστῷ καὶ ἡμέρῳ) a nature," because each viewer thought that he too

---

31. One can only wonder whether the "balance of power" between David and Joab begins to shift after Joab comes in possession of David's letter ordering the death of Uriah. From a modern perspective, this would seem to be analogous to the infamous "blue dress" in the Clinton–Lewinsky fiasco, as politically valuable physical evidence of a leader's abuse of power. Of course, by the end of the Court History David again proves to be the stronger one even when he is moribund, in part due to his "wise" son Solomon's ability to have Joab "justly" executed.

32. Joab refrains from conquering Rabbah in 2 Sam 12:26–30 so that the absent David can get the credit for the victory and have a MacArthuresque photo opportunity, but that is not collusion. Neither is Joab's reluctantly following David's orders to conduct a census in 2 Sam 24. Nor are there cases of collusion between the two in 2 Sam 2, 14, 18–19, or 1 Kgs 1–2. Joab's forcing David to appear before the people in 2 Sam 19 is no exception, since the king is not a willing participant in this staged event.

would be treated that well when he died (*Ant.* 7.43; Thackeray and Marcus 1977, 380–81). Josephus adds that it was quite natural for David to want to merit a good opinion by showing care for the dead, so that no one suspected him of complicity. In this reading, David intentionally creates an image of himself as "gentle" by nature before making the statement about being gentle, and at the same time gives his audience a practical incentive to accept his self-characterization. However, while the people view him as gentle, David does not characterize himself as "weak."[33]

Fokkelman (1990, 117) finds David's use of the adjective *rak* (רך) in 2 Sam 3:39 to be surprising. *Rak*, and the verbal form *rākak*, are only used to describe the dispositions of a few specific individuals, all but one of whom are members of the Davidic family line: David himself, Solomon, Rehoboam, Josiah, and Job.[34] As discussed above, Job's reference to his faintheartedness is entirely a function of his situation and not his basic disposition. Of course, that could be said of David in 2 Sam 3, because he merely claims to be weak "today." But he makes no such qualification when attributing the opposite trait to his nephews. Rather, here and elsewhere (2 Sam 16:10; 19:22) he points to it as a family trait. He may also be implying that it is their hardness which has allowed them to gain power over him in his present situation, that is, the situation as he portrays it for the benefit of his audiences.

33. In Josephus, David continues to talk to the people, saying at one point, "as for me, you know that I can do nothing to Joab and Abishai, the sons of Saruia, who are more powerful than I, but the Deity will inflict upon them just punishment for their lawless deed" (*Ant.* 7.45; Thackeray and Marcus 1977, 383). Rather than referring to himself as soft (or weak) or to his nephews as hard, David speaks in terms of greater and lesser power, with no qualification that this is the case only "today." In this respect Josephus's David resembles King Zedekiah in relation to his nobles in Jer 38:5; see Chapter 3, above. While in 2 Sam 3:39 David is addressing "his servants," here the king's audience is the entire people, all of whom are led to make a dispositional attribution about the king's "nature." David does not call himself soft or weak in the LXX of 3:39 either. Instead, he says that he is a "kinsman."

34. In 1 Chr 22:5; 29:1, David refers to Solomon as young and soft/weak (נער ורך); on these verses, see Lasine 2001, 135–36. In 2 Chr 13:7 Rehoboam's son Abijah claims that Jeroboam and his worthless scoundrels prevailed over Rehoboam because Rehoboam did not have the strength to withstand them because he was a youth and soft/faint-hearted (ורך־לבב). Through the prophetess Huldah, Yahweh himself calls the heart of Zedekiah's father Josiah רך, due to his humble response to the reading of the book of the law (2 Kgs 22:19). In other words, in this situation it is a good thing to be "soft-hearted," and Josiah is "rewarded" for it with an early death and burial in the family tomb.

When we attempt to read the events reported in all of 2 Sam 2–4 in terms of the characters' strength and weakness, ostensible opposites start to mirror one another. 2 Samuel 3 begins with a summary notice of David growing stronger, and Saul's house growing weaker (דל; v. 1). This is followed by a list of the wives and sons David has acquired, a sign of his virile strength. Next we hear that Abner is becoming strong in Saul's house (v. 6). In other words, Abner is getting stronger within a weakening house. Then Ishbosheth alleges that Abner has been demonstrating his strength in the same way that David has just done: by sleeping with royal women—in this case, one of Saul's women. And later we are informed that "Saul's wives" have in fact become David's (2 Sam 12:8).

Should we view Joab's complaint to David about Abner's motives as being analogous to Abner's complaint to Ishbosheth about the latter's making a fuss over a woman? If so, to that extent David is parallel to Ishbosheth and therefore in the role of a weak king who has to deal with a powerful commander. Yet after Abner's death it is David who appears strong when he orders Joab how to behave when mourning the deceased, and Joab complies without any mention of protest. This, in turn, contrasts with the later situation in 2 Sam 19, when David's mourning for the rebel Absalom has turned a day of joy into one of mourning, prompting Joab to force the king to appear before the people. It is not possible to determine whether David had to coerce Joab to appear in Abner's funeral procession, but one similarity stands out: it is Joab who caused the death of both of those who are being lamented. In 2 Sam 19 there is no doubt that David is weak and soft vis-à-vis Joab; Joab himself stresses that fact (2 Sam 19:8). However, we cannot assume that the same power relations obtained when Abner was cast in the role played by Absalom so many years later.

2 Samuel 2 and 3 both present Abner and Joab as strong and decisive. If David does manage to manipulate both of these powerful men in ch. 3, he is anything but soft and weak on that day, as he contends.[35] While

---

35. Of course, we cannot exclude the possibility that David sincerely believes that his present situation makes him weak. The ambiguity resembles that created by Homer when he has Achilles contrast himself to Odysseus in *Iliad* 9 (see above). Just as there is no doubt that Joab is "hard," so there is no doubt that Odysseus is duplicitous. The question is whether the speakers who claim to be the opposite of these two are truly their opposite or just their mirror-image. Achilles does appear to mean what he says when he says it. While commentators have long noted inconsistencies in Achilles' statements even within Book 9, this is most likely a function of the fact that Achilles is reacting differently to different interlocutors in the embassy scene. In Plato's *Lesser Hippias* (370a–371e), Socrates points out that

there is indeed evidence that David is in control, there is little evidence of any real weakness. The chapter is bracketed by the narrator's opening statement that David was growing stronger and the closing scenes in which David tells Joab what to do and heaps dread curses on him and his descendants. On the other hand, Joab himself is not harmed by David and does not even lose his job, which David explains by insisting that he is too weak to take action against his "hard" nephews. If the rest of the chapter undermines David's self-presentation, the probability increases that David planned this series of events, and intended for Joab to survive and stay on as his commander, whether or not Joab willingly played the role of foil. If Joab is *not* playing along with David concerning the funeral, then it is he who is ignorant about what is going on and *David* is the one who is totally in the know.

While David might not have been weak after Abner's assassination, he is described as being weak later in his reign, by the "wise man" Ahithophel. In his new capacity as Absalom's counselor during the rebellion, Ahithophel proposes to lead a force of twelve thousand men to come upon David while "he is weary and weak-handed" (יגע ורפה ידים) and therefore susceptible to panic (2 Sam 17:2). The people with him will then flee, allowing Ahithophel to strike only the king. The expression for weakness used there[36] is also employed by the narrator to describe Ishbosheth in 2 Sam 4:1. In that instance, the reason for Ishbosheth's weakness may be his perception of David's dangerous strength. If so, the weak Ishbosheth is viewing David as hard and strong at the very moment that David claims to be soft (see further in Lasine 2001, 112 n. 10). In the case of the scenario sketched by Ahithophel, the key question is whether David's weak-handedness is due to his situation alone, or the result of a dispositional trait which Ahithophel attributes to him, namely, that David is the kind of person who would feel weak in this kind of situation and therefore panic when attacked.

A number of commentators[37] have questioned the reliability of Ahithophel's advice here, in spite of his reputation for godlike wisdom (2 Sam 16:23). They do so by identifying Ahithophel as Bathsheba's

---

Achilles tells Ajax something different from what he tells Odysseus in this scene, implying that Achilles could outdeceive Odysseus, which would collapse the difference between them. Hippias replies by predicating a different motive to Achilles, based on the assumption that he has a very different character from Odysseus.

36. The phrase describes one's hands dropping down, expressive of weakness or dispiritedness. 2 Sam 4:1 uses the verb רפה, while 2 Sam 17:1 has the adjectival form.

37. E.g. Hertzberg 1964, 350 and the others cited by Bodner 2005, 124–25.

grandfather (an identification which is by no means certain)[38] and suggesting that Ahithophel is motivated by a desire for revenge against his granddaughter's abuser. The most recent and extended version of this argument is put forth by Bodner. He believes that a "grudge" against David is Ahithophel's sole motive for defection (2005, 126, 133). This allows him to interpret all of Ahithophel's words and actions in terms of this single motive, a procedure reminiscent of Mr. Wickfield's use of his "inch-rule" (see Chapter 1, above). Measured by this yard-stick, the fact that Ahithophel's strategy would minimize bloodshed and end the violence quickly is merely the "political side of [his] machination" (2005, 133). The "personal side" is his enmity for David. As result, Bodner hears Ahithophel's proposal as "virulent language" which "adds an element of malignancy to Ahithophel's character" and "evinces a rancorous confidence" (2005, 132, 133). Finally, McCarter (1984, 386) attributes character traits to Ahithophel on the grounds that Ahithophel himself does exactly that: "Ahithophel turns out to be foolish in attributing his own fickleness to other men."[39]

The fact remains that no reason is given in the text for Ahithophel's switch of allegiance to Absalom; many reasons—or a combination of several reasons—are possible. The issue here is how we should evaluate Ahithophel's characterization of David as weak. David had not acted "panicky" in chs. 15–16, even in flight. However, the fact that God ensures Absalom's defeat by leading him to reject Ahithophel's advice implies that God himself assumes that Ahithophel's plan would be successful. Similarly, David's earlier prayer for God to "make foolish" the counselor's advice (15:31) assumes that his advice will *not* be foolish. Ahithophel himself seems to know that the alternate plan accepted by Absalom will not succeed, if the reason that he commits suicide is to avoid having the victorious David execute him for treason, as is often suggested.

A final question about 2 Sam 3: Is the story rhetorically designed to bring readers to the point of challenging David's self-characterization as weak—and by extension, his claim to be innocent of, and morally outraged by, the murder of Abner—or is this reading entirely "against the

38. See, e.g., Schley 1992b, 121–22 and Harris 2000, 35.

39. The idea that Ahithophel is a person of bad character is a commonplace in post-biblical literature. This includes Dante's *Inferno*, where Ahithophel's "wicked goadings" are used as an ancient example of a man who sows discord between a royal father and son (*Inf.* 28.136–38). In English literature, Ahithophel's name became a "conventional tag for traitor, wicked politician, and...[for] political machination" in general (Carver 1992, 27).

grain"? Like the many scholars who believe that the narrator "protests too much," Halpern (2001, 82–83) notes that the story "carefully and categorically denies that David had a motive for the murder." This "elaborate apparatus of defenses" indicates that the murder was "a live issue when this text—and probably Joab—were framed." Similarly, McKenzie notes that "the very fervency with which David's innocence in this matter is asserted can lead a historian[40] to suspect his complicity" (2000, 120). These scholars do not ask whether the text might be designed to "bare the device," that is, to make perceptible its character as apology.[41] After all, how can the story be as carefully crafted as they claim and still fail so miserably at persuading them of David's innocence and ignorance?

Regardless of how this issue is resolved, the definition of character which best suits David in 2 Sam 3 is that given by Goffman (1959, 252–53) about modern Westerners: "in our society the character one performs and one's self are somewhat equated… [T]his self…[is] generated by that attribute of local events which renders them interpretable by witnesses…[it] is a product of a scene that comes off, and is not a cause of it." In short, it is "a dramatic effect." As we have discovered throughout this study, different biblical stories illustrate different conceptions of character, and require different tools to analyze those conceptions.

One social-psychological tool which may be helpful in the study of characters' self-evaluation is the "self-standards" model for reduction of cognitive dissonance (see J. Cooper 2007, 90–116). This focuses on "people's tendency to evaluate their own behavior" (J. Cooper et al. 2005, 74), especially when they view themselves as good and moral but commit acts which are bad by relevant personal standards, or which have unwanted negative consequences. If one becomes aware of the inconsistency between one's high self-esteem and the bad acts which one has chosen to commit, the resulting dissonance will not usually be reduced by concluding that one must actually be a bad person because wicked acts emanate from wicked people (see 1 Sam 24:14). On the contrary,

---

40. Apparently non-historians are too dense to notice a problem. Cf. Halpern (2001, 83), who is surprised when even a "highly critical" historian like Gösta Ahlström takes the story at face value.

41. Polzin (1993, 40–41) believes that the narrator's "piling up of universals" in 3:36–37 communicates "the narrator's distance from the people's wholesale acceptance of David." Nevertheless, Polzin asserts that in this instance confidence in David is justified. The narrator's distancing here is aimed at the people, not David: "However innocent David is in this instance, the narrator is saying, the people appear foolish in their wholesale acceptance of the king." Polzin does not go on to ask whether *David* is "fooling" the people, resulting in their folly.

one will usually seek to justify one's positive view of oneself, either by minimizing the seriousness of the bad act and its consequences, or by judging negatively the person who has been adversely affected by the act (Glass 1964, 533 n. 3).

Aronson (1999, 121) highlights the irony involved in the latter strategy: "It is precisely because I think I am such a nice person that, if I do something that causes you pain, I must convince myself you are a rat."[42] We can also use this strategy when we learn that a bad act has been committed by a moral agent whose character we have assessed positively, by justifying the perpetrator at the expense of his victim. For example, if I am committed to the belief that David is a pious, heroic individual, when I learn that David has betrayed and killed Uriah I may convince myself that Uriah is a rat, as did the rabbis who claim that Uriah was being rebellious against royal authority when he refused David's order to go home to his wife (*b. Šabb.* 56a). In the next and final chapter, I will use a variety of tools to determine what our judgments about biblical figures like David say about our own "self-standards" and the ways in which we seek to maintain *our* positive self-assessments.

---

42. Aronson is referring to Glass's experiment with high self-esteem subjects who choose to administer electric shocks to others; see Glass 1964, 545.

Chapter 9

# ART THOU THE MAN?
# JUDGING KING DAVID AND JUDGING OURSELVES

## 1. Counting Character and Weighing "Heaps" of Facticity

Do not trust in the length of years. They regard a lifetime as[1] an hour. A person remains after death, and his deeds are placed beside him in heaps.
—*Instructions for Merikare* 55–56[2]

[To defend himself before this Court] his entire life—even the smallest actions and events—would have to be recalled, represented, and examined from all angles….how sad was such a task.
—Kafka, *Der Proceß* (1994, 134)

As long as you are alive, your case is doubtful… In order to cease being doubtful, it's necessary to cease being.
—Camus, *La Chute* (1956, 88)

When we judge a person as a whole and forever we are putting ourselves in the position of the underworld judges I discussed in the preface to this book. Plato suggests that a fair judgment is impossible when the judges are themselves alive. In this final chapter I want to ask how we living judges can most responsibly judge others (including literary personages), keeping in mind that such judgments also expose our own moral character, and thereby the meaning of our own lives as a whole.

Insofar as we assume that an individual's actions are caused by stable, robust and enduring dispositional traits, we can subject him or her to a "last judgment" *without* having to wait for that individual to die.[3] Once we have definitively evaluated a person's character at any given point in

---

1. Müller (1967, 118) reads *m wnw.t* as "in an hour"; cf. Quack 1992, 35.
2. Lines numbers refer to the St. Petersburg 1116A papyrus.
3. Kafka expresses this in aphoristic fashion: "Only our concept of time allows us to refer to the Last Judgment as such; in fact it is a *Standrecht*" (1953, 88). *Standrecht* is a German legal term which, in this usage by Kafka, seems to suggest that humans are constantly under judgment, and can be held accountable for their actions at any point in their lives.

time we can reckon all their future deeds on the basis of our prior judgment of their character. This kind of judgment assumes that individuals can commit acts by which they forfeit their right to be pitied, excused, or treated with clemency.[4] Such a judgment is a metaphoric death sentence.

According to the Egyptian text known as the *Instructions for Merikare*, a person's deeds are placed beside them in "heaps" when he or she is judged after death. Scholars disagree about whether this refers to all the person's actions during life, only the good deeds, only the bad deeds, or opposing piles of each.[5] When all the relevant evidence is taken into account, it seems clear that the "heaps" represent the grand total of all one's actions during life, not just the good or wicked deeds. And if one's heart represents "the individual's entire earthly existence" in scenes of afterlife judgment (Silverman 1991, 48), and actually "contained a record of the deceased's actions in life" (J. Taylor 2001, 37), their intentions and spoken words would be included as well.

Thus, when individuals are judged after their lives have ended, all the accumulated elements of their life-history are piled up beside them, and must be "counted." For the Egyptians, afterlife judgment involves "counting (or "reckoning") character" (*ḥsb qd*) or "counting hearts."[6] According to Assmann, "when the judges of the dead view a life-time

---

4.  For example, Philo contends that the Egyptian killed by Moses in Exod 2:11–14 had lived only to destroy men. Since the Egyptian has shed his own humanity, he has no right to clemency or pity. In effect, when Moses strikes the Egyptian he is destroying a vicious beast, not a human being (*Mos.* 1.44).

5.  How one understands the symbolism has much to do with how one interprets the word usually rendered "his deeds" (*sp.w.f*) and the words I translated "in heaps" (*m 'ḫ' '.w*). For the range of meanings denoted by *ḫ'* and *sp* (*zp*), see *CDME* 47, 221–22; J. Wilson in *ANET* 415 n. 12. The plural form *'ḫ'.w* has been understood in a variety of ways. Lichtheim (1973, 101) translates "his deeds are set beside him as a treasure." Brandon (1958, 120) argues that the judgment consists of "setting out in opposing heaps a man's good and bad deeds." Helck (1977, 33) restricts the sense of *sp.w.f* to only a person's misdeeds, which are laid "as heaps." Others who retain the plural sense of *'ḫ'.w* are Breasted (1968, 157; cf. 177, 249, 250) and Müller (1967, 123). Many translators render *m 'ḫ'.w* as singular "in a heap" or "*in einen Haufen*" (e.g. *CDME* 184; Volten 1945, 27). Karenga (2004, 167) believes that the deeds are set beside him "as his portion." Assmann prefers the mathematical sense of *'ḫ'.w*, translating "as a sum" or "*Endbetrag*" (1975, 12; 2005a, 73; cf. Quack 1992, 35).

6.  The heart was often viewed as forming one's character, as in this fragment: "It is the heart (*ib*) that multiplies character traits (*qdw*), a mighty teacher for shaping qualities (*biȝwt*)" (Ramesseum Papyrus II; Lichtheim 1992, 54). The verb *ip* is also used for "counting" in the sense of reckoning character in post-mortem judgment, as in the stela of Pairy: "I was put on the scale, I went forth, having been counted" (*ip.kwi*; Urk. 119.10–11). On counting hearts, see, e.g., *Pyramid Texts*, Utterance 217: "He will count hearts, he will claim hearts" (Lichtheim 1973, 31).

'as an hour,' they consider it under the aspect of 'having-been-ness,' and they reckon up the sum. It is as though an entire lifetime was the pre-history of this moment when the result...was determined" (2005a, 384; cf. 1975, 12 n. 13). This notion of "resultativity" is akin to Sartre's concept of "facticity" (Sartre 1943, 91–102). When a person dies, she or he is reduced to all "facticity" and no "transcendence." That is, one is reduced to the facts of one's past life, although those "facts" are of course still open to interpretation. No longer is that person the sum of her past actions and her future plans and possibilities.[7] As Camus's character Clamence declares in the epigraph to this section, "in order to cease being doubtful, it's necessary to cease being."

In contrast to the afterlife judgment in Egyptian texts, Job is very much alive when he feels that he has been judged and received his sentence. One reason that Job wants God to weigh him in just scales is because he knows that God is already "counting his steps" (31:4) and has already reckoned Job's character from the accumulated heaps of data he has at his disposal. Job himself has audited the records of his own life and calculated that his character has been righteous and that he possesses integrity. In his so-called negative confession (Job 31:5–40), which is so reminiscent of spell 125 of the *Book of the Dead*,[8] Job, in effect, stakes his life on the correctness of his computation.[9]

Job's friends also calculate the moral significance of Job's life experiences and condemn his behavior, his motives and, ultimately, his basic character. Yet they also implore him to change. In a sense, they ascribe to what commentators on Chronicles call the doctrine of "immediate retribution." In this sense, a person can be condemned as a whole for a life which has been heaped with sinful acts, and then go on to repent and live another existence which is morally impeccable. The Chronicler's Manasseh is a case in point. In this scenario, it is as though repentance allows one to alter one's basic character enough to change one's pattern of behavior, unless the repentance was itself prompted by a conversion of character.

7.   Dante's *Inferno* is the model for Camus' novel. Dante places the damned into situations which fit his judgments on their essential nature. These judgments may be based on just one evil (or at least dubious) action committed during their lifetime. As Erich Auerbach puts it, "we behold an intensified image of the essence of their being, fixed for all eternity in gigantic dimensions" (1953, 192; cf. 193, 197). Similarly, Camus' first-person narrator defines hell as "no way of explaining oneself; one is classified once and forever" (1956, 56–57).

8.   On the similarities and differences see, e.g., Kunz 2001, 242–44.

9.   On the risks involved when Job uses the expression חלילה לי in Job 27:5, see Chapter 8, above.

After his oath of clearance, Job refers again to the notion of counting character. He declares that if he were granted a legal hearing he would tell God the "number of his steps" (31:37), that is, the sum of his actions which he believes that God has already tabulated and evaluated.[10] Job's belief in the accuracy of his self-assessment convinces him that the reckoning would vindicate him. One modern fictional character who has often been viewed as a Job-like victim is Josef K. in *The Trial*, one of Kafka's so-called sacred texts.[11] Later in this chapter I will focus on the very un-Job-like flaws in K.'s character. For now, it will suffice to note that Josef K. is not exhilarated by the prospect of compiling the "heaps" of details which constitute his life experience, in order to prove his innocence before the court which is trying him for his moral failings. On the contrary, he envisions this task as "almost endless." Because K. has no insight into the charges against him, even the smallest actions and events of his entire life would have to be recalled, represented, and examined from all angles in his petition. K. sees this as a "sad" business best suited for senile retirees to wile away the time (Kafka 1994, 134).

Later I will discuss moral philosophers who believe that if we are to judge others fairly we must display sympathetic understanding and mercy, which stem from engaging in "participatory identification" with the particulars of individuals' "complex life histories," looking at "the minute details of motive and intention and their social formation" (Nussbaum 1995, 147, 167; cf. Cates 1998, 412). This too may seem like a sad and almost endless task. As Dickens's character David Copperfield puts it, "trifles make the sum of life" (2004, 773). Whether a given reader will regard the sum of Copperfield's narrated trifles as proof that he is "the hero of his own life" (Dickens 2004, 13) depends on a number of

---

10. See Job 14:16; 31:4; cf. 7:17–20, 13:27. Job 14:16 is difficult, and has been interpreted in opposing ways; see Dhorme 1984, 203; Whybray 1998, 79; Clines 1989, 333–34.

11. Both biblical scholars and specialists on Kafka have noted that Kafka's works have been treated as sacred—or claim that they *should* be so treated. Rosenberg remarks that "we…have invested the parables of Kafka with the aura of a sacred text" (1975, 87–88). Corngold quotes the instructions he received from the editor with whom he was working on a translation of one of Kafka's works: "'You must stay with Kafka's actual words,' he said, 'treat them like the Bible'" (2004, 191). Rolleston (1976, 9) declares that "we have to treat Kafka's texts as 'sacred'"; for Rolleston, "sacred texts exist in order to be interpreted." Many commentators agree that the Bible and Kafka's works "invite," "demand," or even "command" interpretation to an unusual degree. However, the concepts of sacred text and scripture involve many factors besides the demand for interpretation; see Lasine 1984d.

factors, as I will discuss below. How could the autobiographer Copperfield or the would-be autobiographer Josef K. (or we ourselves) make the facticity of their lives so convincingly univocal that readers of their stories would conclude only what they (or we) would wish them to conclude? And if such univocality is impossible, how should we evaluate complex literary characters like Copperfield and K., and biblical characters like King David? What *should* constitute the ethics of reading the Bible?

One "ethical reader," Denis Diderot, compares the novels of Samuel Richardson to sacred texts, more specifically, to a gospel designed to separate family members. He assumes that readers identify with virtuous characters and draw away from those who are unjust and vicious. In fact, Diderot (1994, 89, 92–94) says that he has to restrain himself from breaking off relations with people whose judgments of Richardson's characters are opposed to his own. Should we imitate Diderot by "separating" ourselves from those whose judgments on problematic characters like King David differ from our own? Should we, for example, draw conclusions about the moral character of readers who identify with David enough to excuse his crimes on the grounds that he is simply "all-too-human"? Is such an excuse a way to avoid being judged by the text in the way that Nathan's parable judges David? Is identification, or even empathy, a moral *failing* when faced with David's facticity, that is, the heaps of his actions and their devastating aftermath? But if we *do* condemn David are we implying that we are morally superior to the king, as though Nathan were to say to each of us, "Thou art *not* the man!'"? In order to deal with these questions it is first necessary to extend our previous discussions of narrative evaluation and the process of identification, and to add fresh perspectives based on the work of Kierkegaard and others. I will then compare the David and Bathsheba episode with the modern works by Dickens and Kafka mentioned above, works which also challenge readers to "break the spell of identification" with a morally suspect protagonist.

## 2. Identifying the Wicked and the "Negativity Bias"

> So, oft it chances in particular men,...
> Carrying, I say, the stamp of one defect,...
> His virtues else, be they as pure as grace,
> As infinite as man may undergo,
> Shall in the general censure take corruption
> From that particular fault.
>                     —Shakespeare, *Hamlet* (1. 4. 23, 31, 33–36; Q.2)

According to Frank Palmer, "to understand a wicked act is to…link the quality of the deed with the bad intentions that are involved in its execution… [Thus,] to condemn the act is to condemn the man" (1992, 78). Moral philosophers like Cates object that this "reflect[s] a disregard of morally relevant particulars"; she recommends that we foster "a flexible emotional responsiveness" to "the details of a person's unfolding story" (1998, 412). The problem is to decide whether one can justify withholding compassion and condemn a person as a whole and forever because they intentionally committed one or more evil acts, even if they are not "incurable" in Plato's sense (*Gorg.* 525b-d; *Phaed.* 113e; *Resp.* 615e). That is, even if they might go on to rehabilitate themselves like the Chronicler's Manasseh, do "good works," preach the Gospel to other death-row inmates,[12] and so on. To condemn a living person as a whole is to reduce him or her to their facticity, to define them—once and for all—by their evil act, eliminating the relevance of future change in behavior or disposition, regardless of possible extenuating circumstances.

If this mode of judgment sounds unusually harsh, social psychologists have found it to be a consistent mode of human behavior, which they call "negativity bias." The epigraph to this section shows that Shakespeare was well aware that an individual's many virtues can "take corruption" from just one "particular fault." Probably the most dramatic description of this phenomenon in the psychological literature is offered by Riskey and Birnbaum (1974, 171): "the overall goodness of a person is determined mostly by his worst bad deed, with good deeds having lesser influence." In fact, "given a person has done evil, an infinite number of good deeds may not produce a favorable overall impression" (1974, 172).[13] Other researchers have found that if a person commits his first offense, it neutralizes his earlier positive behaviors, even if the one being judged is an acquaintance of the evaluator (Richey et al. 1975, 240; 1972, 67).[14]

12.   I am referring here to the appeal of Scott Panetti; see Greenhouse 2007. On the Supreme Court's 5–4 decision "enforcing its edict against execution of the insane," see Blumenthal 2007.

13.   In support, these psychologists cite Ezek 3:20, in which God declares that if a righteous man turns back from his righteousness and does evil he shall die, and his righteous acts shall not be remembered. However, Skowronski and Carlston (1992, 441, 450–51) find that the impact of morally good behaviors was easily overridden by new information depicting immoral behaviors, but the reverse did not hold. An initial impression based on morally bad behaviors was not easily changed by new information about morally good behaviors.

14.   Richey et al. note that "[these studies] consistently support the hypothesis of negativity with regard to impressions of *character*." The results were shown to hold across four cultures (1975, 240, 233). Cf. Baumeister et al. 2001, 344–48.

According to some proponents of virtue ethics, the virtuous person is someone "for whom proper conduct emanates characteristically from a fixed disposition" (Kosman 1980, 103). King David implies that the same is true for vicious persons, when he cites the *mashal*: "from wicked men emanates wickedness" (1 Sam 24:14). Psychological research indicates that ordinary Westerners today make the same assumption. Lupfer and his colleagues (2000, 1354) note that when people witness immoral behavior they assume that only immoral people would behave in this way. As Bierbrauer puts it, in spite of all the evidence to the contrary accumulated by social scientists, "the naïve man…continues to believe that…*only good men* do good and merit praise[,] and…*only evil men* do evil and deserve punishment" (1979, 82; emphasis added). The important point here is that the tendency to judge others mainly by their worst bad act is exhibited not only by unusually severe and harsh individuals, but by the majority of us.

### 3. *Identifying the Sinner:*
### *Ambiguity, Attribution, and Cognitive Dissonance*

Believing is seeing.
>                               —Ernst Gombrich (1969, 210)

If the facts don't fit the theory, change the facts.
>                               —saying attributed to Albert Einstein

Any explanation is better than none.
>                               —Friedrich Nietzsche (1964b, 112)

We must not overlook the fact that we sometimes condemn people and literary characters not for their worst bad acts, but for actions which do not qualify as "bad" at all. Reader reactions to 2 Sam 24 are a case in point. Many non-academic readers and commentators state as a fact that King David exhibits one or more negative character traits in this story, including "pride," "arrogance," "a self-glorying spirit," self-aggrandizement, self reliance, self-sufficiency, military ambition, boastfulness, a lack of trust in God, and even rebellion.[15] Among academic commentators, Gordon (2000, 316) contends that "the likelihood is that it is David's aspirations after self-sufficiency that are being censured." Peterson (1999, 264) contends that David has committed a prideful act in the service of ambition and power. Similarly, Brueggemann (1990, 352) claims that David had yielded to the seduction of state power. Brooks

---

15.  These examples are taken from the results of a basic Google search using the keywords "david census plague pride."

(2005, 161–62) follows Gelander in assuming that David decides to demonstrate his military and political power.[16] And even though Fokkelman believes that God's plan is "nefarious" and that David is being manipulated, he nevertheless claims that "the king...really does want to quantify his own power" (1990, 310). Among rabbinic commentators, Nachmanides asserts that David's only reason for ordering the census was to express his pride that he ruled over such a large nation (Chavel 1975, 9). And according to one authority in *Midrash Talpiyot*, the danger of a plague is present only when the census is taken by a king for vainglorious motives (#20; Bleich 1989, 327).

In spite of this chorus of condemnation, the text of 2 Sam 24 offers little or no direct evidence which could support such highly negative judgments about King David here. Most of these judgments stem from grave distrust of the individual "self" and various forms of self-assertion. The very first verse is strong evidence against these assessments: "Again the anger of Yahweh was kindled against Israel, and he incited David against them, saying, 'Go, number Israel and Judah.'" Fokkelman (1990, 308) calls v. 1 a "little stick of dynamite" that the author has stuck into the story. He is referring to the theological implications of this verse. The sentence itself is quite simple and unequivocal: Yahweh commanded David to take a census of the two major sections of his kingdom. In other words, Yahweh gives a direct order to the king and David obeys it. How then could David possibly be acting selfishly proud, boastful and distrustful of his God, when he is simply obeying Yahweh's command? As Campbell puts it, "within the narrative, David's sin...consists in having obeyed God's order, when incited by God against Israel." Campbell adds that while David takes full responsibility for this in v. 17, "no court of law would accept such a confession in light of v. 1" (2005, 207; cf. 210).

Campbell believes that this story "does not speak well of God." Steussy (1999, 68) puts it more strongly, charging that God's punishing David for following the command he issued "border[s] on demonic." Yet, as indicated above, many readers conclude that the story does not speak well of *David*, not God. Is this another biblical example of readers justifying God by condemning the humans with whom God interacts, inventing human crimes (and character traits) which fit the punishment?

The narrative is riddled with silences which invite readers to fill in the blanks by reference to the situation or the disposition of the actors. For

---

16.  Brooks (2005, 162) contends that "it was actually *David's own anger*" which was "the factor," not Yahweh's. In this reading, David is angry because Israel doesn't love him! Hertzberg (1964, 411–12) asserts that on "closer examination" it appears that David "intended to alter or disband the levy...a direct inroad into the sacral sphere...a challenge to God himself."

example, in v. 1 we are not told why God is angry at "Israel" or how he transmitted his command to David. Moreover, David does not give any indication that he is aware of having been "incited" by God, let alone that he attempts to shift responsibility for his "sin" onto God. Nor does David tell Joab that the command originates with God, or explain to Joab (and therefore to us) what other reasons he might have for wanting to number the people. Joab also refrains from explaining why he balks at the idea of a census. Nor does David say why his conscience is bothering him after he has done it or why he thinks that the census-taking was foolish and sinful. In fact, the chapter never makes clear why this census is sinful. Since this is the case, we can never claim to know with certainty that David took the census for any reason other than obedience to an order from God. The cumulative effect of these silences is to prompt readers to adopt one of two strategies: either remain silent where the text is silent or add to the story by inserting intentions, motivations, and traits which are not stated or described in the narrative.

These silences would not be so vexing or mysterious if readers did not begin with a specific set of beliefs about God's character traits. Such readers may echo Abraham and say to God, "far be it from you to command one of your faithful followers to commit a sin, let alone reward him for his willingness to sin." Yet that is precisely what God does with Abraham in Gen 22. One might then object that God would not lead someone to commit a sin and then punish him or her for having done it. Yet that is what God does with Baasha, whom Yahweh raises up as king of Israel. Baasha annihilates all of the house of Jeroboam, fulfilling the curse that Yahweh had hurled down against Jeroboam. He is then punished by Yahweh in the same way, in part because he fulfilled Yahweh's curse (1 Kgs 15:27–30; 16:1–6).

In 2 Sam 24:17 David describes the seventy thousand dead as innocent sheep. Is David leaving open the possibility that Yahweh's anger was *not* motivated by a sin committed by Israel? Here a reader might object that God's character would never lead him to be angry at non-sinners, certainly not angry enough to kill them. Yet this is precisely what happened with Uzzah in 2 Sam 6:6–7, although many readers attempt to invent sins that Uzzah committed in order to justify God's anger and Uzzah's death (see Lasine 2010, 41 n. 31). The objecting reader could then retreat to the position that at least God would never kill non-sinners with whom he is not angry, although this is precisely what God does with Job's children and workers.

Admittedly there *is* evidence within 2 Sam 24 that David can act selfishly. For example, instead of choosing the mode of punishment which would cause him the personal discomfort of fleeing from his enemies for three months, he prefers either of the two proposed penalties which entail immense suffering for his people. As a result, many thousands of these innocent "sheep" die like the ewe lamb which the "rich man" David failed to spare in Nathan's parable (vv. 13, 17). Nevertheless, this action does not prove that David was displaying selfishness and pride earlier in ch. 24, when he ordered the census. One could also argue that David is acting selfishly and hypocritically when he offers himself and his family as substitute victims *after* all the deaths have occurred and Yahweh has repented of the evil (v. 16), especially since he could have spared his people earlier by accepting the option of three months of personal suffering Yahweh had offered him. But once again, this does not imply that David's original motivation for calling the census was selfish or proud. Why David did *that* was stated at the start: he was told to do it by Yahweh.

There are many ways of explaining why it is so difficult for readers to refrain from adding motivations and traits to the biblical characters whose actions we are not allowed readily to understand. The epigraphs to this section point in the right direction. From the perspective of social psychology, the ways in which readers attribute negative traits to David in 2 Sam 24 illustrate several of our psychological vulnerabilities. In the present case, readers tend to explain David's call for the census as a function of his prideful character, rather than viewing him as being constrained by his situation, that is, the direct order he has received from God, the ultimate authority figure. If subjects in Milgram's obedience experiments were constrained by the orders they received from a minor authority figure like a lab instructor, how much more would David be constrained by his jealous and wrathful God?

Readers' condemnations of David here can also be explained in terms of the need to reduce the discomfort caused by "cognitive dissonance." This refers to our tendency to reduce the tension between two conflicting cognitions (pieces of information, beliefs, attitudes etc.), by changing one of them to bring it more into conformity with the other (Festinger 1957, 260–66; Harmon-Jones and Mills 1999, 3–4). Because events in the world are often difficult to change or ignore, when an event or completed action conflicts with one's beliefs (including about what kind of person one is), it is easier to change one's attitude or belief (see Beauvois and Joule 1999, 66). However, when one has a strong commitment to a belief, attitude or value, one may ignore, discount or attempt to refute the fact or event which conflicts with it (see Harmon-Jones 1999, 93–95).[17]

---

17. In some cases, the attempt to refute the conflicting cognition is achieved through seeking new cognitions which support the original belief; in others, it may be through persuading other people to agree with one's beliefs and reject the

In the present case, readers may be strongly committed to beliefs such as these: God would never be angry at, or kill, innocent people. Or, God would never incite a person to commit a sin and then punish them for having done it. Or, people's actions stem from their moral character, rather than their situation. Alternatively, one may be strongly committed to a prior judgment about the character of another individual, such as "David is a hero and model of piety," or, conversely, "David is a wicked self-obsessed king," or, "David is a human being, and like all other humans, he is weak, corrupt and sinful by nature, and subject to over-weening pride." The more that readers are committed to beliefs like these, and the more limited is their tolerance for ambiguity, the more likely it is that they will ignore or discount "dissonant" evidence in the text which runs counter to their beliefs, or change the facts of the story to fit their theories about God's character.

### 4. *It Is I to Whom It Is Speaking*

These ways of negatively evaluating others' character tend to place the evaluator in the position of detached observer. In terms of evaluating literary characters, it puts the reader outside the frame of the story. But readers do not usually remain so aloof and detached from the stories they hear or read. Diderot's "scriptural" way of reading Richardson involves taking the people and events in his novels *personally*, thanks to the process of identification. But Diderot does not take the characters per-sonally enough to ask himself whether *he* might share the nature of the vicious villain he condemns, or consider that the story may be speaking to him—personally—about his own faults.

Such questions *are* asked by readers of the Bible such as Kierkegaard. He contends that scripture is a mirror in which we are supposed to see ourselves (1990, 25). Echoing William Tyndale,[18] Kierkegaard advises that when you read God's word, you should "remember to say to yourself incessantly: 'It is I to whom it is speaking; it is I *about whom* it

---

conflicting cognitions (Festinger 1957, 177–96). On the differing experiences of selfhood and dissonance in Western and Eastern cultures, see J. Cooper (2007, 136–52). On individual differences in the experience of dissonance, see, e.g., J. Cooper et al. 2005, 75–76; Aronson 1999, 109–12, 120–23. On the relation between tolerance of ambiguity and dissonance, see Festinger (1957, 266–71) and the studies cited in Furnham and Ribchester 1995, 183–84. For another explanation of the tension produced by perceived dissonance, ill-fit or imbalance, see Heider 1958, 201–12.

18.  In his *Prologue to Genesis*, Tyndale advises that "as thou readest, think that every syllable pertaineth to thine own self, and suck out the pith of the Scripture"; see Greenblatt 1984, 96.

is speaking'" (1990, 35). When we take an impersonal and objective stance toward the text, as does David when he hears Nathan's parable, we turn the Word into something impersonal, and fail to see its application to ourselves in particular. The fact that the biblical David was emotionally involved and far from objective in his reaction to Nathan's story[19] does not affect Kierkegaard's main point: David did not recognize that the story was *about him* personally, and addressed *to him* personally.

Kierkegaard is urging us to place ourselves within the frame of biblical stories, and to cultivate "honest distrust of oneself,...[treating] oneself as a suspicious character" (1990, 44). Most empirical studies of reading indicate that readers and hearers avoid identifying with negative characters; Kierkegaard is suggesting that we distrust ourselves enough to entertain the notion that our mirrors in a story may be the bad guys. Clearly, the way in which we identify with and evaluate biblical characters includes an evaluation of ourselves in relation to those characters. In addition, it may reveal who the reader sees himself as being, or who he does not want to see himself as being.

### 5. *Empathy, the Spell of Identification, and the Process of Character Evaluation*

Indifference towards, and ignorance of, other people's inner lives leads to a totally skewed relationship to reality and breeds blind self-conceit. Since the days of Adam and Eve—since two came from one—no one has ever been able to live who has not wanted to put himself in his neighbor's place and ascertain his true situation by also attempting to see it through different eyes. Imagination and the art of surmising in relation to the emotional life of others—that is, empathy—is not merely praiseworthy insofar as it breaks through the bounds of the ego, it is also an indispensable means of self-preservation.

—Thomas Mann, *Joseph und seine Brüder* (1964, 359)

Because these accounts of ethical reading usually assume the importance of identification, this concept must be examined before proceeding further. The role played by identification with literary characters is not as obvious and unproblematic as it may seem. Traditionally, literary critics have taken for granted that "to some extent...identification is a necessity of all literature, as it is of life" (Watt 1957, 201; cf. Cawelti 1976, 18). More recently, however, the concept has been criticized or rejected. Various reasons are given. For example, "the reader's identificatory fantasies" are said to make people "misrecognize themselves as free

---

19. On David's emotional response, see Lasine 1984a, 112–18.

subjects" (Lynch 1998, 14–15; see Chapter 1, above). Others view identification as prompting "ego confusion." Still others believe that the term "identification" should be abandoned in favor of empathy, which more accurately describes the process (see, e.g., Andringa 2004). Finally, some contend that the concept should be retained, as long as we distinguish between "weak" and "strong" forms of identification (Cupchik 1997, 17).[20]

I cannot agree with Mann's narrator in *Joseph* when he expresses the optimistic view that no one has ever been able to live without wanting to explore his neighbor's true situation by attempting to see it through his eyes. Psychological studies suggest that individuals' "empathic dispositions" differ, both in relation to other people and literary characters (Keen 2006, 214; 2007, 10–12). Hakemulder (2000, 70) argues that "the tendency to put oneself in another's place is a "personality variable... strongly correlat[ed] with certain global personality traits." Some studies indicate that "empathizers are better readers" (Keen 2006, 214; 2007, 87–88), because they are better able to "understand the emotions and motivation of characters" (Hakemulder 2000, 4; cf. 49). Nevertheless, most research has found that empathic reading experiences do *not* change a reader's disposition or attitudes, *or* affect their behavior.[21] Even Diderot eventually came to this conclusion (see Blum 1974, 89–90).

An empathetic reader imaginatively puts him- or herself into the mind and situation of a character. Philosopher Frederick Schoemen (1987, 307) notes that one "reason people have for being morally generous is they can see *themselves* falling prey to a certain line of behavior, and... this act of identification in itself makes them prone to leniency." But he goes on to argue that such identification "offers no excuse..." and "no basis for mitigation." In contrast, Cates (1998, 412) stresses "the moral value of a compassionate demeanor over against one that prefers clarity and simplicity of moral perception and judgment." The question is whether such compassion is appropriate in situations which *do* clearly call for simple moral judgment.

20. According to Cupchik (1997, 17), in weak identification spectators are "witnesses" who adopt the character's perspective and experience events as if through their eyes and ears. This helps to construct a mental representation or what Graesser et al. (1994, 372) call a coherent, "meaningful situation model." In contrast, strong identification is predicated on some kind of resonance between the lived world of the situated character and the emotional needs of the readers and an absorption of one into the other.

21. Keen 2006, 214; 2007, 92; Hakemulder 2000, 36; contrast Collins and Zbikowski 2005, 851, 853; Polichak and Gerrig 2002, 79.

Psychologists like Hakemulder (2000, 153) assume that readers are not likely to take the role of morally objectionable characters. This would seem to preclude judging those characters with "moral generosity." However, Keen (2007, 74) points to cases in which a reader connects emotionally with the "wrong" character. In her research, some "readers confessed not only to disliking certain popular characters, but to empathizing with or identifying with despised characters apparently held up for scorn by authors."[22]

Some theorists describe moral judgments on characters as preceding an emotional disposition toward them, while others envision a process during which "empathic responses are...corrected and redirected by moral judgments" (Hakemulder 2000, 70). The shock of having identified with the "wrong" character—or having recognized oneself in a "bad" character—might itself propel an empathetic withdrawal from them, expressing both a judgment against the character and an assertion of difference between oneself and that character.[23] Whether a given reader will be led to confront the negative aspects of himself reflected in a character, or to assert his difference from the character by condemning him, the fact remains that "we say who we are...when we confess our feelings about characters," as Keen puts it (2007, 77; cf. 80).

This is especially important in collective reading situations, as observers from Diderot to modern scholars have pointed out. Keen notes that "among readers with different emotional reactions to a shared text" we share our opinions "fully conscious that we will be judged by others" (2006, 223; 2007, 77; cf. 91). To philosopher Noël Carroll (1998, 141), "it comes as no surprise that we should want to discuss, to share, and to compare with other readers our reactions to the characters [and] situations" in texts which are designed to elicit "moral responses." To this extent, it is not surprising that Diderot would consider separating himself

---

22. Keen's studies of empathy in novel-reading make use of developmental and social psychology, as well as neuroscience. She also gathers anecdotal evidence from other readers, which she compares to existing empirical studies of reading. According to Keen (2007, 6–9), the notion that women are more empathetic than men is more indicative of culturally sanctioned gender roles than a universal set of traits. Cf. Milgram's mistaken assumption that female subjects would respond differently from males in his obedience experiments (1974, 63).

23. Similarly, Cawelti (1976, 18) notes that the process of identification in a mimetic fiction can make readers confront motives and experiences in themselves which they might prefer to ignore. Andringa (2004, 210) notes that recognition of similarity can cause aversion, but also joy or relief. Desirability may cause eager interest, but also envy, while empathetic understanding may cause pity but also contempt.

from those whose "moral responses" to a shared text were opposed to his own.

Diderot was recommending group reading and re-reading of Richardson's novels in the second half of the eighteenth century, when "intensive" and "empathetic" reading of the literature of sensibility was at its height.[24] This mode of reading had previously been reserved for the Bible, at least within Protestantism.[25] As Chartier (1999, 652) observes, these novels became "a guide to existence," marking the "deplacement of an ancient model of spiritual reading to the novel."[26] In this model, readers are "absorb[ed]...into a reading process that [the novel] governs just as firmly as the religious text had done" (Cavallo and Chartier 1999, 25). Should Jewish and Christian biblical scholars—as academic readers of the Hebrew Bible/Old Testament, our shared "religious text"—make room for this style of reading biblical narratives, and share our moral responses to characters with one another?

### 6. *Judging King David and Ourselves*

> In many ways "know thyself" is not well said. More useful would be "know other people."
>
> —Menander, *Thrasyleon* (Allinson 1959, 360)

I will address this last question by evaluating David as he is portrayed in 1–2 Samuel. As mentioned earlier, David believes that wickedness emanates from wicked men. If we apply this standard to him, is *David* a "wicked man"? David's operating assumption is that his words and deeds are motivated by the "uprightness of his heart" (1 Chr 29:17; cf. 1 Sam 24:12–16).[27] Some of the other characters in this textual world,

24. See Cavallo and Chartier 1999, 24–25; Wittmann 1999, 295–96.

25. In late eighteenth-century paintings, the traditional group reading situation is that of the "extended family gathered together in evening to listen to the patriarch read the Bible aloud" (Cavallo and Chartier 1999, 26).

26. Similarly, Blum (1974, 78) notes that the novel would now "do for the worldly what the Bible did for the pious, provide virtue for those who accepted its words as literally true." Similarly, Darnton (1984, 251) observes that "Rousseau's... public probably applied an old style of religious reading to new materials, notably the novel, which had previously seemed incompatible with it." They "threw themselves into texts with a passion that we can barely imagine."

27. In 1 Sam 24 David quotes the proverb that wickedness comes from wicked men, after saying that there is neither evil nor transgression in *his* hand; *he* has not sinned against Saul by killing him. In v. 18 Saul buys into David's self-characterization, declaring that David has rendered good to him, while he has rendered evil to David.

like Achish of Gath (1 Sam 29:6), share David's positive view of himself, even though readers are given ample reason to question their assessment of David's behavior toward them. Eliab's much more negative evaluation of his brother's character is usually dismissed by readers as an indicator of *Eliab's* bad character rather than David's.[28]

In spite of all the negative information that readers of the Court History are given about David's bad acts—including his murder of Uriah and adultery with Bathsheba—most retain a very positive opinion of David's character. "Negativity bias" does not seem to affect their assessments of the king. Various factors might explain why this is so. Some, like Isser, grossly understate the seriousness of David's sins, saying, for example, that "the Bathsheba affair does not reflect well on [his] character" (2003, 159; cf. 183). Others focus on positive aspects of David's character and deeds at other points in his career. Dante places the sweet inspired psalmist David in Paradise—among the just rulers, no less (*Par* 20.37–42). Tyndale (1992, 8) points to the fact that David "pleased God and [was a] good [man], both before...those things...and also after."

Even modern scholars who acknowledge that David has an "ugly side" and "character flaws"[29] temper their assessment by pointing to his allegedly "complex inner conscience" and stressing that he is "plagued by remorse" after committing bad acts (Noll 1997, 129), in spite of the fact that David expresses no remorse at all after murdering Uriah, prompting Nathan to trap the king into a belated two-word acknowledgment of his already-exposed sin against God (חטאתי ליהוה; 2 Sam 12:13).[30] While this brief admission is made only *after* Nathan made it clear to David that his crimes were known and would be punished in specific ways, U. Simon (1997, 122–23), Aurelius (2004, 10), and others (e.g. Bar Yosef 2006, 961) incorrectly describe the scene as though the king recognizes the "full severity of his sin" and confesses *immediately after* hearing the parable, when he angrily and "sincerely" condemns the rich man in the story.[31] For Bowman (2002, 91), it is David's "anguished

---

28. Bodner argues that the reader of 1 Sam 16–17 is being encouraged "not simply to make a series of psychological pronouncements on Eliab as merely a jealous older sibling on the rampage," but to keep Eliab's judgments on David's character "open-ended as a potential point of insight into David's complex personality" (2005, 23–24; cf. 16–22, and Chapter 3, above).

29. Noll 1997, 61; Bowman 2002, 91; cf. Steussy 1999, 197; Barton 2003, 72.

30. There is no textual basis for Simon's assumption (1997, 122–23) that Nathan knew that David's "insensitivity to the death of Uriah was temporary"; in fact, there is no evidence that David's insensitivity *was* temporary.

31. For Simon (1997, 123–24), the brevity of David's acknowledgment of his sin against Yahweh is not an admission of what has already become obvious, but a way

response" to the illness of his first son by Bathsheba which expresses "repentance...and renewed piety," even though the king's baffling behavior in this scene can, and has, been understood very differently by other readers (see Chapter 3, above). Bowman also asserts that although David is "blind" to his own flaws, he "recognizes and condemns moral failure in others" (2002, 91), even though David's lack of action after Amnon's rape of Tamar indicates the opposite.[32]

Others echo Barth (2004, 467) in saying that David is "like all other men." Many understand this to mean that David is characterized by his "complexity";[33] he is "a very human mix of good, bad, and indeterminate features" (Steussy 1999, 88). "Character," as the term is employed in such statements, has the features of an object. It has many "sides" and can be "circumscribed."[34] It can be "infected" (Bowman 2002, 91). It "emerges" or "surfaces" (Bowman 2002, 95, 97; Noll 1997, 61), becoming readable to the observer. And it *causes* an individual to act in "typical" and "characteristic" ways.[35]

Readers often stress that David is "very human," or "fully human,"[36] in a way that also tends to mitigate the severity of his crimes. And if David is a typically complex and very human character, he must be like *us*—

---

of accentuating the force of the admission. He refers to David's words in v. 13 as his "reply" to Nathan's "that man is you," even though he does not follow commentators who claim that the chapter originally lacked vv. 7b–12. In Simon's reading, David spontaneously and angrily "pronounces judgment on himself," which expresses his "authentic" sincerity (1997, 122–23). Since the king's two words in v. 13 hardly constitute an "angry pronouncement of judgment" on himself, Simon seems to be referring back to the condemnation of the rich man in v. 5. Nevertheless, he goes on to describe David's words in v. 5 as "the death sentence that David has unwittingly passed on himself" (1997, 123). Whether or not Simon's conflation of vv. 5 and 13 is intentional, the effect is to salvage David's character in the usual way, by retaining the traditional image of the king as a man who exhibits immediate, full and spontaneous repentance.

32. Garsiel (1993, 262) assumes that the biblical narrator prevents identification with the victim Uriah, because otherwise we would "find it very difficult to forgive David." This would cause readers to "lose sight of the moral lesson taught by the whole affair," that "repentance is at least partially effectual even after adultery and murder." My discussion does not assume that this is the "moral lesson" of the story, or that it is easy to forgive David in the text as it stands—if one reads the narrative ethically, in the sense described above.

33. E.g. Noll 1997, 38, 63; Bowman 2002, 74, 95; Barton 2003, 72; Whybray 1968, 36.

34. Noll 1997, 61; Barton 2003, 72; Bowman 2002, 91.

35. Bowman 2002, 90–92; also see Chapter 4 n. 52, above.

36. E.g. Steussy 1999, 88; Noll 1997, 182; cf. 63; VanderKam 1980, 534.

and *we* must be like *him*. Thus, Tyndale (1992, 8) insists that we are not "holier than David, though he brake wedlock, and…committed abominable murder." Modern scholars agree, claiming that David is "a person like ourselves," with a heart that "looks remarkably like anyone else's" (Barton 2003, 73; Steussy 1999, 70). For Bowman (2002, 75) this is a "counter-story," designed to present "a confessing community a mirror of ourselves" (2002, 74; cf. 97). Barton (2003, 73) also puts it in a way reminiscent of Kierkegaard, noting that the story of David is told "in such a way that the reader is obliged to look [human emotions and attitudes] in the face and to recognise…her affinity with the characters in whom they are exemplified."

Even apologists for David concede that he acts like a tyrant at times in the books of Samuel. However, this too could exonerate the king if we appeal to attribution theory. In their critiques of tyranny, Herodotus, Plato and others point out that being in power as a monarch is a *situation*, one which would make *anyone* capable of committing evil acts. In this set of circumstances, situation trumps character. Leaders like David, therefore, being "human," must fail morally in that situation. In response, one could cite the social psychologists who claim that situations are largely of one's own making. While Herodotus's Otanes (*Hist.* 3.80) and others contend that the power of kingship creates a necessarily corrupting situation for the monarch, whether a given king becomes a tyrant depends on how he "situates himself" in his role, that is, whether he sets in place practices which acknowledge and correct for the temptations of power, whether he acknowledges his interdependence with others, and so on. The Hebrew Bible acknowledges that royal power does not necessarily corrupt, since many of the kings are not said to commit any of the injustices listed by Herodotus and Plato (*or* by Samuel), the very injustices which David *does* commit.

The idea that David's sins are a mirror for readers has even made its way into discussions of business ethics, where it is been dubbed "the Bathsheba Syndrome."[37] For example, Ludwig and Longenecker advise

---

37. Ludwig and Longenecker 1993, 267; cf. Price 2000, 178–79. This "syndrome" is viewed as the result of both situational and dispositional factors, although the authors do not invoke concepts from attribution theory. Success creates a situation which allows leaders like David to become complacent. It grants them privileged access to information and people, and it often leads to unrestrained control of organizational resources. In terms of disposition, it can "inflate a leader's belief in his or her personal ability to manipulate or control outcomes" and lead to egocentricity (1993, 268–69, 271). Neither these authors nor other exponents of the "Bathsheba Syndrome" pinpoint the narcissistic personality type as most likely to exploit the opportunities given them by their privileged situation, although studies

"successful [business and political] leaders" that "it could happen to you" (1993, 272). These authors begin with the assumption that David is presented as a "good" man of "high moral character…[and] strong personal integrity" (1993, 265–67). David, and analogous modern business leaders, throw away their success "by engaging in an activity which is wrong, which they know is wrong, which they know would lead to their downfall if discovered, and which they mistakenly believe they have the power to conceal." In this scenario, the prophet Nathan becomes "the equivalent of a modern day whistle-blower" (1993, 271), and the reader of their article is to consider him- or herself as having the potential to resemble David at his worst.

*Are* the David narratives a mirror which challenges us to take action to change ourselves—or our business practices? *Should* they lead us to be empathetic and merciful in our assessment of the king, knowing that our judgment can reflect back on us, like David's condemnation of the rich man in Nathan's parable? Is our potential likeness to him a "basis for mitigation"? Barton (2003, 10) contends that the Court History, and in particular Nathan's parable, lead "the reader or hearer to find analogies between the story and his or her own life and to draw appropriate conclusions." For me, the "appropriate" conclusion to draw is that David is a mirror of someone I've tried *not* to become. If Nathan were to tap me on the shoulder, I would hope he'd say "You're *not* the man!" Law (2002, 124), commenting on Kierkegaard, points out the obvious: "most of us, after all, have not arranged for our rivals…to be murdered."

However, Rosenberg (1986, 41) points out the ethical dangers of distancing ourselves too quickly from David: "Nathan's…'you're the man'…is ultimately capable of being turned against the reader, who has thus far been habituated to imagine villainy primarily in the third person, just as has the king himself… [T]he 'you're the man' of allegorical discourse is distressingly contagious but it likewise can appear to quarantine and reassure ('Yes, *he's* the one, all right!'). It much depends on the type of reader facing this material." In Kierkegaard's terms, if "he's the man" and not me, this scripture is *not* addressed to me personally, and is not about me. If that is my conclusion, then I've determined what kind of

linking leadership and narcissism are well known. Ludwig and Longenecker (1993, 271) come closest to making this connection when they cite "the emptiness syndrome" and the "I am the center of the universe phenomenon." Price (2000, 179) faults Ludwig and Longenecker for "the egoistic assumptions at the heart of [their] view." He believes that a cognitive explanation for leaders' failures is stronger than a volitional one. However, Price may be failing to consider the extent to which cognitive mistakes and distorted thinking pander on behalf of desires and personal fantasies stemming from the leader's personality type.

reader *I* am facing is this material. Whatever I might conclude, it's clear that the epigraph from Menander is itself "not well said" in one respect. While at first it might seem more "useful" to know other people than to know oneself, this study has made it abundantly clear that one needs to know oneself *before* one can be capable of knowing (and accurately assessing) other people.

### 7. *Judging Dickens's David and Uriah*

Before reaching any verdict concerning David—or myself—I want to compare this complex king to two modern literary characters whose ethical behavior presents similar challenges to readers. The first of these is Dickens's David Copperfield.[38] Many Dickens scholars have puzzled over the significance of Dickens naming his seemingly virtuous protagonist "David," and Copperfield's odious rival "Uriah," to say nothing of his calling the object of their shared desire "Agnes," whose name recalls the lamb in Nathan's parable. Most argue that the reversal of "good" and "bad" characters in the two narratives "destabilizes" the presentation of characters and events by Dickens's first-person narrator Copperfield, including his moral judgments on his fellow characters. For example, Bar Yosef (2006, 961) asserts that by "constantly" reminding readers of 2 Samuel, Dickens is able to present David Copperfield in an ironic perspective, raising doubts about his "strict moral design for his own history." Other scholars who have *not* considered intertextual links with the Bible have also shown that Dickens exposes the "limitations and self-deceptions of David's perspective" (e.g. Jordan 1985, 64).

Some commentators believe that the parallel to the Court History puts Copperfield into the role of king[39] or representative of the victimizing "ruling classes" (Jordan 1985, 79), making Uriah Heep David's exploited "servant." These scholars tend to castigate David for his refusal to see the extent to which Uriah Heep is a "society-fostered" scapegoat (e.g. Stone 1979, 225; Newey 2004, 132).[40] Others stress that David

38. As late as 1970 Barbara Hardy wrote that she did not know "if anyone had observed the Biblical origins" of the names "David Copperfield" and "Uriah Heep" (1987, 17). Such a statement would be impossible to make now, as will become clear as we proceed. Hardy supposes that Dickens himself was "not conscious of all the ironies of the associations." The Dickens scholars I will discuss in this section would strongly disagree.

39. Hara n.d., 8, 11; Bar Yosef 2006, 962; cf. Stone 1979, 222.

40. Uriah is scapegoated for reminding "smug readers" of the arbitrary and irrational nature of our "privileged categories and power" (Titolo 2003, 184, 186, 191; cf. Tambling 2004, xxxiv).

dehumanizes and demonizes Uriah in order to avoid acknowledging the extent to which Heep mirrors himself, in terms of his aspirations and social status.[41] Hara (n.d., 11) expresses this view most dramatically: "Heep must be the despicable, dastardly vermin that he is which it is the king's pleasure and even duty to trample upon despite, or rather because of, his secret kinship to himself." Stone suggests that Heep not only exposes David's dark side, but "*our* hidden urges and motivations" (1979, 226; emphasis added; cf. 222), implying that Uriah shows the less flattering side of being "totally human."

For one Dickens scholar, the intertextual linkages transform the biblical warrior Uriah into another Uriah Heep. In her reading, Bathsheba's Hittite husband becomes "leech-like...prating...flawed...verbose, tiresome, blind...almost strident...clumsy...queer...self-congratulatory... facile and glib" (Vogel 1976, 9–10)![42] Perry and Sternberg (1986, 293–94) also leave room for Uriah to be something other than "an exemplary soldier, a man of noble spirit and uncompromising conscience." They argue that this interpretation of his character holds only if Uriah does not know what David has done, and if we take his words "at face value." They believe that such idealistic behavior is "strange...unrealistic [and]...*too* heroic to be true," reducing him to "the flat figure of the idealist" (1986, 297–98). However, if Uriah *does* know, he becomes "more alluring" in the "tensions and stresses he lives through than the flat figure of the idealist."[43] Yet this version of Uriah is still far from the sniveling Heep-like Hittite described by Vogel.

In contrast, more than one Dickens scholar finds Uriah *Heep* to be "profoundly sympathetic" (Titolo 2003, 186) at certain points in the novel, in spite of the fact that the narrator David consistently compares him to a menagerie of slimy, creeping, vile subhuman beasts.[44] N. Carroll

41.　E.g. Buckton 1997, 209–11; Stone 1979, 220; Jordan 1985, 78.

42.　According to Vogel (1976, 8), Uriah the Hittite is also like Uriah Heep in that both Davids have to "suffer in silence" a Uriah's "unwanted presence overnight." But in 2 Sam 11, during the first night King David does not even know that Uriah was sleeping with the courtiers in the palace; he learns this only the next day.

43.　U. Simon does not agree with Perry, Sternberg, and Garsiel that Uriah may have been aware of David's actions: "it's precisely the moral superiority of the betrayed husband that frustrates the king's stratagem, and Uriah's guilelessness that gives his words their force... Uriah's integrity confounds David's scheme" (1997, 105, 107).

44.　See the list of David's epithets for Uriah assembled by Newey (2004, 128–29). For readers like Titolo, sympathetic responses to Heep support Suleiman's contention that when a narrator reports the words of a negative character, "these words can acquire an authentic tone that will counteract the condemnation they're supposed to provoke" (Suleiman 1983, 206–7).

is one reader who accepts David's presentation of Uriah uncritically, and universalizes that reading: "anyone who does not find Uriah Heep… repugnant would have missed Dickens's point" (1998, 139). Such a reader gets the narrator *David's* point, but not the author's point, if Dickens is indeed showing David's perspective to be unreliable and unfair.

According to Bar Yosef, "the Old Testament original was imprinted… powerfully on the minds" of Dickens's Victorian readers (2006, 957), allowing us to "gain a better understanding of the Victorian reader response" by comparing the biblical story with Dickens's novel. Specialists on Victorian reading habits do not necessarily agree with Bar Yosef's assumption that "scriptural stories provided a common cultural ground" in nineteenth-century England. For example, Vincent (1982, 110) finds that in many cases the Bible served as "a vague symbol of religious commitment, useful as a primer for young children…, an occasional source of entertainment, [and]…a particularly suitable item for pawning." He points out that English surveys conducted in the late 1830s constantly emphasized that the possession of the books "bore little relation to the practice of reading" during this period. He confirms the statement made by autodidact John Clare that "te Bible, is laid by on its peaceful shelf, and by 9 cottages out of 10 never disturbed or turn'd to further than the minute's reference for reciting the text on a Sunday."[45] Other scholars point to the poor quality of schooling during this period, especially before 1870.[46] Rose (2001, 102–3) notes that memoirs of Bible reading frequently focus on the gaudy illustrations rather than on the text itself.[47]

Against this background, it is illuminating that the word "bible" appears only once in *David Copperfield*, referring to a Bible in a working

45. Vincent notes that in Dunkirk in Kent parents read in the evening in only two of fifty families. On methodological issues involving Vincent and Rose, see Colclough 2007, 149–53.

46. See Webb 1950 and the scholars mentioned in the preceding note. In several novels Dickens describes the hopelessly inadequate way the Bible was used as a primer for reading in Victorian England. In *Great Expectations*, Mr. Wopsle's great-aunt distributes "three defaced Bibles, more illegibly printed at the best than any curiosities of literature I have since met with, speckled all over with ironmould, and having various specimens of the insect world smashed between their leaves." When the students read aloud from a given page, none had "the least notion of, or reverence for, what we were reading about" (Dickens 2003, 73–74); cf. the adult students in *Our Mutual Friend* (Dickens 1971, 264).

47. To Rose, this suggests that the Bible "could be read as a dime novel." He describes Dickens as a "dominating presence" in working-class memoirs (2001, 111). In *David Copperfield*, the walls of Peggoty's room are decorated with "common coloured pictures…of scripture subjects" involving Abraham's sacrifice and Daniel in the lion's den (Dickens 2004, 41).

class home which was used to prevent a tea-tray from tumbling down and smashing the cups and saucers. In fact, the narrator David refers only once to the New Testament and once to the "Greek Testament" (2004, 839, 117), while *Robinson Crusoe* is mentioned five times in the novel.

More importantly, the research indicates that Victorian readers (like readers of the Bible now) did not all read, interpret, and recall stories like those about David and Uriah in the same way. To scholars who compare Dickens's novel to the Bible, King David is "openly" a villain in 2 Sam 11–12 and Uriah is his totally innocent victim. However, many Victorian readers may have had a much more positive image of David, even in this episode. In Anglican Protestant tradition David is a "model for penitents" (Goodblatt 1996, 23), largely because his brief acknowledgment of sin in 2 Sam 12:13 was read together with penitential Ps 51. In nineteenth-century England, this is illustrated by John Keble's poem "Sixth Sunday after Trinity," which uses 2 Sam 12:13 as its epigraph (see Landow 1980, 82–83). This view of David is also illustrated in a much more recent text, Bill Clinton's 1998 Prayer Breakfast speech, in which he subtly compares himself to the contrite adulterer David by using phrases from Ps 51. To illustrate his "genuine repentance," Clinton repeatedly refers to his "broken spirit" and requests that God give him a "clean heart"[48]

In addition to the parallels already noted by scholars, there exist other similarities between the two Davids which are crucial for judging character in terms of ethical behavior. These involve the individual's tendency not to see his true place within the frame of a story, and his failure to intervene effectively or appropriately to perceived injustices. In Copperfield's case, this is most clear in his failure to prevent or condemn the abuse of "little Em'ly" by the narcissistic Steerforth, and his failure to acknowledge his own role as enabler of that abuse. Copperfield refuses to relinquish his idealized image of his adored Steerforth, in spite of recording Steerforth's snobbism, his abuse of Emily, Mr. Mell, and Traddles, and the narcissism which results in his inability to empathize with or care about others. In King David's case, this is most clear in his misdirected "intervention" in the case of the ewe lamb, his failure to identify himself as the rich man in the story, and his failure to intervene when his son rapes his daughter. In effect, King David chooses Amnon over Tamar, as David Copperfield chooses Steerforth over Emily.

Nussbaum also chooses Steerforth over Emily, by excusing him on the grounds of mercy based on imaginative understanding of how his character was formed from childhood. As mentioned above, Nussbaum

---

48. See Ps 51:12, 19 (Heb.) and Ofulue 2005, 129–36. Cf. Lee 2005, 104–6.

and Cates prefer sympathetic understanding of the particulars of a person's complex life history to the "retributive attitude." In this case, Nussbaum concludes that readers are led by David's example to "suspend punitive judgment on Steerforth's acts" (1995, 169–70). Yet Nussbaum herself condemns *another* character, David's "good angel" Agnes, because Agnes does not seem to share Nussbaum's compassionate view of Steerforth. Showing no such sympathetic understanding for the particulars of *Agnes's* troubled life story, Nussbaum misrepresents her as a vengeful and rigid religious dogmatist who is incapable of empathy. She characterizes Agnes as a "reader of religious books" who is guided in life by a "strict moral code" which precludes her looking at events from Steerforth's point of view, and as someone who resents Steerforth's "romantic hold" over David and uses her moral condemnation of Steerforth to gain revenge (1995, 168; 1992: 358–63). *None of this* is supported by evidence in the novel. Nowhere is Agnes said to be a reader of religious books, let alone prefer them to novels. Nor is it said—or shown—that Agnes is guided by a "strict moral code" which ignores empathy and human psychology and which leads to simple, harsh, and unfair judgments. Far from it.

*David* may view Agnes as an angel and religious icon, but, as Peter Gay puts it, "that's his problem, not hers" (1995, 274). Dickens tells his readers almost nothing about Agnes's thoughts and emotions apart from Copperfield's far from objective beliefs about his "good angel." However, Gay shows that Dickens provides readers with enough information about Agnes's life and behavior for them to understand her psychological profile. That profile does not resemble Nussbaum's view of her. All Agnes does is to warn David to be wary of Steerforth's influence, adding that Steerforth is a "dangerous friend" (Dickens 2004, 374–75). Agnes acknowledges that David's attitude is natural, but believes it to be unwise for a number of reasons. David jumps to the conclusion that Agnes is basing her opinion on David's drunkenness with Steerforth shortly before this conversation. Agnes denies this, saying that her judgment is based on "many things," including David's reports about Steerforth, her knowledge of David's character, and the influence Steerforth has over him. Agnes readily concedes that David's affection and admiration for Steerforth is natural and will not be quickly or easily given up, especially given David's "trusting disposition" (Dickens 2004, 373–74). David's attitude is natural, but it is also unwise.[49] Agnes does not utter a harsh and punitive condemnation of Steerforth as a person in this scene.

49. This aspect is stressed in the manuscript version of the scene. See Dickens 2004, 960 n. 3; 1981, 313 n. 2.

Similarly, when David later has Traddles praise Steerforth in Agnes's hearing, all she does is to "very slightly shake her head" when only David was observing her. Later events in the novel—and even those prior to her warning—show that Agnes is entirely correct about Steerforth. In effect, Nussbaum views Agnes, and Agnes's view of Steerforth, in precisely the same way that David does, granting full reliability to David's perspective in spite of all evidence to the contrary discussed earlier.

If sympathetic understanding is to be extended to perpetrators like Steerforth, it must also be extended to their victims. As noted by Sigler (2000, 360), Nussbaum excludes "victim impact statements" from consideration.[50] Bennett argues that taking someone's "Developmental Story" into account does not in itself mitigate responsibility. While no one "chooses their Developmental Story...it is simply not true that one has to have chosen one's desires, beliefs, emotions in order to be responsible for them" (2004, 9). For Bennett, to be responsible is to be called to account. He believes that Nussbaum's view of mercy fails to respect a person's moral agency. For Bennett it is the attitude of mercy, not that of condemnation, which assumes the judge's moral superiority to the person being evaluated.

Do the same arguments apply to those who urge a sympathetic view of Uriah Heep? Titolo (2003, 184) contends that "Heep's transgression might be forgiven more as a violation of decorum than villainous intrigue." But because readers are privy to the "victim impact statements" of Mr. Wickfield, Agnes, and David's aunt Betsy, we are well aware of the severity of Heep's crimes, which are far too serious to be dismissed as "violated decorum." Should David's blanket condemnation of Uriah Heep be accepted by readers of the novel because David is respecting Heep's moral agency? Newey thinks not. In line with Cates and Nussbaum, he points out that in spite of David's "claim to full comprehension" of Uriah's nature and upbringing, David's "language...is everywhere that of indignant condemnation rather than of understanding" (2004, 132). Newey adds the Copperfield

> fails to treat Uriah as the three-dimensional character that the evidence, if only for an interval, presents... He uses terms that suggest some *predetermined and unalterable* process. Baseness runs in the family; conditioning seems to have become unconditional... nowhere does David impugn the system that produced Heep father and son, nor contemplate grounds either for reforming it or for exculpating Uriah. (2004, 132)

50. Sigler rightly concludes that "the exclusion of the victim's story as it bears on the defendant's, if the novel format is to be taken seriously, represents a distortion of the narrative."

Since Dickens has established David's friend Tommy Traddles as the true moral center of the novel, his judgment on Uriah carries much weight. From the time we meet Traddles as a child until the end of Copperfield's story, his words and actions show him to be courageous, selfless, honorable, good-natured, reliable and humane. Whereas the boy Copperfield refused to condemn Steerforth for his "shameful" abuse of Mr. Mell, young Traddles did so, and showed his sympathy for the "ill-used" Mr. Mell in spite of the fact that doing so alienated him from the other boys and earned him Steerforth's scorn and a caning from his cruel schoolmaster (Dickens 2004, 102, 107, 111, 112). Later in life, Traddles speaks of Steerforth "with warmth," while Steerforth has to be reminded who Traddles is. When David reminds him, Steerforth is as disdainful toward Traddles as ever, dismissing him as "soft" and "an odd fish" (2004, 384, 432–33). Once again David fails to criticize Steerforth for his unjust attitude, even though David and Traddles have become friends as adults, and Traddles remains loyal to David throughout the story.

Traddles is also more understanding of Heep. When David's aunt Betsy calls Uriah a "monster of meanness," Traddles replies, "'Really I don't know about that... Many people can be very mean, when they give their minds to it'" (2004, 784). Traddles knows full well the crimes committed by Heep and certainly holds him accountable for those misdeeds. But he refuses to demonize Heep or view him as a "monster." Labeling perpetrators of heinous crimes as monsters is a time-honored way of distancing them and their actions from "us," a way of viewing them as so fundamentally different from us that we couldn't possibly behave as they did.[51] As Rosenberg (1986, 41) says in reference to condemning King David, such judgments can "quarantine and reassure."

Dickens scholar Gerhard Joseph (2000, 686–88) defines as "Heepian" a "hermeneutics of suspicion whereby certain textual clues tempt us to question the benign motives and behavior of all...sympathetic characters." Should we adopt a "Heepian view" of King David's supposedly repentant response to Nathan's parable, even though that may lead to "quarantining" David? And if we give full weight to the "impact statements" of David's victims included in the Court History, would that ultimately lead us to respect the king's moral agency enough to condemn him?

51. Thus, as Chastain (1997, 169) points out, one way observers "distance themselves from atrocity [such as sexual abuse of children] is to demonize the perpetrator."

## 8. *Judging Kafka's Josef K. and King David*

...guilty creatures sitting at a play
have by the very cunning of the scene
been struck so to the soul that presently
they have proclaim'd their malefactions;
for murder, though it have no tongue, will speak
with most miraculous organ."

—Shakespeare, *Hamlet* (2.2.577–83)

There ought to be behind the door of every happy, contented man
someone standing with a hammer continually reminding him with a tap
that there are unhappy people; that however happy he may be, life will
show him her laws sooner or later, trouble will come for him—disease,
poverty, losses, and no one will see or hear, just as now he neither sees
nor hears others. But there is no man with a hammer; the happy man lives
at his ease, and trivial daily cares faintly agitate him like the wind in the
aspen-tree—and all goes well.

—Chekhov, "Gooseberries" (2000, 273)

To help answer these questions, I will compare King David's response to
Nathan's parable with Josef K.'s response to the "doorkeeper parable" in
Kafka's *The Trial* (*Der Proceß*), a novel which has been called "almost a
biblical work" (Haas 1962, 226).[52] In addition, some surprising similarities between Josef K., King David, *and* David Copperfield will become
perceptible by means of this comparison.

Many scholars believe that the key function of both biblical and
Kafkan parables is to "jolt" and "awaken" readers and hearers.[53] In a
letter written when he was twenty years old, Kafka declares that we need
to read books that "wound and stab" us, that upset and sadden us like a
disaster, or like a suicide, books that "wake us up with a punch on the
head," that "affect us like the death of someone we loved more than
ourselves." In short, "a book must be the axe for the frozen sea within
us" (1958, 27–28).

In his characterization of Kafka's method, Adorno uses metaphors
which are equally violent. According to Adorno (1963, 249–50), Kafka
commands interpretation with force and collapses aesthetic distance,

52. Northrop Frye (1983, 195) calls the novel "a kind of 'midrash' on the Book
of Job"; see Lasine 1990, 187–88.

53. See Lasine 1984a for references to such "jolting" by biblical scholars, as well
as for biblicists whose studies of New Testament parable include extensive reference
to Kafka's parables. Suleiman (1983, 46, 53) classifies parables as "exemplary"
narratives, "in which [the]...aim is not only to teach something but also to influence
the receiver's actions or attitudes in a particular way.

pouncing on the supposedly disinterested observer, radically disrupting the contemplative relationship between text and reader. The reader becomes the text's "victim"; his emotions become so agitated that he must fear that the narrative could get loose and come at him like a locomotive heading for the audience in a 1950s "3-d" movie.[54] This "aggressive physical proximity" thwarts the reader's habit of identifying with the personages in the novel. In Adorno's formulation, identification is not a matter of feeling the emotions of, or merging with, the characters in the fictional world; it is the result of remaining aesthetically and safely distant from that world.

One way in which Kafka disrupts "the contemplative relationship between text and reader" is through what Beissner (1952, 28–42) first called the "*Einsinnigkeit*" or "unity of meaning" of Kafka's writing. This strategy limits us to the intellectual and perceptual range of the main character,[55] leading us to identify initially with the character's perspective. As Beicken puts it, Kafka forces identification with his character, and at the same time offers readers the opportunity to "break the spell" of identification (1977, 186; cf. Marson 1975, 20–21). Here "empathy becomes alienation" (Neugroschel 2000, xiii).[56] While Kafka's narrative rhetoric clearly differs in important ways from the techniques employed by the biblical authors and Dickens, *all* their narratives invite readers to identify with the central character and then withdraw empathy from that character, prompting them to judge the character more critically.

One technique used in both 2 Samuel and *The Trial* is to allow readers to judge the protagonist by observing the way in which the protagonist judges a character in a parable. In *The Trial* the Court's prison chaplain uses a story from the Law's introductory "scriptures" (*Schriften*; 1994, 226) to deliver a metaphorical axe-blow to Josef K.'s frozen sea. Like the tale which Nathan relates to King David, the "legend" that Kafka's priest tells Josef K. functions as a "juridical parable,"[57] in the sense that it is

54.  Corngold (2004, 243 n. 13) compares this with a statement by Primo Levi: "I fear him [Kafka], like a great machine that crashes in on you, like the prophet who tells you the day you will die."

55.  Readers can then experience the world of the text as though it possessed the self-evidence of the perceptual world, in this case the character's perceptual world. This accounts for what Beissner describes as the reader's feeling of the "inevitability" of even the most absurd happenings in the narratives (1952, 35).

56.  Neugroschel's argument in support of this conclusion is unpersuasive, since it precludes the possibility that readers could successfully empathize with characters in *any* narrative.

57.  It has been called a "juridical" or "judgment-eliciting" parable, because it is designed to provoke a detached judgment from a particular hearer which can then be

designed to make the intended hearer recognize his personal responsibility and guilt (see further in Lasine 1989b).

This is precisely the function served by the stage-plays described by Hamlet in the epigraph to this section. Later, Hamlet sets up a cunning play within a play for his uncle, King Claudius. Hamlet knows that Claudius has murdered his brother, Hamlet's father. Hamlet tells Horatio to "observe mine uncle: if his occulted guilt/ do not itself unkennel in one speech" (3.2.75–76). However, Claudius does *not* "proclaim his malefactions" when he sees the players act out his murder; rather, he gets up and leaves. Admittedly, this response does "unkennel his occulted guilt" for the onlookers Hamlet and Horatio (3.2.270–74). But there is no prophet Nathan at the Danish king's side. Instead, Claudius recovers his composure, although his guilt shows through for Shakespeare's audience, who hear his private soliloquy and prayer (3.3.36–72). Thus, while Claudius was not oblivious to the significance of the scene as a reflection of his own guilt—as King David had been—he does not confess, as had the malefactors in the cases about which Hamlet had heard. Interestingly, in his soliloquy Claudius expresses more guilt *and* more honesty about the difficulty of contrition than does David, in his two-word acknowledgment of sin against Yahweh. Like Claudius, David too is still "possess'd of the effects" for which he did the murder: the crown, his ambition, and his queen (3.3.53–55).

Both King David and Josef K. mistake their true relation to the stories they are told, so that their vehement responses expose the self-deception which has characterized their behavior in the world. Unlike Nathan, however, Kafka's priest gives his hearer a clue about his relation to the story before telling it. He informs K. that he is deceived about the Court, and that the passage he is about to recite refers to K.'s delusion (Kafka 1994, 225–26). In this story a man from the country comes to "the Law" (*das Gesetz*). When he asks the doorkeeper to be admitted to the Law, he is told that he cannot enter now. The man finally decides to wait for permission to enter. He waits many years, pleading with the doorkeeper and even trying to bribe him. Shortly before he dies, he asks one final

---

turned against that hearer and applied to his own life-situation. See U. Simon 1997, 112–18; Gunn 1989, 40–41, and, most recently, Schipper (2007, 386–91), who argues that David *does* recognize that Nathan's story is a parable and reacts by "overinterpreting" it, identifying the "rich man" in the parable with Joab. Thus, when David says that "the man who has done this" is "a son of death" (2 Sam 12:5), he is referring specifically to Joab. While Schipper's argument is ingenious and imaginative, it is itself an overinterpretation, which lacks both plausibility and textual support.

question, and learns that this entrance was meant for him, and that the doorkeeper is now going to shut it.

In spite of the chaplain's hints, K. can no more recognize that the man from the country deceives himself, and that K. himself shares the delusion, than David can see that he is the unjust rich man in Nathan's tale. Only Nathan uses his hearer's response to force the truth on him; the accused K. must make the connection on his own, if it is to be made at all. K.'s basic assumption, that the country man fails to gain access to the Law because he has been deceived by the doorkeeper,[58] shows that K. has carried his delusion about the Court and its officials into his interpretation of the story. For both K. and the man from the country, fixation on officials constitutes a forgetting of oneself. Just as the country man never asks *why* he cannot enter the Law now, and therefore how he might change himself to gain admittance, K. assumes from the start that the "main question" is *not* why he was arrested, but *by whom* he is being accused (Kafka 1994, 21; contrast 11 and 54).[59]

Just as the analogy between David and the rich man concerns only their callous, tyrannical behavior over the powerless, so does the analogy between K. and the country man hold only for their delusion about their relations with representatives of the Court or Law, and their inability to ask whether it might be something about themselves that is causing their problems. The fact that neither story neatly fits the hearer's situation forces David and K. to reveal whether they have the self-knowledge needed to recognize the stories' message to them, in spite of the differences between their circumstances and those of the characters in the stories. Both parables have been called "traps" for the intended hearer (U. Simon 1997, 112, 295 n. 37; Politzer 1962, 180). Once the hearer is "trapped," he can (theoretically, at least) be "jolted" into increased self-awareness and acknowledgment of his guilt. David and K. fall into the trap by responding with strong feeling and misplaced accusations.

---

58. In the early version of the manuscript this read: "*Der Mann hat sich also vom Türhüter täuschen lassen*" (Kafka 1990, 312). In this phrasing, K. is still blaming the doorkeeper as a deceiver, but he is also blaming the man for not being smart, strong, or vigilant enough to prevent himself being deceived. Is K. quick to judge the country man and the doorkeeper because he assumes that he himself is too smart to be taken in like that? One can only wonder whether Kafka changed the line because he decided that K. wasn't capable of recognizing how the "victim" co-operates in this act of deception. In fact, however, the only real deception involved in *either* case may be the "victim's" *self*-deception.

59. On the failure of K. and the country man to ask crucial questions, see Marson 1975, 19, 306.

However, only Nathan uses his hearer's response to force the truth on him; in *The Trial*, the chaplain merely follows K.'s lead in discussing various interpretations of the story.

The chaplain's strategy is characteristic of the Court's relationship to K. throughout his trial-process (see Lasine 1984c, 124–26). In this instance, the priest goes along with K's tendency to understand the story by attributing character traits to the doorkeeper and country man, and then judging them. K. also makes assumptions about the priest's character, which he uses to gauge how he should take the priest's comments on the story. Their conversation about the parable is commonly described as "talmudic," or as a parody of talmudic discourse.[60] In essence, however, the strategy employed by K. and the priest involves determining the reliability of the speakers in the story, and the meaning of the story itself, by attributing various fixed traits to the characters in the parable, and judging their behavior on the basis of those traits. Their discussion shows readers, if not K himself, the pointlessness of reading the character of others without first reading oneself.

Because the story related by the priest is part of a pre-existent and unalterable body of scripture, it has significance independently of K. and his guilt.[61] Far from applying any general truths from the Court scripture to his own life, K. consistently attempts to evade individual responsibility by viewing himself as nothing more than a human being in general. He tells the priest, "'I am not guilty… How…can a human being ever be guilty? We're all humans here, after all, one like the other.' 'That is correct,' said the priest, 'but that's how the guilty are in the habit of talking'" (Kafka 1994, 223). It is correct that each person has a general identity as a human being, but guilty humans submerge their individual accountability in the collective. As I discussed earlier, this is precisely how many apologists for King David attempt to mitigate the seriousness of his crimes.

The country man in the priest's parable assumes that he should be granted entry into the Law because—he thinks—"the Law should be

---

60.   See, e.g., Kurz 1987, 212–13; Heller 1974, 73, 75; Biderman 1995, 155, 157. In contrast, Sokel believes that the priest is behaving "like a careful New Critic" with K., restraining a hasty student from identifying the text's meaning with the protagonist's point of view. The priest always seeks to bring K. back to the text and points out the need to be faithful to the literal wording (2002, 241).

61.   Coincidentally, the doorkeeper parable also had its own "existence" prior to and independent of the novel, for Kafka published it under the title "Before the Law" (Kafka 1970, 131–32), while the novel remained unpublished until after the author's death.

accessible to everyone and at all times" (1994, 226). Yet, even if "all strive for the Law," as the man says shortly before his death, the fact remains that he must change himself in a specific way if he is to pass through the entrance meant only for him. K. does not learn from the man's failure; just before his own death he is still looking outside himself, wondering whether he sees help in the distance: "Was it a single individual? Was it everybody?" (1994, 241). The man who defended himself as an everyman ends by imagining help from "everybody."

Kafka's understanding of the way scripture can apply to an individual's particular situation is also exhibited by a diary sketch written shortly after the doorkeeper parable (1949, 323–24). In this vignette, a merchant is about to visit an expert in law (*Gesetzeskundigen*) because he can no longer bear his business misfortunes. A custom of the expert has kept the merchant from seeking his advice earlier. The expert, who continually studies in the "*Schrift*" which is open before him, has the habit of greeting everyone who comes for advice with the words "I am just now reading of your case," while pointing with his finger at a passage on the page lying before him. Although this offers the merchant the prospect of help, and relieves him of the fear of suffering something which he can communicate to no one, and with which no one can sympathize, he does not like the custom, for it is too "unbelievable." The fact that whatever page the expert has before him refers specifically to the individual's "case" might seem to imply that people are so similar that everyone falls into the same categories, or that scripture is so general, and therefore vague, that it can be made to "fit" everyone. However, it is also possible that the "scripture" in this fragment, like the Bible, has both universal scope *and*—when read as Kierkegaard recommends—the ability to address everyone as though it were written for each. The merchant would like company for his misery, but he cannot accept that his misfortunes are indistinguishable from those of others. Although characters like K. hide in the collective to avoid personal responsibility, they still demand unique solutions and individual attention from helpers and "scripture," as long as such attention leads to solutions that conform to their expectations and desires. As for the merchant, the legal expert may be showing his "client" that what matters is the latter's appealing for help in spite of his doubts. If so, then any scriptural passage will illumine his case if the "reader" allows himself to be addressed by it.[62]

---

62. Similarly, Buber contends that the Bible "demands that the individual fit (*einbetten*) his own life into this true history" (Buber 1936, 20) and Erich Auerbach claims that the Old Testament "seeks to overcome [our own reality]; we are to fit

Will the story of Josef K. have a "parabolic" effect on individual readers who take Kafka's novel as addressed to them personally and about them personally? Whether this story will break through the frozen sea inside each of us—or serve to *thicken* the ice concealing the K.s inside us—may depend on how each of us exercises his or her role as K.'s judge (see Lasine 1990), that is, whether we choose to identify with K. on the grounds that "we're all humans here" (or because we *are* like K. as an individual!), or break the spell and morally condemn K. as a failed human being.

Similarly, will Nathan's parable jolt its readers like a "punch on the head"? How can scripture, which claims universal meaning, authority, and relevance, be made to apply to the life of an individual reader, especially when the reader, like K., does not have Nathan tapping him on the shoulder saying "Thou art the man!" Can the biblical stories, read by themselves, affect us like a "hammer which breaks the rock in pieces" (Jer 23:29)?

The second epigraph to this section illustrates another way "hammers" might awaken one to self-awareness. Chekhov's character Ivan Ivanovich tells his friends that it would be necessary to have a man standing by to tap one to remind that person of the suffering of others—and the suffering that awaits that person as well. But "there is no man with a hammer." Commentators like Freedman (1988, 7–9) and Kramer (1979, 346–49) point out that Ivan Ivanovich's words are contradicted by his behavior in the story.[63] However, the fact that Ivan may be an "unreliable" narrator does not mean that *everything* he says must be unreliable and incorrect. Are such critics reading the story "objectively" in Kierkegaard's sense, unwilling to take Ivan's insight as addressed to them? Just

---

(*einfügen*) our own life into its world, feel ourselves to be elements in its world-historical structure" (Auerbach 1953, 18). Such statements should not be taken to mean that the Bible's claim to authority and unalterability requires the reader to "fit his life" to the biblical world and history without questioning the text and wrestling with it. By the same token, Kafka's descriptions of himself "submitting to" and being "caught up" and "shaken up" by certain kinds of books (1949, 128–29, 133) should not be taken as evidence that he envisions readers to be essentially passive. While readers must allow themselves to be penetrated in order for the "frozen sea within us" to be destroyed, the force capable of breaking through reification and self-deception is furnished by our coming within the world of the text, and actively giving it the power to affect us.

63.   Some dismiss this speech as a "moralistic diatribe" (Freedman 1988, 8) and judge Ivan's perceptions and argument to be foolish, self-destructive, quixotic, insane, and unreasonable (Slatoff 1970, 256, 260).

as none of us has a Nathan at our shoulder to force us to read personally, so is there no man with a hammer to tap us into acknowledging inconvenient truths, as Ivan points out.

Before deciding my own similarity to these characters, I should note that comparing 2 Sam 12 to these modern narratives reveals a surprising degree of similarity among Josef K., David Copperfield, and King David as moral agents. King David and Josef K. fail to be "awakened" by the parables because they are unable or unwilling to relate the narrated events to their own life situations, let alone take responsibility for what they are witnessing.[64] In an early diary entry, Kafka notes that if an actor is required by the script to flog someone, but in the excitement and excessively large rush of his senses actually flogs the other person, who screams from the pain, then the spectator must become a person and put himself in the middle (1949, 157). Of course we know from the Milgram experiments (and unfortunately many other examples, both staged and unstaged) that even "spectators" who are direct causes of another's pain may not "become a person" and intervene in response to the other's screams. There are, however, cases in which King David, David Copperfield, and Josef K. *do* attempt to intervene when they witness victimizations, and even acknowledge some degree of responsibility for the victimization, although the extent and success of their interventions is at best debatable.

David Copperfield's consistent failure to intervene on behalf of Emily is especially striking, as noted earlier. One telling example in *The Trial* is when K. hears groaning coming from a junk room at the bank, and discovers that the two guards who had arrested him earlier were now being flogged in response to relatively minor charges that K. had made against them at his first hearing (1994, 87–91). K. attempts to prevent the flogging by telling the flogger that he had never intended the guards to be punished as a result of his allegations; he even attempts to bribe[65] the flogger. When these attempts fail K. does not place himself "in the middle" as a "person." He quits without having achieved the release of the guards and fails to understand the implications of the fact that he is the cause of what is occurring. While he envisions the possibility of

64. Although David has been viewed as almost an ideal reader here (see Lasine 1984a, 114 and n. 29), neither he nor K. reacts to the stories in ways which the parable speakers would deem accurate or successful.

65. This contradicts K.'s earlier insistence that he would never resort to bribing the court, although in this case the attempted bribe is ostensibly for the benefit of someone else. K. then proceeds to leave, slamming the door behind him, thereby canceling his earlier resolution not to do precisely this (1994, 65, 89–91).

offering himself as a substitute victim, he does not take this idea seriously and fails to see why it would be appropriate. Finally, he himself uses violence against one of the guards (1994, 91), just as he treats others with physical violence elsewhere.[66] Josef K. cannot accept responsibility for victimizing others, clinging to the view that he is a victim at the same time that he is acting as a victimizer.

K's interventions resemble King David's reaction to the fictional legal case presented by Nathan, as well as David's failure to react to the real case of Tamar's rape. Both K. in the "Flogger" episode and King David as interpreter of Nathan's story construe parabolic displays tailored to themselves as being "real" events.[67] Both attempt to view these "events" from outside, as it were, with David as presiding judge and K. as defender of those against whom he had formerly leveled charges. Of course, K is aware that the guards are being flogged because of his testimony, but he still does not understand how the whole scene is designed to prompt him to see the relation between his personal self and what is displayed before him. K. claims the role of victim, but constantly acts as accuser, prosecutor, and punisher of others. If he had realized his position within the frame of the story, he might have gone ahead and offered himself as the substitute victim. By the same token, should David have accepted the death penalty he had unknowingly pronounced against himself, instead of letting his baby die?

Just as the narrator of the Court History undermines his own declarations of David's *aretē*, and Dickens makes it possible for readers to view David Copperfield more critically than Copperfield's first-person self-presentation may intend, so does Kafka put readers in a position to assess K's self-portrayal critically. In terms of the ethics of reading, it is not only crucial to refrain from judging when identification, empathy, and understanding are called for; it is equally crucial to judge a condemnable character, even when persuasive devices like *Einsinnigkeit* promote our identification with what Hakemulder calls a "nasty" character.

Far from viewing Josef K. as "nasty," many readers (and professional commentators) on *The Trial* have accepted K.'s self-presentation as an innocent victim, as I have discussed elsewhere (Lasine 1990). One recent argument by a Kafka scholar is instructive in this context. Sheppard (1994, 21–22) criticizes a colleague for judging K. "harshly" because the colleague cannot see that the Court speaks to K. in ways which his "calm distributive understanding" (*ruhig einteilender Verstand*) is incapable of

---

66. E.g. Kafka 1994, 45, 70, 193 and 207.
67. *Pace* Schipper (n. 57 above); see Lasine, 1984a, 106–7.

grasping, ways that would require K. to be endowed with just those psychological attributes which he lacks, and for lacking which he's put on trial in the first place. According to Sheppard (1994, 20), it is unreasonable to expect K. to become capable of empathy, because he is narcissistic.

This argument resembles Nussbaum's attempt to mitigate Steerforth's guilt in *David Copperfield* on the grounds that Steerforth was raised by his mother in a way which was sure to make him a narcissist. Leaving aside the fact that King David (if not David Copperfield) could also be described as having narcissistic personalities, Sheppard's argument, like Nussbaum's, is open to objection on several counts. The Court in *The Trial* may assume that one must be held responsible for lack of empathy and any resulting unethical behavior,[68] but it does not assume that the defendants are unable to change themselves, although they may be *unwilling* to undergo the metamorphosis which the Court is inviting them to experience. The Court continues to appeal to K.'s transcendence, his possibility of learning and changing. Only with the repeated failure of their attempts is K. executed.

Even if we go beyond the text and assume that Josef K. had been raised in a way which led to his developing a narcissistic personality,[69] as is the case with Dickens's Steerforth, K., like Steerforth, remains accountable for his failure to become a "*Mensch*" as an adult. Sheppard talks about K. as if he were not capable of developing and changing, as though K. were burdened with an hereditary legacy which precluded his becoming responsive to others' feelings and needs. K. is being judged for having failed in his moral duty to gain (or, at the very least, to simulate) the capacity to empathize. If K. is analogous to the man from the country in the priest's "legend," Sheppard is contradicting what the doorkeeper tells the country man: it *is* possible for the man to enter the Law, *but not now*. Not until the man takes the crucial step and learns what it is about himself which now precludes his entry. The majority view among social psychologists is that people's personalities *can* change as adults, including at Josef K.'s age of thirty.[70] In biblical terms, it *was* possible for K. to circumcise the foreskin of his heart.

---

68. Of course, Josef K. is not said to engage in the kind of flagrantly illegal, immoral, and deceitful behavior exhibited by King David.

69. On narcissism and child development, see Lasine 2001, 214–35.

70. See, e.g., Franz 1994, 228–33, 241–44; Weinberger 1994, 335–36, 338. Josef K. is "arrested" on his thirtieth birthday and executed just before his thirty-first.

## 9. *Conclusion*

It would be a very great wrong...if one were to give profane persons grounds to object that as soon as a man has been party to God's inspiration one must consider his behavior as a model for good morals (*comme le regle des mœurs*); or that we dare not condemn public deeds completely opposed to ideas of justice (*l'équité*) if it is he who has committed them. There is no middle ground: either these actions are unworthy, or actions similar to them are not wicked...since one must choose... [I]s it not better for us to favor the interests of morality (*la morale*) than the glory of an individual?

> —Pierre Bayle, "David" (2000, 52–53; cf. 42)

Our association with other people mainly consists of discussing and evaluating (*värderar*) our neighbors' character and behavior. For me, this has led to a voluntary withdrawal from virtually all so-called being together with others (*samvaro*). Because of this, I have become a bit lonely in my old age.

> —Ingmar Bergman, *Wild Strawberries* (film; 1957)[71]

Having viewed King David against several different backgrounds in this chapter, as well as earlier in the book and in my previous work on David,[72] it is finally time to decide whether David's response to Nathan's parable, and the king's subsequent behavior, indicate that *his* internal sea is still solidly frozen. Does David deserve the kind of blanket condemnation which Copperfield gives to his Uriah, or which Kafka's Court gives to Josef K.? In making this decision it is wise to keep in mind the counsel of Pierre Bayle, in what Rex calls his "dangerous article" on King David in the *Dictionnaire* (Rex 1965, 198). Bayle fully acknowledges David's greatness and piety (the latter particularly in the Psalms), but he also makes a frank assessment of the king's crimes, betrayals and cruelties. For Bayle it would be a very great wrong to excuse David's many sins simply because of the favor and glory which God has bestowed upon him. One must choose; either we condemn his unworthy acts or conclude that those actions are not really wicked at all. There is "no middle ground."[73] A judgment must be made.

---

71. Quotation from Bergman 1960, 169; translation modified.
72. E.g. Lasine 1984a, 1989b, and 2001, 39–50, 93–125.
73. Bayle took the traditional French Calvinist position that "without ethics, there was no true faith" (Rex 1965, 205; cf. 208, 212, 246). Bayle's approach to ethical reading influences his method of argumentation. After formulating "the laws of equity and ethics...by which the individual could set himself up as judge of the actions recounted in the Bible," Bayle lets "the mere recounting of fact constrain the reader to draw enlightened inferences from the text" (Rex 1965, 199).

This study has certainly established that we humans have a "vocation for judgment." Bergmann's Professor Borg goes so far as to claim that our intercourse with others consists mainly of discussing and evaluating our neighbors' character and behavior.[74] However, before I succumb to the negativity bias and reduce my "neighbor" David to his "worst bad act," I should ask myself: "Who am I to cast judgment on anyone?" And I should recall Jesus' warning not to judge, lest I be judged (Matt 7:1). But must one always assume that one has a log in one's eye which removes our right to call attention to the speck in our neighbor's eye (Matt 7:2–5)? In Jesus' name many have advised us to view ourselves as suspicious characters or preached our abysmal sinfulness. But is self-abasement the only safeguard against hypocrisy and arrogance?[75] Must we always judge ourselves harshly in order *not* to have the right to judge anyone else?

Whether or not I have a cord of wood in my reattached retinas, I can still spot the splinters of murder and betrayal making David's pretty eyes bloodshot. Admittedly, making the kind of personal judgment I've described also means reducing *my own* nature, stifling my empathy toward the person being judged, and ceasing to look at their situation from their perspective.

It is certainly true that someone might condemn another person in order to create a comfortable difference between herself and that person, as Job's friends do. But if one shows compassion to David because he too is human, one is letting both David *and oneself* off the hook. On the other hand, to condemn David for actions which I have *not* committed is to assert my belief in my own integrity, as did Job. In communal reading situations, this is asserting to my auditors that I have the right to condemn David, implying that I'm "better" than he, in this respect.

So when I assign David to at least three circles of Dante's Hell,[76] I am exposing who I am, the sources of my moral standards, and—*or*—my inability to resist the negativity bias. I do this in full knowledge that David is loved by many of the other characters within his textual world, and that the biblical narrators show David to be a charming narcissist who has some spectacular successes—and the ability to write some damned good poetry. And I make this judgment in spite of the fact that I would like to see myself as an empathetic and forgiving sort of fellow

74. In his opinion, social interaction is basically gossip, a form of moral evaluation which characteristically exhibits the negativity bias (see Chapter 1 n. 32, above).

75. On this strategy, see Chapter 5 n. 12, above.

76. Specifically, circles two and seven through nine. These zones include those guilty of lust, violence, murder, fraud, seduction, theft, and treachery to guests.

(after all, I'm an INFP according to Myers-Briggs[77]). To the extent that narrators can put a reading community into the role of a jury (see Lasine 1989b; 1990), I urge my fellow jurors to join me in breaking the spell of identification, find the defendant David guilty as an incorrigible moral failure, and separate ourselves from him—not because he is all-too-human, but because he is not-human-enough.

To the extent that evaluating biblical characters reveals our self-construal, an ethical reading of the Hebrew Bible conforms to the famous[78] description of reading given by Proust's narrator: "In reality, every reader is, while he is reading, the reader of his own self. The... work is...a kind of optical instrument which he [*sic*] offers to the reader to enable him to discern what, without this book, he would perhaps never have perceived in himself" (Proust 2003, 276; cf. 424). As this study has made clear, Proust's Marcel could have added that it is our expectations and assumptions about character and human behavior which partly determine what we see when we look at—and through—the textual optic, and what kind of self we reveal to ourselves (and to others) when we do so.

---

77. Myers-Briggs Type Indicator (MBTI). "INFP" stands for "introverted-intuitive-feeling-perceiving." According to Paul (2004, 128), the inventor of this personality profile (Isabel Myers) was also INFP, and Jesus was a "classic ENTP" (extraverted-intuitive-thinking-perceiving).

78. This passage has been quoted by a wide variety of writers, in articles concerning everything from Jewish Bible education (Holtz 2002) to business research methods (Bannister and Remenyi 2003, 46). Proust scholars disagree about the meaning of "self-reading" for Proust's narrator, and the degree to which it reflects the narrator's final view, let alone the author's (see, e.g., Bailey 1997, 7, 11). The very open-endedness of the passage allows it to take on different shades of meaning in different contexts.

# BIBLIOGRAPHY

Aberbach, Moses, and Leivy Smolar. 1968. Jeroboam and Solomon: Rabbinic Interpretations. *JQR* 59:118–32.

Ackroyd, Peter R. 1977. *The Second Book of Samuel: Commentary*. CBC. Cambridge: Cambridge University Press.

Adkins, Arthur W. H. 1965. *Merit and Responsibility: A Study in Greek Values*. Oxford: Clarendon.

———. 1970. *From the Many to the One: A Study of Personality and Views of Human Nature in the Context of Ancient Greek Society, Values, and Beliefs*. Ithaca, N.Y.: Cornell University Press.

———. 1973. *Moral Values and Political Behaviour in Ancient Greece: From Homer to the End of the Fifth Century*. New York: Norton.

Adorno, Theodore W. 1963. Aufzeichnungen zu Kafka. Pages 248–81 in *Prismen: Kulturkritik und Gesellschaft*. Munich: Deutscher Taschenbuch.

Ahlström, Gösta W. 1993. *The History of Ancient Palestine*. Edited by Diana Edelman. Minneapolis: Fortress.

Albertz, Rainer. 2003. *Israel in Exile: The History and Literature of the Sixth Century B.C.E.* Translated by David Green. Atlanta: SBL.

Albrecht, Jason E., and Edward J. O'Brien. 1993. Updating a Mental Model: Maintaining Both Local and Global Coherence. *Journal of Experimental Psychology: Learning, Memory and Cognition* 19:1061–70.

Allen, James P. 2000. *Middle Egyptian: An Introduction to the Language and Culture of Hieroglyphs*. Cambridge: Cambridge University Press.

Allinson, Francis G., trans. 1959. *Menander: The Principal Fragments*. LCL. Cambridge, Mass.: Harvard University Press.

Allport, Gordon W. 1937. *Personality: A Psychological Interpretation*. New York: Henry Holt.

Alter, Robert. 1981. *The Art of Biblical Narrative*. New York: Basic.

Aly, Wolf. 1929. *Volksmärchen, Sage, und Novelle bei Herodot und seinen Zeitgenossen: eine Untersuchung über die volkstümlichen Elemente der altergriechischen Prosaerzählung*. Göttingen: Vandenhoeck & Ruprecht.

Ames, Roger T., and Wimal Dissanayake, eds. 1996. *Self and Deception: A Cross-Cultural Philosophical Enquiry*. Albany: State University of New York Press.

Amit, Yairah. 2006. The Delicate Balance in the Image of Saul and Its Place in the Deuteronomistic History. Pages 71–79 in *Saul in Story and Tradition*. Edited by Carl S. Ehrlich and Marsha C. White. Tübingen: Mohr Siebeck.

Andrewes, Antony. 1956. *The Greek Tyrants*. London: Hutchinson University Library.

Andringa, Els. 2004. The Interface between Fiction and Life: Patterns of Identification in Reading Autobiographies. *PT* 25:205–40.

Angel, Hayyim. 2005. When God's Will Can and Cannot Be Altered: The Relationship Between the Balaam Narrative and 1 Kings 13. *JBQ* 33:31–39.

Annas, Julia. 2003. Virtue Ethics and Social Psychology. *A Priori* 2:20–34. Online: http://www.stolaf.edu/people/huff/classes/GoodnEvil/Readings/julia_annas1.pdf.

Anscombe, G. E. M. 1997. Modern Moral Philosophy. Pages 26–44 in Crisp and Slote 1997.

Anzengruber, Ludwig. 1980. *Die Kreuzelschreiber: Bauernkomödie mit Gesang in drei Akten.* Pages 2–74 in *Anzengrubers Werke in zwei Bänden, Erster Band.* Edited by Manfred Kuhne. 3d ed. Berlin: Aufbau-Verlag.

Applegate, John. 1998a. The Fate of Zedekiah: Redactional Debate in the Book of Jeremiah, Part I. *VT* 48:137–60.

———. 1998b. The Fate of Zedekiah: Redactional Debate in the Book of Jeremiah, Part II. *VT* 48:301–8.

Appler, Deborah A. 1999. From Queen to Cuisine: Food Imagery in the *Jezebel* Narrative. *Semeia* 86:55–73.

———. 2000. Ahab. Pages 30–31 in *EDB.*

Aronson, Elliot. 1999. Dissonance, Hypocrisy, and the Self-Concept. Pages 103–26 in Harmon-Jones and Mills 1999.

Ash, Mitchell G. 1995. *Gestalt Psychology in German Culture, 1890–1967: Holism and the Quest for Objectivity.* Cambridge: Cambridge University Press.

Ash, Paul S. 1998. Jeroboam I and the Deuteronomistic Historian's Ideology of the Founder. *CBQ* 60:16–24.

Assmann, Jan. 1975. *Zeit und Ewigkeit im alten Ägypten: Ein Beitrag zur Geschichte der Ewigkeit.* Heidelberg: Winter.

———. 1993a. Zur Geschichte des Herzens im Alten Ägypten. Pages 81–113 in *Die Erfindung des inneren Menschen: Studien zur religiösen Anthropologie.* Edited by Jan Assmann. Gütersloh: Gerd Mohn.

———. 1993b. Zitathaftes Leben. Thomas Mann und die Phänomenologie der kulturellen Erinnerung. *Thomas Mann Jahrbuch* 6:133–58.

———. 1999. Confession in Ancient Egypt. Pages 231–44 in *Transformations of the Inner Self in Ancient Religions.* Edited by Jan Assmann and Guy G. Stroumsa. Leiden: Brill.

———. 2005a. *Death and Salvation in Ancient Egypt.* Translated by David Lorton. Ithaca, N.Y.: Cornell University Press.

———. 2005b. Axial "Breakthroughs" and Semantic "Relocations" in Ancient Egypt and Israel. Pages 133–56 in *Axial Civilizations and World History.* Edited by J. P. Arnason, S. N. Eisenstadt, and B. Wittrock. Leiden: Brill.

Auerbach, Elias. 1975. *Moses.* Translated by Robert A. Barclay and Israel O. Lehman. Detroit: Wayne State University Press.

Auerbach, Erich. 1953. *Mimesis: The Representation of Reality in Western Literature.* Translated by Willard Trask. Princeton: Princeton University Press.

Auld, A. Graeme. 1984. Prophets and Prophecy in Jeremiah and Kings. *ZAW* 96:66–82.

———. 1986. *I & II Kings.* DSB. Louisville: Westminster John Knox.

Aurelius, Erik. 2004. *"Du bist der Mann": Zum Charakter biblischer Texte.* Translated by Dietz Lange. Göttingen: Vandenhoeck & Ruprecht.

Avigad, Nahman. 1993. Samaria (City). Pages 1300–1310 in *NEAEHL*, vol. 4.

Azevedo, Joaquim. 1999. At the Door of Paradise: A Contextual Interpretation of Gen 4:7. *BN* 100:45–59.

Babbitt, Frank C., trans. 1956. *Plutarch's Moralia, II: 86B–171F*. LCL. Cambridge, Mass.: Harvard University Press.

Bailey, Phillip. 1997. *Proust's Self-Reader: The Pursuit of Literature as Privileged Communication*. Birmingham, Ala.: Summa.

Bakker, Egbert J., Irene J. F. De Jong, and Hans Van Wees, eds. 2002. *Brill's Companion to Herodotus*. Leiden: Brill.

Bannister, Frank and Dan Remenyi. 2003. Echoes in the Mind: The Use, Misuse and Abuse of Language in Business Research. Pages 43–50 in *European Conference on Research Methodology for Business and Management Studies*. Edited by Dan Remenyi and Ann Brown. Reading: Academic Conferences Limited.

Baranger, Willy. 1991. Narcissism in Freud. Pages 108–30 in *Freud's "On Narcissism: An Introduction."* Edited by J. Sandler, E. S. Person, and P. Fonagy. New Haven, Conn.: Yale University Press.

Bar-Efrat, Shimon. 1989. *Narrative Art in the Bible*. Translated by Dorothy Shefer-Vanson. JSOTSup 70. Sheffield: Almond.

Barolini, Teodolinda. 1998. Canto XX: True and False See-ers. Pages 275–86 in Mandelbaum et al. 1998.

Barr, James. 1961. *The Semantics of Biblical Language*. Oxford: Oxford University Press.

Barrett, Charles K. 1978. *The Gospel According to St. John: An Introduction With Commentary and Notes on The Greek Text*. 2d ed. Philadelphia: Westminster.

Barth, Karl. 1955. *Exegese von 1 Könige 13*. Neukirchen: Neukirchen Kreis Moers.

———. 2004. *Church Dogmatics*. Vol. 4, *The Doctrine of Reconciliation, Pt. 2*. Translated by G. W. Bromiley. Edited by G. W. Bromiley and T. F. Torrance. London: T. & T. Clark.

Barthes, Roland. 1974. *S/Z*. Translated by Richard Miller. New York: Hill & Wang.

Bar Yosef, Eitan. 2006. "It's the Same Old Story": David and Uriah in II Samuel and *David Copperfield*. *MLR* 101:957–65.

Barton, John. 2003. *Understanding Old Testament Ethics: Approaches and Explorations*. Louisville: Westminster John Knox.

Batson, C. Daniel, Nadia Ahmad, and E. L. Stocks. 2004. Benefits and Liabilities of Empathy-Induced Altruism. Pages 359–85 in *The Social Psychology of Good and Evil*. Edited by Arthur G. Miller. New York: Guilford.

Baumeister, Roy F., Ellen Bratslavsky, Catrin Finkenauer, and Kathleen D. Vohs. 2001. Bad Is Stronger than Good. *Review of General Psychology* 5:323–70.

Bayle, Pierre. 2000. *Political Writings*. Translated and edited by Sally L. Jenkinson. CTHPT. Cambridge: Cambridge University Press.

Bayley, John. 1960. *The Characters of Love: A Study in the Literature of Personality*. New York: Basic.

Beauvois, Jean-Léon, and Robert Vincent Joule. 1999. A Radical Point of View on Dissonance Theory. Pages 43–70 in Harmon-Jones and Mills 1999.

Becker, Ernest. 1973. *The Denial of Death*. New York: Free Press.

Beicken, Peter U. 1977. Kafka's Narrative Rhetoric. Pages 178–87 in *The Kafka Debate: New Perspectives for Our Time*. Edited by Angel Flores. New York: Gordian.

Beissner, Friedrich. 1952. *Der Erzahler Franz Kafka: Ein Vortrag.* Stuttgart: Kohl-hammer.

Belsey, Catherine. 2002. *Critical Practice.* 2d ed. London: Routledge.

Bendix, Reinhard. 1952. Compliant Behavior and Individual Personality. *American Journal of Sociology* 58:292–303.

Benjamin, Walter. 2002. *Selected Writings of Walter Benjamin.* Vol. 3, *1935–1938.* Translated by Harry Zohn et al. Edited by M. W. Jennings, H. Eiland, and G. Smith. Cambridge, Mass.: Belknap.

Bennett, Christopher. 2004. The Limits of Mercy. *Ratio* NS 17:1–11.

Bergen, Wesley J. 1999. *Elisha and the End of Prophetism.* JSOTSup 286. Sheffield: Sheffield Academic.

Bergman, Ingmar. 1960. *Four Screenplays.* Translated by Lars Malmstrom and David Kushner. New York: Simon & Schuster.

Bergmann, Jörg R. 1993. *Discreet Indiscretions: The Social Organization of Gossip.* Translated by John Bednarz Jr. and Eva Kafka Barron. New York: Aldine de Gruyter.

Bergson, Henri. 1959. *Le Rire: Essai sur la signification du comique.* Pages 387–485 in *Oeuvres.* Edited by André Robinet. Édition du centenaire. Paris: Presses universitaires de France.

Berke, Joseph H. 1988. *The Tyranny of Malice: Exploring the Dark Side of Character and Culture.* New York: Summit.

Berlin, Adele. 1983. *Poetics and Interpretation of Biblical Narrative.* Sheffield: Almond.

Bernard, Tristan. 1909. Lectures d'Occasion. Pages 124–28 in *Auteurs, Acteurs, Spectateurs.* Paris: Lafitte.

Bersani, Leo. 1976. *A Future for Astyanax: Character and Desire in Literature.* Boston: Little, Brown.

Bettelheim, Bruno. 1976. *The Uses of Enchantment: The Meaning and Importance of Fairy Tales.* New York: Knopf.

Biderman, Shlomo. 1995. *Scripture and Knowledge: An Essay on Religious Episte-mology.* Leiden: Brill.

Bierbrauer, Günter. 1979. Why Did He Do It? Attribution of Obedience and the Phenomenon of Dispositional Bias. *EJSP* 9:67–84.

Bishop, Paul. 1996. *Jung-Joseph*: Thomas Mann's Reception of Jungian Thought in the *Joseph* Tetralogy. *MLR* 91:138–58.

Blackman, Philip. 1985. *Pirke Avoth: Ethics of the Fathers.* Gateshead: Judaica.

Blasi, A. 2005. Moral character: A Psychological Approach. Pages 67–100 in Lapsley and Power 2005.

Blass, Thomas, ed. 2000. *Obedience to Authority: Current Perspectives on the Milgram Paradigm.* Mahwah, N.J.: Erlbaum.

Bleich, J. David. 1989. *Contemporary Halakhic Problems*, vol. 3. New York: KTAV.

Blenkinsopp, Joseph. 1988. *Ezra–Nehemiah: A Commentary.* OTL. Philadelphia: Westminster.

Blum, Carol. 1974. *Diderot: The Virtue of a Philosopher.* New York: Viking.

Blumenthal, Ralph. 2007. Supreme Court Blocks Execution of Delusional Killer. *New York Times,* 6/19/07. Online: http://www.nytimes.com/2007/06/29/washington/29execution.html.

Bodner, Keith. 2005. *David Observed: A King in the Eyes of His Court.* Sheffield: Sheffield Phoenix.

Boecker, Hans Jochen. 1964. *Redeformen des Rechtslebens im Alten Testament.* WMANT 14. Neukirchen–Vluyn: Neukirchener Verlag.

Boedeker, Deborah. 2002. Epic Heritage and Mythical Patterns in Herodotus. Pages 97–116 in Bakker et al. 2002.

Bonaventure, St. 1978. The Life of St. Francis. Translated by Ewert Cousins. Pages 179–327 in *Bonaventure: The Soul's Journey into God, The Tree of Life, The Life of St. Francis.* CWS. New York: Paulist.

Booth, Wayne C. 1974. *A Rhetoric of Irony.* Chicago: University of Chicago Press.

———. 1988. *The Company We Keep: An Ethics of Fiction.* Berkeley: University of California Press.

Boshoff, Willem. 2000. Jeroboam ben Nebat in the Deuteronomistic History: Recovering the Northern Kingdom from the Deuteronomistic Historians Against the Background of Recent South African History. Pages 19–35 in *Past, Present, Future: The Deuteronomistic History and the Prophets.* Edited by Johannes de Moor and Harry Van Rooy. Leiden: Brill.

Bousset, Jacque-Bénigne. 1990. *Politics Drawn from the Very Words of Holy Scripture.* Translated and edited by Patrick Riley. CTHPT. Cambridge: Cambridge University Press.

Bowman, Richard G. 2002. The Complexity of Character and the Ethics of Complexity: The Case of King David. Pages 73–97 in W. Brown 2002.

Brandon, S. G. F. 1958. A Problem of the Osirian Judgment of the Dead. *Numen* 5:110–27.

Braude, William G., and Israel J. Kapstein, trans. 1981. *Tanna debe Eliyyahu: The Lore of the School of Elijah.* Philadelphia: JPS.

Braun, Roddy L. 1986. *1 Chronicles.* WBC 14. Waco, Tex.: Word.

Breasted, James H. 1968. *The Dawn of Conscience.* New York: Charles Scribner's Sons.

Breden, Hugh. 1982. The Displacement of Character in Narrative Theory. *British Journal of Aesthetics* 22:291–300.

Brenneman, James E. 2000. Debating Ahab: Characterization in Biblical Theology. Pages 89–107 in *Reading the Hebrew Bible for a New Millennium.* Edited by W. Kim D. Ellens, M. Floyd, and M. A. Sweeney. Harrisburg, Pa.: Trinity Press International.

Brenner, Athalia. 1997. Job the Pious? The Characterization of Job in the Narrative Framework of the Book. Pages 298–313 in *The Poetical Books: A Sheffield Reader.* Edited by David J. A. Clines. Sheffield: Sheffield Academic.

Brenninkmeijer, Veerle, Nico VanYeren, and Bram Buunk. 2001. Burnout and Depression Are Not Identical Twins: Is Superiority a Distinguishing Feature? *Personality and Individual Differences* 30:873–80.

Brichto, Herbert Chanan. 1992. *Toward a Grammar of Biblical Poetics: Tales of the Prophets.* New York: Oxford University Press.

Briggs, Richard S. 2010. *The Virtuous Reader: Old Testament Narrative and Interpretive Virtue.* Studies in Theological Interpretation. Grand Rapids, Mich.: Baker Academic.

Brooks, Simcha Shalom. 2005. *Saul and the Monarchy: A New Look.* SOTSMS. Aldershot: Ashgate.

Brown, Raymond E. 1966. *The Gospel According to John, Chapters 1–12.* AB 29. Garden City, N.Y.: Doubleday.

Brown, William P., ed. 2002. *Character and Scripture: Moral Formation, Community, and Biblical Interpretation.* Grand Rapids, Mich.: Eerdmans.

———.2002. Preface. Pages xi–xvi in W. Brown 2002.

Brownlee, William H. 1977. The Ineffable Name of God. *BASOR* 226:39–46.

Brueggemann, Walter. 1990. *First and Second Samuel.* IBC. Louisville: John Knox.

———. 2000. *1 & 2 Kings.* Smyth & Helwys Bible Commentary. Macon, *Ga.:* Smyth & Helwys.

Bruner, Jerome. 1986. *Actual Minds, Possible Worlds.* Cambridge, Mass.: Harvard University Press.

Brunner-Traut, Emma. 1990. *Frühformen des Erkennens am Beispiel Altägyptens.* Darmstadt: Wissenschaftliche Buchgesellschaft.

Buber, Martin. 1936. Der Mensch von heute and die jüdische Bibel. Pages 13–45 in *Die Schrift und ihre Verdeutschung.* Berlin: Schocken.

Buckton, Oliver S. 1997. "The Reader Whom I Love": Homoerotic Secrets in *David Copperfield. ELH* 64:189–222.

Bultmann, Rudolph. 1971. *The Gospel of John: A Commentary.* Translated by G. R. Beasley-Murray. Philadelphia: Westminster.

Bury, R. G. 1967. *Plato: The Laws*, vol. 1. LCL. Cambridge, Mass.: Harvard University Press.

Butler, Trent. 1979. An Anti-Moses Tradition. *JSOT* 12:9–15.

Button, Mark. 2005. A Monkish Kind of Virtue? For and Against Humility. *Political Theory* 33:840–68.

Campbell, Antony F. 2005. *2 Samuel.* FOTL 8. Grand Rapids, Mich.: Eerdmans.

Camus, Albert. 1956. *La Chute.* Paris: Gallimard.

Canetti, Elias. 1980. *Masse und Macht.* Frankfurt: Fischer Taschenbuch.

Carasik, Michael. 2000. The Limits of Omniscience. *JBL* 119:221–32.

Carroll, Noël. 1998. Art, Narrative, and Moral Understanding. Pages 126–59 in *Aesthetics and Ethics: Essays at the Intersection.* Edited by Jerrold Levinson. Cambridge: Cambridge University Press.

Carroll, Robert P. 1977. The Aniconic God and the Cult of Images. *ST* 31:51–64.

———. 1981. *From Chaos to Covenant: Prophecy in the Book of Jeremiah.* New York: Crossroad.

———. 1986. *The Book of Jeremiah: A Commentary.* OTL. Philadelphia: Westminster.

Carugati, Giuliana. 1998. Canto XXII: Poets as Scoundrels. Pages 297–305 in Mandelbaum 1998.

Carver, Larry. 1992. Ahithophel. Pages 27–28 in *A Dictionary of Biblical Tradition in English Literature.* Edited by David L. Jeffrey. Grand Rapids, Mich.: Eerdmans.

Cassuto, Umberto. 1967. *A Commentary on the Book of Exodus.* Translated by Israel Abrahams. Jerusalem: Magnes.

———. 1978. *A Commentary on the Book of Genesis, Pt. 1. From Adam to Noah.* Translated by Israel Abrahams. Jerusalem: Magnes.

Cates, Diana Fritz. 1998. Ethics, Literature, and the Emotional Dimension of Moral Understanding: A Review Essay. *JRE* 26:409–31.

Cavallo, Guglielmo, and Roger Chartier. 1999. Introduction. Pages 1–36 in *A History of Reading in the West.* Edited by Guglielmo Cavallo and Roger Chartier. Amherst: University of Massachusetts Press.

Cawelti, John G. 1976. *Adventure, Mystery, and Romance: Formula Stories as Art and Popular Culture.* Chicago: University of Chicago Press.

Cervone, Daniel. 1999. Bottom-Up Explanation in Social Psychology: The Case of Cross-Situational Coherence. Pages 303–41 in Cervone and Shoda 1999.

Cervone, Daniel, and Yuichi Shoda, eds. 1999. *The Coherence of Personality: Social-Cognitive Bases of Consistency, Variability, and Organization.* New York: Guilford.

———. 1999. Social-Cognitive Theories and the Coherence of Personality. Pages 3–33 in Cervone and Shoda 1999.

Chartier, Roger. 1999. Richardson, Diderot et la lectrice impatiente. *Modern Language Notes* 114:647–66.

Chastain, Kimberly Parsons. 1997. The Dying Art of Demon-Recognition: Victims, Systems, and the Book of Job. Pages 161–78 in *Power, Powerlessness, and the Divine: New Inquiries in Bible and Theology.* Edited by Cynthia L. Rigby. Atlanta: Scholars Press.

Chatman, Seymour. 1978. *Story and Discourse: Narrative Structure in Fiction and Film.* Ithaca, N.Y.: Cornell University Press.

Chavel, Charles B., trans. 1975. *Ramban: Commentary on the Torah, Numbers.* New York: Shilo.

Chekhov, Anton. 2000. Gooseberries. Pages 265–75 in *The Essential Tales of Chekhov.* Translated by Constance Garnett. Edited by Richard Ford. New York: Ecco/Harper Collins.

Choi, Incheol, Richard E. Nisbett, and Ara Norenzayan. 1999. Causal Attribution Across Cultures: Variation and Universality. *PB* 125:47–63.

Church, A. Timothy, and Walter J. Lonner. 1998. The Cross-Cultural Perspective in the Study of Personality. *Journal of Cross-Cultural Psychology* 29:32–62.

Cixous, Hélène. 1974. The Character of "Character." *New Literary History* 5:383–402.

Clark, J. O. A. 1893. *Elijah Vindicated: The Answer By Fire.* Rev. ed. Nashville: Publishing House of the M. E. Church, South.

Clark, Maudemarie, and Alan J. Swensen, trans. and eds. 1998. *Nietzsche: On the Genealogy of Morality.* Indianapolis: Hackett.

Clines, David J. A. 1989. *Job 1–20.* WBC 17. Dallas: Word.

———. 2006. *Job 21–37.* WBC 18A. Nashville: Nelson.

Coats, George W. 1981. Parable, Fable, and Anecdote: Storytelling in the Succession Narrative. *Int* 35:368–82.

———. 1982. The Way of Obedience: Traditio-Historical and Hermeneutical Reflections on the Balaam Story. *Semeia* 24:53–79.

Cogan, Mordechai, and Hayim Tadmor. 1988. *II Kings: A New Translation with Introduction and Commentary.* AB 11. Garden City, N.Y.: Doubleday.

Cogan, Mordechai. 2000. *1 Kings.* AB 10. New York: Doubleday.

Cohan, Steven. 1990. Figures Beyond the Text: A Theory of Readable Character in the Novel. Pages 113–36 in Spilka and McCracken-Flesher 1990.

Cohen, Abraham, trans. and ed. 1945. *The Psalms.* London: Soncino.

Cohn, Robert L. 1985. Literary Technique in the Jeroboam Narrative. *ZAW* 97:23–35.

Colclough, Stephen. 2007. *Consuming Texts: Readers and Reading Communities, 1695–1870.* Basingstoke: Palgrave Macmillan.

Collins, Barry E., and Laura Ma. 2000. Impression Management and Identity Construction in the Milgram Social System. Pages 61–90 in Blass 2000.

Collins, Jerre, and John Zbikowski. 2005. Literature as the Laboratory of the Moral Life: Building Moral Communities Through Literary Study. *Analecta Husserliana* 85:845–63.

Conners, Quinn R. 1997. Elijah and Elisha: A Psychologist's Perspective. Pages 235–42 in Egan and Morrison 1997.

Cooper, Arnold M. 1986. Narcissism. Pages 112–43 in *Essential Papers on Narcissism*. Edited by A. P. Morrison. New York: New York University Press.

Cooper, Joel. 2007. *Cognitive Dissonance: Fifty Years of a Classic Theory*. Los Angeles: Sage.

Cooper, Joel, Robert Mirabile, and Steven J. Scher. 2005. Actions and Attitudes: The Theory of Cognitive Dissonance. Pages 63–79 in *Persuasion: Psychological Insights and Perspectives*. Edited by Timothy C. Brock and Melanie C. Green. 2d ed. Thousand Oaks: Sage.

Corngold, Stanley. 2004. *Lambent Traces: Franz Kafka*. Princeton: Princeton University Press.

Costa, Paul T., Jr., and Robert R. McCrae. 1994. Set Like Plaster? Evidence for the Stability of Adult Personality. Pages 21–40 in Heatherton and Weinberger 1994.

Cox, Damian, Marguerite La Caze, and Michael P. Levine. 2003. *Integrity and the Fragile Self*. Aldershot: Ashgate.

Crenshaw, James L. 1971. *Prophetic Conflict: Its Effect Upon Israelite Religion*. BZAW 124. Berlin: de Gruyter.

———. 1987. *Ecclesiastes: A Commentary*. OTL. Philadelphia: Westminster.

Crisp, Roger, and Michael Slote, eds. 1997. *Virtue Ethics*. New York: Oxford University Press.

Crisp, Roger, and Michael Slote. 1997. Introduction. Pages 1–25 in Crisp and Slote 1997.

Cronauer, Patrick T. 2003. The Many Faces of Elijah. *TBT* 41:340–47.

Cross, Frank Moore. 1973. *Canaanite Myth and Hebrew Epic: Essays in the History of the Religion of Israel*. Cambridge, Mass., Harvard University Press.

Culler, Jonathan. 1975. *Structuralist Poetics: Structuralism, Linguistics, and the Study of Literature*. Ithaca, N.Y.: Cornell University Press.

Cupchik, Gerald C. 1997. Identification as a Basic Problem for Aesthetic Reception. Pages 11–22 in *The Systemic and Empirical Approach to Literature and Culture as Theory and Application*. Edited by Steven Tötösy de Zepetnek and Irene Sywenky. Edmonton: University of Alberta Research Institute for Comparative Literature.

Currie, Gregory. 2009. Narrative and the Psychology of Character. *Journal of Aesthetics and Art Criticism* 67:61–71.

Dahood, Mitchell. 1966. *Psalms I: 1–50*. AB 16. Garden City, N.Y.: Doubleday.

Danelius, Eva. 1967. The Sins of Jeroboam Ben-Nabat. *JQR* NS 58:95–114.

Darnton, Robert. 1984. *The Great Cat Massacre and Other Episodes in French Cultural History*. New York: Basic.

Davis, Avrohom and Yosef Rabinowitz, trans. 2004. *The Metsudah Chumash/Rashi: IV, Bamidbar*. The Ellen and David Scheinfeld Edition. New York: Metsudah.

Davis, Colin. 2004. *After Poststructuralism: Reading, Stories and Theory*. London: Routledge.

de Buck, Adriaan. 1935. *ECT, VI: Texts of Spells 472–786*. Chicago: University of Chicago Press.

Dell, Katharine J. 1991. *The Book of Job as Sceptical Literature*. BZAW 197. Berlin: de Gruyter.

de Vaux, Roland. 1971. *The Bible and the Ancient Near East*. Garden City, N.Y.: Doubleday.

De Vries, Simon J. 1985. *1 Kings*. WBC 12. Waco, Tex.: Word.

Dewald, Carolyn. 2003. Form and Content: The Question of Tyranny in Herodotus. Pages 25–58 in Morgan 2003.

Dhorme, Edouard. 1984. *A Commentary on the Book of Job*. Translated by Harold Knight. Nashville: Nelson.

Diamond, A. R. Pete. 1996. Portraying Prophecy: Of Doublets, Variants and Analogies in the Narrative Representation of Jeremiah's Oracles—Reconstructing the Hermeneutics of Prophecy. Pages 313–33 in *The Prophets: A Sheffield Reader*. Edited by Philip R. Davies. Sheffield: Sheffield Academic.

Diamond, Cora. 1998. Martha Nussbaum and the Need for Novels. Pages 39–64 in *Renegotiating Ethics in Literature, Philosophy and Theory*. Edited by J. Adamson, R. Freadman, and D. Parker. Cambridge: Cambridge University Press.

Dickens, Charles. 1971. *Our Mutual Friend*. Edited by Stephen Gill. Harmondsworth: Penguin.

———. 1981. *David Copperfield*. Edited by Nina Burgis. Oxford: Clarendon.

———. 2003. *Great Expectations*. Edited by Charlotte Mitchell. London: Penguin.

———. 2004. *David Copperfield*. Edited by Jeremy Tambling. Rev. ed. London: Penguin.

Diderot, Denis. 1994. *Éloge de Richardson*. Pages 80–97 in *Selected Writings on Art and Literature*. Translated by Geoffrey Bremner. London: Penguin.

Dillon, Matthew, and Lynda Garland. 1994. *Ancient Greece: Social and Historical Documents from Archaic Times to the Death of Socrates (c. 800–399 BC)*. London: Routledge.

Di Vito, Robert A. 1997. Here One Need Not Be One's Self: The Concept of "Self" in the Old Testament. Pages 49–88 in *The Whole and Divided Self: The Bible and Theological Anthropology*. Edited by David E. Aune and John McCarthy. New York: Crossroad.

Dodds, E. R., ed. 1960. *Euripides: Bacchae*. 2d ed. Oxford: Clarendon.

Donlan, Walter. 1971. Homer's Agamemnon. *CW* 65:109–15.

Doris. John M. 2002. *Lack of Character: Personality and Moral Behavior*. New York: Cambridge University Press.

Driver, Samuel R. 1902. *Deuteronomy*. 3d ed. ICC. Edinburgh: T. & T. Clark.

Driver, Samuel R., and George Buchanan Gray. 1977. *A Critical and Exegetical Commentary on the Book of Job, Parts I and II*. ICC. Edinburgh: T. & T. Clark.

Dumbrell, William J. 1986. What Are You Doing Here? Elijah at Horeb. *Crux* 22:12–19.

Eaglestone, Robert. 1997. *Ethical Criticism: Reading After Levinas*. Edinburgh: Edinburgh University Press.

Eagleton, Terry. 2003. *After Theory*. New York: Basic.

Easterling, P. E. 1990. Constructing Character in Greek Tragedy. Pages 83–99 in Pelling, ed., 1990.

Edelman, Diana Vikander. 1991. *King Saul in the Historiography of Judah*. JSOTSup 121. Sheffield: JSOT Press.

Egan, Keith J., and Craig E. Morrison, eds. 1997. *Master of the Sacred Page: Essays and Articles in Honor of Roland E. Murphy on the Occasion of His Eightieth Birthday.* Washington, D.C.: Carmelite Institute.

Eissfeldt, Otto. 1965. *The Old Testament: An Introduction.* Translated by Peter R. Ackroyd. New York: Harper & Row.

Elias, Norbert. 1970. *Was ist Soziologie?* Grundlagen der Soziologie 1. Munich: Juventa.

———. 1997a. *Über den Prozeß der Zivilisation: Soziogenetische und psychogenetische Untersuchungen.* Band 1. Frankfurt: Suhrkamp Taschenbuch.

———. 1997b. *Über den Prozeß der Zivilisation: Soziogenetische und psychogenetische Untersuchungen.* Band 2. Frankfurt: Suhrkamp Taschenbuch.

———. 2002. *Die höfische Gesellschaft: Untersuchungen zur Soziologie des Königtums und der höfischen Aristokratie, mit einer Einleitung: Soziologie und Geschichtswissenschaft.* Gesammelte Schriften 2. Frankfurt: Suhrkamp.

Ellis, Steve. 1998. Canto XXII: Controversial Comedy. Pages 287–96 in Mandelbaum et al. 1998.

Elms, Alan C. 2001. Apocryphal Freud: Sigmund Freud's Most Famous "Quotations" and Their Actual Sources. Pages 83–104 in *Sigmund Freud and His Impact on the Modern World.* Edited by Jerome A. Winer and James W. Anderson. Annual of Psychoanalysis 29. Hillsdale, N.J.: Analytic.

Eskin, Michael. 2004. Introduction: The Double "Turn" to Ethics and Literature? *PT* 25:557–62.

Evans, William McKee. 1980. From the Land of Canaan to the Land of Guinea: The Strange Odyssey of the "Sons of Ham." *AHR* 85:15–43.

Eynikel, Erik. 1990. Prophecy and Fulfillment in the Deuteronomistic History: 1 Kgs 13; 2 Kgs 23, 16–18. Pages 227–37 in *Pentateuchal and Deuteronomistic Studies: Papers Read at the XIIIth IOSOT Congress, Leuven 1989.* Edited by C. Brekelmans and Johan Lust. Leuven: Leuven University Press.

Falvo, Joseph D. 1988. The Irony of Deception in *Malebolge*: *Inferno* XXI–XXII. *LD* 2:55–72.

Faulkner, Raymond, and Ogden Goelet, trans. 1998. *The Egyptian Book of the Dead: The Book of Going Forth by Day.* Edited by Eva von Dassow. San Francisco: Chronicle Books.

Feldman, Louis H. 1994. Josephus' Portrait of Elijah. *SJOT* 8:61–86.

Felsenstein, Frank. 1995. *Anti-Semitic Stereotypes: A Paradigm of Otherness in English Popular Culture, 1660–1830.* Baltimore: The Johns Hopkins University Press.

Ferrill, Arthur. 1978. Herodotus on Tyranny. *Historia* 22:385–98.

Festinger, Leon. 1957. *A Theory of Cognitive Dissonance.* Evanston, Ill.: Row, Peterson & Co.

Fitzmyer, Joseph A. 1967. *The Aramaic Inscriptions of Sefire.* Rome: Pontifical Biblical Institute.

———. 1993. *Romans: A New Translation with Introduction and Commentary.* AB 33. New York: Doubleday.

Fleming, Diana. 2006. The Character of Virtue: Answering the Situationist Challenge to Virtue Ethics. *Ratio* NS 19:24–42.

Fokkelman, J. P. 1981. *Narrative Art and Poetry in the Books of Samuel: A Full Interpretation Based on Stylistic and Structural Analyses.* Vol. 1, *King David (II Sam. 9–20 & I Kings 1–2).* SSN 20. Assen: Van Gorcum.

————. 1990. *Narrative Art and Poetry in the Books of Samuel: A Full Interpretation Based on Stylistic and Structural Analyses*. Vol. 3, *Throne and City (II Sam. 2–8 & 21–24)*. Translated by L. Waaning-Wardle. SSN. Assen: Van Gorcum.

Ford, Charles V. 1996. *Lies! Lies!! Lies!!! The Psychology of Deceit*. Washington, D.C.: American Psychiatric Press.

Forsdyke, Sara. 2002. Greek History, *c.* 525–480 BC. Pages 521–49 in Bakker et al. 2002.

Forster, E. M. 1927. *Aspects of the Novel*. New York: Harcourt, Brace & Company.

Försterling, Friedrich. 2001. *Attribution: An Introduction to Theories, Research, and Applications*. Philadelphia: Taylor & Francis.

Fowler, Robert. 1993. Characterizing Character in Biblical Narrative. *Semeia* 63:97–104.

Fox, Michael V. 1989. *Qohelet and his Contradictions*. JSOTSup 71. Sheffield: Almond.

Fränkel, Hermann F. 1951. *Dichtung und Philosophie des Frühen Griechentums: Eine Geschichte der griechischen Literatur von Homer bis Pindar*. Philological Monographs 13. New York: American Philological Association.

Frankfurt Institute for Social Research. 1972. *Aspects of Sociology*. Translated by John Viertel. Boston: Beacon.

Franz, Carol E. 1994. Does Thought Content Change as Individuals Age? A Longitudinal Study of Midlife Adults. Pages 227–49 in Heatherton and Weinberger 1994.

Freedman, John. 1988. Narrative Technique and the Art of Story-Telling in Anton Chekhov's "Little Trilogy." *South Atlantic Review* 53:1–18.

Fretheim, Terence E. 1999. *First and Second Kings*. WBCom. Louisville: Westminster John Knox.

Freud, Sigmund. 1940a. *Jenseits des Lustprinzips*. Pages 3–69 in vol. 13 of *GW*.

————. 1940b. *Das Ich und das Es*. Pages 237–89 in vol. 13 of *GW*.

————. 1940c. *Massenpsychologie und Ich-Analyse*. Pages 73–161 in vol. 13 of *GW*.

————. 1941. Der Dichter und Das Phantasieren. Pages 213–23 in vol. 7 of *GW*.

————. 1946a. Einige Charaktertypen aus der Psychoanalytischen Arbeit. Pages 364–91 in vol. 10 of *GW*.

————. 1946b. Zeitgemäßes über Krieg und Tod. Pages 324–55 in vol. 10 of *GW*.

————. 1946c. Zür Einführung des Narzissmus. Pages 138–70 in vol. 10 of *GW*.

————. 1947. Eine Schwierigkeit der Psychoanalyse. Pages 3–12 in vol. 12 of *GW*.

————. 1948a. *Die Zukunft einer Illusion*. Pages 325–80 in vol. 14 of *GW*.

————. 1948b. Die Verneinung. Pages 11–15 in vol. 14 of *GW*.

————. 1950. *Der Mann Moses und die monotheistische Religion*. Pages 103–246 in vol. 16 of *GW*.

————. 1953a. *Das Unbehagen in der Kultur*. Pages 65–129 in *Abriß der Psycho-analyse/Das Unbehagen in der Kultur*. Bücher des Wissens. Frankfurt: Fischer Taschenbuch.

————. 1953b. Psychopathic Characters on the Stage. Pages 305–10 in vol. 7 of *SE*.

————. 1963. *Introductory Lectures on Psycho-Analysis, Part III*. Pages 243–463 in vol. 16 of *SE*.

Friedlander, Gerald, trans. 1965. *Pirḵê de Rabbi Eliezer: (The Chapters of Rabbi Eliezer the Great) According to the Text of the Manuscript Belonging to Abraham Epstein of Vienna*. 2d ed. New York: Sepher-Hermon.

Fromm, Erich. 1975. *The Anatomy of Human Destructiveness*. Greenwich, Conn.: Fawcett Crest.

Frye, Northrop. 1983. *The Great Code: The Bible and Literature*. New York: Harcourt.

Furnham, Adrian, and Tracy Ribchester. 1995. Tolerance of Ambiguity: A Review of the Concept, Its Measurement and Applications. *Current Psychology* 14:179–99.

Ganss, George E., ed. 1991. *Ignatius of Loyola: The* Spiritual Exercises *and Selected Works*. New York: Paulist.

Garsiel, Moshe. 1993. The Story of David and Bathsheba: A Different Approach. *CBQ* 55:244–62.

Gay, Peter. 1995. *The Bourgeois Experience, Victoria to Freud*. Vol. 4, *The Naked Heart*. New York: Norton.

Geddes, A. G. 1998. Homer in Translation. Pages 186–98 in McAuslan and Walcot 1998.

Geertz, Clifford. 1973. *The Interpretation of Cultures*. New York: Basic.

———. 1983. "From the Native's Point of View": On the Nature of Anthropological Understanding. Pages 55–70 in *Local Knowledge: Further Essays in Interpretive Anthropology*. New York: Basic.

Geiringer, Erich. 1952. Fear of Death. *The Spectator* 189:179–80.

Geller, Stephen A. 1996. *Sacred Enigmas: Literary Religion in the Hebrew Bible*. London: Routledge.

———. 2000. The God of the Covenant; Discussion and Conclusions. Pages 273–319 and 321–42 in *One God or Many? Concepts of Divinity in the Ancient World*. Edited by Barbara N. Porter. Transactions of the Casco Bay Assyriological Institute 1. Chebeague Island: CDL.

Gerleman, Gillis. 1977. Schuld und Sühne. Erwägungen zu 2. Samuel 12. Pages 132–39 in *Beiträge zur Alttestamentlichen Theologie. Festschrift für W. Zimmerli zum 70. Geburtstag*. Edited by H. Donner, R. Hanhart, and R. Smend. Göttingen: Vandenhoeck & Ruprecht.

Gibson, Andrew 1999. *Postmodernity, Ethics and the Novel: From Leavis to Levinas*. London: Routledge.

Gilbert, Daniel T., and Patrick S. Malone. 1995. The Correspondence Bias. *PB* 117:21–38.

Gill, Christopher. 1990. The Character–Personality Distinction. Pages 1–31 in Pelling 1990.

———. 1996. *Personality in Greek Epic, Tragedy, and Philosophy: The Self in Dialogue*. Oxford: Clarendon.

Gilmore, D. D. 1982. Anthropology of the Mediterranean Area. *Annual Review of Anthropology* 11:175–205.

Gilsenan, Michael. 1976. Lying, Honor and Contradiction. Pages 191–219 in *Transaction and Meaning: Directions in the Anthropology of Exchange and Symbolic Behavior*. Edited by Bruce Kapferer. Philadelphia: Institute for the Study of Human Issues.

Ginzberg, Louis. 1968. *The Legends of the Jews*, vols. 1, 4, 5, 6. Translated by Henrietta Szold. Philadelphia: JPS.

Glass, David C. 1964. Changes in Liking as a Means of Reducing Cognitive Discrepancies between Self-Esteem and Aggression. *Journal of Personality* 32:531–49.

Goelet, Ogden. 1998. A Commentary on *The Book of Going Forth by Day*. Pages 137–70 in Faulkner and Goelet 1998.

Goffman, Erving. 1959. *The Presentation of Self in Everyday Life.* Garden City, N.Y.: Doubleday Anchor.

———. 1974. *Frame Analysis: An Essay on the Organization of Experience.* Boston: Northeastern University Press.

Goldingay, John. 2001. Death and Afterlife in the Psalms. Pages 61–85 in *Judaism in Late Antiquity, Part 4: Death, Life-After-Death, Resurrection and the World-to-Come in the Judaisms of Antiquity.* Edited by Alan J. Avery-Peck and Jacob Neusner. Boston: Brill.

Gombrich, Ernst H. 1969. *Art and Illusion: A Study in the Psychology of Pictorial Representation.* 2d ed. Princeton, N.J.: Princeton University Press.

Good, Edwin M. 1981. *Irony in The Old Testament.* 2d ed. Sheffield: Almond.

———. 1990. *In Turns of Tempest: A Reading of Job.* Stanford: Stanford University Press.

Goodblatt, Chanita. 1996. An Intertextual Discourse on Sin and Salvation: John Donne's Sermon on Psalm 51. *Renaissance and Reformation / Renaissance et Réforme* 20:23–40.

Gooding, D. W. 1964. Ahab according to the Septuagint. *ZAW* 76:269–80.

Gordis, Robert. 1978. *The Book of Job: Commentary, New Translation, and Special Studies.* New York: Jewish Theological Seminary.

Gordon, Robert P. 2000. David's Rise and Saul's Demise: Narrative Analogy in 1 Samuel 24–26. Pages 319–39 in *Reconsidering Israel and Judah: Recent Studies on the Deuteronomistic History.* Edited by Gary N. Knoppers and J. Gordon McConville. Winona Lake, Ind.: Eisenbrauns.

Gouldner, Alvin W. 1965. *Enter Plato: Classical Greece and the Origins of Social Theory.* New York: Basic.

Graesser, Arthur C., Murray Singer, and Tom Trabasso. 1994. Constructing Inferences During Narrative Text Comprehension. *PR* 101:371–95.

Gray, John. 1970. *I & II Kings: A Commentary.* 2d ed. OTL. Philadelphia: Westminster.

Gray, Vivienne J. 1996. Herodotus and Images of Tyranny: The Tyrants of Corinth. *AJP* 117:361–89.

———. 2001. Herodotus' Literary and Historical Method: Arion's Story (1.23–24). *AJP* 122:11–28.

Green, André. 1983. *Narcissisme de Vie—Narcissisme de Mort.* Paris: Éditions de Minuit.

Green, Christopher D., and Philip R. Groff. 2003. *Early Psychological Thought: Ancient Accounts of Mind and Soul.* Westport, Conn.: Praeger.

Green, Melanie C., Jeffrey J. Strange, and Timothy C. Brock, eds. 2002. *Narrative Impact: Social and Cognitive Foundations.* Mahwah, N.J.: Erlbaum.

Greenberg, Moshe. 1969. *Understanding Exodus.* New York: Behrman House.

Greenberg, Nathan A. 1993. The Attitude of Agamemnon. *CW* 86:193–205.

Greenblatt, Stephen. 1984. *Renaissance Self-Fashioning: From More to Shakespeare.* Chicago: University of Chicago Press.

Greenhouse, Linda G. 2007. Justices to Consider Impact of Mental Illness on Death Penalty. *New York Times* 1/6/07. Online: http://query.nytimes.com/gst/fullpage.html?res=9C06EED91430F935A35752C0A9619C8B63.

Gregory, Richard L. 1974. Social Implications of Intelligent Machines. Pages 630–42 in *Concepts and Mechanisms of Perception.* New York: Charles Scribner's Sons.

Gregory, Russell. 1990. Irony and the Unmasking of Elijah. Pages 93–169 in Hauser and Gregory 1990.

Gressmann, Hugo. 1913. *Mose und seine Zeit: Ein Kommentar zu den Mose-Sagen.* Göttingen: Vandenhoeck & Ruprecht.

Griffin, Jaspar. 1980. *Homer on Life and Death.* Oxford: Clarendon.

Griffin, Jaspar, and Martin Hammond. 1998. Critical Appreciation: Homer, *Iliad* 1.1–52. Pages 65–82 in McAuslan and Walcot 1998.

Gross, Walter. 1979. Lying Prophet and Disobedient Man of God in 1 Kings 13: Role Analysis as an Instrument of Theological Interpretation of an OT Narrative Text. *Semeia* 15:97–135.

Gunkel, Hermann. 1928. *What Remains of the Old Testament and Other Essays.* Translated by A. K. Dallas. New York: Macmillan.

Gunn, David M. 1989. *The Story of King David: Genre and Interpretation.* JSOTSup 6. Sheffield: JSOT.

Gunn, David M., and Danna Nolan Fewell. 1993. *Narrative in the Hebrew Bible.* Oxford Bible Series. New York: Oxford University Press.

Haas, Willy. 1962. *Gestalten: Essays zur Literatur und Gesellschaft.* Berlin: Im Propylaen.

Habel, Norman C. 1985. *The Book of Job: A Commentary.* OTL. Philadelphia: Westminster.

———. 1995. *The Land Is Mine: Six Biblical Land Ideologies.* Minneapolis: Fortress.

Hahn, Joachim. 1981. Das "Goldene Kalb": Die Jahwe-Verehrung bei Stierbildem in der *Geschichte Israels.* Frankfurt: Lang.

Hainsworth, Bryan. 1993. *The Iliad: A Commentary, Volume III, Books 9–12.* Cambridge: Cambridge University Press.

Hakemulder, Jèmeljan (Frank). 2000. *The Moral Laboratory: Experiments Examining the Effects of Reading Literature on Social Perception and Moral Self-Concept.* Amsterdam: Benjamins.

Hall, David L. 1996. Our Names Are Legion for We Are Many: On the Academics of Deception. Pages 241–61 in Ames and Dissanayake 1996.

Halleran, Michael R. 1992. Review of Ruth Padel, *In and Out of the Mind. BRCW* 03.06.14. Online: http://bmcr.brynmawr.edu/1992/03.06.14.html.

Halliwell, Stephen. 1990. Traditional Greek Conceptions of Character. Pages 32–59 in Pelling 1990.

———. 1998. *Aristotle's Poetics.* 2d ed. Chicago: University of Chicago Press.

Halpern, Baruch. 1991. Jerusalem and the Lineages in the Seventh Century BCE: Kinship and the Rise of Individual Moral Liability. Pages 11–107 in *Law and Ideology in Monarchic Israel.* Edited by Baruch Halpern and Deborah W. Hobson. JSOTSup 124. Sheffield: Sheffield Academic.

———. 2001. *David's Secret Demons: Messiah, Murderer, Traitor, King.* Grand Rapids. Mich.: Eerdmans.

Hamburger, Käte. 1965. *Der Humor bei Thomas Mann: Zum Joseph-Roman.* Munich: Nymphenburger Verlagshandlung.

Hamilton, Victor P. 1995. *The Book of Genesis, Chapters 18–50.* NIBCOT. Grand Rapids, Mich.: Eerdmans.

Hankiss, Agnes. 1980. Games Con Men Play: The Semiosis of Deceptive Interaction. *Journal of Communication* 30:104–12.

Hanson, Paul D. 1987. Israelite Religion in the Early Postexilic Periods. Pages 485–508 in *Ancient Israelite Religion: Essays in Honor of Frank Moore Cross*. Edited by P. D. Miller et al. Philadelphia: Fortress.

Hara, Eiichi. n. d. The King and the Apprentice: Writing *David Copperfield*. Online: http://wwwsoc.nii.ac.jp/dickens/archive/dc/dc-hara.pdf.

Hardy, Barbara. 1987. The Moral Art of Dickens: *David Copperfield*. Pages 9–19 in *Charles Dickens's David Copperfield*. Edited by Harold Bloom. Modern Critical Interpretations. New York: Chelsea House.

Harman, Gilbert. 2000. The Nonexistence of Character Traits. *Proceedings of the Aristotelian Society for the Systematic Study of Philosophy* 100:223–26.

Harmon-Jones, Eddie. 1999. Toward an Understanding of the Motivation Underlying Dissonance Effects: Is the Production of Aversive Consequences Necessary? Pages 71–99 in Harmon-Jones and Mills 1999.

Harmon-Jones, Eddie, and Judson Mills, eds. 1999. *Cognitive Dissonance: Progress on a Pivotal Theory in Social Psychology*. Washington, D.C.: American Psychological Association.

———. 1999. An Introduction to Cognitive Dissonance Theory and an Overview of Current Perspectives on the Theory. Pages 3–21 in Harmon-Jones and Mills 1999.

Harris, John L. 2000. Ahithophel. Pages 34–35 in *EDB*.

Harrison, Thomas. 2000. Divinity and History: The Religion of Herodotus. Oxford: Clarendon.

Hauser, Alan. 1990. Yahweh Versus Death—The Real Struggle in 1 Kings 17–19. Pages 9–89 in Hauser and Gregory 1990.

Hauser, Alan J., and Russell Gregory. 1990. *From Carmel to Horeb: Elijah in Crisis*. Bible and Literature, 19; JSOTSup, 85. Sheffield: Almond.

Hayes, Christine E. 2004. Golden Calf Stories: The Relationship of Exodus 32 and Deuteronomy 9–10. Pages 45–93 in *The Idea of Biblical Interpretation: Essays in Honor of James L. Kugel*. Edited by Hindy Najman and Judith H. Newman. Leiden: Brill.

Heatherton, Todd F., and Joel L. Weinberger, eds. 1994. *Can Personality Change?* Washington, D.C.: American Psychological Association.

Heider, Fritz. 1944. Social Perception and Phenomenal Causality. *PR* 51:358–74.

———. 1958. *The Psychology of Interpersonal Relations*. New York: Wiley & Sons.

Helck, H. Wolfgang. 1977. *Die Lehre für König Merikarê*. Wiesbaden: Harrassowitz.

Heller, Erich. 1974. *Franz Kafka*. New York: Viking.

Herman, David. 1999. Introduction: Narratologies. Pages 1–30 in *Narratologies: New Perspectives on Narrative Analysis*. Edited by David Herman. Columbus: Ohio State University Press.

Hertz, J. H. 1960. *The Pentateuch and Haftorahs*. 2d ed. London: Soncino.

Hertzberg, Hans Wilhelm. 1964. *I and II Samuel: A Commentary*. Translated by J. S. Bowden. OTL. Philadelphia: Westminster.

Heschel, Abraham J. 1969. *The Prophets, I*. New York: Harper Torchbooks.

Hirsch, E. D., Jr. 1976. *The Aims of Interpretation*. Chicago: University of Chicago Press.

Hobbs, T. R. 1985. *2 Kings*. WBC 13. Waco, Tex.: Word.

Hochman, Baruch. 1985. *Character in Literature*. Ithaca, N.Y.: Cornell University Press.

Hoffman, Yair. 1996. A Blemished Perfection: The Book of Job in Context. JSOTSup 213. Sheffield: Sheffield Academic.

Hoffmann, Hans-Detlef. 1980. *Reform und Reformen: Untersuchungen zu einen Grundthema der deuteronomistischen Geschichtsschreibung.* ATANT 66. Zurich: Theologischer Verlag.

Hoffner, Cynthia, and Joanne Cantor. 1991. Perceiving and Responding to Mass Media Characters. Pages 63–101 in *Responding to the Screen: Reception and Reaction Processes.* Edited by Jennings Bryant and Dolf Zillmann. Hilldale, N.J.: Erlbaum.

Holladay, William L. 1989. *Jeremiah 2: A Commentary on the Book of the Prophet Jeremiah, Chapters 26–52.* Hermeneia. Minneapolis: Fortress.

Hollander, Robert. 1989. Dante's Virgil: A Light That Failed. *LD* 4:3–9.

Holmes, Oliver Wendell, Jr. 1881. *The Common Law.* Boston: Little, Brown & Co.

Holt, Else K. 1995. "…Urged on By his Wife Jezebel": A Literary Reading of 1 Kgs 18 in Context. *SJOT* 9:83–96.

———. 1999. The Potent Word of God: Remarks on the Composition of Jeremiah 37–44. Pages 161–70 in *Troubling Jeremiah.* Edited by A. R. P. Diamond, K. M. O'Connor and L. Stulman. JSOTSup 260. Sheffield: Sheffield Academic.

Holtz, Barry W. 2002. The Torah as Truth: Teaching the Bible in a Skeptical Age. *Journal of Jewish Education* 68:105–12.

Horn, Siegfried H., and P. Kyle McCarter. 1999. The Divided Monarchy: The Kingdoms of Judah and Israel. Pages 129–99 in *Ancient Israel: From Abraham to the Roman Destruction of the Temple.* Edited by Hershel Shanks. Rev. ed. Upper Saddle River, N.J.: Prentice Hall.

Houtman, Cornelis. 2000. *Exodus*, vol. 3. Translated by Sierd Woudstra. HCOT. Leuven: Peeters.

Howell, J. Dwayne, and Susan H. Howell. 2008. Journey to Mount Horeb: Cognitive Theory and 1 Kings 19:1–18. *Mental Health, Religion & Culture* 11/7: 1–6; online version: http://dx.doi.org/10.1080/13674670801930445.

Hugo, Victor. 1982. *Les Misérables.* Translated by Norman Denny. London: Penguin.

Hursthouse, Rosalind. 1997. Virtue Theory and Abortion. Pages 217–38 in Crisp and Slote 1997.

Hyatt, J. Philip. 1980. *Commentary on Exodus.* NCBC. London: Marshall, Morgan & Scott.

Hyppolite, Jean. 1966. Commentaire parlé sur la "*Verneinung*" de Freud. Pages 879–87 in Jacques Lacan, *Écrits.* Paris: Seuil.

Isser, Stanley. 2003. *The Sword of Goliath: David in Heroic Literature.* Studies in Biblical Literature 6. Leiden: Brill.

Izre'el, Shlomo. 2001. *Adapa and the South Wind: Language Has the Power of Life and Death.* Winona Lake, Ind.: Eisenbrauns.

Jacob, Benno. 1924. Gott and Pharao. *Monatschrift für Geschichte and Wissenschaft des Judentums* 32:268–89.

———. 1992. *The Second Book of the Bible: Exodus.* Translated by Walter Jacob and Yaakov Elman. Hoboken, N.J.: KTAV.

Jaeger, Werner. 1965. *Paideia: The Ideals of Greek Culture.* Vol. 1, *Archaic Greece, The Mind of Athens.* Translated by Gilbert Highet. 2d ed. New York: Oxford University Press.

Janzen, J. Gerald. 1990. The Character of the Calf and its Cult in Exodus 32. *CBQ* 52:597–607.

Jenks, Alan W. 1977. *The Elohist and North Israelite Traditions.* SBLMS 22. Missoula, Mont.: Scholars Press.

Jobling, David. 1986. *The Sense of Biblical Narrative: Structural Analyses in the Hebrew Bible, I.* 2d ed. JSOTSup 7. Sheffield: JSOT.

———. 1998. *1 Samuel.* Berit Olam. Collegeville, Minn.: Liturgical.

Johnson, Aubrey R. 1957. Jonah II. 3–10: A Study in Cultic Phantasy. Pages 82–102 in *Studies in Old Testament Prophecy presented to Professor Theodore H. Robinson.* Edited by H. H. Rowley. Edinburgh: T. & T. Clark.

———. 1964. *The Vitality of the Individual in the Thought of Ancient Israel.* 2d ed. Cardiff: University of Wales Press.

Johnson, David M. 2001. Herodotus' Storytelling Speeches: Socles (5.92) and Leotychides (6.86). *CJ* 97:1–26.

Johnson, Samuel. 1990. The History of Rasselas, Prince of Abyssinia. Pages 7–176 in *Rasselas and Other Tales.* Edited by Gwin J. Kolb. New Haven: Yale University Press.

Jones, Gwilym H. 1984. *1 and 2 Kings*, vol. 2. NCBC. Grand Rapids: Eerdmans.

Jones, Michael. 2008. *Leningrad: State of Siege.* New York: Basic.

Jordan, John O. 1985. The Social Sub-text of *David Copperfield.* Pages 61–92 in *Dickens Studies Annual: Essays on Victorian Fiction.* Edited by M. Timko, F. Kaplan, and E. Guiliano. New York: AMS.

Joseph, Gerhard. 2000. Prejudice in Jane Austen, Emma Tennant, Charles Dickens—and Us. *Studies in English Literature* 40:679–93.

Kadushin, Max. 1969. *A Conceptual Approach to the Mekilta.* New York: Jewish Theological Seminary of America.

Kafka, Franz. 1949. *Tagebücher 1910–1923.* Edited by Max Brod. Frankfurt: Fischer.

———. 1953. *Hochzeitsvorbereitungen auf dem Lande und andere Prosa aus dem Nachlass.* Frankfurt: Fischer.

———. 1958. *Briefe 1902–1924.* Frankfurt: Fischer.

———. 1970. *Sämtliche Erzählungen.* Edited by Paul Raabe. Frankfurt: Fischer.

———. 1990. *Der Proceß: Apparatband.* Kritische Ausgabe. Edited by Malcolm Pasley. Frankfurt: Fischer Taschenbuch.

———. 1994. *Der Proceß.* Originalfassung. Frankfurt: Fischer Taschenbuch.

Karenga, Maulana. 2004. *Maat, the Moral Ideal in Ancient Egypt: A Study in Classical African Ethics.* New York: Routledge.

Kawashima, Robert S. 2004. *Biblical Narrative and the Death of the Rhapsode.* Indiana Studies in Biblical Literature. Bloomington: Indiana University Press.

Keen, Suzanne. 2006. A Theory of Narrative Empathy. *Narrative* 14:207–36.

———. 2007. *Empathy and the Novel.* New York: Oxford University Press.

Keinänen, Jyrki. 2001. *Traditions in Collision: A Literary and Redaction-Critical Study on the Elijah Narratives 1 Kings 17–19.* Helsinki: Finnish Exegetical Society.

Kennedy, A. R. S. 1901. Calf, Golden Calf. Pages 340–43 in *A Dictionary of the Bible*, vol. 1. Edited by J. Hastings. 4th ed. Edinburgh: T. & T. Clark.

Kernberg, Otto F. 1985. *Borderline Conditions and Pathological Narcissism.* Northvale, N.J.: Aronson.

Kierkegaard, Søren. 1990. *For Self-Examination/Judge for Yourself!* Edited and translated by Howard V. Hong and Edna H. Hong. Princeton, N.J.: Princeton University Press.

Kindt, Tom, and Hans-Harald Müller. 2003. Narratology and Interpretation: A Rejoinder to David Darby. *PT* 24:413–21.

Kirk, Geoffrey S. 1962. *The Songs of Homer.* Cambridge: Cambridge University Press.

———. 1985. *The Iliad: A Commentary, Volume I: Books 1–4.* New York: Cambridge University Press.

Kissling, Paul J. 1996. *Reliable Characters in the Primary History: Profiles of Moses, Joshua, Elijah and Elisha.* JSOTSup 224. Sheffield: Sheffield Academic.

Klopfenstein, Martin A. 1966. 1 Könige 13. Pages 639–72 in ΠΑΡΡΗΣΙΑ: *Karl Barth zum achtzigsten Geburtstag am 10. Mai 1966.* Edited by E. Busch et al. Zurich: Evz-Verlag.

Knights, L. C. 1933. *How Many Children Had Lady Macbeth? An Essay in the Theory and Practice of Shakespeare Criticism.* Cambridge: Minority.

Knoppers, Gary N. 1994. *Two Nations under God: The Deuteronomic History of Solomon and the Dual Monarchies.* Vol. 2, *The Reign of Jeroboam, the Fall of Israel, and the Reign of Josiah.* HSM 53. Atlanta: Scholars Press.

Koch, Klaus. 1969. *The Growth of the Biblical Tradition: The Form-Critical Method.* Translated by S. M. Cupitt. 2d ed. New York: Scribner.

Kohut, Heinz. 1972. Thoughts on Narcissism and Narcissistic Rage. *The Psychoanalytic Study of the Child* 27:360–400.

———. 1977. *The Restoration of the Self.* New York: International Universities Press.

Kosman, L. A. 1980. Being Properly Affected: Virtues and Feelings in Aristotle's Ethics. Pages 103–16 in *Essays on Aristotle's Ethics.* Edited by Amélie Oksenberg Rorty. Berkeley: University of California Press.

Kramer, Karl. 1979. Stories of Ambiguity. Pages 338–51 in *Anton Chekhov's Short Stories: Texts of the Stories, Backgrounds, Criticism.* Edited and translated by Ralph E. Matlaw. Norton Critical Editions. New York: Norton.

Kruger, Paul A. 2005. Depression in the Hebrew Bible: An Update. *JNES* 64:187–92.

Krummacher, Friedrich Wilhelm. 1870. *Elisha.* Translated by Samuel Jackson. London: Nelson & Sons.

Kselman, J., and M. L. Barré. 1998. Psalm 55: Problems and Proposals. *CBQ* 60:440–62.

Kugel, James L. 1998. *Traditions of the Bible: A Guide to the Bible as It Was at the Start of the Common Era.* Cambridge, Mass.: Harvard University Press.

———. 2007. How to Read the Bible: A Guide to Scripture, Then and Now. New York: Free Press/Simon & Schuster.

Kuhn, Thomas. 1996. *The Structure of Scientific Revolutions.* 3d ed. Chicago: University of Chicago Press.

Kuiken, Don, David S. Miall, and Shelley Sikora. 2004. Forms of Self-Implication in Literary Reading. *PT* 25:171–203.

Kuiper, N. A., and M. R. McDonald. 1982. Self and Other Perceptions in Mild Depressives. *Social Cognition* 1:223–39.

Kunz, Andreas. 2001. Der Mensch auf der Waage: Die Vorstellung vom Gerichtshandeln Gottes im ägyptischen Totenbuch (Tb 125) und bei Hiob (Ijob 31). *BZ* 45:235–50.

Kurz, Gerhard. 1987. Meinungen zur Schrift: Zur Exegese der Legende "Vor dem Gesetz" im Roman *Der Prozeß.* Pages 209–23 in *Kafka und das Judentum.* Edited by K. E. Grözinger, S. Mosès, and H. D. Zimmermann. Frankfurt: Jüdischer Verlag bei Athenäum.

LaBarbera, Robert 1984. The Man of War and the Man of God: Social Satire in 2 Kings 6:8–6:20. *CBQ* 46:637–51.

Landow, George P. 1980. *Victorian Types, Victorian Shadows: Biblical Typology in Victorian Literature, Art, and Thought.* Boston: Routledge & Kegan Paul.

Lapsley, Daniel K., and Darcia Narvaez. 2005. Moral Psychology at the Crossroads. Pages 18–35 in Lapsley and Power 2005.

Lapsley, Daniel K., and F. C. Power, eds. 2005. *Character Psychology and Character Education.* Notre Dame, Ind.: University of Notre Dame Press.

La Rochefoucauld, François, duc de. 1950. *Œuvres Complètes.* Edited by L. Martin-Chauffier. Paris: Librairie Gallimard.

Lasine, Stuart. 1977. Sight, Body, and Motion in Plato and Kafka: A Study of Projective and Topological Experience. Ph.D. diss. University of Wisconsin-Madison. University Microfilms International, Ann Arbor, Mich.

———. 1984a. Melodrama as Parable: The Story of the Poor Man's Ewe-Lamb and the Unmasking of David's Topsy-Turvy Emotions. *HAR* 8:101–24.

———. 1984b. Guest and Host in Judges 19: Lot's Hospitality in an Inverted World. *JSOT* 29:37–59.

———. 1984c. Kafka's "Sacred Texts" and the Hebrew Bible. *Papers in Comparative Studies* 3:121–35.

———. 1984d. Fiction, Falsehood, and Reality in Hebrew Scripture. *HS* 25:24–40.

———. 1986. Indeterminacy and the Bible: A Review of Literary and Anthropological Theories and Their Application to Biblical Texts. *HS* 27:48–80.

———. 1987. Solomon, Daniel and the Detective Story: The Social Functions of a Literary Genre. *HAR* 11:247–66.

———. 1988. Bird's-Eye and Worm's-Eye Views of Justice in the Book of Job. *JSOT* 42:29–53.

———. 1989a. The Riddle of Solomon's Judgment and the Riddle of Human Nature in the Hebrew Bible. *JSOT* 45:61–86.

———. 1989b. Judicial Narratives and the Ethics of Reading: The Reader as Judge of the Dispute Between Mephibosheth and Ziba. *HS* 30:49–69.

———. 1990. The Trials of Job and Kafka's Josef K. *The German Quarterly* 63:187–98.

———. 1991. Jehoram and the Cannibal Mothers (2 Kings 6:24–33): Solomon's Judgment in an Inverted World. *JSOT* 50:27–53.

———. 1992. Reading Jeroboam's Intentions: Intertextuality, Rhetoric and History in 1 Kings 12. Pages 133–52 in *Reading between Texts: Intertextuality and the Hebrew Bible.* Edited by Danna Nolan Fewell. Louisville: Westminster John Knox.

———. 1993. The Ups and Downs of Monarchical Justice: Solomon and Jehoram in an Intertextual World. *JSOT* 59:37–53.

———. 1994. Levite Violence, Fratricide, and Sacrifice in the Bible and Later Revolutionary Rhetoric. Pages 204–29 in *Curing Violence.* Edited by Mark I. Wallace and Theophus H. Smith. Sonoma, Calif.: Polebridge.

———. 2001. *Knowing Kings: Knowledge, Power and Narcissism in the Hebrew Bible.* SemeiaSt 40. Atlanta: SBL.

———. 2002. Divine Narcissism and Yahweh's Parenting Style. *BibInt* 10:36–56.

———. 2004a. Matters of Life and Death: The Story of Elijah and the Widow's Son in Comparative Perspective. *BibInt* 12:117–44.

———. 2004b. From Ahab to Obadiah. Pages 75–78 in *Yours Faithfully: Virtual Letters from the Bible.* Edited by Philip R. Davies. London: Equinox.

―――. 2005. Wordsworth Brooding Over Elijah: Immortality, Death and Narcissism. Pages 29–70 in *From Wordsworth to Stevens: Essays in Honor of Robert Rehder*. Edited by Anthony Mortimer. Bern: Lang.

―――. 2010. "Everything Belongs To Me": Holiness, Danger, and Divine Kingship in the Post-Genesis World. *JSOT* 35:31–62.

―――. 2011a. Review of Richard S. Briggs, *The Virtuous Reader: Old Testament Narrative and Interpretive Virtue*. *CBQ* 73:115–16.

―――. 2011b. "Go in peace" or "Go to Hell"? Elisha, Naaman and the Meaning of Monotheism in 2 Kings 5. *SJOT* 25:3–28.

―――. forthcoming. Holy Men in Space. In *Constructions of Space III: Biblical Spaces and the Sacred*. Edited by J. Økland, C. de Vos, and K. Wennell. LHBOTS. New York: Continuum.

Launderville, Dale. 2003. *Piety and Politics: The Dynamics of Royal Authority in Homeric Greece, Biblical Israel, and Old Babylonian Mesopotamia*. Grand Rapids, Mich.: Eerdmans.

Lauterbach, Jacob Z. 1933a. *Mekilta de-Rabbi Ishmael*, vol. 1. Philadelphia: JPS.

―――. 1933b. *Mekilta de-Rabbi Ishmael*, vol. 2. Philadelphia: JPS.

Lavelle, B. M. 1994. Review of James F. McGlew, *Tyranny and Political Culture in Ancient Greece*. *BRCW* Oct. 21. Online: http://bmcr.brynmawr.edu/1994/94.10.21.html.

Laver, A. B. 1972. Precursors of Psychology in Ancient Egypt. *Journal of the History of the Behavioral Sciences* 8:181–95.

Law, David R. 2002. Cheap Grace and the Cost of Discipleship in Kierkegaard's *For Self-Examination*. Pages 111–42 in *International Kierkegaard Commentary: For Self-Examination and Judge for Yourself!* Edited by Robert L. Perkins. Macon, Ga.: Mercer University Press.

Lee, Ronald. 2005. The Force of Religion in the Public Sphere. Pages 99–108 in *The Political Pulpit Revisited*. Edited by Roderick P. Hart and John L. Pauley. West Lafayette, Ind.: Purdue University Press.

Leibowitz, Nehama. 1976. *Studies in Shemot, Part 2*. Translated by Aryeh Newman. Jerusalem: World Zionist Organization.

―――. 1981. *Studies in Bereshit (Genesis)*. Translated by Aryeh Newman. 4th ed. Jerusalem: World Zionist Organization.

Lemke, Werner E. 1976. The Way of Obedience: 1 Kings 13 and the Structure of the Deuteronomistic History. Pages 301–26 in *Magnalia Dei: The Mighty Acts of God. Essays on the Bible and Archaeology in Memory of G. Ernest Wright*. Edited by F. M. Cross, W. E. Lemke, and P. D. Miller. Garden City, N.Y.: Doubleday.

Leuchter, Mark. 2006. Jeroboam the Ephratite. *JBL* 125:51-72.

Levenson, Jon D. 1985. *Sinai and Zion: An Entry into the Jewish Bible*. Minneapolis: Winston.

Levine, Baruch. 1993. *Numbers 1–20: A New Translation with Introduction and Commentary*. AB 4. New York: Doubleday.

Lewis, Michael. 2000. The Emergence of Human Emotions. Pages 265–80 in *Handbook of Emotions*. Edited by Michael Lewis and Jeannette M. Haviland-Jones. 2d ed. New York: Guilford.

Lichtheim, Miriam. 1973. *The Old and Middle Kingdoms*. Vol. 1 of *AEL*.

―――. 1976. *The New Kingdom*. Vol. 2 of *AEL*.

——. 1988. *Ancient Egyptian Autobiographies Chiefly of the Middle Kingdom: A Study and an Anthology*. OBO 84. Göttingen: Vandenhoeck & Ruprecht.

——. 1992. *Maat in Egyptian Autobiographies and Related Studies*. OBO 120. Göttingen: Vandenhoeck & Ruprecht.

Liess, Kathrin. 2004. *Der Weg des Lebens: Psalm 16 und das Lebens- und Todesverständnis der Individualpsalmen*. FAT 2/5. Tübingen: Mohr Siebeck.

Lightfoot, J. L., ed. 1999. *Parthenius of Nicaea: The Poetical Fragments and the Erotica Pathemata*. Oxford: Clarendon.

Liverani, Mario. 2005. *Israel's History and the History of Israel*. Translated by Chiara Peri and Philip R. Davies. London: Equinox.

Lockwood, Peter F. 2004. The Elijah Syndrome: What is Elijah Up to at Mt. Horeb? *Lutheran Theological Journal* 38:51–62.

Lohfink, Norbert. 1989. *Das Jüdische am Christentum: Die verlorene Dimension*. Freiburg: Herder.

Long, Burke O. 1984. *1 Kings, with an Introduction to Historical Literature*. FOTL 9. Grand Rapids, Mich.: Eerdmans.

——. 1991. *2 Kings*. FOTL 10. Grand Rapids, Mich.: Eerdmans.

Ludwig, Dean C., and Clinton O. Longenecker. 1993. The Bathsheba Syndrome: The Ethical Failure of Successful Leaders. *Journal of Business Ethics* 12:265–73.

Lupfer, Michael B., and Bryan E. Gingrich. 1999. When Bad (Good) Things Happen to Good (Bad) People: The Impact of Character Appraisal and Perceived Controllability on Judgments of Deservingness. *Social Justice Research* 12:165–88.

Lupfer, Michael, Matthew Weeks, and Susan Dupuis. 2000. How Pervasive is the Negativity Bias in Judgments Based on Character Appraisal? *Personality and Social Psychology Bulletin* 26:1353–66.

Lynch, Deidre Shauna. 1998. *The Economy of Character: Novels, Market Culture, and the Business of Inner Meaning*. Chicago: University of Chicago Press.

MacLean, H. B. 1962a. Ahab. Pages 61–63 in *IDB*, vol. 1.

——. 1962b. Joram. Pages 971–73 in *IDB*, vol. 2.

Maclean, Jennifer K. Berenson and Ellen Bradshaw Aitken, trans. 2002. *Flavius Philostratus: On Heroes*. Atlanta: SBL.

Malle, Bertram F. 2004. *How the Mind Explains Behavior: Folk Explanations, Meaning, and Social Interaction*. Cambridge, Mass.: MIT.

Mandelbaum, Allen, Anthony Oldcorn, and Charles Ross, eds. 1998. *Lectura Dantis: Inferno*. Berkeley: University of California Press.

Mann, Thomas. 1960. Joseph und seine Brüder: Ein Vortrag. Pages 654–69 in *Gesammelte Werke in Zwölf Bänden, Band XI: Reden und Aufsätze 3*. Frankfurt: Fischer.

——. 1964. *Joseph und seine Brüder*. Frankfurt: Fischer.

——. 1972. Freud und die Zukunft. Pages 133–51 in Sigmund Freud, *Abriß der Psychoanalyse und Das Unbehagen in der Kultur, mit einer Rede von Thomas Mann als Nachwort*. Frankfurt: Fischer Taschenbuch.

——. 2003. Address Delivered in the Coolidge Auditorium in the Library of Congress, November 17, 1942. Pages 3–19 in *Thomas Mann's Addresses Delivered at the Library of Congress*. Edited by Don Heinrich Tolzmann. Oxford: Lang.

Marcus, David. 1995. *From Balaam to Jonah: Anti-Prophetic Satire in the Hebrew Bible*. BJS 301. Atlanta: Scholars Press.

Markus, Hazel Rose, and Shinobu Kitayama. 1991. Culture and the Self: Implications for Cognition, Emotion, and Motivation. *PR* 98:224–53.

Marson, Eric Lawson. 1975. *Kafka's Trial: The Case Against Josef K.* St. Lucia, Q.: University of Queensland Press.

Masson, Michel. 2001. Rois et prophètes dans la cycle d'Élie. Pages 119–31 in *Prophètes et Rois: Bible et Proche-Orient.* Edited by André Lemaire. Lectio Divina Hors Série. Paris: Cerf.

Matthews, Gerald, Ian J. Deary, and Martha C. Whiteman. 2003. *Personality Traits.* 2d ed. Cambridge: Cambridge University Press.

Mauss, Marcel. 1968. Rapports réels et pratiques de la psychologie et de la sociologie. Pages 281–310 in Marcel Mauss, *Sociologie et anthropologie.* Paris: Presses Universitaires de France.

May, Herbert G., and Bruce M. Metzger, eds. 1977. *The New Oxford Annotated Bible with the Apocrypha.* New York: Oxford.

McAdams, Dan P. 1994. Can Personality Change? Levels of Stability and Growth in Personality Across the Life Span. Pages 299–313 in Heatherton and Weinberger 1994.

McAuslan, Ian, and Peter Walcot, eds. 1998. *Homer.* Oxford: Oxford University Press.

McCarter, P. Kyle. 1984. *II Samuel: A New Translation with Introduction, Notes, and Commentary.* AB 9. New York: Doubleday.

McConville, J. Gordon. 1984. *I & II Chronicles.* DSB. Louisville: Westminster John Knox.

McKane, William. 1970. *Proverbs: A New Approach.* OTL. Philadelphia: Westminster.

McKenzie, Steven L. 2000. *King David: A Biography.* New York: Oxford University Press.

Mead, James K. 1999. Kings and Prophets, Donkeys and Lions: Dramatic Shape and Deuteronomistic Rhetoric in 1 Kings XIII. *VT* 49:191–205.

Meier, Sam. 1989. Job I–II: A Reflection of Genesis I–III. *VT* 39:183–93.

Meier, Samuel A. 2009. *Themes and Transformations in Old Testament Prophecy.* Downers Grove, Ill.: InterVarsity.

Meinhold, Arndt. 2002. Mose und Elia am Gottesberg und am Ende des Prophetenkanons. *leqach* 2:22–38.

Merleau-Ponty, Maurice. 1964. *Le Visible et l'invisible.* Paris: Gallimard.

Meyer, Wulf-Uwe. 1988. Die Rolle von Überraschung im Attributionsprozeß. *Psychologische Rundschau* 39:136–47.

Meyer, Wulf-Uwe, Rainer Reisenzein, and Achim Schützwohl. 1997. Toward a Process Analysis of Emotions: The Case of Surprise. *Motivation and Emotion* 21:251–74.

Michotte, Albert. 1963. *The Perception of Causality.* Translated by T. R. Miles and Elaine Miles. London: Methuen.

Milgram, Stanley. 1974. *Obedience to Authority: An Experimental View.* New York: Harper & Row.

———. 1977. *The Individual in a Social World: Essays and Experiments.* Reading, Mass.: Addison-Wesley.

Milgrom, Jacob. 1976. *Cult and Conscience: The* Asham *and the Priestly Doctrine of Repentance.* Leiden: Brill.

———. 1990. *Numbers: The Traditional Hebrew Text With the New JPS Translation.* JPS Torah Commentary. Philadelphia: JPS.

———. 1992. Numbers, Book of. Pages 1146–55 in *ABD*, vol. 4.

Miller, Arthur G., ed. 1986. *The Obedience Experiments: A Case Study of Controversy in Social Science.* New York: Praeger.

Miller, J. Maxwell. 1966. The Elisha Cycle and the Accounts of the Omride Wars. *JBL* 85:441–54.

Miller, J. Maxwell, and John H. Hayes. 1986. *A History of Ancient Israel and Judah.* Philadelphia: Westminster.

Miller, Joan G. 1984. Culture and the Development of Everyday Social Explanation. *Journal of Personality and Social Psychology* 46:961–78.

Millon, Theodore. 1975. Reflections on Rosenhan's "On Being Sane in Insane Places." *JAP* 84:456–61.

Milton, John. 1889. Of Reformation Touching Church Discipline in England. Pages 51–108 in *English Prose Writings of Milton.* Edited by Henry Morley. London: Routledge.

Mintz, Alan. 1984. *Ḥurban: Responses to Catastrophe in Hebrew Literature.* New York: Columbia University Press.

Moberly, R. W. L. 1982. *At the Mountain of God: Story and Theology in Exodus 32–34.* JSOTSup 22. Sheffield: JSOT.

———. 2003. Does God Lie to His Prophets? The Story of Micaiah ben Imlah as a Test Case. *HTR* 96:1–23.

Moles, John. 2007. "Saving" Greece from the "Ignominy" of Tyranny? The "Famous" and "Wonderful" Speech of Socles (5.92). Pages 245–68 in *Reading Herodotus: A Study of the Logoi in Book 5 of Herodotus' Histories.* Edited by Elizabeth K. Irwin and Emily Greenwood. Cambridge: Cambridge University Press.

Momigliano, Arnaldo. 1985. Marcel Mauss and the Quest for the Person in Greek Biography and Autobiography. Pages 83–92 in *The Category of the Person: Anthropology, Philosophy, History.* Edited by M. Carrithers, S. Collins, and S. Lukes. Cambridge: Cambridge University Press.

Montgomery, James A., and Henry S. Gehman. 1951. *A Critical and Exegetical Commentary on the Books of Kings.* Edinburgh: T. & T. Clark.

Moore, Stephen D., and Yvonne Sherwood. 2011. *The Invention of the Biblical Scholar: A Critical Manifesto.* Minneapolis: Fortress.

Morgan, Kathryn A., ed. 2003. *Popular Tyranny: Sovereignty and Its Discontents in Ancient Greece.* Austin: University of Texas Press.

Morgenstern, Julian. 1948. The *Chanukkah* Festival and the Calendar of Ancient Israel (Continued). *HUCA* 21:365–496.

Morrison, Craig E. 1997. Handing on the Mantle: The Transmission of the Elijah Cycle in the Biblical Versions. Pages 109–29 in Egan and Morrison 1997.

Mowinckel, Sigmund. 1914. *Zur Komposition des Buches Jeremia.* Kristiania: Dybwad.

Mulder, Martin J. 1998. *1 Kings.* Vol. 1, *1 Kings 1–11.* Translated by John Vriend. HCOT. Leuven: Peeters.

Müller, Dieter. 1967. Grabausstattung und Totengericht in der Lehre für König Merikare. *ZÄS* 94:117–24.

Murdoch, Iris. 1993. *Metaphysics as a Guide to Morals.* New York: Allen Lane/Penguin.

———. 1999. *Existentialists and Mystics: Writings on Philosophy and Literature.* Edited by Peter Conradi and George Steiner. New York: Penguin.

Murray, A. T., and William F. Wyatt. 1999. *Homer: The Iliad, Books 1–12.* LCL 170. Cambridge, Mass.: Harvard University Press.

Musil, Robert. 1978a. Der Dichter und diese Zeit oder: Der Dichter und seine Zeit. Pages 1349–52 in *Gesammelte Werke 8: Essays und Reden.* Reinbek bei Hamburg: Rowohlt.

———. 1978b. *Der Mann ohne Eigenschaften. Gesammelte Werke 1.* Edited by Adolf Frisé. Reinbek bei Hamburg: Rowohlt.

Nell, Victor. 2002. Mythic Structures in Narrative: The Domestication of Immortality. Pages 17–37 in Green et al. 2002.

Nelson, Richard D. 1987. *First and Second Kings.* IBC. Atlanta: John Knox.

———. 1988. The Anatomy of the Book of Kings. *JSOT* 40:39–48.

Neugroschel, Joachim. 2000. Introduction. Pages vii–xxiii in *Franz Kafka: The Metamorphosis, In the Penal Colony, and Other Stories.* Translated by Joachim Neugroschel. Scribner Paperback Fiction ed. New York: Simon & Shuster.

Neusner, Jacob. 1981. *Judaism: The Evidence of the Mishnah.* Chicago: University of Chicago Press.

Newey, Vincent. 2004. *The Scriptures of Charles Dickens: Novels of Ideology, Novels of the Self.* The Nineteenth Century Series. Aldershot: Ashgate.

Newsom, Carol A. 1996. The Book of Job. Pages 319–637 in *NIB*, vol. 4.

———. 2002. Narrative Ethics, Character, and the Prose Tale of Job. Pages 121–34 in *Character and Scripture: Moral Formation, Community, and Biblical Interpretation.* Edited by William P. Brown. Grand Rapids, Mich.: Eerdmans.

Nietzsche, Friedrich. 1964a. *Ecce Homo: Wie Man Wird, Was Man Ist.* Pages 293–409 in *Götzendämmerung, Der Antichrist, Ecce Homo, Gedichte.* Stuttgart: Kröner.

———. 1964b. *Götzen-dämmerung oder Wie Man Mit Dem Hammer Philosophiert.* Pages 79–183 in *Götzendämmerung, Der Antichrist, Ecce Homo, Gedichte.* Stuttgart: Kröner.

———. 1964c. Vom Nutzen und Nachteil der Historie für das Leben. Pages 97–195 in *Unzeitgemässe Betrachtungen. SWZB*, vol. 2.

———. 1964d. Über Wahrheit und Lüge im aussermoralischen Sinne. Pages 605–22 in *Unzeitgemässe Betrachtungen. SWZB*, vol. 2.

———. 1964e. *Der Wille zur Macht: Versuch einer Umwertung aller Werte. SWZB*, vol. 9.

———. 1999. *Zur Genealogie der Moral.* Pages 247–412 in *Sämtliche Werke, 5: Jenseits von Gut und Böse und Zur Genealogie der Moral.* Kritische Studienausgabe. Edited by Giorgio Colli and Mazzino Montinari. Berlin: de Gruyter.

Noll, Kurt L. 1997. *The Faces of David.* JSOTSup 242. Sheffield: Sheffield Academic.

———. 2007a. Deuteronomistic History or Deuteronomic Debate? (A Thought Experiment). *JSOT* 31:311–45.

———. 2007b. Is the Book of Kings Deuteronomistic? And is it a History? *SJOT* 21:49–72.

Noth, Martin. 1960. *The History of Israel.* 2d ed. New York: Harper.

———. 1968. *Könige.* BKAT 9/1. Neukirchen–Vluyn: Neukirchener Verlag.

Nussbaum, Martha C. 1992. *Love's Knowledge: Essays on Philosophy and Literature.* Oxford: Oxford University Press.

———. 1995. Equity and Mercy. Pages 145–87 in *Punishment: A Philosophy and Public Affairs Reader.* Edited by A. J. Simmons, M. Cohen, J. Cohen, and C. R. Beitz. Princeton: Princeton University Press.

Ofulue, Nneka Ifeoma. 2005. President Clinton and the White House Prayer Breakfast. Pages 127–36 in *The Political Pulpit Revisited*. Edited by Roderick P. Hart and John L. Pauley. West Lafayette, Ind.: Purdue University Press.

Olley, John W. 1998. YHWH and His Zealous Prophet: The Presentation of Elijah in 1 and 2 Kings. *JSOT* 80:25–51.

Otto, Rudolf. 2004. *Das Heilige: Über das irrationale in der Idee des Göttlichen und sein Verhältnis zum rationalen*. Munich: Beck.

Ottosson, M. 1974. *'ākhal*. Pages 236–41 in *TDOT*, vol. 1.

Padel, Ruth. 1992. *In and Out of the Mind: Greek Images of the Tragic Self*. Princeton, N.J.: Princeton University Press.

Pakkala, Juha. 2002. Jeroboam's Sin and Bethel in 1 Kgs 12:25–33. *BN* 112:86–94.

———. 2006. Zedekiah's Fate and the Dynastic Succession. *JBL* 125:443–52.

———. 2008. Jeroboam Without Bulls. *ZAW* 120:501–25.

Palmer, Frank. 1992. *Literature and Moral Understanding: A Philosophical Essay on Ethics, Aesthetics, Education, and Culture*. Oxford: Clarendon.

Parker, David. 1994. *Ethics, Theory, and the Novel*. Cambridge: Cambridge University Press.

Patrick, Dale, and Allen Scult. 1990. *Rhetoric and Biblical Interpretation*. Bible and Literature 26. Sheffield: Sheffield Academic.

Paul, Annie Murphy. 2004. *The Cult of Personality Testing: How Personality Tests are Leading Us to Miseducate our Children, Mismanage our Companies, and Misunderstand Ourselves*. New York: Free Press.

Payne, Michael, and John Schad. 2003. *Life. After. Theory*. London: Continuum.

Peake, Arthur S. 1905. *Job: Introduction, Revised Version with Notes and Index*. New Century Bible. New York: Henry Frowde.

Pearson, Lionel. 1954. Real and Conventional Personalities in Greek History. *JHI* 15:136–45.

Pelling, Christopher, ed. 1990. *Characterization and Individuality in Greek Literature*. Oxford: Clarendon.

———. 1990. "Conclusion." Pages 245–62 in Pelling 1990.

———. 2006. Speech and Narrative in the *Histories*. Pages 103–21 in *The Cambridge Companion to Herodotus*. Edited by Carolyn Dewald and John Marincola. Cambridge: Cambridge University Press.

Penchansky, David. 1995. *The Politics of Biblical Theology: A Postmodern Reading*. Macon, Ga.: Mercer University Press.

Perry, Menahem, and Meir Sternberg. 1986. The King Through Ironic Eyes: Biblical Narrative and the Literary Reading Process. *PT* 7:275–322.

Pervin, Lawrence A. 1994. Personality Stability, Personality Change, and the Question of Process. Pages 315–30 in Heatherton and Weinberger 1994.

Peterson, Eugene H. 1999. *First and Second Samuel*. WBCom. Louisville: Westminster John Knox.

Pfeiffer, Robert H. 1941. *Introduction to the Old Testament*. New York: Harper & Brothers.

Pinch, Geraldine. 1995. *Magic in Ancient Egypt*. Austin: University of Texas Press.

Pitard, Wayne T. 1987. *Ancient Damascus: A Historical Study of the Syrian City-State from Earliest Times Until Its Fall to the Assyrians in 732 BCE*. Winona Lake, Ind.: Eisenbrauns.

Plotz, Judith. 2001. *Romanticism and the Vocation of Childhood*. New York: Palgrave.

Polichak, James W., and Richard J. Gerrig. 2002. "Get Up and Win!" Participatory Responses to Narrative. Pages 71–95 in Green et al. 2002.

Politzer, Heinz. 1962. *Franz Kafka: Parable and Paradox*. Ithaca, N.Y.: Cornell University Press.

Polk, Timothy. 1984. *The Prophetic Persona: Jeremiah and the Language of Self*. JSOTSup 32. Sheffield: JSOT.

Polzin, Robert. 1993. *David and the Deuteronomist: A Literary Study of the Deuteronomic History, Part III, 2 Samuel*. Bloomington: Indiana University Press.

Price, Terry L. 2000. Explaining Ethical Failures of Leadership. *The Leadership and Organization Development Journal* 21:177–84.

Propp, William H. C. 1998. Why Moses Could Not Enter The Promised Land. *BRev* 14:37–43.

———. 2006. *Exodus 19–40*. AB 2A. New York: Doubleday.

Proust, Marcel. 2003. *Time Regained*. Translated by A. Mayor, T. Kilmartin, and D. J. Enright. New York: Modern Library.

Provan, Iain W. 1995. *1 and 2 Kings*. NIBCOT. Peabody, Mass.: Hendrickson.

Pyper, Hugh. 1993. Judging the Wisdom of Solomon: The Two-Way Effect of Intertextuality. *JSOT* 59:25–36.

Quack, Joachim Friedrich. 1992. *Studien zur Lehre für Merikarê*. Wiesbaden: Harrassowitz.

Rabinowitz, Peter J. 1977. Truth in Fiction: A Reexamination of Audiences. *Critical Inquiry* 4:121–41.

———. 1987. *Before Reading: Narrative Conventions and the Politics of Interpretation*. Ithaca, N.Y.: Cornell University Press.

Rad, Gerhard von. 1962. *Old Testament Theology*. Vol. 1, *The Theology of Israel's Historical Traditions*. Translated by D. M. G. Stalker. New York: Harper & Row.

———. 1972. *Genesis: A Commentary*. Translated by John H. Marks. Rev. ed. OTL. Philadelphia: Westminster.

Raffa, Guy P. 1995. Dante's Beloved Yet Damned Virgil. Pages 267–85 in *Dante's Inferno: The Indiana Critical Edition*. Edited by Mark Musa. Bloomington: Indiana University Press.

Raleigh, Sir Walter. 1829. *The History of the World, Bk. 2, Ch. 1–13,4 (The Works of Sir Walter Raleigh, Kr., vol. 3)*. Oxford: Oxford University Press.

Rank, Otto. 1989. *The Double: A Psychoanalytic Study*. Translated by Harry Tucker, Jr. Maresfield Library. London: Karnac.

Rashkow, Ilona N. 1993. In Our Image We Create Him, Male and Female We Create Them: The E/Affect of Biblical Characterization. *Semeia* 63:105–13.

Redfield, James. 1975. *Nature and Culture in the Iliad: The Tragedy of Hector*. Chicago: University of Chicago Press.

Reich, Annie. 1973. *Annie Reich: Psychoanalytic Contributions*. New York: International Universities Press.

Reinhartz, Adele. 1998. *"Why Ask My Name?": Anonymity and Identity in Biblical Narrative*. New York: Oxford University Press.

Reis, Pamela Tamarkin. 1994. Vindicating God: Another Look at 1 Kings XIII. *VT* 44:376–86.

Reiss, Moshe. 2005. The Fall and Rise of Job the Dissenter. *JBQ* 33:257–66.

Rex, Walter. 1965. *Essays on Pierre Bayle and Religious Controversy*. The Hague: Nijhoff.

Richey, Marjorie H., Robert J. Koenigs, Harold W. Richey, and Richard Fortin. 1975. Negative Salience in Impressions of Character: Effects of Unequal Proportions of Positive and Negative Information. *Journal of Social Psychology* 97:233–41.

Richey, Marjorie H., Harold W. Richey, and Gregory Thieman. 1972. Negative Salience in Impression of Character: Effects of New Information on Established Relationships. *Psychonomic Science* 28:65–67.

Ricks, Christopher. 1988. *T. S. Eliot and Prejudice*. Berkeley: University of California Press.

Ricoeur, Paul. 1983. *Temps et récit*, vol. 1. Paris: Seuil.

———. 1990. *Soi-même comme un autre*. Paris: Seuil.

Riskey, Dwight R., and Michael H. Birnbaum. 1974. Compensatory Effects in Moral Judgment: Two Rights Don't Make Up for a Wrong. *Journal of Experimental Psychology* 103:171–73.

Robins, Richard W., Mark D. Spranca, Gerald A. Mendelsohn. 1996. The Actor–Observer Effect Revisited: Effects of Individual Differences and Repeated Social Interactions on Actor and Observer Attributions. *Journal of Personality and Social Psychology* 71:375–89.

Robinson, Bernard P. 1991 Elijah at Horeb, 1 Kings 19:1–18: A Coherent Narrative? *RB* 98:513–36.

Robinson, H. Wheeler. 1911. *The Christian Doctrine of Man*. Edinburgh: T. & T. Clark.

Robinson, Joseph. 1976. *The Second Book of Kings*. CBC. Cambridge: Cambridge University Press.

Rofé, Alexander. 1974. Classes in the Prophetical Stories: Didactic Legenda and Parable. Pages 143–64 in *Studies on Prophecy: A Collection of Twelve Papers*. Edited by G. W. Anderson et al. VTSup 26. Leiden: Brill.

———. 1988a. *The Prophetical Stories: The Narratives About the Prophets in the Hebrew Bible, Their Literary Types and History*. Jerusalem: Magnes.

———. 1988b. The Vineyard of Naboth: The Origin and Message of the Story. *VT* 38:89–104.

Rohde, Erwin. 1966. *Psyche: The Cult of Souls and Belief in Immortality Among the Greeks*, vols. 1 and 2. Translated by W. B. Hillis. New York: Harper Torchbooks.

Rolleston, James. 1976. Introduction: On Interpreting *The Trial*. Pages 1–9 in *Twentieth Century Interpretations of* The Trial. Edited by James Rolleston. Englewood Cliffs, N.J.: Prentice-Hall.

Römer, Thomas, ed. 2000. *The Future of the Deuteronomistic History*. Leuven: Peeters.

Romm, James. 1998. *Herodotus*. New Haven: Yale University Press.

Roncace, Mark. 2005. *Jeremiah, Zedekiah, and the Fall of Jerusalem*. JSOTSup 423. New York: T. & T. Clark.

Rose, Jonathan. 2001. *The Intellectual Life of the British Working Classes*. New Haven: Yale University Press.

Rosenberg, Joel. 1975. Meanings, Morals, and Mysteries: Literary Approaches to Torah. *Response: A Contemporary Jewish Review* 9:67–94.

———. 1986. *King and Kin: Political Allegory in the Hebrew Bible*. Bloomington, Ind.: Indiana University Press.

Rosenhan, David L. 1973. On Being Sane in Insane Places. *Science* 179:250–58.
———. 1975. The Contextual Nature of Psychiatric Diagnosis. *JAP* 84:462–74.
Ross, Lee. 1977. The Intuitive Psychologist and His Shortcomings: Distortions in the Attribution Process. Pages 173–220 in *Advances in Experimental Social Psychology 10*. Edited by L. Berkowitz. New York: Academic.
Ross, Lee, and Richard E. Nisbett. 1991. *The Person and the Situation: Perspectives of Social Psychology*. New York: McGraw-Hill.
Rowley, Harold H. 1980. *Job*. 2d ed. NCBC. Grand Rapids: Eerdmans.
Ryan, C. J. 1982. *Inferno* XXI: Virgil and Dante, a Study in Contrasts. *Italica* 59:16–31.
Salmon, John B. 1984. *Wealthy Corinth: A History of the City to 338 BC*. Oxford: Clarendon.
———. 1997. Lopping off the Heads? Tyrants, Politics and the *Polis*. Pages 60–73 in *The Development of the* Polis *in Archaic Greece*. Edited by Lynette G. Mitchell and P. J. Rhodes. London: Routledge.
Šanda, A. 1912. *Die Bücher der Könige*. EHAT 2. Münster: Aschendorff.
Sandbank, Shimon. 1970. Surprise Techniques in Kafka's Aphorisms. *Orbis Litterarum* 25:261–64.
Sandmel, Samuel. 1961. The Haggada within Scripture. *JBL* 80:105–22.
———. 1972. The Ancient Mind and Ours. Pages 29–44 in *Understanding the Sacred Text: Essays in Honor of Morton S. Enslin on the Hebrew Bible and Christian Beginnings*. Edited by John Reumann. Valley Forge: Judson.
Sarna, Nahum M. 1986. *Exploring Exodus: The Heritage of Biblical Israel*. New York: Schocken.
Sartre, Jean-Paul. 1943. *L'être et le néant: Essai d'ontologie phénoménologique*. Paris: Gallimard.
Sasson, Jack M. 1990. *Jonah: A New Translation with Introduction, Commentary, and Interpretation*. AB 24b. New York: Doubleday.
Schacht, Richard. 1994. Of Morals and *Menschen*. Pages 427–48 *Nietzsche, Genealogy, Morality: Essays on Nietzsche's On the Genealogy of Morals*. Edited by Richard Schacht. Berkeley: University of California Press.
Schipper, Jeremy. 2007. Did David Overinterpret Nathan's Parable in 2 Samuel 12:1–6? *JBL* 126:381–89.
Schley, D. G. 1992a. Abishai. Pages 24–26 in *ABD*, vol 1.
———. 1992b. Ahithophel. Pages 121–22 in *ABD*, vol. 1.
Schneewind, J. B. 1997. The Misfortunes of Virtue. Pages 178–200 in Crisp and Slote 1997.
Schoemen, Ferdinand. 1987. Statistical Norms and Moral Attributions. Pages 287–315 in *Responsibility, Character, and the Emotions: New Essays in Moral Psychology*. Edited by Ferdinand Schoemen. Cambridge: Cambridge University Press.
Schopenhauer, Arthur. 1960. *Sämtliche Werke, Band I: Die Welt als Wille und Vorstellung, I*. Edited by Wolfgang von Löhneysen. Stuttgart: Cotta-Insel.
Schwartz, Matthew B., and Kalman J. Kaplan. 2004. *Biblical Stories for Psychotherapy and Counseling: A Sourcebook*. New York: Haworth.
Schweizer, H. 1974. *Elischa in den Kriegen. Literaturwissenschaftliche Untersuchungen von 2 Kön. 3; 6:8–23; 6:24–7:20*. SANT 37. Munich: Kösel.
Seaford, Richard. 2003. Tragic Tyranny. Pages 95–115 in Morgan 2003.

Seale, Clive. 1998. *Constructing Death: The Sociology of Dying and Bereavement.* Cambridge: Cambridge University Press.

Seow, Choon-Leong. 1999. The First and Second Books of Kings. Pages 3–295 in *NIB*, vol. 3.

Sheehan, Jonathan. 2006. Sacred and Profane: Idolatry, Antiquarianism and the Polemics of Distinction in the Seventeenth Century. *Past & Present* 192:35–66.

Shemesh, Yael. 2008. The Elisha Stories As Saints' Legends. *Journal of Hebrew Scriptures* 8:1–41 Online: http://www.arts.ualberta.ca/JHS/jhs-article.html#vol8.

Sheppard, Richard. 1994. Kafka's *Vor dem Gesetz*: Hermeneutic Pluralism or the Significance of Uninterpretability. Pages 13–30 in *Franz Kafka "Vor dem Gesetz"*: *Aufsätze und Materialien*. Edited by Manfred Voigts. Würzburg: Königshausen & Neumann.

Shorey, Paul, trans. 1969. *Plato: The Republic*, vol. 1. LCL. Cambridge, Mass.: Harvard University Press.

Sigler, Mary. 2000. The Story of Justice: Retribution, Mercy, and the Role of Emotions in the Capital Sentencing Process. *Law and Philosophy* 19:339–67.

Silverman, David P. 1991. Divinity and Deities in Ancient Egypt. Pages 7–87 in *Religion in Ancient Egypt: Gods, Myths, and Personal Practice*. Edited by Byron E. Shafer. Ithaca, N.Y.: Cornell University Press.

Simmel, Georg. 1918. Die Transzendenz des Lebens. Pages 1–27 in *Lebensanschauung: Vier metaphysische Kapitel*. Munich: Duncker & Humblot.

———. 1957. Die Großstädte und das Geistesleben. Pages 227–42 in *Brücke und Tür: Essays des Philosophen zur Geschichte, Religion, Kunst und Gesellschaft*. Stuttgart: Koehler.

Simon, Maurice. 1939. *Midrash Rabbah: Song of Songs*. London: Soncino.

Simon, Uriel. 1967. The Poor Man's Ewe-Lamb: An Example of a Juridical Parable. *Bib* 48:207–42.

———. 1997. *Reading Prophetic Narratives*. Translated by Lenn J. Schramm. Bloomington: Indiana University Press.

———. 1999. *Jonah*. JPS Bible Commentary. Philadelphia: JPS.

Sinclair, John D. 1961. *The Divine Comedy of Dante Alighieri, with Translation and Comment: Inferno*. New York: Oxford University Press.

Ska, Jean Louis. 1990. *"Our Fathers Have Told Us": Introduction to the Analysis of Hebrew Narratives*. SubBi 13. Rome: Editrice Pontificia Università Gregoriana.

Skowronski, J. J., and D. E. Carlston. 1992. Caught in the Act: When Impressions Based on Highly Contradictory Information are Resistant to Contradiction. *EJSP* 22:435–52.

Slatoff, Walter. 1970. Against Detachment. *College English* 32:255–60.

Smith, Carol. 1998. "Queenship" in Israel: The Cases of Bathsheba, Jezebel and Athaliah. Pages 142–62 in *King and Messiah in Israel the Ancient Near East*. Edited by John Day. JSOTSup 270. Sheffield: Sheffield Academic.

Snell, Bruno. 1960. *The Discovery of the Mind: The Greek Origins of European Thought*. Translated by T. G. Rosenmeyer. New York: Harper Torchbook.

———. 1975. *Die Entdeckung des Geistes: Studien zur Entstehung des europäischen Denkens bei den Griechen*. 4th ed. Göttingen: Vandenhoeck & Ruprecht.

Sokel, Walter H. 2002. *The Myth of Power and the Self: Essays on Franz Kafka*. Detroit: Wayne State University Press.

Solomon, Robert C. 1994. One Hundred Years of *Ressentiment*: Nietzsche's *Genealogy of Morals*. Pages 95–126 in *Nietzsche, Genealogy, Morality: Essays on Nietzsche's On the Genealogy of Morals*. Edited by Richard Schacht. Berkeley: University of California Press.

———. 1996. Self, Deception, and Self-Deception in Philosophy. Pages 91–121 in Ames and Dissanayake 1996.

Sommer, Benjamin D. 1999. Reflecting on Moses: The Redaction of Numbers 11. *JBL* 118:601–24.

Sourvinou-Inwood, Christine. 1991. *"Reading" Greek Culture: Texts and Images, Rituals and Myths*. Oxford: Clarendon.

Spacks, Patricia M. 1990. The Novel as Ethical Paradigm. Pages 199–206 in Spilka and McCracken-Flesher 1990.

Spilka, Mark, and Caroline McCracken-Flesher, eds. 1990. *Why the Novel Matters: A Postmodern Perplex*. Bloomington, Ind.: Indiana University Press.

Stanford, William B., ed. 1958. *The Odyssey of Homer, Vol. II (Books XIII–XXIV)*. 2d ed. London: St. Martin's.

———. 1968. *The Ulysses Theme: A Study in the Adaptability of a Traditional Hero*. Ann Arbor: University of Michigan Press.

Stein, Martin H. 1969. The Problem of Character Theory. *Journal of the American Psychoanalytic Association* 17:675–701.

Steiner, George. 1975. *After Babel: Aspects of Language and Translation*. New York: Oxford University Press.

Sternberg, Meir. 1985. *The Poetics of Biblical Narrative: Ideological Literature and the Drama of Reading*. Bloomington, Ind.: Indiana University Press.

Steussy, Marti J. 1999. *David: Biblical Portraits of Power*. Columbia, S. C.: University of South Carolina Press.

Stipp, Hermann-Josef. 1996. Zedekiah in the Book of Jeremiah: On the Formation of a Biblical Character. *CBQ* 58:627–48.

Stone, Harry. 1979. *Dickens and the Invisible World: Fairy Tales, Fantasy, and Novel-Making*. Bloomington: Indiana University Press.

Stulman, Louis. 2004. Jeremiah the Prophet: Astride Two Worlds. Pages 41–56 in *Reading the Book of Jeremiah: A Search for Coherence*. Edited by Martin Kessler. Winona Lake, Ind.: Eisenbrauns.

———. 2005. *Jeremiah*. Abingdon Old Testament Commentaries. Nashville: Abingdon.

Suleiman, Susan Rubin. 1983. *Authoritarian Fictions: The Ideological Novel as a Literary Genre*. Princeton, N.J.: Princeton University Press.

Sullivan, Shirley Darcus. 1988. *Psychological Activity in Homer: A Study of Phrēn*. Ottawa: Carleton University Press.

Švrakić, Dragan M. 1990. The Functional Dynamics of the Narcissistic Personality. *American Journal of Psychotherapy* 44:189–203.

Sweeney, Marvin A. 2007a. Review of Mark Roncace, *Jeremiah, Zedekiah, and the Fall of Jerusalem CBQ* 69:131–32.

———. 2007b. *I & II Kings: A Commentary*. OTL. Louisville: Westminster John Knox.

Talmon, Shemaryahu. 1958. Divergences in Calendar-Reckoning in Ephraim and Judah. *VT* 8:48–74.

Tambling, Jeremy. 2004. Introduction. Pages xi–xli in *David Copperfield*, by Charles Dickens. Edited by Jeremy Tambling. Rev. ed. London: Penguin.

Taplin, Oliver. 1990. Agamemnon's Role in the *Iliad*. Pages 60–82 in Pelling 1990.

Tarnow, Eugen. 2000. Self-destructive Obedience in the Airplane Cockpit and the Concept of Obedience Optimization. Pages 111–23 in Blass 2000.

Tartakoff, Helen H. 1966. The Normal Personality in Our Culture and the Nobel Prize Complex. Pages 222–52 in *Psychoanalysis—A General Psychology: Essays in Honor of Heinz Hartmann*. Edited by R. M. Loewenstein, L. M. Newman, M. Schur, and A. J. Solnit. New York: International Universities.

Tawil, Hayim. 2005. The Semantic Range of the Biblical Hebrew חלל: Lexicographical Note X. *ZAW* 117:91–94.

Taylor, Charles. 1989. *Sources of the Self: The Making of the Modern Identity*. Cambridge, Mass.: Harvard University Press.

Taylor, John H. 2001. *Death and the Afterlife in Ancient Egypt*. Chicago: University of Chicago Press.

Telford, Kenneth A. 1961. *Aristotle's Poetics: Translation and Analysis*. South Bend, Ind.: Gateway.

Thackeray, H. St. J., and Ralph Marcus, trans. 1977. *Josephus*. Vol. 5, *Jewish Antiquities, Books V–VIII*. LCL. Cambridge, Mass.: Harvard University Press.

Thompson, Henry O. 1992. Carmel, Mount. Pages 874–75 in *ABD*, vol. 1.

Titolo, Matthew. 2003. The Clerks' Tale: Liberalism, Accountability, and Mimesis in *David Copperfield*. *ELH* 70:171–95.

Todorov, Tzvetan. 1990. *Genres in Discourse*. Translated by Catherine Porter. Cambridge: Cambridge University Press.

Toews, Wesley I. 1993. *Monarchy and Religious Institution in Israel Under Jeroboam*. SBLMS 47. Atlanta: Scholars Press.

Tolstoy, Leo. 2002. *Anna Karenina*. Translated by David Magarshack. New York: Signet.

Trachtenberg, Joshua. 1943. *The Devil and the Jews: The Medieval Conception of the Jew and its Relation to Modern Antisemitism*. New Haven: Yale University Press.

Travers Herford, R. 1962. *The Ethics of the Talmud: Sayings of the Fathers*. New York: Schocken.

Trible, Phyllis. 1978. *God and the Rhetoric of Sexuality*. Philadelphia: Fortress.

———. 1994. The Odd Couple: Elijah and Jezebel. Pages 166–79 in *Out of the Garden: Women Writers on the Bible*. Edited by Christina Büchmann and Celina Spiegel. New York: Fawcett.

Tyndale, William. 1992. A Prologue Showing the Use of the Scripture. Pages 7–11 in *Tyndale's Old Testament: being the Pentateuch of 1530, Joshua to 2 Chronicles of 1537, and Jonah*. Edited by David Daniell. New Haven: Yale University Press.

Uffenheimer, Benjamin. 1999. *Early Prophecy in Israel*. Jerusalem: Magnes.

Urbach, Ephraim E. 1987. *The Sages: Their Concepts and Beliefs*. Translated by Israel Abrahams. Cambridge, Mass.: Harvard University Press.

VanderKam, James C. 1980. Davidic Complicity in the Deaths of Abner and Eshbaal: A Historical and Radactional Study. *JBL* 99:521–39.

———. 1984. *Enoch and the Growth of an Apocalyptic Tradition*. CBQMS 16. Washington, D.C.: Catholic Biblical Association.

Van Krieken, Robert. 1998. *Norbert Elias*. London: Routledge.

Van Seters, John. 1999. On Reading the Story of the Man of God from Judah in 1 Kings 13. Pages 225–34 in *The Labour of Reading: Desire, Alienation, and Biblical Interpretation*. Edited by F. C. Black, R. Boer, and E. Runions. SemeiaSt 36. Atlanta: SBL.

————. 2000. The Deuteronomistic History: Can it Avoid Death by Redaction? Pages 213–22 in *The Future of the Deuteronomistic History*. Edited by Thomas Römer. Leuven: Peeters.

Van Winkle, D. W. 1989. 1 Kings xiii: True and False Prophecy. *VT* 39:31–43.

Vauhkonen, Kauko. 1968. *On the Pathogenesis of Morbid Jealousy, with Special Reference to the Personality Traits of and Interaction between Jealous Patients and their Spouses*. Copenhagen: Munksgaard.

Vermeule, Emily. *1979. Aspects of Death in Early Greek Art and Poetry*. Sather Classical Lectures 46. Berkeley: University of California Press.

Veyne, Paul. 1988. *Did the Greeks Believe in Their Myths? An Essay on the Constitutive Imagination*. Translated by Paula Wissing. Chicago: University of Chicago Press.

Vincent, David. 1982. *Bread, Knowledge, and Freedom: A Study of Nineteenth-Century Working Class Autobiography*. London: Methuen.

Vogel, Jane. 1976. *Allegory in Dickens*. University, Ala.: University of Alabama Press.

Volten, Aksel. 1945. *Zwei Altägyptische politische Schriften: Die Lehre für König Merikarê (Pap. Carlsberg VI) und die Lehre des Königs Amenemhet*. Copenhagen: Munksgaard.

Volz, Paul. 1924. *Das Dämonische in Jahwe*. Tübingen: Mohr (Paul Siebeck).

Wachtel, Paul L. 1973. Psychodynamics, Behavior Therapy, and the Implacable Experimenter: An Inquiry into the Consistency of Personality. *JAP* 82:324–34.

Wagner, Siegfried. 1996. Elia am Horeb: Methodologische und theologische Überlegungen zu I Reg 19. Pages 213–25 in *Ausgewählte Aufsätze zum Alten Testament*. Edited by Dietmar Mathias. Berlin: de Gruyter.

Walcot, Peter. 1978. *Envy and the Greeks: A Study of Human Behaviour*. Warminster, Eng.: Aris & Phillips.

Waldman, Nahum M. 1988. Ahab in Bible and Talmud. *Judaism* 37:41–47.

Waller, James. 2002. *Becoming Evil: How Ordinary People Commit Genocide and Mass Killing*. Oxford: Oxford University Press.

Walsh Jerome T. 1989. The Contexts of 1 Kings XIII. *VT* 39:355–70.

————. 1996. *1 Kings*. Berit Olam. Collegeville, Minn.: Liturgical.

Watson, David. 1982. The Actor and the Observer: How Are Their Perceptions of Causality Divergent? *PB* 92:682–700.

Watson, J. B. 1928. *The Ways of Behaviorism*. New York: Harper.

Watt, Ian. 1957. *The Rise of the Novel: Studies in Defoe, Richardson and Fielding*. Berkeley: University of California Press.

Webb, Robert K. 1950. Working Class Readers in Early Victorian England. *The English Historical Review* 65:333–51.

Weber, Max. 1934. *Die protestantische Ethik und der Geist des Kapitalismus*. Tübingen: Mohr (Siebeck).

Weinberger, Joel L. 1994. Can Personality Change? Pages 333–50 in Heatherton and Weinberger 1994.

Weiner, Bernard. 1975. On Being Sane in Insane Places: A Process (Attributional) Analysis and Critique. *JAP* 84:433–41.

Werlitz, Jürgen. 2001. Was hat der Gottesmann aus Juda mit dem Propheten Amos zu tun? Überlegungen zu 1 Kön 13 und den Beziehungen des Textes zu Am 7.10–17. Pages 109–23 in *Steht Nicht Geschrieben? Studien zur Bibel und ihrer Wirkungsgeschichte. Festschrift für Georg Schmuttermayr*. Edited by J. Frühwald-König, F. Prostmeier, and R. Zwick. Regensburg: Pustet.

Westermann, Claus. 1994. *Genesis 1–11: A Continental Commentary*. Translated by John J. Scullion. Minneapolis: Fortress.

Weitzman, Steven. 2007. Before and After *The Art of Biblical Narrative*. *Proof* 27:191–210.

White, Gregory L., and Paul E. Mullen. 1989. *Theory, Research, and Clinical Strategies*. New York: Guilford.

White, Marsha C. 1997. *The Elijah Legends and Jehu's Coup*. BJS 311. Atlanta: Scholars Press.

Whitelam, Keith. 1979. *The Just King: Monarchical Judicial Authority in Ancient Israel*. Sheffield: JSOT.

Whitman, Cedric H. 1965. *Homer and the Heroic Tradition*. New York: Norton.

Whybray, R. Norman. 1968. *The Succession Narrative: A Study of II Samuel 9–20; I Kings 1 and 2*. London: SCM.

———. 1998. *Job*. Readings, A New Biblical Commentary. Sheffield: Sheffield Academic.

Wiener, Aharon. 1978. *The Prophet Elijah in the Development of Judaism: A Depth-Psychological Study*. London, Routledge & Kegan Paul.

Wiesel, Elie. 1981. *Five Biblical Portraits*. Notre Dame, Ind.: University of Notre Dame Press.

Williams, Bernard. 1993. *Shame and Necessity*. Berkeley: University of California Press.

Williams, Raymond. 1983. *Keywords: A Vocabulary of Culture and Society*. Rev. ed. New York: Oxford University Press.

Wilson, Donna F. 2002. *Ransom, Revenge, and Heroic Identity in the* Iliad. Cambridge: Cambridge University Press.

Winnicott, Donald W. 1965. *The Maturational Processes and the Facilitating Environment: Studies in the Theory of Emotional Development*. Madison, Conn.: International Universities.

Wiseman, Donald J. 1993. *1 and 2 Kings: An Introduction and Commentary*. Leicester: InterVarsity.

Wittmann, Reinhard. 1999. Was there a Reading Revolution at the End of the Eighteenth Century? Pages 284–312 in *A History of Reading in the West*. Edited by Guglielmo Cavallo and Roger Chartier. Amherst: University of Massachusetts Press.

Wolff, Hans W. 1964. Das Zitat im Prophetenspruch: eine Studie zur prophetischen Verkündigungsweise. Pages 36–129 in *Gesammelte Studien zum Alten Testament*. Munich: Kaiser.

———. 1981. *Anthropology of the Old Testament*. Philadelphia: Fortress.

Woloch, Alex. 2003. *The One vs. the Many: Minor Characters and the Space of the Protagonist in the Novel*. Princeton, N.J.: Princeton University Press.

Wordsworth, William. 1947. *The Poetical Works of William Wordsworth*. Edited by Ernest de Selincourt and Helen Darbishire. Oxford: Clarendon.

———. 1974. Essay Upon Epitaphs, I. Pages 49–62 in *The Prose Works of William Wordsworth*, vol. 2. Edited by W. J. B. Owen and Jane Worthington Smyser. Oxford: Oxford University Press.

———. 1979. *The Prelude: 1799, 1805, 1850*. Edited by J. Wordsworth, M. H. Abrams, and S. Gill. Norton Critical ed. New York: Norton.

Worman, Nancy. 2003. *The Cast of Character: Style in Greek Literature*. Austin: University of Texas Press.

Würthwein, Ernst. 1984. *Die Bücher der Könige, 1. Kön. 17–2. Kön. 25.* ATD 11/2. Göttingen: Vandenhoeck & Ruprecht.

———. 1985. *Die Bücher der Könige, 1. Kön. 1–16.* 2d ed. ATD 11/1. Göttingen: Vandenhoeck & Ruprecht.

Yeivin, S. 1979. The Divided Kingdom: Rehoboam-Ahaz/Jeroboam-Pekah. Pages 126–78 in *WHJP.* Vol. 4/1, *The Age of the Monarchies: Political History.* Edited by Abraham Malamat. Jerusalem: Masada.

Young, William J., ed. and trans. 1959. *Letters of St. Ignatius of Loyola.* Chicago: Loyola University Press.

Zakovitch, Yair. 1991. *"And You Shall Tell Your Son": The Concept of the Exodus in the Bible.* Jerusalem: Magnes.

Zanker, Graham. 1994. *The Heart of Achilles: Characterization and Personal Ethics in the* Iliad. Ann Arbor: University of Michigan Press.

# INDEX OF AUTHORS